Stephen Johnson

JOHNSON'S
ATLAS & GAZETTEER OF THE
RAILWAYS OF IRELAND

This book
is dedicated to Susan,
for encouraging my obsession
and for putting up with it
and to Poppy for keeping my lap warm.

Johnson's Atlas & Gazetteer
of the Railways of Ireland

© 1997 Stephen M Johnson
ISBN 1 85780 044 3

Published by
Midland Publishing Limited
24 The Hollow, Earl Shilton
Leicester, LE9 7NA, England
Tel: 01455 847815 Fax: 01455 841805
E-mail: midlandbooks@compuserve.com

Worldwide distribution by
Midland Counties Publications
Unit 3 Maizefield, Hinckley, Leics.
LE10 1YF, England
Tel: 01455 233747 Fax: 01455 233737
E-mail: midlandbooks@compuserve.com

Maps originated by Stephen M Johnson
on a PC using CorelDraw software

Book design concept and layout
© Midland Publishing Limited
and Stephen Thompson Associates.

Maps typeset in
Frankfurt Gothic and Avalon.
Atlas & Gazetteer typeset
in ITC Garamond and Gill Sans.

Printed in England by
Woolnough Bookbinding Limited
Irthlingborough, Northants

Stephen Johnson

JOHNSON'S
ATLAS & GAZETTEER OF THE
RAILWAYS OF IRELAND

Midland Publishing
Limited

FORWARD

As MY INTEREST in the railways of Ireland developed over the years, I began to look around for a comprehensive atlas on the subject; preferably one backed up by a gazetteer to provide detailed information on the opening and closing dates of lines and stations. Unable to find one source of reference which would satisfy my requirements, it seemed a very good idea when my wife Sue suggested that I compile my own.

With hindsight, it is fortunate that I did not realise the enormity of the task I was embarking on or I might never have started the research which has gone into this book. The number of railway companies involved, the hundreds of stations, the seemingly endless catalogue of level crossings and other features which had to be listed and whose locations had to be checked, have taken more time than I care to think about and occupied more of my life over the last few years than I could ever have imagined.

As I sought information and assistance from a growing number of people, the one thing above all else which encouraged me to carry on with the work, was the support of those who were helping me with the project and the realisation that they were as much in need of the finished product as I had been myself when I started out on the research.

Every effort has been made to verify the information contained within the book, but it will be appreciated that in a work of this scale and complexity some omissions have possibly occurred or errors may inadvertently have slipped through.

I would be most grateful if readers noting anything untoward, or with additional information to offer, would contact me, through my publisher, so that these may be incorporated in a future edition.

Stephen Johnson
Warwick, November 1997

ACKNOWLEDGEMENTS

In COMPILING this Atlas & Gazetteer I received help from many people, and I would like to take this opportunity to gratefully acknowledge the assistance of the following individuals: Bob Ayres, Ken Boyd, Joe Carroll, Desmond Coakham, Colm Creedon, Jimmy Donnelly, Frank Dunlop, Eugene Field, Steve Flanders of the South Donegal Railway Restoration Society, Fiona Hamilton, Ivor Hughes, Jonathan James, Peter Jones of the Irish Traction Group, Mark Kennedy of the Ulster Folk & Transport Museum, Michael Kennedy, Robin Linsley, Leslie McAllister, Alex McConnell, Michael McMahon, Eamonn Maher of Bord na Móna, David Murray, the Narrow Gauge Railway Society (in particular Dr Peter Lee), Padraig O'Cuimin, David Parks, Ernie Shepherd, John J. Smith, Neil Sprinks, Nick Wakeford and Francis Walls.

I owe a very special debt of gratitude to John Langford. He originally agreed to proof-read the Atlas for me, but then became very involved in the project to the extent of making much of his own invaluable research available for inclusion in this book. In addition to checking much of the information in the Gazetteer, he also provided useful refinements to the map pages.

Last but not least I would like to thank Tom Ferris for encouraging me to complete the book and for dangling the carrot of its eventual publication before me. I am also grateful to his colleagues at Midland Publishing, Chris Salter and Russell Strong, for the care and attention with which they have fine-tuned the design of the book and guided it through its production phases.

If anyone has been overlooked, I offer my apologies.

CONTENTS

Half-title page:
Limerick Junction, in County Tipperary, over 20 miles from Limerick City, is one of the most celebrated railway locations in Ireland. This view was taken looking north, in August 1959.
John Langford

Title page:
Castlemaine Station was 6½ miles from Farranfore on the branch line to Valentia Harbour, in County Kerry. The track was still intact when this photograph was taken on 6th June 1961.
John Langford

USING THIS BOOK

IN COMPILING this book I have endeavoured to include as much information as possible and present it in a manner which is both clear and comprehensible. I hope this brief explanation of the methods employed may be of assistance to those using the book.

The core of the book is in the map pages and the Route Tables. These are linked and cross referenced by the Index & Gazetteer. There is also a separate numerical index to the Route Tables.

The Atlas

The Atlas consists of 36 pages which cover the whole of Ireland to a scale of approximately 5 miles to the inch. In addition to these there are three smaller scale maps which provide greater detail on the railway networks around Ireland's biggest cities – Dublin, Belfast and Cork.

A fourth map is devoted to Inchicore Works and the Atlas section is completed by a single page map showing the routes which are still in existence in 1997.

On the map pages, solid lines indicate those routes built to the Irish standard gauge of 5ft 3in, whereas broken lines show narrow gauge tracks. An exception to this applies to the industrial railways and urban tramways, which are shown in solid lines. These were built to many different gauges and readers are advised to consult the Route Tables for further information. The number of the relevant Route Table is displayed in green in a box adjacent to the route to which it refers. Various colours are used to differentiate between the owning companies and a key is used on each double page spread to relate these colours to the railway companies they represent on that pair of pages.

The owning companies listed are those operating that route in 1922, except where a line closed before or opened after that date. A full list of company abbreviations precedes the map pages.

The Atlas sets out to display all the significant features which have existed over the life span of a line. Thus, Gaggin Viaduct on the Cork, Bandon & South Coast Railway is shown, even though it was later replaced by an embankment; as are the numerous level crossings which once existed on the Great Northern main line out of Great Victoria Street station, Belfast, even though many of these were later replaced by bridges.

Careful reference to the Route Tables is essential to ascertain the current status of the features shown.

Stations which are open at the time of going to press in October 1997, are easily recognised by the use of a solid circle to mark their position. Closed stations on lines which are still open and also on routes which are closed, are identified by a circle with a white centre. Reference to the relevant Route Table is again essential to determine the opening and closing dates.

From the 1930s onwards the GNR(I) and other companies made increasing use of railcars and railbuses in an attempt to counter the increasing competition from road transport. These railcars could stop at level crossings to pick up and set down passengers. Where these railcar stopping places have been listed in timetables or leaflets produced by the railway companies, they are indicated on the maps by the letter 'R' in red. On the County Donegal Railway, railcars would stop virtually anywhere it was safe to do so, if there was some custom to be had. These unlisted stopping places have not been indicated on the maps.

Some features on the maps may look too large or not quite in the right place. This is particularly noticeable in the case of level crossings and short sidings and has been brought about by the scale of the maps and the size of the symbols used, in order for them to be legible. For an accurate indication of the true distances between features, please refer to the Route Tables.

The appearance of a yellow diamond symbol on a map indicates the position of a small and probably very obscure industrial system. In these instances evidence of the sometime existence of the system has come to light during the course of the research, but precise information as to its layout or indeed in some cases its exact location, has not been uncovered. It was felt better to acknowledge these systems, however imprecise and unsatisfactory the information, rather than ignore them.

A further point worth noting about industrial lines is the temporary nature of some of the installations. This is still very relevant in relation to Ireland's railways today. In terms of route mileage, the second largest railway operator on the island is Bord na Móna. At most of its locations, the Bord has a network of permanent tracks linking the main areas

of bog being worked to the processing plant or the power station where the peat is needed. In addition there can be many miles of temporary track, off the main routes to the sites where the peat is being harvested. For example, the Bord na Móna system at Blackwater has 96 miles of permanent track, though as much as 55 miles of temporary track is also normally in use – the precise location of which can change almost on a weekly basis. Only the permanent track at such places in shown in the Atlas.

The endemic spelling inconsistencies in Irish place names present many hazards for those engaged on enterprises such as this. Throughout the book I have employed the names as used by the railway companies. Where alternative names were sometimes applied, both the usual version and the alternatives are listed individually, followed by the other version(s), in the Index & Gazetteer. On the map pages, an asterisk (*) after a name indicates that another name or names were used at some time. For details of this please refer to the Route Tables.

A full exposition of the symbols used appears on the first of the map pages, and provides the key to that section of the book.

The Index & Gazetteer

This follows the map pages and provides the link between them and the Route Tables. The Index provides an alphabetical listing of every feature in the Atlas, cross-referenced to the Route Tables. Each entry states the map page on which the feature appears, the grid reference and the relevant Route Table.

The Route Tables

These are preceded by a numerical index indicating the section of railway covered. The route numbers appear on both the map pages and in the Index & Gazetteer; thus information on a particular feature can be sourced from either the maps or the Index. Each Route Table begins with a brief history, including opening and closing dates. It then lists stations, level crossings, junctions and other features along its length. Additional information on certain of the stations or features may also be included. Distances are given in terms of railway mileposts and, where known or relevant, also in miles and chains. Page and grid references to the map section are shown, as are the numbers of route tables for adjoining lines.

ABBREVIATIONS

AEJR	Athenry & Ennis Junction Railway
ATECLR	Athenry & Tuam Extension to Claremorris Light Railway
ATR	Athenry & Tuam Railway
AVR	Arigna Valley Railway
BBCPJR	Belfast, Ballymena, Coleraine & Portrush Junction Railway
BBER	Bantry Bay Extension Railway
BBR	Belfast & Ballymena Railway
BCDR	Belfast & County Down Railway
BCER	Buncrana & Carndonagh Extension Railway
BCLR	Ballinrobe & Claremorris Light Railway
BCR	Belfast Central Railway
BCRBR	Ballymena, Cushendall & Red Bay Railway
BCT	Belfast Corporation Tramways
BELR	Bray & Enniskerry Light Railway
BER	Baltimore Extension Railway
BHBR	Belfast, Holywood & Bangor Railway
BHC	Belfast Harbour Commissioners
BJR	Banbridge Junction Railway
BLBR	Banbridge, Lisburn & Belfast Railway
BLR	Ballymena & Larne Railway
BLJR	Belfast & Londonderry Junction Railway
BNCR	Belfast & Northern Counties Railway
BnM	Bord na Móna
BNT	Bessbrook & Newry Tramway
BoW	Board of Works
BPT	Blessington & Poulaphouca Steam Tramway Company
BR	Ballycastle Railway
BTJLR	Ballinascarthy & Timoleague Junction Light Railway
BWR	Bagenalstown & Wexford Railway
CBPR	Cork, Blackrock & Passage Railway
CBR	Cork & Bandon Railway
CBaR	Clara & Banagher Railway
CBSCR	Cork, Bandon & South Coast Railway
CCR	Cork City Railways
CCER	Clones & Cavan Extension Railway
CDJR	City of Dublin Junction Railway
CDRJC	County Donegal Railways Joint Committee
CDSPC	City of Dublin Steam Packet Company
CDT	City of Derry Tramways
CER	Carndonagh Extension Railway
CExR	Clonakilty Extension Railway
CHC	Coleraine Harbour Commissioners
CHJR	Carrickfergus Harbour Junction Railway
CIE	Córas Iompair Éireann
CIR	Central Ireland Railway
CKAR	Catleblayney, Keady & Armagh Railway
CKJR	Cork & Kinsale Junction Railway
CLR	Cavan & Leitrim Railway
CLRLRTC	Cavan, Leitrim & Roscommon Light Railway & Tramway Company
CLaR	Carrickfergus & Larne Railway
CLDR	Cork & Limerick Direct Railway
CMLR	Cork & Muskerry Light Railway
CMDR	Cork & Macroom Direct Railway
CR	Castleisland Railway
CSET	Comhlucht Suicre Éireann Teoranta
CT	Cork Tramways
CTGL	Cumann Traenach na Gaeltachta Láir
CVBT	Castlederg & Victoria Bridge Tramway
CVR	Clogher Valley Railway
CVT	Clogher Valley Tramway
CYR	Cork & Youghal Railway
DAR	Downpatrick & Ardglass Railway
DAJR	Dublin & Antrim Junction Railway
DBJR	Dublin & Belfast Junction Railway
DBT	Dublin & Blessington Steam Tramway Company
DCR	Dungannon & Cookstown Railway
DCeR	Derry Central Railway
DDNR	Downpatrick, Dundrum & Newcastle Railway
DDR	Dublin & Drogheda Railway
DELR	Donoughmore Extension Light Railway
DER	Dundalk & Enniskillen Railway
DGR	Dundalk & Greenore Railway
DKALR	Downpatrick, Killough & Ardglass Light Railway
DKR	Dublin & Kingstown Railway
DLT	Dublin & Lucan Tramway
DLET	Dublin & Lucan Electric Tramway
DMR	Dublin & Meath Railway
DNGR	Dundalk, Newry & Greenore Railway
DPDB	Dublin Port & Docks Board
DR	Donegal Railway
DrR	Draperstown Railway
DSER	Dublin & South Eastern Railway
DSR	Downpatrick Steam Railway
DUTC	Dublin United Tramways Company
DWR	Dublin & Wicklow Railway
DWWR	Dublin, Wicklow & Wexford Railway
EBSR	Enniskillen, Bundoran & Sligo Railway
ESB	Electricity Supply Board
FLR	Fermoy & Lismore Railway
FMR	Fermoy & Mitchelstown Railway
FPHC	Fenit Pier & Harbour Commissioners
FRRHC	Fishguard & Rosslare Railways & Harbours Company
FVR	Finn Valley Railway
GALT	Glen Anne & Loughgilly Tramway
GCPBVT	Giants Causeway, Portrush & Bush Valley Tramway
GNR(I)	Great Northern Railway (Ireland)
GNRB	Great Northern Railway Board
GNWR	Great Northern & Western railway
GSR	Great Southern Railways
GSWR	Great Southern & Western Railway
GST	Galway & Salthill Tramway
HHT	Hill of Howth Tramway
IE	Iarnród Éireann
INWR	Irish North Western Railway
IR	Irish Rail
ISER	Irish South Eastern Railway
ISPS	Irish Steam Preservation Society
ITG	Irish Traction Group

IVR	Ilen Valley Railway	RPR	Roscrea & Parsonstown Railway
KaJR	Killarney Junction Railway	RPSI	Railway Preservation Society of Ireland
KJR	Kilkenny Junction Railway	SBJR	Sligo & Ballaghaderreen Junction Railway
KNR	Kanturk & Newmarket Railway	SCR	South Clare Railway
LALR	Loughrea & Attymon Light Railway	SCaR	Shane's Castle Railway
LBR	Listowel & Ballybunion Railway	SLNCR	Sligo, Leitrim & Northern Counties Railway
LBER	Letterkenny & Burtonport Extension Railway	SLR	Strabane & Letterkenny Railway
LCKR	Limerick, Castleconnell & Killaloe Railway	SR	Southern of Ireland Railway
LCR	Londonderry & Coleraine Railway	SSR	Schull & Skibbereen Tramway & Light Railway
LCaR	Limerick & Castleconnell Railway	TCELR	Timoleague & Courtmacsherry Extenstion
LDR	Limavady & Dungiven Railway		Light Railway
LER	Limerick & Ennis Railway	TDR	Tralee & Dingle Light Railway
LEnR	Londonderry & Enniskillen Railway	TDSR	Tralee & Dingle Steam Railway
LFR	Limerick & Foynes Railway	TFPHC	Tralee & Fenit Pier & Harbour Commissioners
LKR	Limerick & Kerry Railway	TFR	Tralee & Fenit Railway
LLCT	Lucan, Leixlip & Celbridge Steam Tramway	TKR	Tralee & Killarney Railway
LLER	Lucan & Leixlip Electric Railway	TNCR	Town of Newry Connecting Railway
LLSR	Londonderry & Lough Swilly Railway	UR	Ulster Railway
LNWR	London & North Western Railway	UTA	Ulster Transport Authority
LPHC	Londonderry Port & Harbour Commisioners	UTR	Ulster Transport Railways
LR	Letterkenny Railway	WCLRTC	West Carbery Light Railways & Tramway Company
MGWR	Midland Great Western Railway	WCR	West Clare Railway
MIC	Ministry of Industry & Commerce	WCoR	West Cork Railway
NAR	Newry & Armagh Railway	WD	War Department
NCC	Northern Counties Committee	WDLR	Waterford, Dungarvan & Lismore Railway
NER	Newry & Enniskillen Railway	WDR	West Donegal Railway
NIR	Northern Ireland Railways	WKR	Waterford & Kilkenny Railway
NKR	Navan & Kingscourt Railway	WLR	Waterford & Limerick Railway
NWRR	Newry, Warrenpoint & Rostrevor Railway	WLWR	Waterford, Limerick & Western Railway
PDOR	Portadown, Dungannon & Omagh Railway	WNRWJR	Waterford, New Ross & Wexford Junction Railway
PPBR	Parsonstown & Portumna Bridge Railway	WRT	Warrenpoint & Rostrevor Tramway
PT	Portstewart Tramway	WTR	Waterford & Tramore Railway
RNJR	Rathkeale & Newcastle Junction Railway	WWR	Waterford & Wexford Railway

SOURCES

To LIST all the sources consulted in the course of the research leading to the compilation of this book, would have taken up many valuable pages and I hope this brief note will provide an acceptable alternative. Over the last ten years or so I have read virtually every book that was listed in published bibliographies as relating to the railways of Ireland. I have consulted several series of OS maps published over a time span from before the First World War, to the present day. In some instances, depending upon the complexity of the detail which needed to be resolved, the use of large scale maps relating to parts of urban areas or townlands in the countryside, were called upon. In many cases the maps produced by the Railway Clearing House were also invaluable in clarifying both the layout and ownership of lines at junctions and stations. Where none of the sources resolved matters conclusively, communication with railway employees, from managers to permanent way lengthsmen and operating staff often filled in the necessary detail.

Both public and working timetables yielded valuable information, as did back issues of the *Journal of the Irish Railway Record Society*, and of *Five Foot Three* – the journal of the Railway Preservation Society of Ireland; also *Irish Railfans News* and other specialist publications. Useful sources for confirming details of narrow gauge and industrial lines were the archival publications and the journals of the Narrow Gauge Railway Society and the Industrial Railway Society. Officials of Bord na Móna also provided invaluable assistance in resolving the complexities of their extensive railway systems, as they evolved over the last half century or so. Some of the information which I sought simply did not seem to be extant despite my efforts to track it down.

Any contributions which readers may be able to make to fill in any gaps will be very gratefully received, and should be directed through the publishers, for possible inclusion in a future edition of this book.

Part One

THE ATLAS

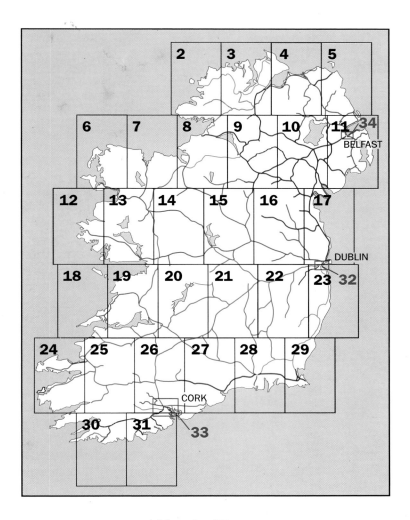

Key to Maps

Standard Gauge (5'3")	
Narrow Gauge †	
Stations (open)	
Stations (closed)	
Stopping Places, Junctions, etc	
Non-Passenger places (open)	
Non-Passenger places (closed)	
Private/Special Platforms	
Level Crossings	
Bridges and Viaducts	
Tunnel	
County Boundary	
National Border	

DRIMOLEAGUE	Passenger places (upper case)
Myroe	Non-Passenger places (lower case)
Brimmages R	Railcar Stop
LISNAGRY ✳	Indicates place is known by more than one name (see index)
67	Route Table numbers
18	Adjoining page numbers
◇	Other railway sites (detail too small or unknown)
CORK	County name

The different coloured lines represent different railway companies.
A key to each colour used is to found on each pair of pages.

† Tramways and industrial railways excluded, see relevant route tables

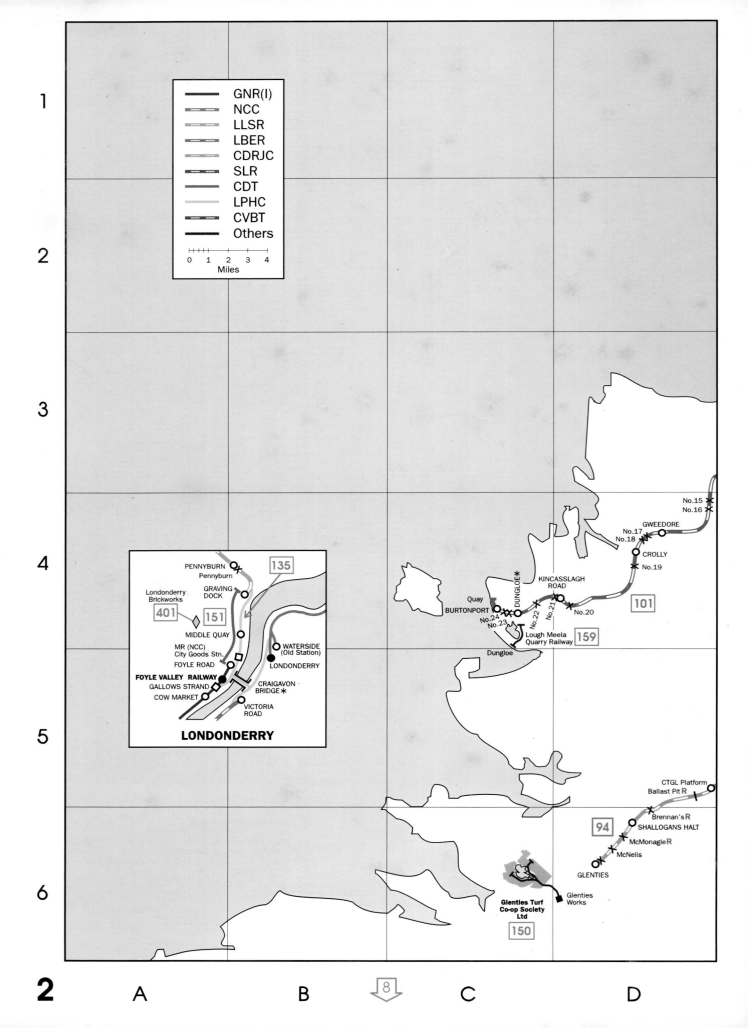

Legend:
- GNR(I)
- NCC
- LLSR
- LBER
- CDRJC
- SLR
- CDT
- LPHC
- CVBT
- Others

0 1 2 3 4
Miles

LONDONDERRY (inset)

PENNYBURN
Pennyburn
135
GRAVING DOCK
Londonderry Brickworks
401
151
MIDDLE QUAY
MR (NCC) City Goods Stn.
FOYLE ROAD
WATERSIDE (Old Station)
FOYLE VALLEY RAILWAY
LONDONDERRY
GALLOWS STRAND
COW MARKET
CRAIGAVON BRIDGE *
VICTORIA ROAD

No.15
No.16
GWEEDORE
No.17
No.18
CROLLY
No.19
DUNGLOE *
KINCASSLAGH ROAD
Quay
BURTONPORT
No.24
No.23
No.22
No.21
No.20
101
Lough Meela Quarry Railway
159
Dungloe

CTGL Platform
Ballast Pit R
Brennan's R
94
SHALLOGANS HALT
McMonagle R
McNelis
GLENTIES
Glenties Turf Co-op Society Ltd
Glenties Works
150

2 A   B   8   C   D

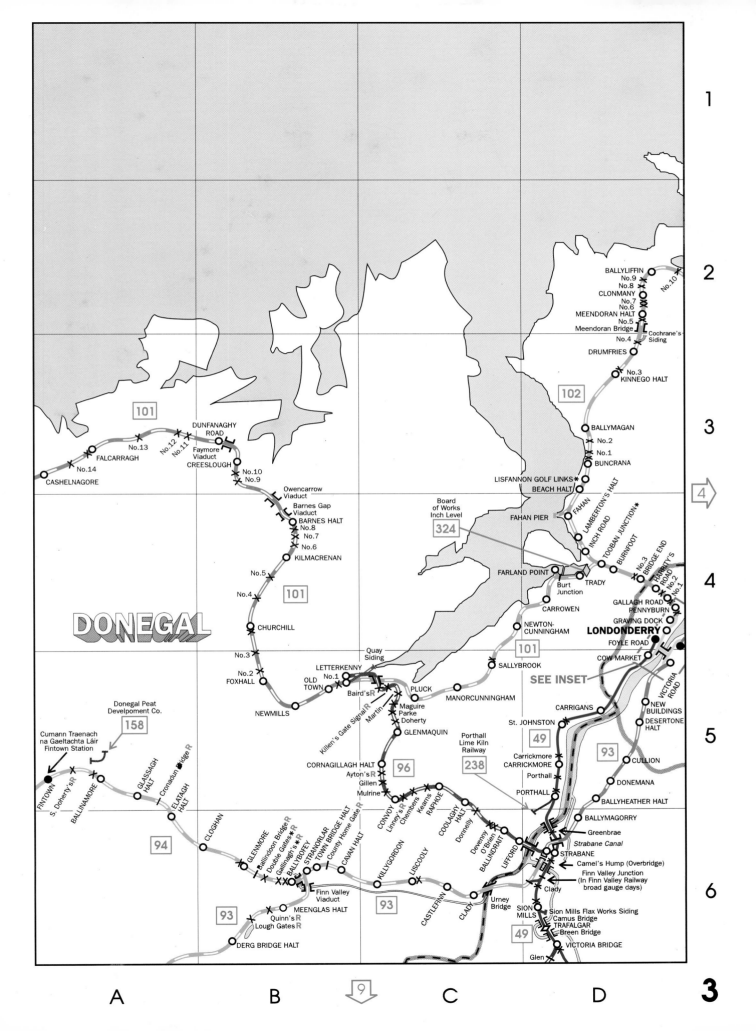

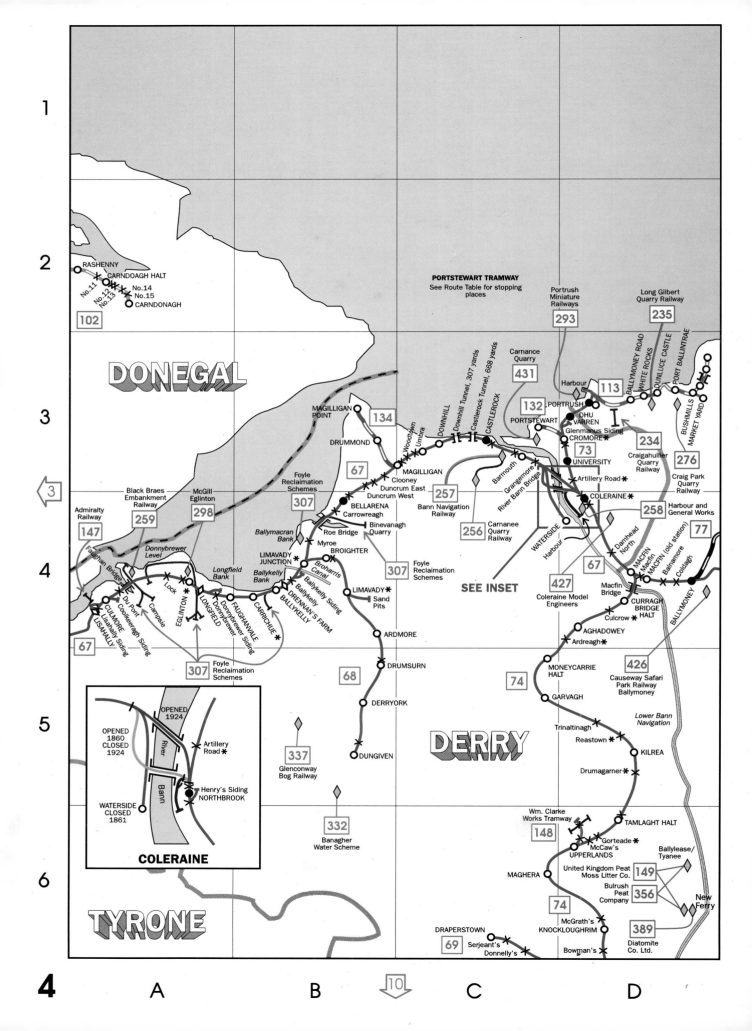

4

1

2

RASHENNY
CARNDOAGH HALT
No.11 No.14
No.12 No.15
No.13 CARNDONAGH
102

DONEGAL

PORTSTEWART TRAMWAY
See Route Table for stopping
places

Portrush
Miniature Railways
293

Long Gilbert
Quarry Railway
235

3

MAGILLIGAN
POINT
134

DRUMMOND

Woodtown
Umbra
DOWNHILL
Downhill Tunnel, 307 yards
Castlerock Tunnel, 668 yards
CASTLEROCK

Carnance
Quarry
431

Harbour
113
PORTRUSH
PORTSTEWART
DHU
VARREN
Glenmanus Siding
CROMORE
73
UNIVERSITY

BALLYMONEY ROAD
WHITE ROCKS
DUNLUCE CASTLE
PORT BALLINTRAE

BUSHMILLS
MARKET YARD

132

234
Craigahullier
Quarry Railway
276
Craig Park
Quarry Railway

MAGILLIGAN
Clooney
Duncrum East
Duncrum West
67

Foyle
Reclaimation
Schemes
307

BELLARENA
Carrowreagh
Roe Bridge

*Ballymacran
Bank*
Binevanagh
Quarry
Myroe
BROIGHTER

Bann Navigation
Railway
257

Barmouth
Grangemore
River Bann Bridge
256
Carnanee
Quarry Railway

Artillery Road *
COLERAINE *

Harbour and
General Works
258

4

Admiralty
Railway
147

Black Braes
Embankment
Railway
259

McGill
Eglinton
298

Faughan Bridge
*Donnybrewer
Level*
*Longfield
Bank*
LIMAVADY
JUNCTION
Broharris
Canal
Ballykelly Siding
*Ballykelly
Bank*
DRENNAN'S FARM
BALLYKELLY

LIMAVADY *
Sand
Pits

WATERSIDE
Damhead
North
MACFIN
MACFIN
MACFIN (old station)
Ballnamore
Coldagh
67
Coleraine Model
Engineers
427
Macfin
Bridge
CURRAGH
BRIDGE
HALT
Culcrow
Culcrow *
77

Lock
Campsie
Du Pont
Coolkeeragh Siding
EGLINTON
LONGFIELD
FAUGHANVALE
CARRICHUE *
Donnybrewer Siding
Lisahally Siding
CULMORE
LISAHALLY
67

Foyle Reclaimation
Schemes
307

ARDMORE

DRUMSURN
68

AGHADOWEY
Ardreagh *

MONEYCARRIE
HALT
74

GARVAGH

Causeway Safari
Park Railway
Ballymoney
426

Lower Bann
Navigation

5

OPENED
1924
Artillery
Road *
OPENED
1860
CLOSED
1924
River
Bann

Henry's Siding
NORTHBROOK
WATERSIDE
CLOSED
1861

COLERAINE

Glenconway
Bog Railway
337

DERRYORK

DUNGIVEN

DERRY

Trinaltinagh
Reastown

KILREA

Drumagarner *

Banagher
Water Scheme
332

6

TYRONE

DRAPERSTOWN
69
Serjeant's
Donnelly's

Wm. Clarke
Works Tramway
148

McCaw's
UPPERLANDS

MAGHERA

74

United Kingdom Peat
Moss Litter Co.
Bulrush
Peat
Company

McGrath's
KNOCKLOUGHRIM
Bowman's

TAMLAGHT HALT
Gorteade *

149
356

Ballylease/
Tyanee

New
Ferry

Diatomite
Co. Ltd.
389

A   B   C   D

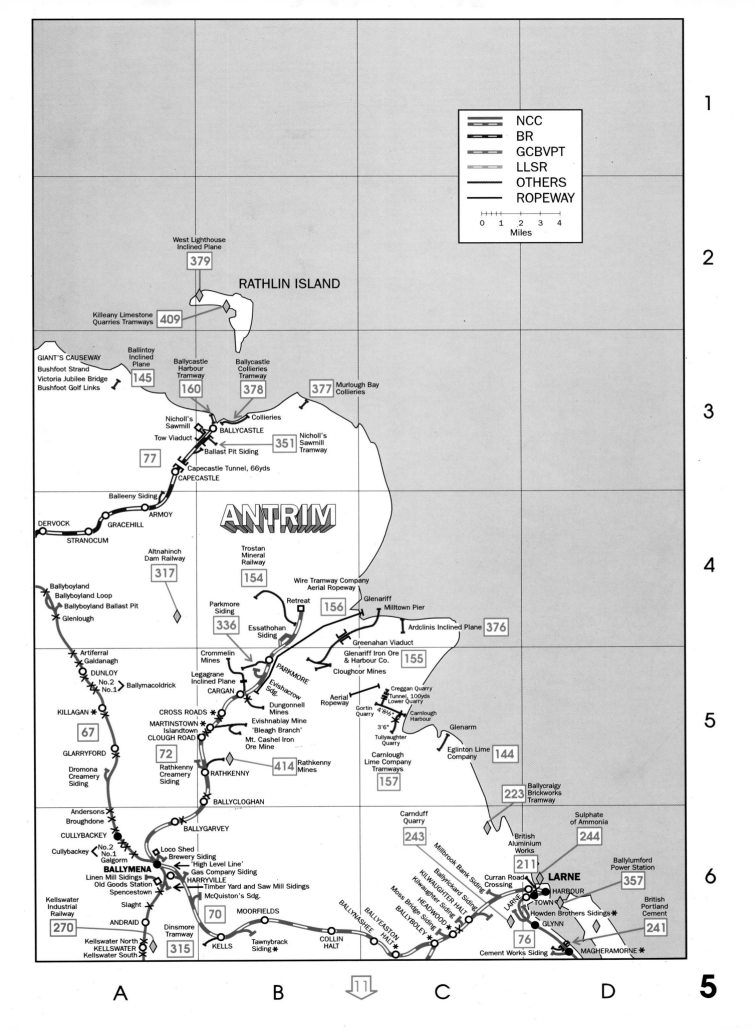

Map legend:

NCC	
BR	
GCBVPT	
LLSR	
OTHERS	
ROPEWAY	

0 1 2 3 4
Miles

1

2

West Lighthouse
Inclined Plane
379

RATHLIN ISLAND

Killeany Limestone
Quarries Tramways 409

GIANT'S CAUSEWAY
Bushfoot Strand
Victoria Jubilee Bridge
Bushfoot Golf Links

Ballintoy
Inclined
Plane
145

Ballycastle
Harbour
Tramway
160

Ballycastle
Collieries
Tramway
378

Murlough Bay
Collieries
377

3

Nicholl's
Sawmill
Tow Viaduct
BALLYCASTLE
Collieries

77
Ballast Pit Siding

351
Nicholl's
Sawmill
Tramway

Capecastle Tunnel, 66yds
CAPECASTLE

Balleeny Siding
ARMOY

ANTRIM

DERVOCK GRACEHILL
STRANOCUM

Altnahinch
Dam Railway
317

Trostan
Mineral
Railway
154

Wire Tramway Company
Aerial Ropeway

4

Ballyboyland
Ballyboyland Loop
Ballyboyland Ballast Pit
Glenlough

Parkmore
Siding
336
Essathohan
Siding

Retreat

156

Glenariff
Milltown Pier

Ardclinis Inclined Plane 376

Greenahan Viaduct

Artiferral
Galdanagh
DUNLOY
No.2
No.1 Ballymacoldrick

Crommelin
Mines

Legagrane
Inclined Plane
CARGAN

PARKMORE

Evishacrow
Sdg.

Glenariff Iron Ore
& Harbour Co.
Cloughcor Mines
155

Creggan Quarry
Tunnel, 100yds
Lower Quarry
4'8½"
3'6"

KILLAGAN

67

CROSS ROADS
MARTINSTOWN
Islandtown
CLOUGH ROAD

Dungonnell
Mines
Evishnablay Mine
'Bleagh Branch'
Mt. Cashel Iron
Ore Mine

Aerial
Ropeway
Gortin
Quarry

Carnlough
Harbour

Glenarm

5

GLARRYFORD

72

Rathkenny
Creamery
Siding

RATHKENNY
414
Rathkenny
Mines

Tullyaughter
Quarry

Carnlough
Lime Company
Tramways
157

Eglinton Lime
Company
144

Dromona
Creamery
Siding

BALLYCLOGHAN

Andersons
Broughdone
CULLYBACKEY
Cullybackey
No.2
No.1
Galgorm

BALLYGARVEY

Ballycraigy
Brickworks
Tramway
223

Carnduff
Quarry
243

Sulphate
of Ammonia
244

Ballylumford
Power Station
357

6

Loco Shed
Brewery Siding
'High Level Line'
Gas Company Siding
BALLYMENA
Linen Mill Sidings
Old Goods Station
Spencestown
Slaght

HARRYVILLE
Timber Yard and Saw Mill Sidings
McQuiston's Sdg.

Millbrook Bank Siding
Ballyrickard Siding
KILWAUGHTER HALT
Kilwaughter Siding
Moss Bridge Siding
HEADWOOD
BALLYBOLEY
BALLYNASHEE HALT
BALLYEASTON

British
Aluminium
Works
211

Curran Road
Crossing

LARNE
LARNE
HARBOUR
TOWN

Howden Brothers Sidings

British
Portland
Cement

Kellswater
Industrial
Railway
270

ANDRAID

Dinsmore
Tramway
315

70
MOORFIELDS

Kellswater North
KELLSWATER
Kellswater South

KELLS

Tawnybrack
Siding

COLLIN
HALT

76

GLYNN

Cement Works Siding

241

MAGHERAMORNE

A   **B**   **C**   **D**   **5**

11

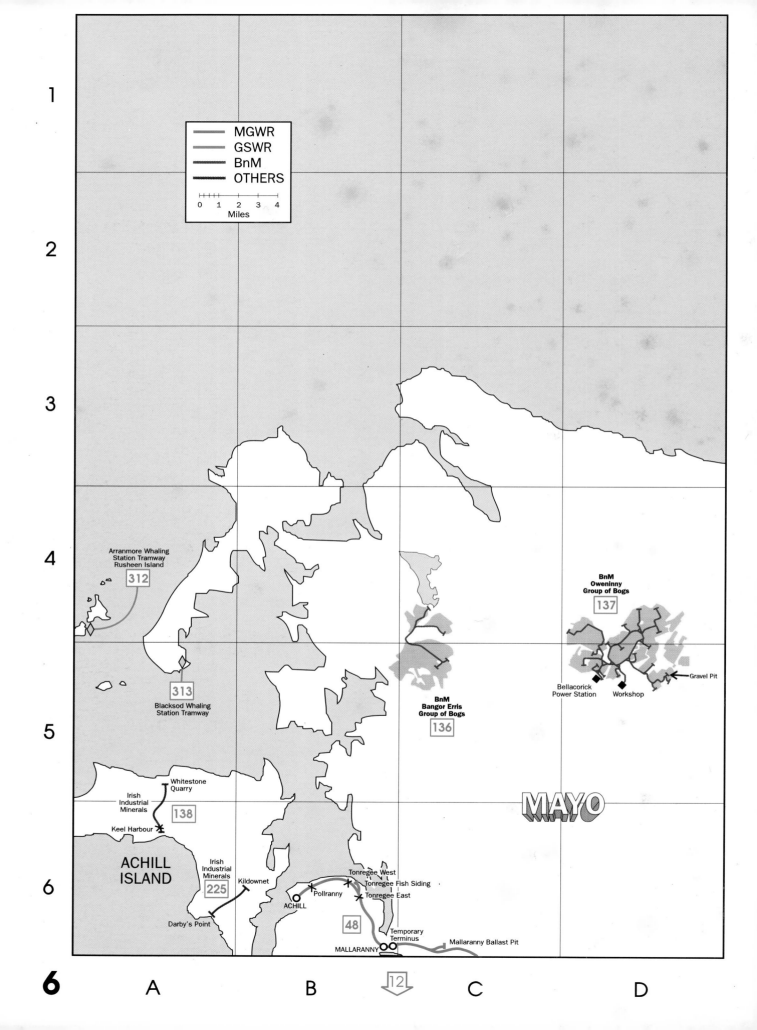

1

2

3

MGWR
GSWR
BnM
OTHERS

0 1 2 3 4
Miles

4

Arranmore Whaling
Station Tramway
Rusheen Island
312

313

Blacksod Whaling
Station Tramway

BnM
Bangor Erris
Group of Bogs
136

BnM
Oweninny
Group of Bogs
137

Bellacorick
Power Station   Workshop   ← Gravel Pit

5

Whitestone
Quarry
Irish
Industrial
Minerals   138

Keel Harbour

MAYO

ACHILL
ISLAND

Irish
Industrial
Minerals   Kildownet
225

Darby's Point

Tonregee West
Tonregee Fish Siding
Pollranny   Tonregee East
ACHILL
48
Temporary
Terminus   Mallaranny Ballast Pit
MALLARANNY

6   A   B   12   C   D

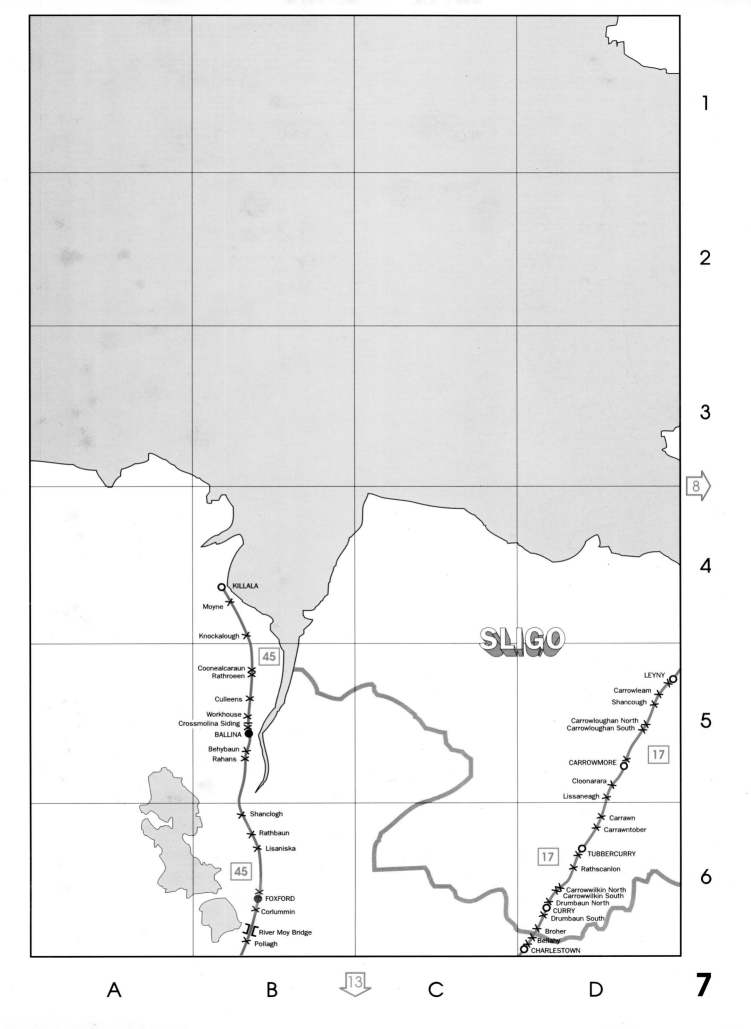

SLIGO

1

2

3

8 ➡

4

KILLALA
Moyne
Knockalough
45
Coonealcaraun
Rathroeen
Culleens
Workhouse
Crossmolina Siding
BALLINA
Behybaun
Rahans

LEYNY
Carrowleam
Shancough
Carrowloughan North
Carrowloughan South
CARROWMORE
Cloonarara
Lissaneagh

17

5

Shanclogh
Rathbaun
Lisaniska

Carrawn
Carrawntober

17 TUBBERCURRY
Rathscanlon

45 FOXFORD
Corlummin

River Moy Bridge
Pollagh

Carrowwilkin North
Carrowwilkin South
Drumbaun North
CURRY
Drumbaun South
Broher
Bellahy
CHARLESTOWN

6

A   B   C   D   **7**

13

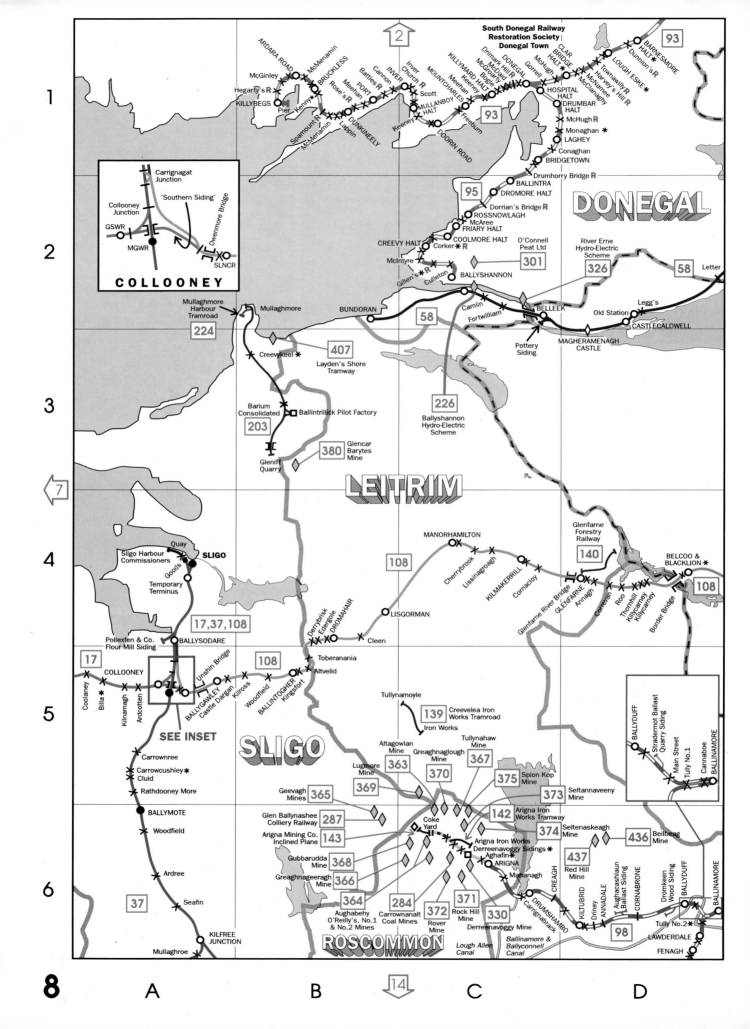

COLLOONEY (inset)

Carrignagat Junction
'Southern Siding'
Colloony Junction
GSWR
MGWR
Owenmore Bridge
SLNCR

DONEGAL

South Donegal Railway
Restoration Society
Donegal Town

ARDARA ROAD
McMenamin
McGinley
BRUCKLESS
Hegarty's **R**
KILLYBEGS
Kenny
Pier
Spamount **R**
McMenamin
Lappin
Battles **R**
Rose's **R**
Cannon
Meehan
DUNKINEELY
PORT
INVER
Inver
Church **R**
Scott
MOUNTCHARLES
KILLYMARD HALT
Meehan
McGrady
McGhee
Drimark Hill **R**
McDaid
Gorrell
DONEGAL
McHugh
CLAR BRIDGE
Townawilly
Dunnion's **R**
Harvey's Hill **R**
McNamee
McClanaghy
LOUGH ESKE **R**
BARNESMORE HALT
93
Keeney
Freeburn
MULLANBOY HALT
Keeney
DOORIN ROAD
93
HOSPITAL HALT
DRUMBAR HALT
McHugh **R**
Monaghan *
LAGHEY
Conaghan
BRIDGETOWN
Drumhorry Bridge **R**
BALLINTRA
DROMORE HALT
95
Dorrian's Bridge **R**
ROSSNOWLAGH
McAree
FRIARY HALT
Corker * **R**
COOLMORE HALT
CREEVY HALT
O'Connell Peat Ltd
McIntyre
Gillen's * **R**
Culleton
301
BALLYSHANNON
River Erne Hydro-Electric Scheme
326
58
Letter
Camlin
Fortwilliam
BELLEEK
Pottery Siding
Old Station
Legg's
CASTLECALDWELL
MAGHERAMENAGH CASTLE

LEITRIM

Mullaghmore Harbour Tramroad
Mullaghmore
224
Creevykeel *
407
Layden's Shore Tramway
Barium Consolidated
Ballintrillick Pilot Factory
203
Gleniff Quarry
380
Glencar Barytes Mine
BUNDORAN
58
226
Ballyshannon Hydro-Electric Scheme

SLIGO

Quay
SLIGO
Sligo Harbour Commissioners
Goods
Temporary Terminus
Pollexfen & Co. Flour Mill Siding
BALLYSODARE
17,37,108
17
COLLOONEY
Unshin Bridge
108
SEE INSET
BALLYGAWLEY
Castle Dargan
Kilross
Woodfield
BALLINTOGHER
Kingsfort
Altvelid
Toberanania
Derrybrisk
Edergole
DROMAHAIR
Cleen
LISGORMAN
108
MANORHAMILTON
Cherrybrook
Lissinagroagh
KILMAKERRILL
Cornacloy
140
Glenfarne Forestry Railway
Glenfarne River Bridge
GLENFARNE
Annagh
Corravan
Roo
Thornhill
Kilfycarney
Kilfycarney
Border Bridge
BELCOO & BLACKLION *
108
Coolaney
Billa
Kilnamagh
Ardcotten
Carrownree
Carrowcushley * Cluid
Rathdooney More
BALLYMOTE
Woodfield
37
Ardree
Seafin
KILFREE JUNCTION
Mullaghroe
Tullynamoyle
139
Creevelea Iron Works Tramroad
Iron Works
Altagowlan Mine
Lugmore Mine
363
Greaghnaglough Mine
370
Tullynahaw Mine
367
Spion Kop Mine
375
373
Seltannaveeny Mine
142
Arigna Iron Works Tramway
Geevagh Mines
365
369
Glen Ballynashee Colliery Railway
287
Coke Yard
Arigna Mining Co. Inclined Plane
143
Gubbarudda Mine
368
Greaghnageeragh Mine
366
364
Aughabehy O'Reilly's, No.1 & No.2 Mines
284
Carrownanalt Coal Mines
372
Rover Mine
371
Rock Hill Mine
330
Derreenavoggy Mine
Arigna Iron Works
Derreenavoggy Sidings *
Aghafin
ARIGNA
Mahanagh
CREAGH
Carrignabrack
DRUMSHAMBO
374
Seltenaskeagh Mine
437
Red Hill Mine
Aughacashlaun Ballast Siding
436
Beilbeag Mine
CORNABRONE
Dromkeen Wood Siding
BALLYDUFF
98
Tully No.2
LAWDERDALE
FENAGH
KILTUBRID
Driney
ANNADALE
BALLYDUFF
Stradermot Ballast Quarry Siding
Main Street
Tully No.1
Cannaboe
BALLINAMORE
Lough Allen Canal
Ballinamore & Ballyconnell Canal

ROSCOMMON

---

8   A   B   C   D

2
14
7

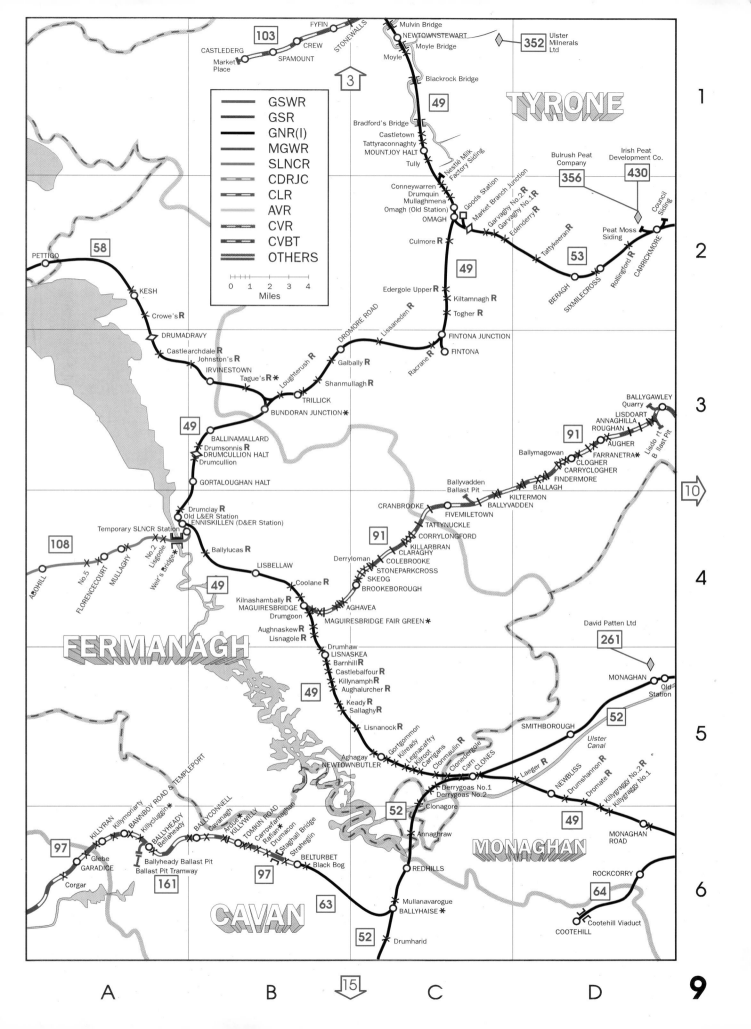

Legend:
- GSWR
- GSR
- GNR(I)
- MGWR
- SLNCR
- CDRJC
- CLR
- AVR
- CVR
- CVBT
- OTHERS

Miles: 0 1 2 3 4

TYRONE

3

FYFIN
103
CASTLEDERG
CREW
SPAMOUNT
Market Place
STONEWALLS

Mulvin Bridge
NEWTOWNSTEWART
Moyle Bridge
Moyle
Blackrock Bridge
49

352 Ulster Minerals Ltd

Bradford's Bridge
Castletown
Tattyraconnaghty
MOUNTJOY HALT
Tully
Nestlé Milk Factory Siding

Conneywarren
Drumquin
Mullaghmena
Omagh (Old Station)
OMAGH
Goods Station
Market Branch Junction
Garvaghy No.2 **R**
Garvaghy No.1 **R**
Edenderry **R**

Bulrush Peat Company
356
Irish Peat Development Co.
430

Peat Moss Siding
Council Siding
CARRICKMORE
Rollingford **R**
SIXMILECROSS
BERAGH
Tattykeeran **R**
53

Culmore **R**

49

Edergole Upper **R**
Kiltamnagh **R**
Togher **R**

58
PETTIGO

KESH
Crowe's **R**

DRUMADRAVY
Castlearchdale **R**
Johnston's **R**
IRVINESTOWN
Tague's **R** *
Loughterush **R**
Galbally **R**
Shanmullagh **R**
TRILLICK
BUNDORAN JUNCTION *

DROMORE ROAD
Lissaneden **R**
Racrane **R**
FINTONA JUNCTION
FINTONA

BALLYGAWLEY Quarry
LISDOART
ANNAGHILLA
ROUGHAN
91
Ballymagowan
AUGHER
FARRANETRA *
CLOGHER
CARRYCLOGHER
FINDERMORE
BALLAGH
Lisdo rt B llast Pit

49
BALLINAMALLARD
Drumsonnis **R**
DRUMCULLION HALT
Drumcullion

GORTALOUGHAN HALT

Drumclay **R**
Old L&ER Station
ENNISKILLEN (D&ER Station)
Temporary SLNCR Station

108
ARDOHILL
No.5
FLORENCECOURT
MULLAGHY
No.2
Lisgoole
Weir's Bridge
Ballylucas **R**

49
LISBELLAW
Coolane **R**
Kilnashambally **R**
MAGUIRESBRIDGE
Drumgoon
AGHAVEA
MAGUIRESBRIDGE FAIR GREEN *
Aughnaskew **R**
Lisnagole **R**

CRANBROOKE
Ballyvadden Ballast Pit
FIVEMILETOWN
TATTYNUCKLE
CORRYLONGFORD
KILLARBRAN
CLARAGHY
Derryloman
COLEBROOKE
STONEPARKCROSS
SKEOG
BROOKEBOROUGH

91

KILTERMON
BALLYVADDEN

10

FERMANAGH

Drumhaw
LISNASKEA
Barnhill **R**
Castlebalfour **R**
Killynamph **R**
Aughalurcher **R**
Keady **R**
Sallaghy **R**
Lisnanock **R**

49

Gortgommon
Kilready
Legnacaffry
Kilroot
Carrigans
Aghagay
NEWTOWNBUTLER
Cloncermaulin **R**
Clonedergole
Carn
CLONES
Derrygoas No.1
Derrygoas No.2
Clonagore

52

David Patten Ltd
261

MONAGHAN
Old Station

SMITHBOROUGH
Ulster Canal
52

Laeger **R**
NEWBLISS
Drumshannon **R**
Dromate **R**
Killygraggy No.2 **R**
Killygraggy No.1

49
MONAGHAN ROAD

ROCKCORRY
64

97
KILLYRAN
Killymoriarty
BAWNBOY ROAD & TEMPLEPORT
Killycluggin *
BALLYHEADY
Bellaheady
Glebe
GARADICE
Corgar
Ballyheady Ballast Pit
Ballast Pit Tramway
161

BALLYCONNELL
Cavanagh
Ardue
KILLYWILLY
TOMKIN ROAD
Carrowfarnaghan
Rafran
Drumacon
Staghall Bridge
Straheglin
97

BELTURBET
Black Bog

63

Annaghraw

REDHILLS

Mullanavarogue
BALLYHAISE *

MONAGHAN

CAVAN

52
Drumharid

COOTEHILL
Cootehill Viaduct

1
2
3
4
5
6

A
15
B
C
D

9

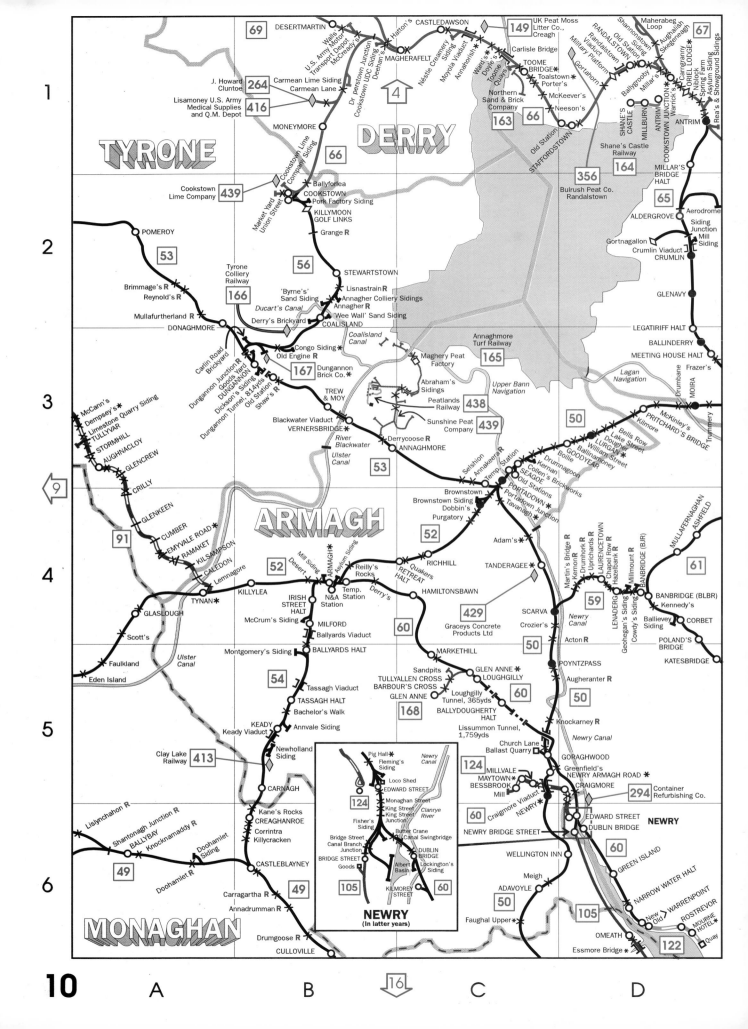

10

TYRONE   **DERRY**   **ARMAGH**   **MONAGHAN**

NEWRY
(In latter years)

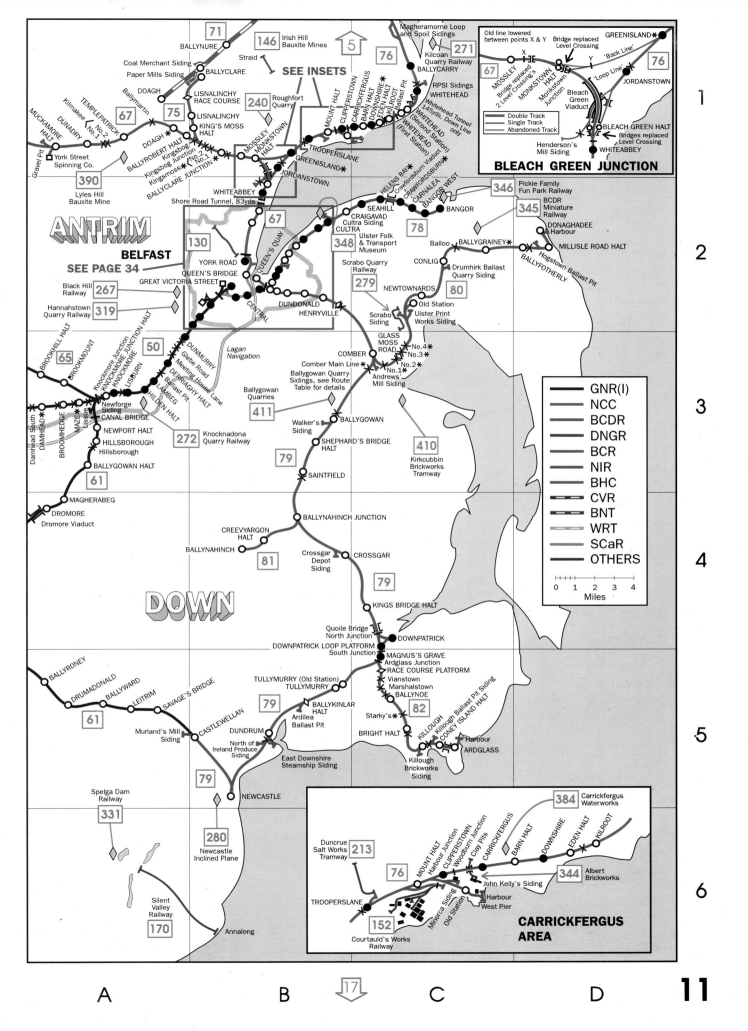

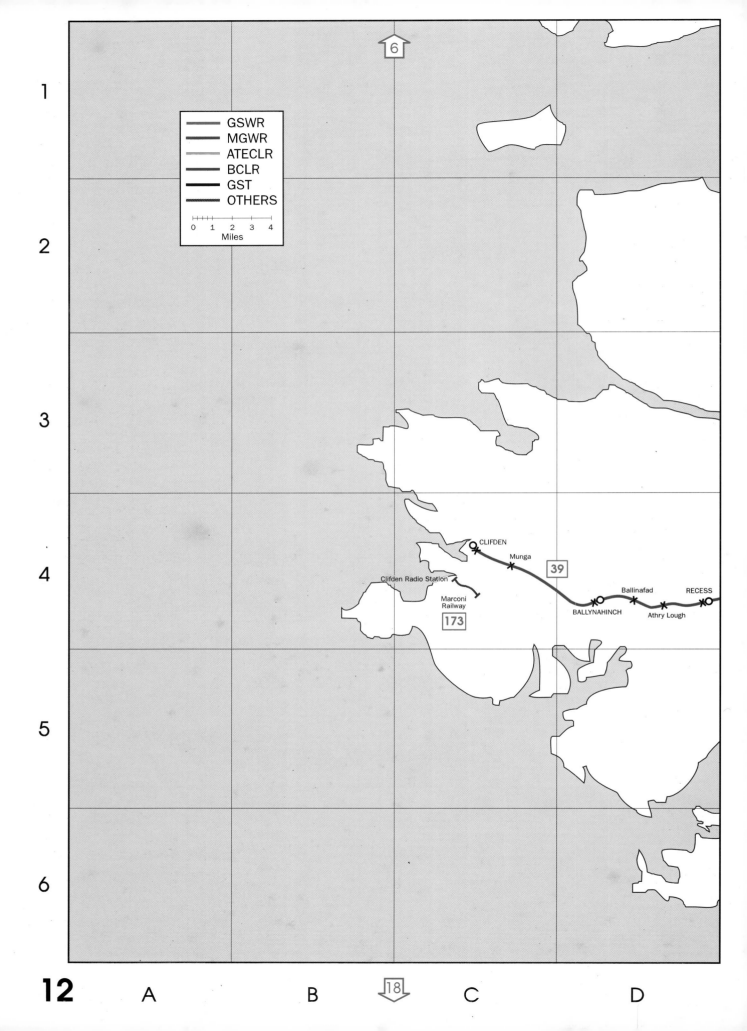

GSWR
MGWR
ATECLR
BCLR
GST
OTHERS

0 1 2 3 4
Miles

CLIFDEN
Munga
39
Clifden Radio Station
Marconi
Railway
173
Ballinafad
RECESS
BALLYNAHINCH
Athry Lough

6

18

12

A   B   C   D

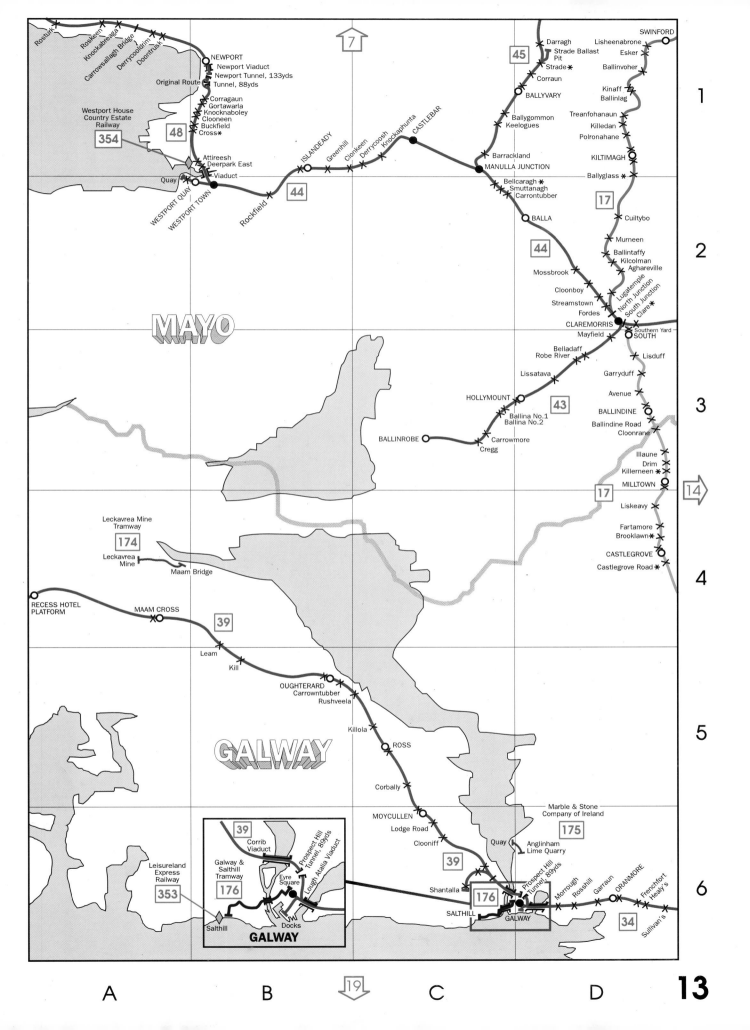

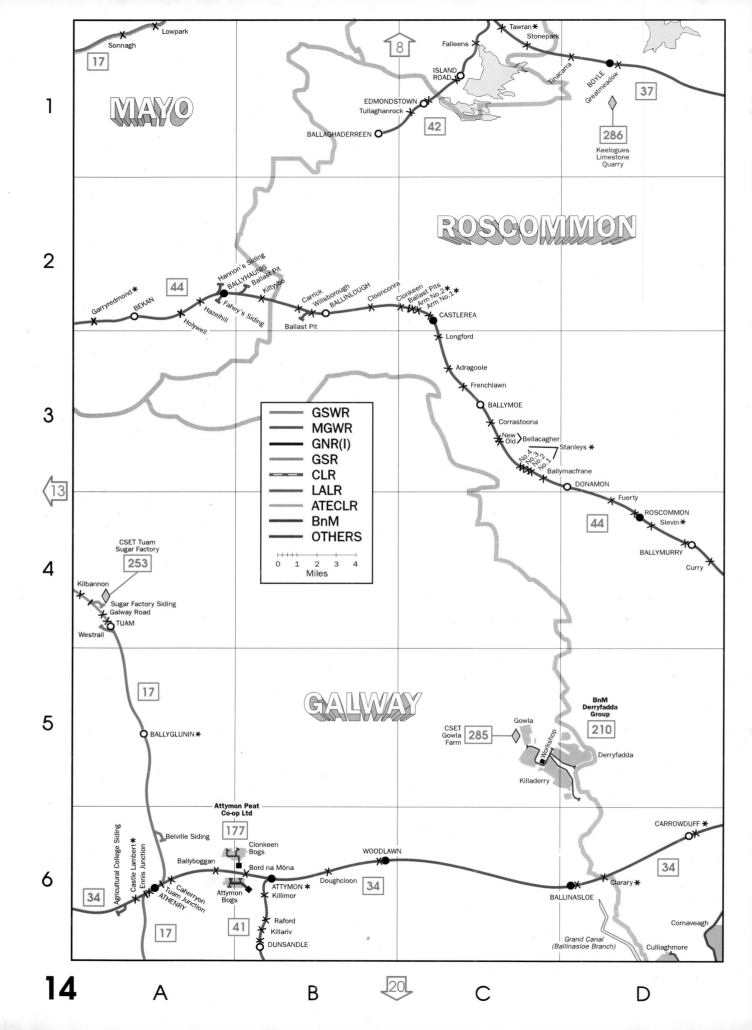

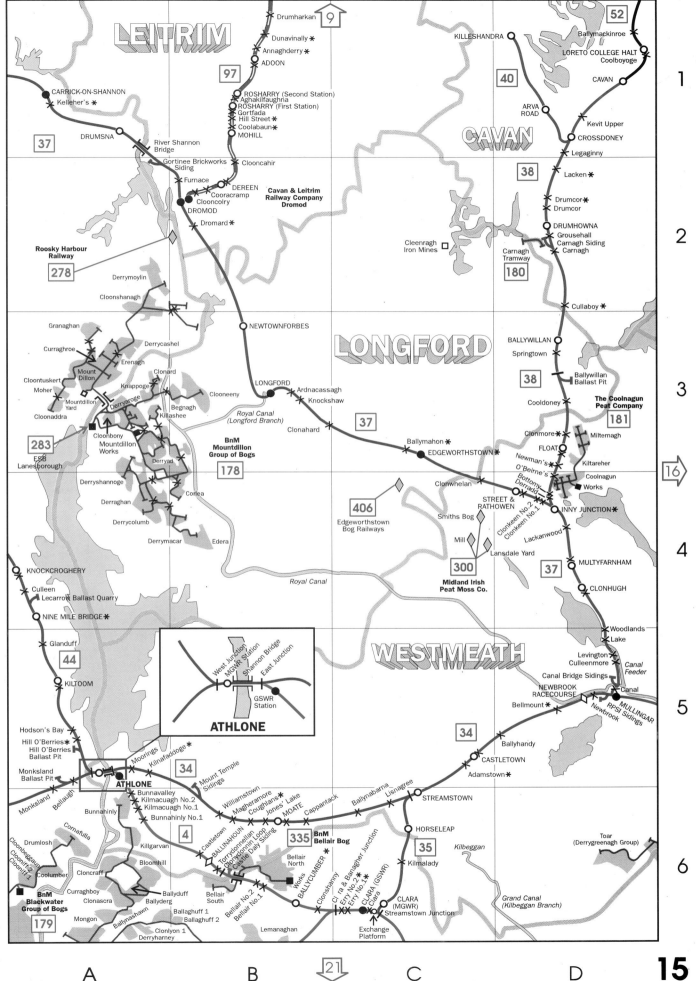

LEITRIM

* Drumharkan
⬆ 9
* Dunavinally
* Annaghderry
○ ADOON
97

● CARRICK-ON-SHANNON
Kelleher's *

DRUMSNA
37
River Shannon Bridge
Gortinee Brickworks Siding
* Clooncahir
* Furnace
○ DEREEN
Cooracramp
Clooncolry
● DROMOD
* Dromard *

Roosky Harbour Railway
278

Derrymoylin
Cloonshanagh

Granaghan
Curraghroe
Derrycashel
Erenagh
Clonard
Mount Dillon
Knappoge
Clooneeny
Cloontuskert
Moher
Mountdillon Yard
Derryaroge
Begnagh
Cloonaddra
Killashee
Cloonbony
Mountdillon Works
283
Derryad
ESB Lanesborough
Derryshannoge
Corlea
Derraghan
Derrycolumb
Derrymacar
Edera
178
BnM Mountdillon Group of Bogs

● NEWTOWNFORBES

LONGFORD

● LONGFORD
Ardnacassagh
Knockshaw
Royal Canal (Longford Branch)
Clonahard
37

* Ballymahon *
● EDGEWORTHSTOWN *
Clonwhelan

406
Edgeworthstown Bog Railways
Smiths Bog
Mill
300
Midland Irish Peat Moss Co.
Lansdale Yard

● KNOCKCROGHERY
Culleen
Lecarrow Ballast Quarry
○ NINE MILE BRIDGE *

Glanduff
44
KILTOOM

Hodson's Bay
Hill O'Berries
Hill O'Berries Ballast Pit
Monksland Ballast Pit
Monksland
Bellaugh
34
● ATHLONE
Bunnavalley
Kilmacuagh No.2
Kilmacuagh No.1
Bunnahinly
Bunnahinly No.1
Moorings
Kilnafaddoge *
Mount Temple Sidings
34

West Junction
MGWR Station
Shannon Bridge
East Junction
GSWR Station
ATHLONE

Williamstown
Magheramore
Coughlans *
Jones' Lake
MOATE
Cappantack
Ballynabarna
Lisnagree
● STREAMSTOWN

Castletown
BALLINAHOUN
Torrydonnellan
Clonydonnin Loop
Castle Daly Siding
335
BnM Bellair Bog
Bellair North

4
Killgarvan
Bloomhill
Ballyduff
Bellair South
Bellair No.2
Bellair No.1
Works
BALLYCUMBER
Clonshanny
Cl ra & Banagher Junction
Ery No.2 *
Ery No.1 *
CLARA (MGWR)
Streamstown Junction
CLARA (GSWR)
Clara
Exchange Platform

Cloonbeggaun
Cloonlf 2
Cloonlf 1
Drumlosh
Cornafulla
Coolumber
BnM Blackwater Group of Bogs
179
Curraghboy
Clonascra
Clancraft
Ballyderg
Mongon
Ballynashawn
Clonlyon 1
Derryharney

Lemanaghan
Kilmalady
35
Kilbeggan

○ HORSELEAP
Kilbeggan

Toar (Derrygreenagh Group)
Grand Canal (Kilbeggan Branch)

Royal Canal

WESTMEATH

Ballyhandy
Adamstown *
○ CASTLETOWN
Bellmount
NEWBROOK RACECOURSE
Newbrook
RPSI Sidings
● MULLINGAR
Canal
Canal Bridge Sidings
Levington
Culleenmore
Canal Feeder
Woodlands
Lake
CLONHUGH
MULTYFARNHAM
37
Lackanwood
INNY JUNCTION *
Clonkeen No.2
Clonkeen No.1
STREET & RATHOWEN
Derrado
Bottomy
O'Beirne's
Newman's
FLOAT
Coolnagun
Works
181
Kiltareher
Milternagh
Clonmore *
The Coolnagun Peat Company
Cooldoney
38
Ballywillan Ballast Pit
Springtown
BALLYWILLAN
* Cullaboy *

Carnagh Tramway
180
Carnagh
Carnagh Siding
Grousehall
DRUMHOWNA
* Drumcor
Drumcor *
Lacken *
Legaginny
CROSSDONEY
Kevit Upper
ARVA ROAD
38
CAVAN
40
CAVAN
Coolboyoge
LORETO COLLEGE HALT
52
Ballymackinroe
● KILLESHANDRA

Cleenragh Iron Mines
Cavan & Leitrim Railway Company Dromod

⬇ 21

1

2

3

◄ 16

4

5

6

A   B   C   D

15

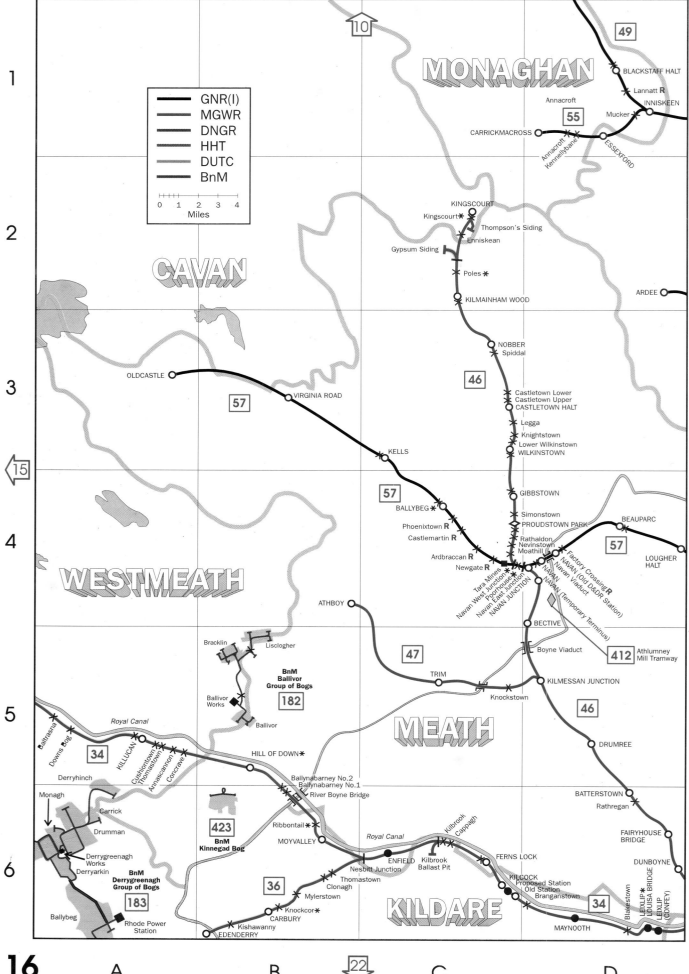

GNR(I)
MGWR
DNGR
HHT
DUTC
BnM

0 1 2 3 4
Miles

16
A   B   C   D
1 2 3 4 5 6

MONAGHAN

49
BLACKSTAFF HALT
Lannatt **R**
INNISKEEN
Annacroft
55
Mucker
CARRICKMACROSS
Annacroft
Kennellybane
ESSEXFORD

CAVAN

KINGSCOURT
Kingscourt
Thompson's Siding
Enniskean
Gypsum Siding
Poles
KILMAINHAM WOOD
ARDEE
NOBBER
Spiddal
46
Castletown Lower
Castletown Upper
CASTLETOWN HALT
OLDCASTLE
57
VIRGINIA ROAD
Legga
Knightstown
Lower Wilkinstown
WILKINSTOWN

15
KELLS
57
GIBBSTOWN
Simonstown
BEAUPARC
57
Ballybeg
Phoenixtown **R**
PROUDSTOWN PARK
Rathaldon
Nevinstown
LOUGHER
HALT
Castlemartin **R**
Moathill
Ardbraccan **R**
Factory Crossing **R**
Newgate **R**
NAVAN (Old D&DR Station)
Navan Viaduct
Tara Mines
NAVAN (Temporary Terminus)
Navan West Junction
Poorhouse
Navan East Junction
NAVAN JUNCTION

WESTMEATH

ATHBOY
BECTIVE
Boyne Viaduct
412
Athlumney
Mill Tramway
Bracklin
Lisclogher
47
TRIM
KILMESSAN JUNCTION
BnM
Ballivor
Group of Bogs
Ballivor
Works
182
Knockstown
46
Ballivor

MEATH

Baltrasna
Royal Canal
DRUMREE
Downs Bog
34
KILLUCAN
Cushiontown
Thomastown
Annascannon
Concrave
HILL OF DOWN
Derryhinch
Ballynabarney No.2
Ballynabarney No.1
River Boyne Bridge
BATTERSTOWN
Monagh
Carrick
423
Ribbontail
Rathregan
Drumman
BnM
Kinnegad Bog
MOYVALLEY
Royal Canal
Kilbrook
Cappagh
FAIRYHOUSE
BRIDGE
Derrygreenagh
Works
Derryarkin
Nesbitt Junction
ENFIELD
Kilbrook
Ballast Pit
FERNS LOCK
DUNBOYNE
BnM
Derrygreenagh Group of Bogs
Thomastown
Clonagh
KILCOCK
Proposed Station
Old Station
Branganstown
Ballybeg
183
36
Mylerstown
Blakestown
LEIXLIP
LOUISA BRIDGE
34
Rhode Power
Station
Knockcor
CARBURY
LEIXLIP
(CONFEY)
Kishawanny
EDENDERRY
KILDARE
MAYNOOTH

10
15
22
49

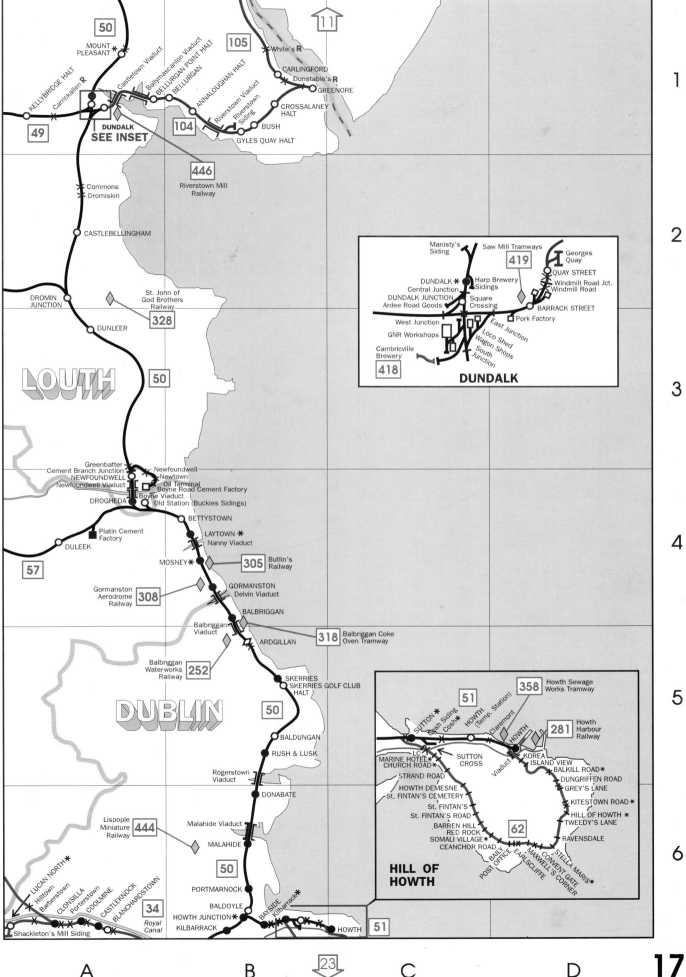

MOUNT PLEASANT

50

KELLYBRIDGE HALT

49

Carrickallen R

Castletown Viaduct

DUNDALK
SEE INSET

Commons
Dromiskin

CASTLEBELLINGHAM

DROMIN JUNCTION

DUNLEER

328

St. John of God Brothers Railway

LOUTH

50

104

446

Riverstown Mill Railway

Ballymascanlon Viaduct

BELLURGAN POINT HALT
BELLURGAN

ANNALOUGHAN HALT

Riverstown Viaduct
Riverstown Siding

105

White's R

CARLINGFORD

Dunstable's R

GREENORE

CROSSALANEY HALT

BUSH

GYLES QUAY HALT

11

DUNDALK inset:

Manisty's Siding

Saw Mill Tramways

419

Georges Quay

QUAY STREET

DUNDALK
Central Junction

Harp Brewery Sidings

Windmill Road Jct.
Windmill Road

DUNDALK JUNCTION
Ardee Road Goods

Square Crossing

BARRACK STREET

West Junction

East Junction

Pork Factory

GNR Workshops

Loco Shed
Wagon Shops
South Junction

Cambricville Brewery

418

DUNDALK

Greenbatter
Cement Branch Junction
NEWFOUNDWELL
Newfoundwell Viaduct

Newfoundwell
Newtown
Oil Terminal
Boyne Road Cement Factory
Boyne Viaduct

DROGHEDA

Old Station (Buckies Sidings)

Platin Cement Factory

DULEEK

57

50

BETTYSTOWN

LAYTOWN

Nanny Viaduct

MOSNEY

305

Butlin's Railway

Gormanston
Aerodrome Railway

308

GORMANSTON
Delvin Viaduct

BALBRIGGAN

Balbriggan Viaduct

ARDGILLAN

318

Balbriggan Coke Oven Tramway

Balbriggan Waterworks Railway

252

DUBLIN

50

SKERRIES
SKERRIES GOLF CLUB HALT

BALDUNGAN

RUSH & LUSK

Rogerstown Viaduct

DONABATE

Lispople Miniature Railway

444

Malahide Viaduct

MALAHIDE

50

PORTMARNOCK

BALDOYLE

HOWTH JUNCTION

KILBARRACK

34

Royal Canal

Lucan North
Hilltown
Baberstown
CLONSILLA
Porterstown
COOLMINE
CASTLEKNOCK
BLANCHARDSTOWN

Shackleton's Mill Siding

BAYSIDE
Kilbarrack

HOWTH

51

HILL OF HOWTH inset:

51

SUTTON

Bush Siding
Cosh

HOWTH (Temp. Station)

Claremont

358

Howth Sewage Works Tramway

281

Howth Harbour Railway

HOWTH

MARINE HOTEL
CHURCH ROAD

SUTTON CROSS

STRAND ROAD

HOWTH DEMESNE
St. FINTAN'S CEMETERY

St. FINTAN'S

St. FINTAN'S ROAD

BARREN HILL
RED ROCK
SOMALI VILLAGE
CEANCHOR ROAD

62

Korea
ISLAND VIEW
BALKILL ROAD
DUNGRIFFEN ROAD
GREY'S LANE
KITESTOWN ROAD
HILL OF HOWTH
TWEEDY'S LANE
RAVENSDALE

STELLA MARIS
CONVENT GATE
MAXWELL'S CORNER
EARLSCLIFFE

BAILY
POST OFFICE

HILL OF HOWTH

23

A   B   C   D

17

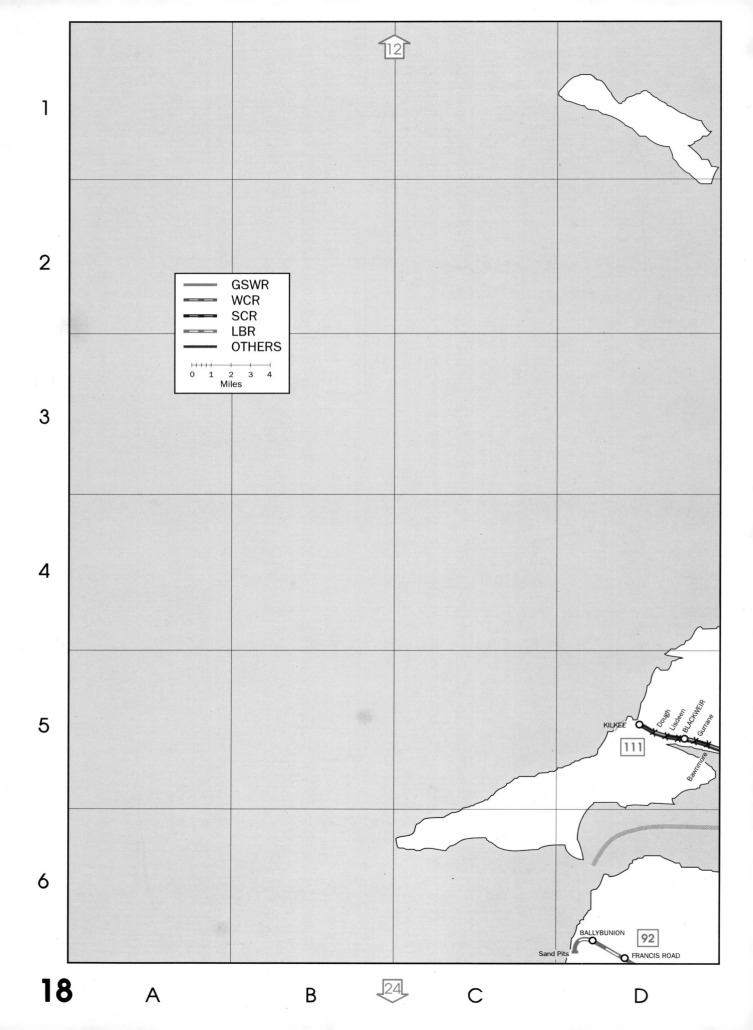

18

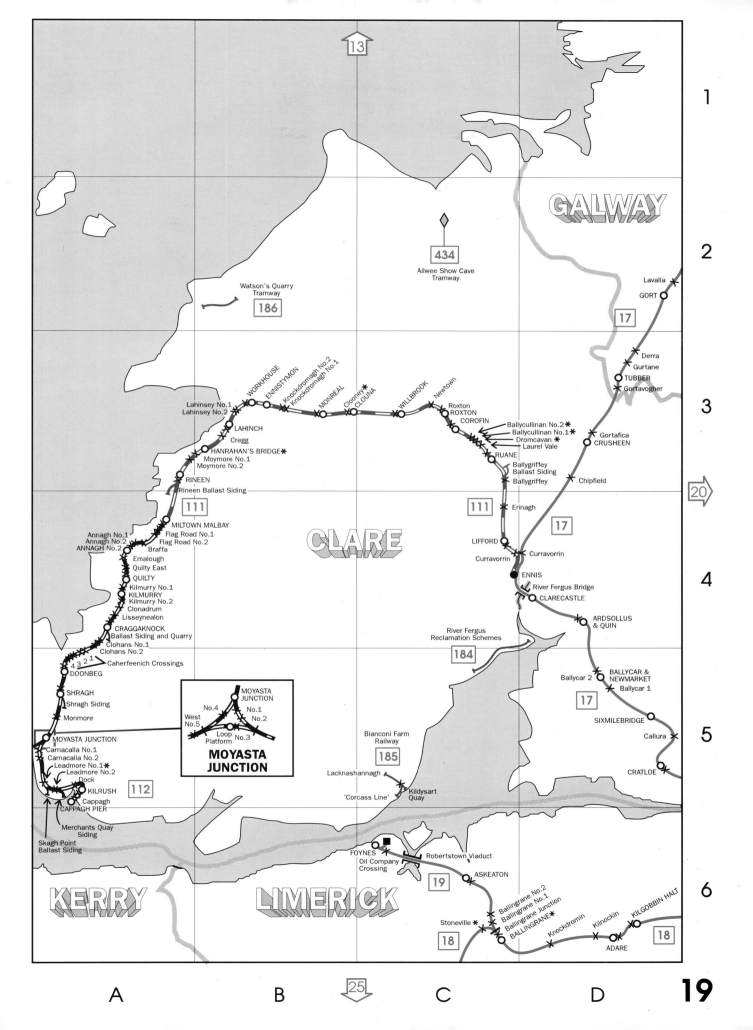

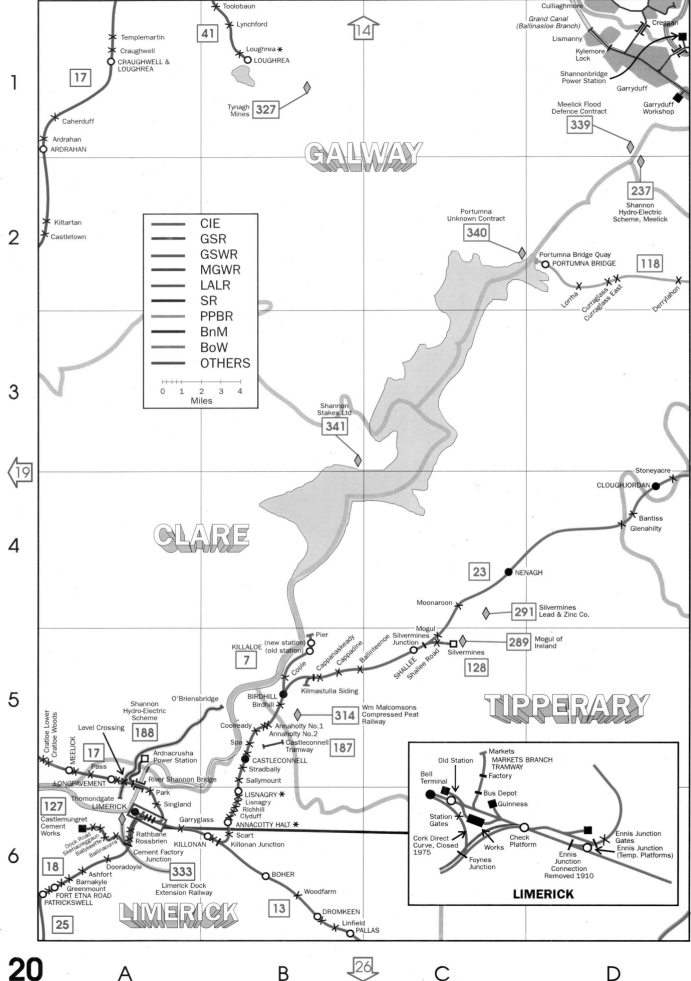

Legend (key):
- CIE
- GSR
- GSWR
- MGWR
- LALR
- SR
- PPBR
- BnM
- BoW
- OTHERS

Scale: 0 1 2 3 4 Miles

GALWAY

Toolabaun
Lynchford
41
Loughrea
LOUGHREA
Templemartin
Craughwell
CRAUGHWELL & LOUGHREA
17
Caherduff
Ardrahan
ARDRAHAN
Tynagh Mines 327
14

Culliaghmore
Grand Canal (Ballinasloe Branch)
Creggan
Lismanny
Kylemore Lock
Shannonbridge Power Station
Garryduff
Garryduff Workshop
Meelick Flood Defence Contract 339
237
Shannon Hydro-Electric Scheme, Meelick

Portumna Unknown Contract 340
Portumna Bridge Quay
PORTUMNA BRIDGE
118
Lorrha
Curraglass
Curraglass East
Derrylahon

Kiltartan
Castletown

CLARE

Shannon Stakes Ltd 341

19

Stoneyacre
CLOUGHJORDAN
Bantiss
Glenahilty

23
NENAGH
Moonaroon
Silvermines Lead & Zinc Co. 291

TIPPERARY

Mogul
Silvermines Junction
SHALLEE
Shallee Road
Silvermines
289 Mogul of Ireland
128

Pier
KILLALOE (new station) (old station)
7
Coole
Cappanaskeady
Cappadine
Ballinteenoe
Kilmastulla Siding

BIRDHILL
Birdhill
O'Briensbridge
Shannon Hydro-Electric Scheme 188
Coolready
Annaholty No.1
Annaholty No.2
Spa
314 Wm Malcomsons Compressed Peat Railway
Castleconnell Tramway 187

Cratloe Lower
Cratloe Woods
MEELICK
Level Crossing
17
Pass
Ardnacrusha Power Station
River Shannon Bridge
LONGPAVEMENT
Thomondgate
LIMERICK
127
Park
Singland
CASTLECONNELL
Stradbally
Sallymount
LISNAGRY
Lisnagry
Richhill
Clyduff
ANNACOTTY HALT
Garryglass
Scart
KILLONAN
Killonan Junction

Castlemungret Cement Works
Dock Road
Skenacreggaun
Ballykeeffe
Ballinacurra
Rathbane
Rossbrien
Cement Factory Junction
Dooradoyle
18
Ashfort
Barnakyle
Greenmount
FORT ETNA ROAD
PATRICKSWELL
25
333 Limerick Dock Extension Railway
BOHER
13
Woodfarm
DROMKEEN
Linfield
PALLAS
26

LIMERICK (inset):
Markets
MARKETS BRANCH TRAMWAY
Old Station
Factory
Bell Terminal
Bus Depot
Guinness
Station Gates
Check Platform
Cork Direct Curve, Closed 1975
Works
Foynes Junction
Ennis Junction Gates
Ennis Junction (Temp. Platforms)
Ennis Junction Connection Removed 1910
LIMERICK

20   A   B   C   D

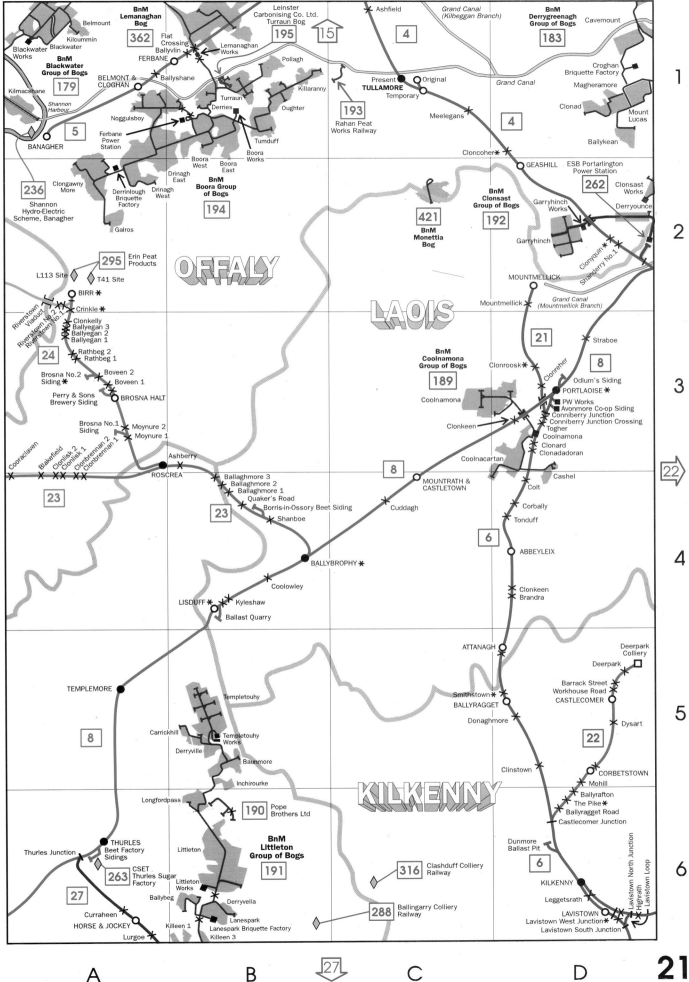

BnM Lemanaghan Bog
362
Flat
Crossing
Ballyvlin
FERBANE
Leinster
Carbonising Co. Ltd.
Turraun Bog
195
Lemanaghan
Works
Pollagh
Ashfield
Grand Canal
(Kilbeggan Branch)
4
15
BnM
Derrygreenagh
Group of Bogs
183
Cavemount

Belmount
Kilcummin
Blackwater Blackwater
Blackwater
Works
BnM
Blackwater
Group of Bogs
179
Ballyshane
Killaranny
Turraun
Derries
Present
TULLAMORE
Temporary
Original
Grand Canal
4
Croghan
Briquette Factory
Magheramore
Clonad
Mount
Lucas
1

Kilmacshane
Shannon
Harbour
5
BANAGHER
BELMONT &
CLOGHAN
Noggulsboy
Ferbane
Power
Station
Ferbane
Power Station
Boora
West
Boora
East
Boora
Works
Tumduff
Oughter
193
Rahan Peat
Works Railway
Meelegans
Cloncoher
GEASHILL
ESB Portarlington
Power Station
262
Clonsast
Works
Derryounce
Ballykean

236
Clongawny
More
Shannon
Hydro-Electric
Scheme, Banagher
Derrinlough
Briquette
Factory
Drinagh
East
Drinagh
West
Galros
Boora
West
BnM
Boora Group
of Bogs
194
OFFALY
421
BnM
Monettia
Bog
BnM
Clonsast
Group of Bogs
192
Garryhinch
Works
Garryhinch
MOUNTMELLICK
Mountmellick
Garryhinch
Clonyquin
Shanderry No.1
Grand Canal
(Mountmellick Branch)
21
Straboe
8
2

295
Erin Peat
Products
L113 Site
T41 Site
BIRR
Crinkle
24
Riverstown
Viaduct
Riverstown No. 2
Riverstown No. 1
Clonkelly
Ballyegan 3
Ballyegan 2
Ballyegan 1
Rathbeg 2
Rathbeg 1
Brosna No.2
Siding
Boveen 2
Boveen 1
BROSNA HALT
Perry & Sons
Brewery Siding
LAOIS
BnM
Coolnamona
Group of Bogs
189
Coolnamona
Clonkeen
Clonroosk
Clonreher
Odlum's Siding
PORTLAOISE
PW Works
Avonmore Co-op Siding
Conniberry Junction
Conniberry Junction Crossing
Togher
Coolnamona
Clonard
Clonadadoran
8
3

Cooraclaven
Blakefield
Clonlisk 1
Clonlisk 2
Clonbrennan 2
Clonbrennan 1
23
Brosna No.1
Siding
Moynure 2
Moynure 1
Ashberry
ROSCREA
Ballaghmore 3
Ballaghmore 2
Ballaghmore 1
Quaker's Road
Borris-in-Ossory Beet Siding
Shanboe
23
Cuddagh
8
MOUNTRATH &
CASTLETOWN
Coolnacartan
Colt
Corbally
Tonduff
6
Cashel
Clonkeen
Brandra
22
4

BALLYBROPHY
Coolowley
LISDUFF
Kyleshaw
Ballast Quarry
ABBEYLEIX

TEMPLEMORE
8
Carrickhill
Templetouhy
Templetouhy
Works
Derryville
Baunmore
Inchirourke
ATTANAGH
Smithstown
BALLYRAGGET
Donaghmore
Clinstown
Deerpark
Colliery
Deerpark
Barrack Street
Workhouse Road
CASTLECOMER
Dysart
22
CORBETSTOWN
Mohill
Ballyrafton
The Pike
Ballyragget Road
Castlecomer Junction
5

Longfordpass
190
Pope
Brothers Ltd
Littleton
BnM
Littleton
Group of Bogs
191
KILKENNY
316
Clashduff Colliery
Railway
288
Ballingarry Colliery
Railway
Dunmore
Ballast Pit
6
KILKENNY
Leggetsrath
LAVISTOWN
Lavistown West Junction
Lavistown South Junction
Lavistown North Junction
Highrath
Lavistown Loop
6

THURLES
Thurles Junction
Beet Factory
Sidings
263
CSET
Thurles Sugar
Factory
27
Curraheen
HORSE & JOCKEY
Lurgoe
Littleton
Littleton
Works
Ballybeg
Killeen 1
Lanespark
Lanespark Briquette Factory
Killeen 3
Derryvella

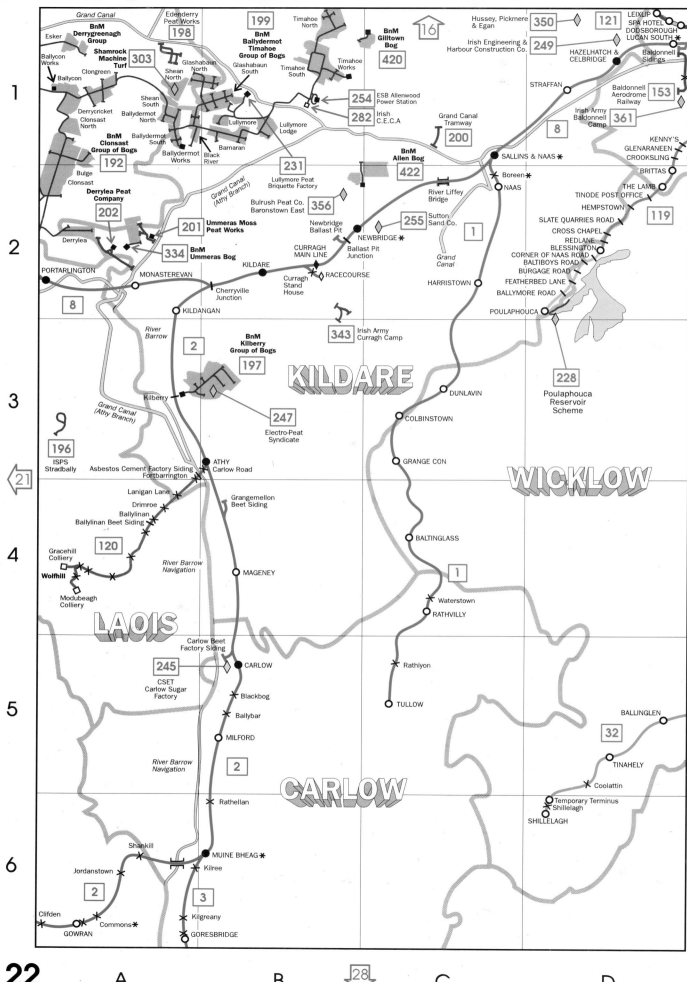

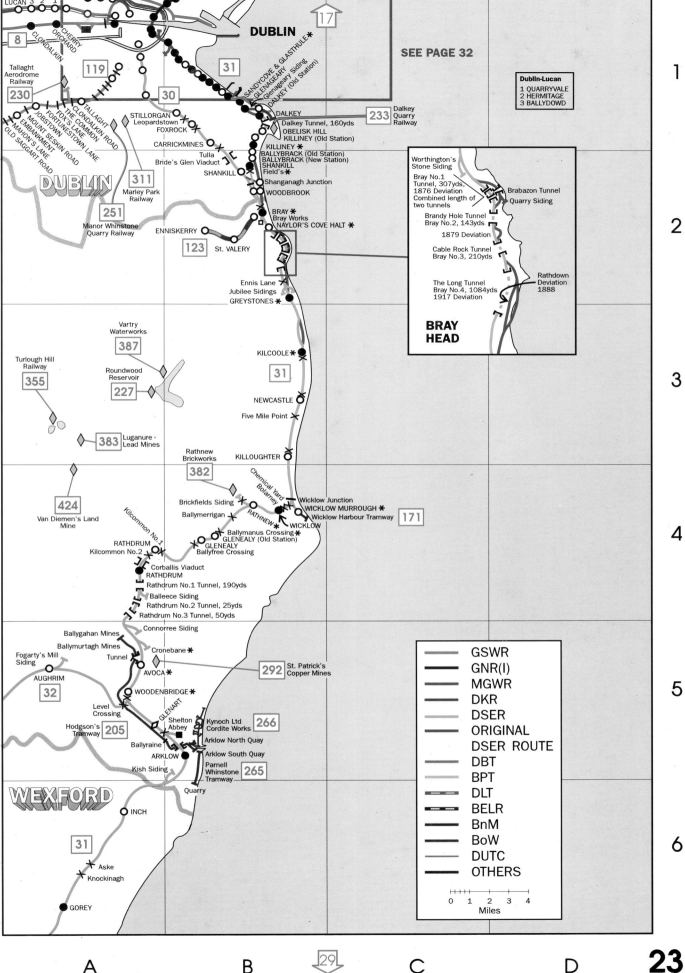

LUCAN 3 2 1
8 CLONDALKIN
CHERRY ORCHARD

DUBLIN

↑ 17

SEE PAGE 32

SANDYCOVE & GLASTHULE ✳
GLENAGEARY
Glenageary Siding
DALKEY (Old Station)

Dublin-Lucan
1 QUARRYVALE
2 HERMITAGE
3 BALLYDOWD

1

119
Tallaght Aerodrome Railway
230
31
30

TALLAGHT
CLONDALKIN
FOX'S LANE
THE COMMON
FORTUNESTOWN LANE
MOUNT SESKIN ROAD
JOBSTOWN
EMBANKMENT
MAHON'S LANE
OLD SAGGART ROAD
CLONDALKIN ROAD

STILLORGAN
Leopardstown
FOXROCK
CARRICKMINES
Tulla
Bride's Glen Viaduct
SHANKILL

311

DUBLIN

251
Manor Whinstone Quarry Railway
Marley Park Railway

ENNISKERRY
123
St. VALERY

DALKEY
233 Dalkey Quarry Railway
Dalkey Tunnel, 160yds
OBELISK HILL
KILLINEY (Old Station)
KILLINEY
BALLYBRACK (Old Station)
BALLYBRACK (New Station)
SHANKILL
Field's
Shanganagh Junction
WOODBROOK
BRAY ✳
Bray Works
NAYLOR'S COVE HALT ✳

Worthington's Stone Siding
Bray No.1 Tunnel, 307yds, 1876 Deviation Combined length of two tunnels
Brabazon Tunnel
Quarry Siding
Brandy Hole Tunnel Bray No.2, 143yds
1879 Deviation
Cable Rock Tunnel Bray No.3, 210yds
Rathdown Deviation 1888
The Long Tunnel Bray No.4, 1084yds 1917 Deviation

BRAY HEAD

2

Ennis Lane
Jubilee Sidings
GREYSTONES ✳

Vartry Waterworks
387

Turlough Hill Railway
355

Roundwood Reservoir
227

KILCOOLE ✳
31

NEWCASTLE
Five Mile Point

3

383 Luganure Lead Mines

424
Van Diemen's Land Mine

Rathnew Brickworks
KILLOUGHTER

382
Brickfields Siding
Ballymerrigan
Chemical Yard
Bolarney
RATHNEW
Wicklow Junction
WICKLOW MURROUGH ✳
Wicklow Harbour Tramway
WICKLOW
171

4

Kilcommon No.1
RATHDRUM
Kilcommon No.2
Corballis Viaduct
RATHDRUM
Rathdrum No.1 Tunnel, 190yds
Balleece Siding
Rathdrum No.2 Tunnel, 25yds
Rathdrum No.3 Tunnel, 50yds

Ballymanus Crossing
GLENEALY (Old Station)
GLENEALY
Ballyfree Crossing

Ballygahan Mines
Ballymurtagh Mines
Tunnel
Connorree Siding
Cronebane ✳
AVOCA ✳
St. Patrick's Copper Mines
292

Fogarty's Mill Siding
AUGHRIM
32

WOODENBRIDGE ✳
Level Crossing
GLENART
Hodgson's Tramway
205
Shelton Abbey
Ballyraine
ARKLOW
Kish Siding
Kynoch Ltd Cordite Works
Arklow North Quay
266
Arklow South Quay
Parnell Whinstone Tramway
265
Quarry

5

WEXFORD

INCH

31

Aske
Knockinagh

GOREY

GSWR
GNR(I)
MGWR
DKR
DSER
ORIGINAL DSER ROUTE
DBT
BPT
DLT
BELR
BnM
BoW
DUTC
OTHERS

0 1 2 3 4
Miles

6

A   B   C   D   23

↓ 29

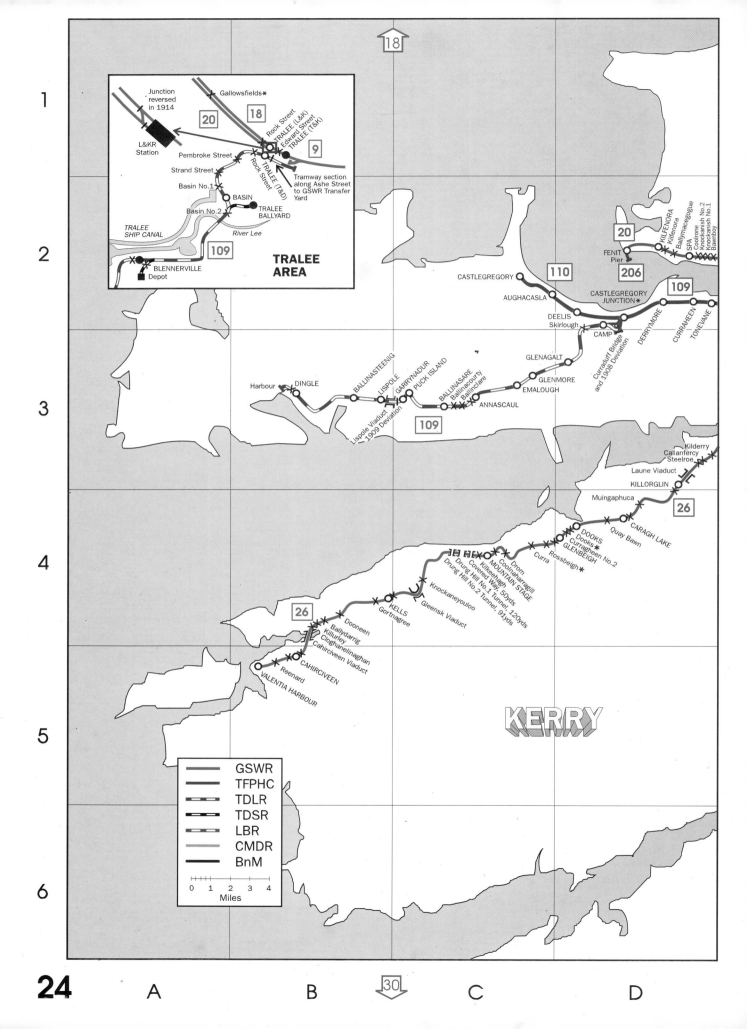

TRALEE AREA

Junction reversed in 1914

Gallowsfields*

20

18

L&KR Station

Rock Street
TRALEE (L&K)
Edward Street
TRALEE (T&K)

9

Pembroke Street

TRALEE (T&D)

Strand Street

Rock Street

Tramway section along Ashe Street to GSWR Transfer Yard

Basin No.1

BASIN

Basin No.2

TRALEE BALLYARD

TRALEE SHIP CANAL

River Lee

109

BLENNERVILLE
Depot

KILFENORA
Kilfenora
Ballymacegogue
SPA
Coolrone
Knockanish No.2
Knockanish No.1
Bawnboy

20

FENIT Pier

206

CASTLEGREGORY

110

CASTLEGREGORY JUNCTION *

109

AUGHACASLA

DEELIS
Skirlough

CAMP

DERRYMORE

CURRAHEEN
TONEVANE

Curraduff Bridge and 1908 Deviation

GLENAGALT

GLENMORE

EMALOUGH

Harbour

DINGLE

BALLINASTEENIG
LISPOLE
GARRYNADUR
PUCK ISLAND

Lispole Viaduct
1909 Deviation

BALLINASARE
Ballinacourty
Ballinclare

ANNASCAUL

109

Kilderry
Callanfercy
Steelroe

Laune Viaduct

KILLORGLIN

Muingaphuca

26

CARAGH LAKE

Quay Bawn

DOOKS
Dooks
Curragheen No.2
GLENBEIGH
Rossbeigh*

Curra

Drom
Coolnaharragill
MOUNTAIN STAGE
Killeenagh
Covered Way, 50yds
Drung Hill No.1 Tunnel, 120yds
Drung Hill No.2 Tunnel, 91yds

Knockaneyouloo

Gleensk Viaduct

KELLS
Gortnagree

26

Dooneen
Ballydarrig
Killurley
Cloghanelinaghan
Cahirciveen Viaduct

CAHIRCIVEEN

Reenard

VALENTIA HARBOUR

KERRY

	GSWR
	TFPHC
	TDLR
	TDSR
	LBR
	CMDR
	BnM

0 1 2 3 4
Miles

30

A   B   C   D

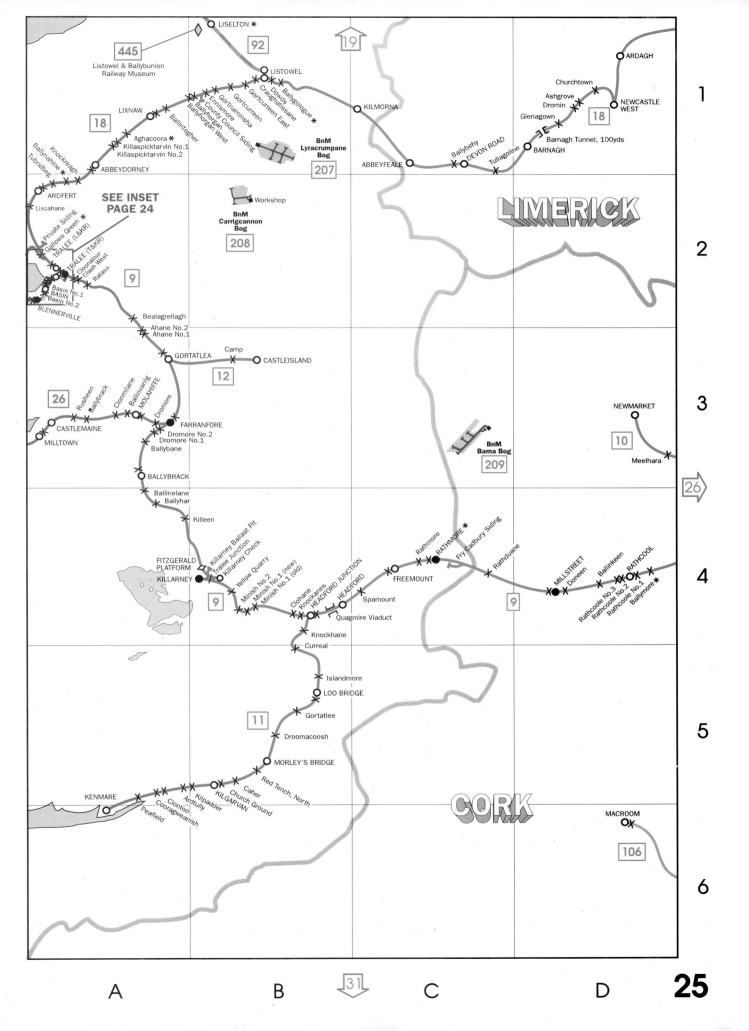

LISELTON ✳

445
Listowel & Ballybunion
Railway Museum

92

19

LISTOWEL
Ballygologue
Dowds
Craughatissane
Gortcurreen East
Gortcurreen
County Council Siding
Ballyhorgan
Ballyhorgan West
Gortnaminsha
Ennismore

KILMORNA

ARDAGH
Churchtown
Ashgrove
Glenagown   Dromin
NEWCASTLE
WEST
18
Barnagh Tunnel, 100yds
BARNAGH
Ballybehy   DEVON ROAD
Tullagoline
ABBEYFEALE

LIMERICK

LIXNAW
18
Ballintogher
Aghacoora ✳
Killaspicktarvin No.1
Killaspicktarvin No.2
ABBEYDORNEY

Knockreagh
Ballynahine
Tubridbeg
ARDFERT
Liscahane
Private Siding ✳
Gallows Green (L&KR)
TRALEE (L&KR)
TRALEE (T&KR)
Clonalour
Clash West
Ratass
BASIN No.1
BASIN
Basin No.2
BLENNERVILLE

SEE INSET
PAGE 24

BnM
Lyracrumpane
Bog
207

Workshop
BnM
Carrigcannon
Bog
208

9

Bealagrellagh
Ahane No.2
Ahane No.1
GORTATLEA   Camp   CASTLEISLAND
12

26
Rusheen
Ballybrack
Clonmilane
Ballinvarrig
MOLAHIFFE
Dromore
CASTLEMAINE
MILLTOWN
FARRANFORE
Dromore No.2
Dromore No.1
Ballybane

BALLYBRACK
Ballinelane
Ballyhar
Killeen

NEWMARKET

BnM
Barna Bog
209

10
Meelhara

26

FITZGERALD
PLATFORM
KILLARNEY

Killarney Ballast Pit
Tralee Junction
Killarney Check
Yellow Quarry
Minish No.2
Minish No.1 (new)
Minish No.1 (old)
9
Clohane
Knockanes
HEADFORD JUNCTION
HEADFORD
Spamount
Quagmire Viaduct

Rathmore
RATHMORE ✳
Fry Cadbury Siding
Rathduane
FREEMOUNT

MILLSTREET
Doneen
Ballinkeen
Rathcoole No.3
Rathcoole No.2
RATHCOOL
Rathcoole No.1
Ballymore ✳
9

Knockhane
Curreal

Islandmore
LOO BRIDGE

11
Gortatlee
Droomacoosh
MORLEY'S BRIDGE

KENMARE
Peafield
Cooragweanish
Clontoo
Ardtully
Kilpadder
KILGARVAN
Church Ground
Caher
Red Tench, North

CORK

MACROOM

106

A   B   C   D

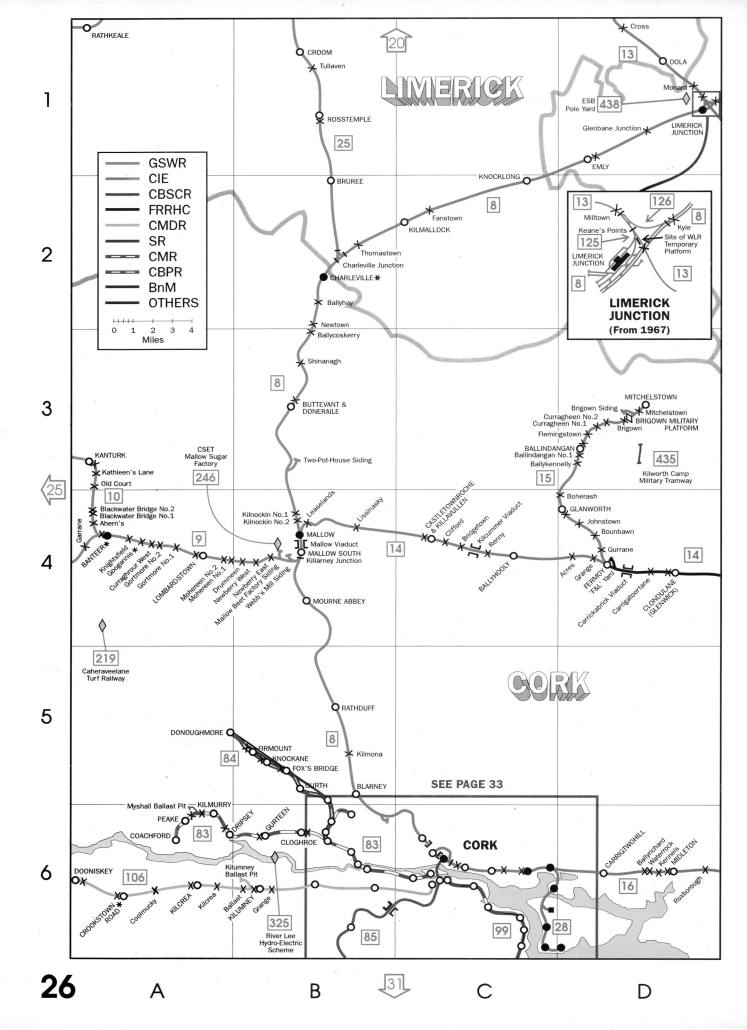

RATHKEALE

CROOM
Tullaven

ROSSTEMPLE
25

BRUREE

Fanstown
KILMALLOCK
8

Thomastown
Charleville Junction
CHARLEVILLE

Ballyhay

Newtown
Ballycoskerry

Shinanagh
8

BUTTEVANT & DONERAILE

Two-Pot-House Siding

LIMERICK

Cross
13 OOLA

Monard
ESB 438
Pole Yard
Glenbane Junction
LIMERICK JUNCTION
EMLY

KNOCKLONG

LIMERICK JUNCTION (From 1967)

13   126
Milltown   Kyle
Keane's Points   8
125   Site of WLR
                    Temporary Platform
LIMERICK
JUNCTION
8   13

MITCHELSTOWN
Brigown Siding   Mitchelstown
Curragheen No.2   BRIGOWN MILITARY
Curragheen No.1   PLATFORM
Flemingstown   Brigown
BALLINDANGAN
Ballindangan No.1   435
Ballykennelly
15   Kilworth Camp
                    Military Tramway
Boherash
GLANWORTH
Johnstown
Bounbawn

KANTURK
Kathleen's Lane
Old Court
10
Blackwater Bridge No.2
Blackwater Bridge No.1
Ahern's

CSET
Mallow Sugar
Factory
246

Leaselands
Kilnockin No.1   Lissinasky
Kilnockin No.2
9   MALLOW
                    Mallow Viaduct
                    MALLOW SOUTH
                    Killarney Junction

Garrane
BANTEER
Knightsfield
Googamis
Curraghrour West
Gortmore No.2
Gortmore No.1
LOMBARDSTOWN
Mohereen No.2
Mohereen No.1
Drumineen
Newberry West
Newberry East
Mallow Beet Factory Siding
Webb's Mill Siding

CASTLETOWNROCHE
& KILLAVULLEN
Clifford
Bridgetown
Kilcummer Viaduct
Renny
14

BALLYHOOLY

Gurrane
Acres   Grange
         FERMOY
         F&L Yard
Carrickabrick Viaduct
Carrigatoortane
CLONDULANE
(GLENWICK)
14

MOURNE ABBEY

219
Caheraveelane
Turf Railway

CORK

RATHDUFF
8

DONOUGHMORE
84   FIRMOUNT
        KNOCKANE
        FOX'S BRIDGE
        GURTH
Kilmona
BLARNEY

Myshall Ballast Pit   KILMURRY
PEAKE   DRIPSEY GURTEEN
COACHFORD
83   CLOGHROE

SEE PAGE 33

CARRIGTWOHILL
Ballyrichard
Waterrock
Kennels
MIDLETON

CORK

83

DOONISKEY
106
CROOKSTOWN
ROAD   Coolmucky KILCREA Kilcrea Ballast Grange
                                     KILUMNEY

Kilumney
Ballast Pit

325
River Lee
Hydro-Electric
Scheme

85

99

16
Roxborough

28

26   A   B   C   D

20

31

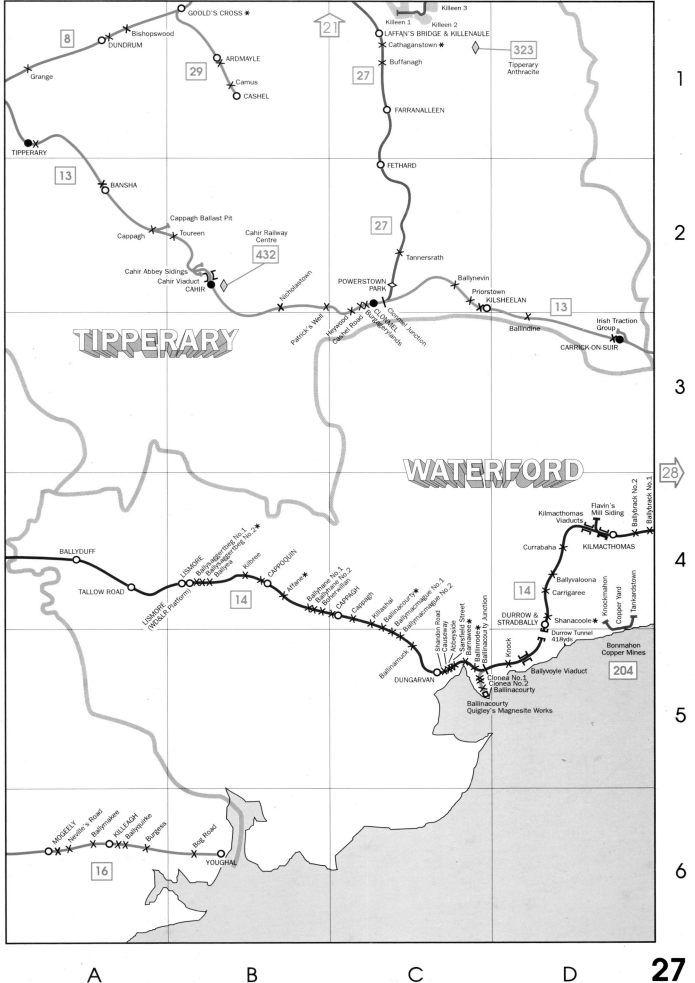

GOOLD'S CROSS

Bishopswood

DUNDRUM

8

Grange

TIPPERARY

13

BANSHA

ARDMAYLE

29

Camus

CASHEL

Cappagh Ballast Pit

Cappagh
Toureen

Cahir Railway
Centre

432

Cahir Abbey Sidings
Cahir Viaduct
CAHIR

Nicholastown

Patrick's Well
Heywood
Cashel Road
Burgagerylands
CLONMEL

Clonmel Junction

POWERSTOWN
PARK

Tannersrath

Ballynevin

Priorstown
KILSHEELAN

Ballindine

13

Irish Traction
Group

CARRICK-ON-SUIR

TIPPERARY

Killeen 3

Killeen 1   Killeen 2

LAFFAN'S BRIDGE & KILLENAULE

21

Cathaganstown

Buffanagh

27

323

Tipperary
Anthracite

FARRANALLEEN

FETHARD

27

WATERFORD

28

BALLYDUFF

TALLOW ROAD

LISMORE
(WD&LR Platform)

LISMORE
Ballysaggertbeg No.1
Ballysaggertbeg No.2
Ballyea
Kilbree
CAPPOQUIN

Affane

14

Ballyhane No.1
Ballyhane No.2
Boherwillan
CAPPAGH

Cappagh
Killashal
Ballinacourty
Ballymacmague No.1
Ballymacmague No.2

Ballinamuck

Shandon Road
Causeway
Abbeyside
Sarsfield Street
Barnawee
Ballinroad
Ballinacourty Junction

DUNGARVAN

Clonea No.1
Clonea No.2
Ballinacourty

Ballinacourty
Quigley's Magnesite Works

Knock

Durrow Tunnel
418yds

DURROW &
STRADBALLY

Shanacoole

14

Carrigaree

Ballyvaloona

Currabaha

Kilmacthomas
Viaducts

Flavin's
Mill Siding

KILMACTHOMAS

Ballybrack No.2
Ballybrack No.1

Knockmahon
Copper Yard
Tankardstown

Ballyvoyle Viaduct

Bonmahon
Copper Mines

204

MOGEELY
Neville's Road
Ballymakee
KILLEAGH
Ballyquirke
Burgess

Bog Road

YOUGHAL

16

1

2

3

4

5

6

A   B   C   D

27

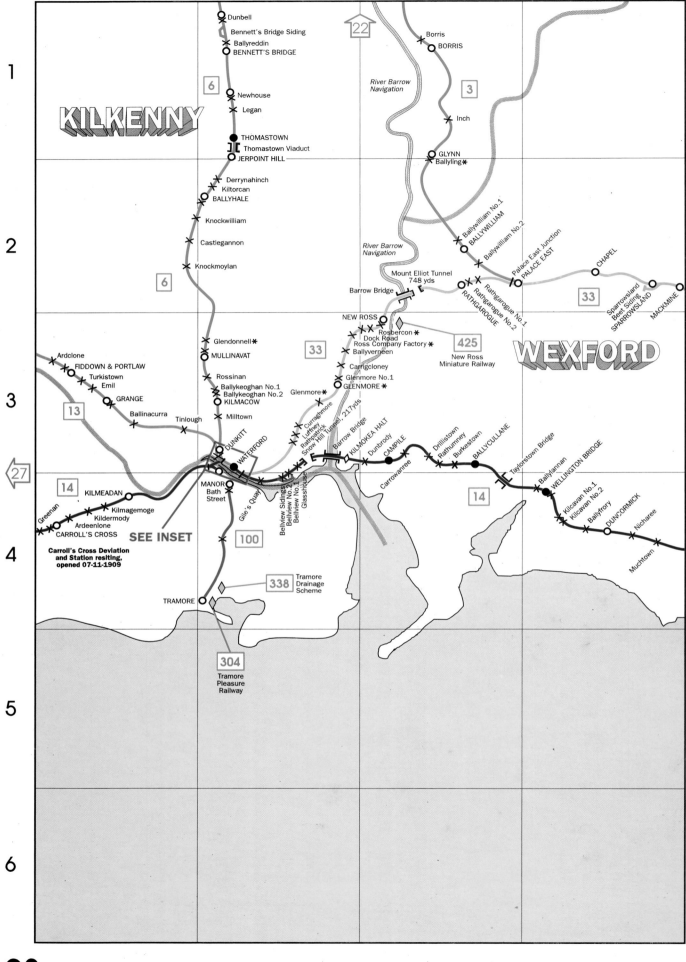

KILKENNY

WEXFORD

Dunbell
Bennett's Bridge Siding
Ballyreddin
BENNETT'S BRIDGE

6

Newhouse
Legan

THOMASTOWN
Thomastown Viaduct
JERPOINT HILL

Derrynahinch
Kiltorcan
BALLYHALE

Knockwilliam

Castlegannon

Knockmoylan

6

Glendonnell
MULLINAVAT

Rossinan
Ballykeoghan No.1
Ballykeoghan No.2
KILMACOW

Milltown

33

Ardclone
FIDDOWN & PORTLAW
Turkistown
Emil
GRANGE

13

Ballinacurra

Tinlough

DUNKITT
WATERFORD

Curraghmore
Luffney
Rathpatrick
Snow Hill Tunnel, 217yds
Barrow Bridge

MANOR
Bath Street

Gile's Quay

SEE INSET

14
KILMEADAN

Greenan
Kilmagemoge
Kildermody
Ardeenlone
CARROLL'S CROSS

Carroll's Cross Deviation
and Station resiting,
opened 07-11-1909

100

Bellview Sidings
Bellview No.2
Bellview No.1
Glasshouse

KILMOKEA HALT
Dunbrody
CAMPILE

Carrowanree

Drillistown
Rathumney
Burkestown
BALLYCULLANE

Taylorstown Bridge
Ballylannan
WELLINGTON BRIDGE

14

Kilcavan No.1
Kilcavan No.2
Ballyfrory
DUNCORMICK

Nicharee

Muchtown

338
Tramore
Drainage
Scheme

TRAMORE

304
Tramore
Pleasure
Railway

22

Borris
BORRIS

River Barrow
Navigation

3

Inch

GLYNN
Ballyling

River Barrow
Navigation

Ballywilliam No.1
BALLYWILLIAM
Ballywilliam No.2

Palace East Junction
PALACE EAST

Mount Elliot Tunnel
748 yds

Barrow Bridge

Rathgarogue No.1
RATHGAROGUE
Rathgarogue No.2

CHAPEL

33

Sparrowsland
Beet Siding
SPARROWSLAND

MACKMINE

NEW ROSS
Rosbercon
Dock Road
Ross Company Factory
Ballyverneen

Carrigcloney

Glenmore No.1
GLENMORE

Glenmore

425
New Ross
Miniature Railway

27

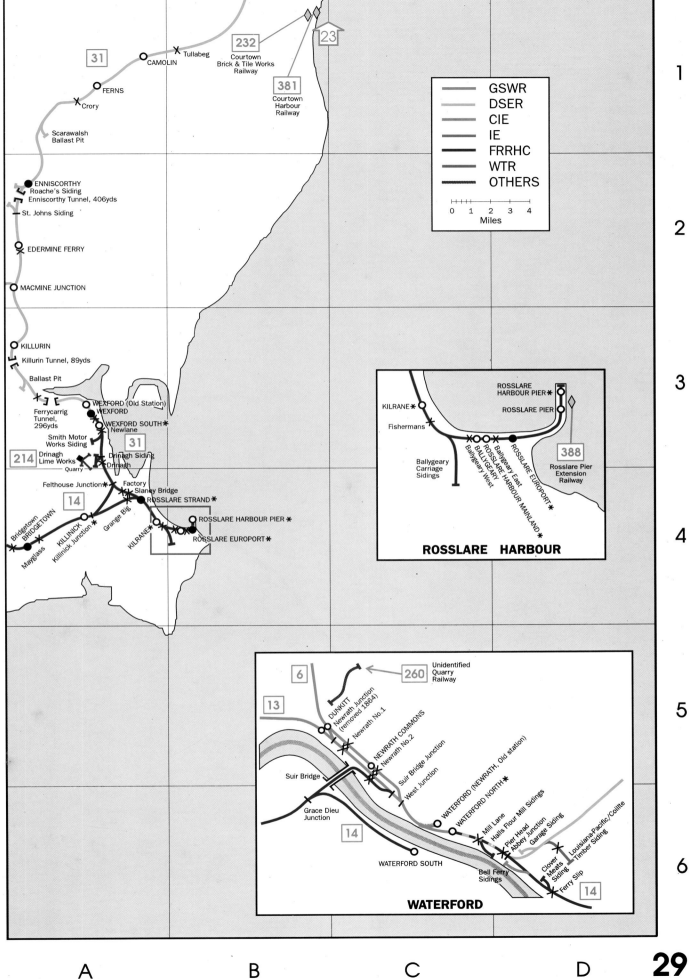

Map labels

Legend:
- GSWR
- DSER
- CIE
- IE
- FRRHC
- WTR
- OTHERS

0 1 2 3 4
Miles

31
CAMOLIN
× Tullabeg
FERNS
× Crory
Scarawalsh
Ballast Pit

232
Courtown
Brick & Tile Works
Railway

23

381
Courtown
Harbour
Railway

ENNISCORTHY
Roache's Siding
Enniscorthy Tunnel, 406yds
St. Johns Siding

EDERMINE FERRY

MACMINE JUNCTION

KILLURIN
Killurin Tunnel, 89yds
Ballast Pit

Ferrycarrig
Tunnel,
296yds

WEXFORD (Old Station)
WEXFORD
WEXFORD SOUTH ✱
Newlane

Smith Motor
Works Siding

31
Drinagh Siding
214
Drinagh
Lime Works
Quarry
Drinagh

Felthouse Junction ✱
Factory
Slaney Bridge
ROSSLARE STRAND ✱

14
Bridgetown
BRIDGETOWN
KILLINICK
Killinick Junction
Grange Big
KILRANE
ROSSLARE HARBOUR PIER ✱
ROSSLARE EUROPORT ✱
Mayglass

ROSSLARE HARBOUR

KILRANE ✱
Fishermans
ROSSLARE
HARBOUR PIER ✱
ROSSLARE PIER
Ballygeary
Carriage
Sidings
Ballygeary East
ROSSLARE HARBOUR MAINLAND
BALLYGEARY
Ballygeary West
ROSSLARE EUROPORT ✱

388
Rosslare Pier
Extension
Railway

WATERFORD

6
13
260
Unidentified
Quarry
Railway

DUNKITT
Newrath Junction
(removed 1864)
Newrath No.1
NEWRATH COMMONS
Newrath No.2
Suir Bridge Junction
West Junction
Suir Bridge
Grace Dieu
Junction
14
WATERFORD SOUTH
WATERFORD (NEWRATH, Old station)
WATERFORD NORTH ✱
Mill Lane
Halls Flour Mill Sidings
Pier Head
Abbey Junction
Garage Siding
Louisiana-Pacific/Coillte
Timber Siding
Clover
Meats
Siding
Bell Ferry
Sidings
Ferry Slip
14

A   B   C   D   **29**

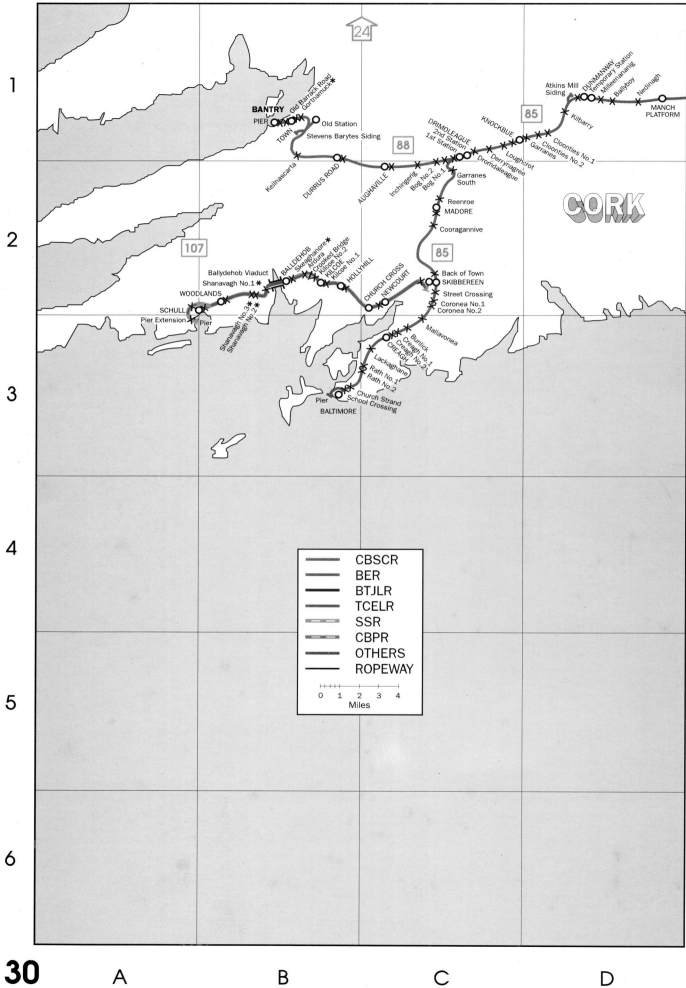

BANTRY
PIER
TOWN
Old Barrack Road
Gortnamuck
Old Station
Stevens Barytes Siding

Kellnascarta
DURRUS ROAD
AUGHAVILLE
Inchingerig
Bog No.2
Bog No.1

DRIMOLEAGUE
2nd Station
1st Station
Derrynagree
Dromdaleague
Garranes
South

KNOCKBUE
Loughcrot
Garranes
Cloonties No.1
Cloonties No.2

Atkins Mill
Siding
DUNMANWAY
Temporary Station
Milleenanahig
Ballyboy
Nedinagh
Kilbarry
MANCH
PLATFORM

CORK

Reenroe
MADORE

Cooragannive

107

Ballydehob Viaduct
Shanavagh No.1
WOODLANDS
SCHULL
Pier Extension
Pier
Shanavagh No.3
Shanavagh No.2

BALLDEHOB
Skeaghanore
Ardura
Crooked Bridge
Kilcoe No.2
KILCOE
Kilcoe No.1
HOLLYHILL

CHURCH CROSS
NEWCOURT

85

Back of Town
SKIBBEREEN
Street Crossing
Coronea No.1
Coronea No.2

Mallavonea
Bumlick
Creagh No.1
Creagh No.2
CREAGH
Lackaghane
Rath No.1
Rath No.2

Pier
BALTIMORE
Church Strand
School Crossing

	CBSCR
	BER
	BTJLR
	TCELR
	SSR
	CBPR
	OTHERS
	ROPEWAY

0 1 2 3 4
Miles

30 A B C D

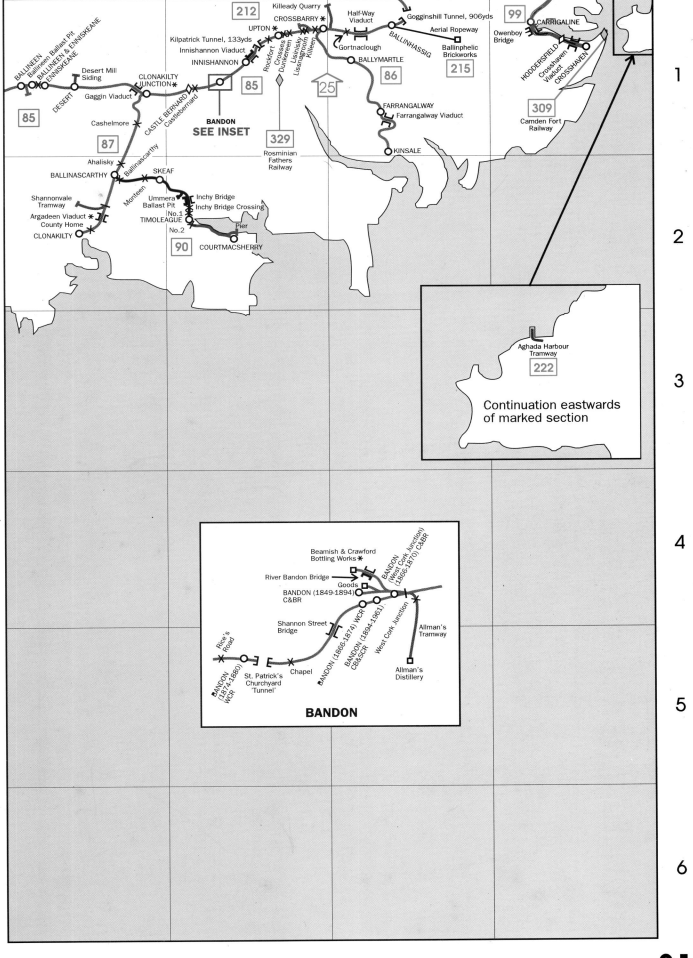

BALLINEEN
Ballineen Ballast Pit
BALLINEEN & ENNISKEANE
ENNISKEANE
Desert Mill Siding
DESERT
Gaggin Viaduct
CLONAKILTY JUNCTION

85

Cashelmore

87

Ahalisky
Ballinascarthy
BALLINASCARTHY
SKEAF
Monteen
Shannonvale Tramway
Argadeen Viaduct
County Home
CLONAKILTY
Ummera Ballast Pit
No.1
TIMOLEAGUE
No.2

90
COURTMACSHERRY

Inchy Bridge
Inchy Bridge Crossing
Pier

Kilpatrick Tunnel, 133yds
Innishannon Viaduct
INNISHANNON
Rockfort
Crosses
Dunkereen

85

CASTLE BERNARD
Castlebernard

BANDON
SEE INSET

329
Rosminian Fathers Railway

212
UPTON

Killeady Quarry
CROSSBARRY

Lisinisky
Lissnagroom
Killeen
Gortnaclough

25

Half-Way Viaduct
Gogginshill Tunnel, 906yds
Aerial Ropeway

BALLINHASSIG
BALLYMARTLE
Ballinphelic Brickworks

215

86

FARRANGALWAY
Farrangalway Viaduct

KINSALE

99
Owenboy Bridge
CARRIGALINE

HODDERSFIELD
Crosshaven Viaduct
CROSSHAVEN

309
Camden Fort Railway

1

Aghada Harbour Tramway

222

Continuation eastwards
of marked section

3

BANDON

Beamish & Crawford Bottling Works
River Bandon Bridge
Goods
BANDON (West Cork Junction) C&BR
BANDON (1866-1870) C&BR
BANDON (1849-1894) C&BR
Rice's Road
BANDON (1874-1880) WCR
St. Patrick's Churchyard 'Tunnel'
Shannon Street Bridge
Chapel
BANDON (1866-1874) WCR
BANDON (1894-1961) CB&SCR
West Cork Junction
Allman's Tramway
Allman's Distillery

4

5

6

A   B   C   D   **31**

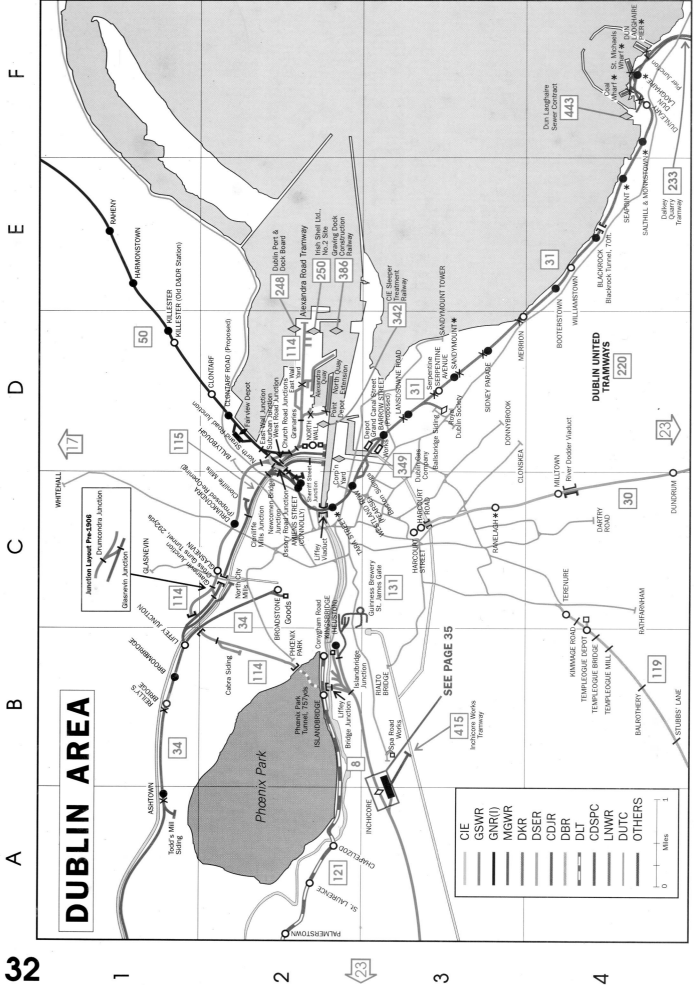

DUBLIN AREA

32

Legend:
- CIE
- GSWR
- GNR(I)
- MGWR
- DKR
- DSER
- CDJR
- DBR
- DLT
- CDSPC
- LNWR
- DUTC
- OTHERS

Miles
0   1

Phoenix Park

DUBLIN UNITED TRAMWAYS

Locations and labels:
- ASHTOWN
- Todd's Mill Siding
- REILLY'S BRIDGE
- BROOMBRIDGE
- LIFFEY JUNCTION
- Cabra Siding
- BROADSTONE Goods
- PHOENIX PARK
- Phoenix Park Tunnel, 757yds
- ISLANDBRIDGE
- Liffey Bridge Junction
- Islandbridge Junction
- Conygham Road
- KINGSBRIDGE (HEUSTON)
- RIALTO BRIDGE
- Spa Road Works
- Inchicore Works Tramway
- INCHICORE
- CHAPELIZOD
- St. LAURENCE
- PALMERSTOWN
- WHITEHALL
- GLASNEVIN
- North City Mills
- Cloniffe Mills Junction
- Drumcondra (proposed Reopening)
- Glasnevin Junction, cross Guns tunnel, 292yds
- Cloniffe Mills
- Newcomen Bridge Junction
- Ossory Road Junction
- AMIENS STREET (CONNOLLY)
- Sheriff Street Junction
- Liffey Viaduct
- North Strand Road Junction
- CLONTARF ROAD (Proposed)
- Fairview Depot
- East Wall Junction
- Suburban Junction
- West Road Junction
- Church Road Junctions
- Granaries
- East Wall Yard
- NORTH WALL
- Point Depot
- North Quay Extension
- Alexandra Quay
- Dublin Port & Dock Board
- Alexandra Road Tramway
- Irish Shell Ltd., No.2 Site
- Graving Dock Construction Railway
- CIE Sleeper Treatment Railway
- RAHENY
- HARMONSTOWN
- KILLESTER
- KILLESTER (Old D&DR Station)
- CLONTARF
- Corp'n Yard
- TARA STREET
- WESTLAND ROW (PEARSE)
- Boston Sidings
- Depot
- Grand Canal Street Works
- BARROW STREET
- LANSDOWNE ROAD
- SANDYMOUNT TOWER
- SANDYMOUNT
- Serpentine Avenue
- SIDNEY PARADE
- Royal Dublin Society
- Ballsbridge Siding
- Dublin Gas Company
- HARCOURT ROAD
- HARCOURT STREET
- Guinness Brewery St. James Gate
- DONNYBROOK
- CLONSKEA
- RANELAGH
- MILLTOWN
- River Dodder Viaduct
- DARTRY ROAD
- TERENURE
- RATHFARNHAM
- KIMMAGE ROAD
- TEMPLEOGUE DEPOT
- TEMPLEOGUE BRIDGE
- TEMPLEOGUE MILL
- BALROTHERY
- STUBBS' LANE
- MERRION
- BOOTERSTOWN
- WILLIAMSTOWN
- BLACKROCK
- Blackrock Tunnel, 70ft.
- SEAPOINT
- SALTHILL & MONKSTOWN
- Dalkey Quarry Tramway
- Dun Laoghaire Sewer Contract
- DUN LAOGHAIRE
- DUN LAOGHAIRE PIER
- St. Michaels Wharf
- Coal Wharf
- Pier Junction
- DUNDRUM

Route numbers:
50, 17, 115, 114, 34, 8, 121, 415, 131, 349, 31, 220, 23, 30, 119, 114, 248, 114, 250, 386, 342, 443, 233, 31

SEE PAGE 35

Junction Layout Pre-1906
Drumcondra Junction
Glasnevin Junction

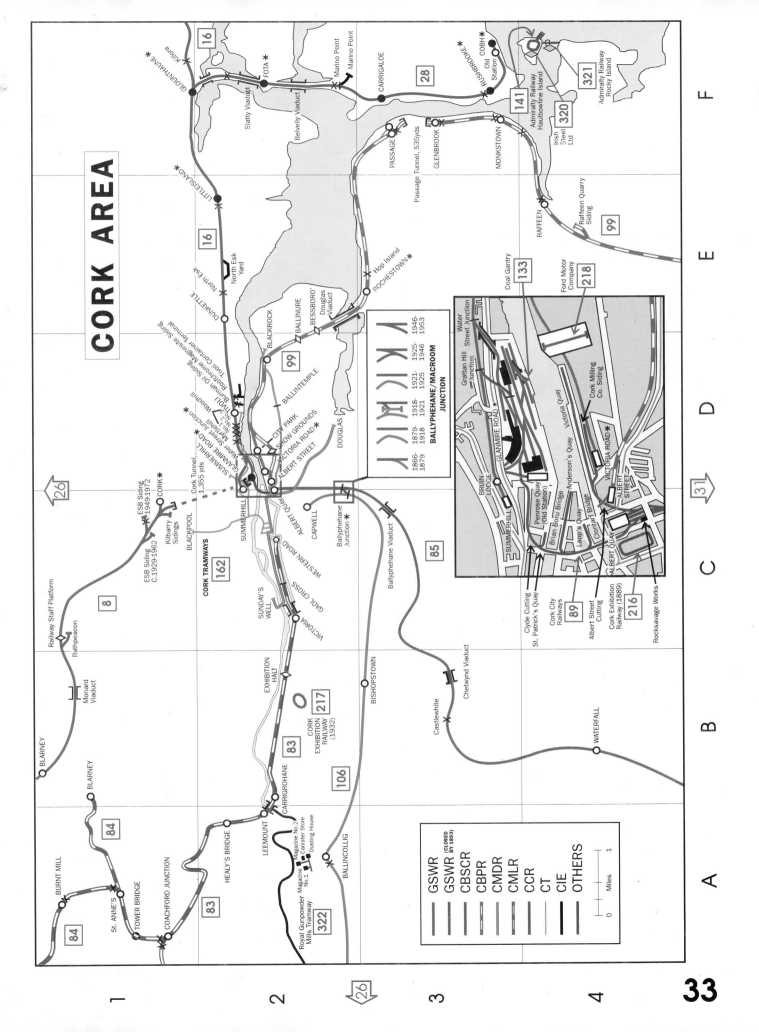

CORK AREA

BALLYPHEHANE/MACROOM JUNCTION

1866-1879	1879-1918	1918-1921	1921-1925	1925-1946	1946-1953

BLARNEY

84 BLARNEY

BURNT MILL

St. ANNE'S

TOWER BRIDGE

COACHFORD JUNCTION

84

83

Monard Viaduct

Rathpeacon

Railway Staff Platform

8

26

ESB Siding 1949-1972

ESB Siding C.1929-1962

CORK *

Kilbarry Sidings

BLACKPOOL

Cork Tunnel, 1,355 yds

SUMMERHILL

162 CORK TRAMWAYS

GLANMIRE ROAD

WATER STREET *

Burnt Oil Siding No.2 *

Tivoli Oil Siding No.1 *

Rochestown Magnesite Siding

Tivoli Container Terminal

KILLORA

GLOUNTHAUNE *

16

FOTA *

Slatty Viaduct

Belvelly Viaduct

Marino Point

Marino Point

CARRIGALOE

28

RUSHBROOKE *

COBH *

Old Station *

Admiralty Railway Haulbowline Island

141

320

321

Admiralty Railway Rocky Island

Irish Steel Ltd

16

LITTLEISLAND *

DUNKETTLE

North Esk

North Esk Yard

BLACKROCK

BALLINURE

Douglas Viaduct

Bessboro'

99

BALLINTEMPLE

CITY PARK

SHOW GROUNDS

VICTORIA ROAD *

ALBERT STREET

DOUGLAS

Hop Island

ROCHESTOWN *

PASSAGE

Passage Tunnel, 535yds

GLENBROOK

MONKSTOWN

RAFFEEN

Raffeen Quarry Siding

99

Coal Gantry

133

Ford Motor Company

218

85

Ballyphehane Junction *

Ballyphehane Viaduct

7

CAPWELL

SUMMERHILL

SUNDAY'S WELL

GAOL CROSS

VICTORIA

WESTERN ROAD

ALBERT QUAY

EXHIBITION HALT

CORK EXHIBITION RAILWAY (1932)

217

83

106

BISHOPSTOWN

Castlewhite

Chetwynd Viaduct

WATERFALL

CARRIGROHANE

LEEMOUNT

HEALY'S BRIDGE

83

BALLINCOLLIG

Magazine No.2

Canister Store

Dusting House

Magazine No.1

Royal Gunpowder Mills Tramway

322

Inset map

BRUIN LODGE

SUMMERHILL

Water Street Junction

Grattan Hill Junction

GLANMIRE ROAD

Penrose Quay (Old Station)

Brian Boru Bridge

Victoria Quay

Anderson's Quay

Lapp's Quay

Clontarf Bridge

Cork Milling Co. Siding

VICTORIA ROAD *

ALBERT QUAY

ALBERT STREET

216

Clyde Cutting St. Patrick's Quay

Cork City Railways

89

Albert Street Cutting

Cork Exhibition Railway (1889)

Rocksavage Works

Legend

GSWR	
GSWR (CLOSED BY 1893)	
CBSCR	
CBPR	
CMDR	
CMLR	
CCR	
CT	
CIE	
OTHERS	

0 Miles 1

33

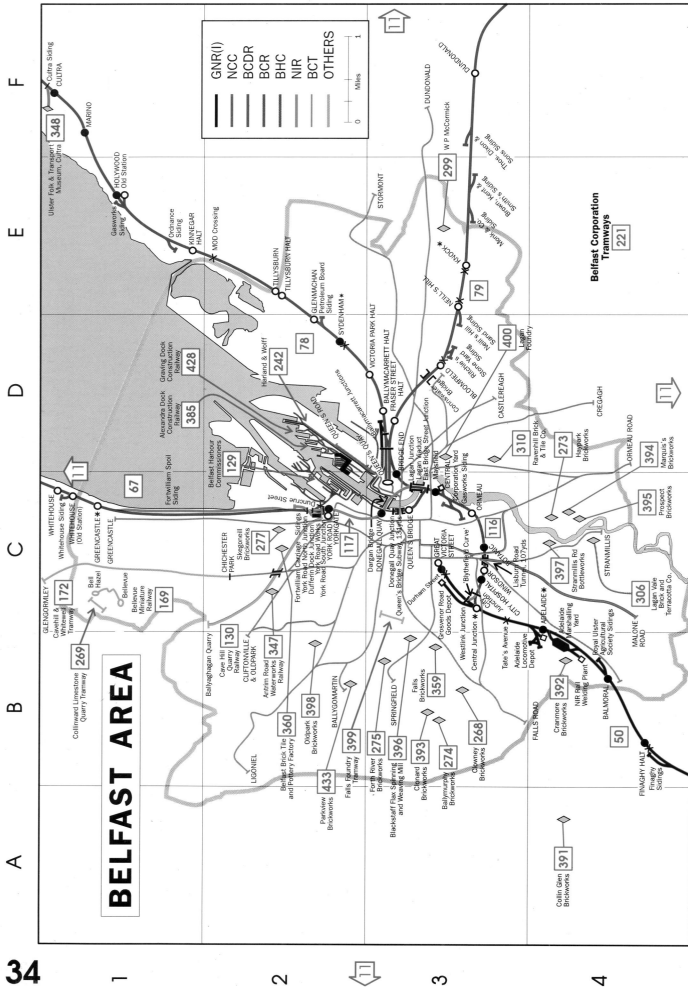

BELFAST AREA

Belfast Corporation Tramways

Legend	
GNR(I)	
NCC	
BCDR	
BCR	
BHC	
NIR	
BCT	
OTHERS	

Miles 0 — 1

348 CULTRA — Cultra Siding — Ulster Folk & Transport Museum, Cultra
MARINO
HOLYWOOD Old Station
Gasworks Siding
KINNEGAR HALT
Ordnance Siding
MOD Crossing
TILLYSBURN
TILLYSBURN HALT
GLENMACHAN Petroleum Board Siding
78
SYDENHAM *
242 Harland & Wolff
VICTORIA PARK HALT
BALLYMACARRETT HALT
FRASER STREET HALT
Ballymacarrett Junctions
QUEEN'S ROAD
428 Graving Dock Construction Railway
385 Alexandra Dock Construction Railway
129 Belfast Harbour Commissioners
Fortwilliam Spoil Siding
67
QUEEN'S QUAY
BRIDGE END
Lagan Viaduct
East Bridge Street Junction
Lagan Junction
MAISFIELD
CENTRAL
Corporation Yard
Gasworks Siding
Comber Bridge
299 W P McCormick
Thos. Dixon & Sons Siding
DUNDONALD
Brown, Kent & Co.
Smith's Siding
Monk & Co.
221
NEILL'S HILL
Neill's Hill Sand Siding
KNOCK *
79
BLOOMFIELD
Ritchie's Store Yard
400 Lagan Foundry
STORMONT
CASTLEREAGH
310 Ravenhill Brick & Tile Co.
273 Haypark Brickworks
CREGAGH
394 Marquis's Brickworks
ORMEAU ROAD
116
ORMEAU
395 Prospect Brickworks
STRANMILLIS
397 Stranmillis Rd Bottleworks
306 Lagan Vale Brick and Terracotta Co.
MALONE ROAD
WHITEHOUSE
Whitehouse Siding
WHITEHOUSE (Old Station)
GREENCASTLE *
GREENCASTLE
277 Skegoneill Brickworks
CHICHESTER PARK
Fortwilliam Carriage Sidings
York Road North Junction
Dufferin Dock Junction
York Road Junction
York Road South Junction
YORKGATE
YORK ROAD
117
Duncrue Street
Dargan Bridge
DONEGALL QUAY
Donegall Quay Junction
Queen's Bridge Subway, 134 yds
QUEEN'S BRIDGE
GREAT VICTORIA STREET
'Blythefield Curve'
CITY HOSPITAL
Lisburn Road Tunnel, 107 yds
WINDSOR
BOTANIC
GLENGORMLEY
Cavehill & Whitewell Tramway 172
Bell Hazel
Bellevue
Bellevue Miniature Railway 169
Collinward Limestone Quarry Tramway 269
Ballyaghagan Quarry
130 Cave Hill Quarry Railway
347 Antrim Road Waterworks Railway
CLIFTONVILLE & OLDPARK
LIGONIEL
Belfast Brick Tile and Pottery Factory 360
398 Oldpark Brickworks
BALLYGOMARTIN
Parkview Brickworks
433
399 Falls Foundry Tramway
275 Forth River Brickworks
SPRINGFIELD
396 Falls Brickworks
393 Clonard Brickworks
274 Ballymurphy Brickworks
268 Clowney Brickworks
359
Grosvenor Road Goods Depot
Durham Street
Westlink Junction
Central Junction *
Tate's Avenue
Adelaide Locomotive Depot
ADELAIDE *
Adelaide Marshalling Yard
Royal Ulster Agricultural Society Sidings
FALLS ROAD
392 Cranmore Brickworks
NIR Rail Welding Plant
BALMORAL
50
FINAGHY HALT
Finaghy Sidings
391 Collin Glen Brickworks
34

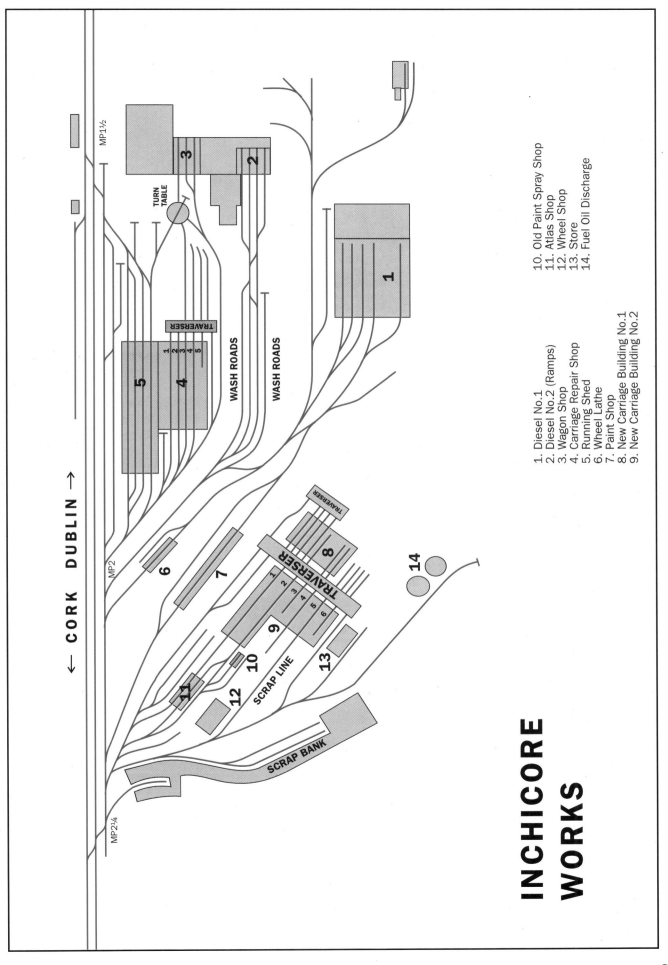

INCHICORE
WORKS

1. Diesel No.1
2. Diesel No.2 (Ramps)
3. Wagon Shop
4. Carriage Repair Shop
5. Running Shed
6. Wheel Lathe
7. Paint Shop
8. New Carriage Building No.1
9. New Carriage Building No.2
10. Old Paint Spray Shop
11. Atlas Shop
12. Wheel Shop
13. Store
14. Fuel Oil Discharge

← CORK DUBLIN →

MP1½

MP2

MP2¼

TURN TABLE

TRAVERSER

WASH ROADS

WASH ROADS

TRAVERSER

TRAVERSER

SCRAP LINE

SCRAP BANK

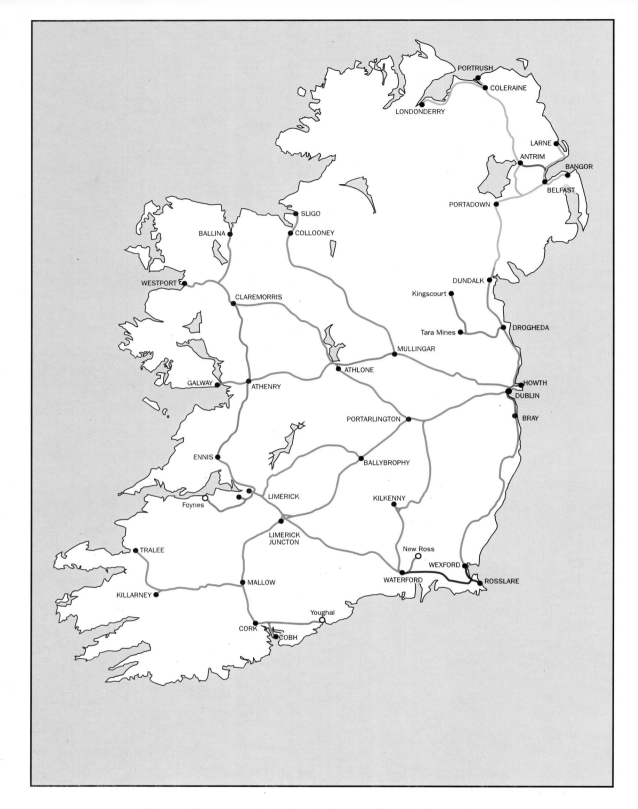

The Current Mainline Rail System

Iarnród Éireann

All Traffic
Freight only
Overhead electric
FRRHC Worked by IE

Northern Ireland Railways

All Traffic
Freight only

36

Part Two

INDEX & GAZETTEER

THIS PART of the book provides a full index to the places and features shown on the maps which precede it, and to those mentioned in the Route Tables which begin on page 68. Passenger stations and halts are printed in capital letters; other features – such as level crossings, bridges and junctions – are printed in 'upper and lower case' type. If the place was known by another name, then this is given in brackets. Where two or more places share the same name, these can be distinguished by the initials of the railway or owning company which served them and/or by the county in which they were located. A list of the abbreviations used appears before the Atlas section, on pages vii and viii.

The first number in each line refers to the page in the Atlas section on which the place or feature appears. The letter and number which follow this is a grid reference needed to locate it on that map page. The number(s) in the right hand column, which complete each entry, denote the Route Table(s) on which the place or feature appears.

Some features (often level crossings) had at some time a passenger service provided by a railcar or railbus. Where this was either listed in the public timetables or in other railway company literature, it is indicated by [R]. Places and/or features that appear in any of the inset maps are suffixed by a '‡'.

A

Name	Railway	Map	Page
Antrim Showground Siding	NCC	10 D1	67
ARDAGH	GSWR	25 D1	18
ARDARA ROAD	CDRJC	8 B1	93
Ardara Road Crossing, (Gillespie, No.28)	CDRJC	8 B1	93
Ardbraccan Crossing [R]	GNR(I)	16 C4	57
Ardclinis Inclined Plane		5 C4	376
Ardclone Crossing	GSWR	28 A3	13
ARDEE	GNR(I)	16 D2	56
Ardee Road Goods Yard ‡	IE	17 A1	50
Ardeenlone Crossing	FRRHC	28 A4	14
ARDFERT	GSWR	25 A2	18
Ardfert Station Gates	GSWR	25 A2	18
ARDGLASS	BCDR	11 C5	82
Ardglass Junction	BCDR	11 C5	79,82
Ardglass Harbour	BCDR	11 C5	82
Ardilea Ballast Pit	BCDR	11 B5	79
ARDMAYLE	GSWR	27 B1	29
Ardmayle Crossing	GSWR	27 B1	29
ARDMORE	NCC	4 B4	68
Ardnacrusha Power Station	GSR	20 A5	17,188
Ardnacrusha Siding	GSR	20 A5	17
Ardshanbally Crossing	GSWR	19 D6	18
ARDRAHAN	GSWR	20 A1	17
Ardrahan Crossing	GSWR	20 A1	17
Ardreagh Crossing (Clinton's)	NCC	4 D4	74
Ardree Crossing	MGWR	8 A6	37
ARDSOLLUS & QUIN	GSWR	19 D4	17
Ardtully Crossing	GSWR	25 A5	11
Ardue Crossing (Killywilly)	CLR	9 B6	97
Ardura Crossing	SSR	30 B2	107
Argadeen Viaduct (Shannonvale Viaduct)	CBSCR	31 A2	87
ARIGNA	CLR	8 C6	98
Arigna Iron Works Tramroad		8 C6	142
Arigna Mining Company Railway	DSER	8 C6	143
ARKLOW	DSER	23 B5	31
Arklow North Key	Hodgson's Tramway	23 B5	205
Arklow South Quay	Hodgson's Tramway	23 B5	205
Arm No.1 Crossing (Meyers)	MGWR	14 C2	44
Arm No.2 Crossing (Meyers)	MGWR	14 C2	44
ARMAGH			
Asylum Siding	GNR(I)	10 B4	52,60
IRISH STREET HALT	GNR(I)	10 B4	54
Mill Siding	GNR(I)	10 B4	52,54
N&A Temporary Station		10 B4	60
RAILWAY STREET	GNR(I)	10 B4	52,54,60
Railway St Station Gates	GNR(I)	10 B4	52,54
ARMAGH ROAD (NEWRY)	GNR(I)	10 C5	50
ARMOY	BR	5 A4	77
Armstrong's Crossing [R] (Aughnaskew)	GNR(I)	9 B4	49
Armstrong No.1 Crossing, (Erry)	GSWR	15 C6	4
Armstrong No.2 Crossing, (Erry)	GSWR	15 C6	4
Arranmore Whaling Station, Rusheen Island		6 A4	312
Artiferral Crossing	NCC	5 A5	67
Artillery Road Crossing (Millburn or Calf Lane) ‡	NCC	4 D3	73
ARVA ROAD	MGWR	15 D1	40
Asbestos Factory Siding (Tegral Siding)	GSWR	22 B3	2,120
ASHFIELD	GNR(I)	10 D4	61
Ashfield Crossing	GSWR	21 C1	4
Ashfort Crossing	GSWR	20 A6	18
ASHTOWN	MGWR	32 A1	34
Ashtown Crossing	MGWR	32 A1	34
ASKEATON	GSWR	19 C6	19
Askeaton Station Gates	GSWR	19 C6	19
Assaly Junction (Killinick Jct, Orriston Jct)	FRRHC	29 A4	14
Asylum Siding, Co Antrim	NCC	10 D1	67
Asylum Siding, Co Armagh	GNR(I)	10 B4	52,60
ATHBOY	MGWR	16 B4	47
ATHENRY (ATHENRY & ENNIS JUNCTION, ATHENRY & TUAM JUNCTION)	GSWR, MGWR	14 A6	17,34
Athenry Station Gates	GSWR, MGWR	14 A6	17,34
ATHLONE, current station ‡	GSWR	15 A5	4
ATHLONE ‡	MGWR	15 A5	34,44
Athlone East Junction ‡	GSWR, MGWR	15 A5	4,34
Athlone Weir Tramway		15 A5	265
Athlone West Junction ‡	MGWR	15 A5	34,44
Athlumney Mill Tramway		16 D4	412

Name	Railway	Map	Page
ATHY	GSWR	22 B3	2
Athry Lough Crossing	MGWR	12 D4	39
Atkins Mill Siding	CBSCR	30 D1	85
ATTANAGH	GSWR	21 D5	6
Attanagh Station Gates	GSWR	21 D5	6
Attireesh Crossing	MGWR	13 B1	48
Attymon Group of Bogs	BnM	14 B6	177
ATTYMON JUNCTION	MGWR, LALR	14 B6	34,41
Attymon Peat Co-op Ltd		14 B6	177
Aughabehy	Arigna Valley Extension Railway	8 C6	98
Aughabehy	Arigna Ironworks Tramway	8 C6	142
Aughabehy Colliery Railway (Noone's)		8 C6	327
Aughabehy Mine		8 C6	160
Aughabehy Coke Yard	Arigna Valley Extension Rly	8 C6	98,142
Aughacashlaun Ballast Siding	CLR	8 D6	98
AUGHACASLA	TDR	24 C2	110
Aughalish Crossing	NCC	10 D1	67
Aughalurcher Crossing [R]	GNR(I)	9 B5	49
AUGHAVILLE	CBSCR	30 C2	88
Aughaville Station Gates	CBSCR	30 C2	88
AUGHER	CVR	9 D3	91
Augheranter Crossing [R]	GNR(I)	10 C5	50
AUGHACASLA	TDR	24 C2	110
AUGHNACLOY	CVR	10 A3	91
Aughnaskew Crossing [R], (Armstrong's)	GNR(I)	9 B4	49
AUGHRIM	DSER	23 A5	32
Avenue Crossing	ATECLR	13 D3	17
AVOCA (Ovoca)	DSER	23 A5	31
Avoca Mines Ltd		23 A5	292
Avonmore Co-op Siding	CIE	21 D3	6
AYLEWARDSTOWN (GLENMORE &)	DSER	28 B3	33
Aytons Gates [R], (Kelly, Vance, Cannon)	SLR	3 C5	96

B

Name	Railway	Map	Page
Bachelor's Walk Crossing	GNR(I)	10 B5	54
'Back Line'	NCC	11 B1	76
Back of Town Crossing	CBSCR	30 C2	85
BAGENALSTOWN (MUINE BHEAG)	GSWR	22 B6	3
BAILY POST OFFICE ‡	GNR(I) HoH	17	62
BAILY VIEW (STELLA MARIS, BAY VIEW) ‡	GNR(I) HoH	17	62
Baird's (No.62) Gates [R]	SLR	3 C5	96
BAKER'S LANE (KITESTOWN ROAD)	GNR(I) HoH	17	62
BALBRIGGAN	GNR(I)	17 B4	50
Balbriggan Coke Oven Tramway	DDR	17 B4	318
Balbriggan Water Works Railway		17 B5	252
Balbriggan Viaduct	GNR(I)	17 B5	50
Baldonnell Aerodrome Railway	WD	22 D1	153
Baldonnell Camp, Irish Army		22 D1	361
Baldonnell Siding	GSWR	22 D1	8
BALDOYLE	GNR(I)	17 B6	50
BALDOYLE (SUTTON &)	GNR(I)	17 B6	51
Baldoyle Road Crossing (Kilbarrack)	GNR(I)	17 B6	51
BALDUNGAN	GNR(I)	17 B5	50
BALGLASS (BALKILL ROAD) ‡	GNR(I) HoH	17	62
BALKILL ROAD (BALGLASS)	GNR(I)	17	62
BALLA	MGWR	13 D2	44
BALLAGH	CVR	9 D3	91
BALLAGHADERREEN	MGWR	14 B1	42
Ballaghmore No.1 Crossing	GSWR	21 B4	23
Ballaghmore No.2 Crossing	GSWR	21 B4	23
Ballaghmore No.3 Crossing	GSWR	21 B4	23
Ballaghuff 1 Bog	Blackwater Group, BnM	15 A6	179
Ballaghuff 2 Bog	Blackwater Group, BnM	15 B6	179
Ballast Crossing	CMDR	26 B6	106
BALLAST PIT [R]	CDR	3 A5	94
Ballast Pit Crossing	GNR(I)	11 A3	50
Ballast Pit Junction	GSWR	22 B2	8
Ballast Pit Siding	BR	5 B3	77
Balleece Siding	DSER	23 A4	31
Ballievey Siding	GNR(I)	10 D4	61
BALLINA	MGWR	7 B5	45
Ballina No.1 Crossing	BCLR	13 C3	43
Ballina No.2 Crossing	BCLR	13 C3	43
Ballina Station Gates	MGWR	7 B5	45
Ballinacourty, Co Waterford	CIE	27 C5	14

Clooney Crossing, Co Londonderry	NCC	4 B3	67
Clooniff 1 Bog	Blackwater Group, BnM	15 A6	179
Clooniff 2 Bog	Blackwater Group, BnM	15 A6	179
Clooniff Crossing	MGWR	13 C6	39
Cloonkeen Crossing	MGWR	13 C1	44
Cloonrane Crossing	ATECLR	13 D3	17
Cloonshanagh Bog	Mountdillon Group, BnM	15 A2	178
Cloonties No.1 Crossing	CBSCR	30 D1	85
Cloonties No.2 Crossing	CBSCR	30 D1	85
Cloontusker Bog	Mountdillon Group, BnM	15 A3	178
Cloughcor Mines	Glenariff Iron Ore & Harbour Co	5 B5	155
CLOUGHJORDAN	GSWR	20 D4	23
CLOUGH ROAD	NCC	5 B5	72
CLOUNA (CLOONEY)	WCR	19 B3	111
Clouna Crossing (Clooney Crossing)	WCR	19 B3	111
Clover Meats Siding ‡	FRRHC	28 B4	14
Clowney Brickworks Railway		34 B3	268
Cluid Crossing	MGWR	8 A5	37
Clyduff Crossing	GSWR	20 B6	23
COACHFORD	CMR	26 A6	83
COACHFORD JUNCTION	CMR	33 A1	83,84
Coal Wharf (Mineral Wharf, Traders Wharf), (Dun Laoghaire)	DK	32 F4	31
COALISLAND	GNR(I)	10 B2	56
Coalisland Colliery Siding	GNR(I)	10 B2	56
Coalisland Colliery Waggonway (Drumglass Colliery)		10 B2	166
Coal Quay Crossing	DK	32 F4	31
COBH (QUEENSTOWN)	GSWR	33 F3	28
COBH JUNCTION (QUEENSTOWN JUNCTION, GLOUNTHAUNE)	GSWR	33 F1	16,28
Coke Yard, (Aughabehy)	AVR	8 C6	98,142
COLBERT (LIMERICK) ‡	GSWR	20 A6	13,17,18 23
COLBINSTOWN	GSWR	22 C3	1
COLEBROOKE	CVR	9 C4	91
COLERAINE			
Crossing ‡	NCC	4 D4	67
Current Station (NORTHBROOK) ‡	NCC	4 D4	67,73
Harbour ‡	NCC	4 D4	67
NORTHBROOK (Current Station) ‡	NCC	4 D4	67,73
WATERSIDE ‡	NCC	4 D4	67
Coldagh Crossing	NCC	4 D4	67
COLDBLOW & LUCAN (LUCAN NORTH)	MGWR	17 A6	34
Collen's Brickworks Siding	GNR(I)	10 C3	50
COLLIN HALT	NCC	5 B6	70
Colin Glen Brickworks Tramway, Belfast		34 A4	391
Collinward Limestone Quarry Railway		11 B2	269
COLLOONEY ‡	GSWR, MGWR, SLNCR	8 A5	17,37,108
Collooney (No.28) Station Gates	SLNCR	8 A5	108
Collooney Junction ‡	GSWR, MGWR	8 A5	17,37
Colt Crossing	GSWR	21 D4	6
COMBER	BCDR	11 C3	79,80
Comber Main Line Crossing, (Carr's Lane Maxwell's Court)	BCDR	11 C3	79
Comber No.1 Crossing, (Killinchy Road)	BCDR	11 C3	80
Comber No.2 Crossing, (Cherryvalley)	BCDR	11 C3	80
Comber No.3 Crossing, (Glass Moss)	BCDR	11 C3	80
Comber No.4 Crossing, (Orr's Road)	BCDR	11 C3	80
Comhlucht Suicre Eireann Teoranta			245,246 253,263,285
COMMON, THE	DBT	23 A1	119
Commons Bog Crossing (Commons), Co Kilkenny	GSWR	22 A6	2
Commons Crossing (Commons Bog), Co Kilkenny	GSWR	22 A6	2
Commons Crossing Co Louth	GNR(I)	17 A2	50
Commons Road Crossing (Poorhouse), (Co Meath)	GNR(I), MGWR	16 C4	46,57
Conaghan Gates [R], (Inver Church, No.18)	CDRJC	8 C1	93
Conaghan Gates, (No.43)	CDRJC	8 C1	93
Concrave Crossing	MGWR	16 A5	34
CONEY ISLAND HALT	BCDR	11 C5	82
Congo Siding (Tyrone Co Council Siding)	GNR(I)	10 B3	56
Conianstown Crossing (Starkey's, Whighamstown)	BCDR	11 C5	82
CONLIG	BCDR	11 C2	80
Conneywarren Crossing	GNR(I)	9 C1	49
Conniberry Junction	GSWR	21 D3	6,21
Conniberry Junction Crossing	GSWR	21 D3	6
CONNOLLY STATION (DUBLIN AMIENS ST)	CDJ, GNR(I)	32 C2	31,50
Connorree Siding	DSER	23 A5	31
Connswater Bridge	BCDR	34 D3	79
Container Refurbishing		10 D5	294
CONVENT GATE	GNR(I) HoH	17	62
CONVOY	SLR	3 C5	96
COOKSTOWN	GNR(I), NCC	10 B2	53,66
Cookstown Junction (Drumsough)	NCC	10 D1	66,67
Cookstown Junction Station Gates	NCC	10 D1	66,67
Cookstown Lime Company		10 B2	439
Cookstown Lime Company Siding	NCC	10 B2	66
Cookstown Market Yard	NCC	10 B2	66
Cookstown UDC Siding	NCC	10 B1	66
Coolabaun Crossing (Mohill Station Gates)	CLR	15 B1	97
COOLAGHY HALT	SLR	3 C5	96
Coolane Crossing [R]	GNR(I)	9 B4	49
Coolaney Crossing	GSWR	8 A5	17
Coolattin Crossing	DSER	22 D5	32
Coolboyoge Crossing	GNR(I)	15 D1	52
Cooldoney Crossing	MGWR	15 D3	38
Coole Crossing	GSWR	20 D5	7
Coolkeeragh Siding	NCC	4 B4	67
COOLMINE	CIE	17 A6	34
Coolmine Crossing	MGWR	17 A6	34
COOLMORE HALT	CDRJC	8 C2	95
Coolmucky Crossing	CMDR	26 A6	106
Coolnacartan Bog	Coolnamona Group, BnM	21 D3	189
Coolnagan Crossing (Newman's)	MGWR	15 D3	38
Coolnagun Bog	Coolnagun Group, BnM	15 D4	181
Coolnagun Group of Bogs	BnM	15 D4	181
Coolnaharrigill Crossing	GSWR	24 C4	26
Coolnamona	BnM, GSWR	21 D3	6,189
Coolnamona Bog	Coolnamona Group, BnM	21 C3	189
Coolnamona Group of Bogs	BnM	21 D3	189
Cooloughra Crossing	MGWR	14 B2	44
Coolowley Crossing	GSWR	21 B4	8
Coolready Crossing	GSWR	20 B5	23
Coolrone Crossing	GSWR	24 D2	20
Coolumber Bog	Blackwater Group, BnM	15 A6	179
Coonealcaraun Crossing	MGWR	7 B5	45
Cooper, H J	Drinagh Limeworks Railway	29 A3	214
Cooraclaven Crossing	GSWR	21 A4	23
Cooracramp Crossing	CLR	15 B2	97
Cooragannive Crossing	CBSCR	30 C2	85
Cooragweanish Crossing	GSWR	25 A5	11
COOTEHILL	GNR(I)	9 D6	64
Cootehill Viaduct	GNR(I)	9 D6	64
Copper Yard	Bonmahon Copper Mine Rly	27 D4	204
Corballis Viaduct (Rathdrum Viaduct)	DSER	23 A4	31
Corbally Crossing, Co Laois	GSWR	21 D4	6
Corbally Crossing, Co Galway	MGWR	13 C5	39
CORBET	GNR(I)	10 D4	61
CORBETSTOWN	GSWR	21 D5	22
Corbetstown Station Gates	GSWR	21 D5	22
Corcass Line	BFR	19 C5	185
Cordarragh Crossing (Ballyglass)	GSWR	13 D1	17
Corgar Crossing	CLR	9 A6	97
Corgarry Crossing (Kingscourt)	MGWR	16 C2	46
CORK			
ALBERT STREET ‡	CBPR	33 D2	99
ALBERT QUAY	CBSCR	33 D2	85
BLACKPOOL (VICTORIA)	GSWR	33 C1	8
BRUIN LODGE ‡	CYR	33 D2	16
CAPWELL	CMDR	33 C2	106
CITY PARK ‡	CBPR	33 D2	99
City Railway ‡	CCR	33 D2	89
Coal Gantry ‡	GSWR	33 D2	133
Exhibition Halt	CMR	33 B2	83
Exhibition Railway (1889) ‡		33 D2	217
Exhibition Railway (1932)		33 B2	218
GLANMIRE ROAD (KENT) ‡	GSWR	33 D2	8,16
Grattan Hill Junction ‡	GSWR	33 D2	16
KENT (GLANMIRE ROAD) ‡	GSWR	33 D2	8,16
Milling Company ‡		33 D2	85
PENROSE QUAY ‡	GSWR	33 D2	8
SHOW GROUND	CBPR	33 D2	99

Name	Operator	Grid	Page
Garryhinch Works	Clonsast Group, BnM	21 D2	192
GARRYNADUR	TDR	24 C3	109
Garryredmond Crossing (Cloondin, High Lodge)	MGWR	14 A2	44
GARVAGH	NCC	4 C5	74
Garvaghy No.1 Crossing [R]	GNR(I)	9 C2	53
Garvaghy No.2 Crossing [R]	GNR(I)	9 C2	53
Gasworks Siding, Belfast	BCR	34 C3	116
GEASHILL	GSWR	21 D2	4
Geevagh Coal Mine Tramway		8 B6	365
Geohegan's Siding	GNR(I)	10 D4	59
Georges Quay (Dundalk) ‡	DNGR	17 A1	104
Geraghty's Crossing (Ribbontail)	MGWR	16 B6	34
GIANTS CAUSEWAY	GCPBVT	4 D3	113
Giant's Head Loop (Not Shown)	GCPBVT	4 D3	113
Giant's Causeway Columner Basalt Co Rly		4 D3	234
GIBBSTOWN	MGWR	16 C4	46
Gibbstown Station Gates	MGWR	16 C4	46
Giles Quay Crossing	FRRHC	28 B4	14
GILFORD (TANDERAGEE &, MADDEN BRIDGE)	GNR(I)	10 C4	50
Gill's Siding	BCDR	11 B3	79
Gillen's Crossing [R], (Kildoney)	CDRJC	8 C2	95
Gillen's Gates (No.55)	SLR	3 C5	96
Gillen's Gates (No.61)	SLR	3 C5	96
Gillespie's Gates (Ardara Rd Stn, No.28)	CDRJC	8 B1	93
Gilltown Bog	BnM	22 C1	420
Gilltown Works	Gilltown Bog, BnM	22 C1	420
Glanduff Crossing	MGWR	15 A5	44
GLANMIRE ROAD (Cork) ‡	Kent, GSWR	33 D2	8,16,133
GLANWORTH	GSWR	26 D4	15
Glanworth Station Gates	GSWR	26 D4	15
GLARRYFORD	NCC	5 A5	67
Glarryford Crossing	NCC	5 A5	67
Glashabaun North Bog	Ballydermot-Timahoe Group, BnM	22 B1	199
Glashabaun South Bog	Ballydermot-Timahoe Group, BnM	22 B1	199
GLASLOUGH	GNR(I)	10 A4	52
Glaslough Station Gates	GNR(I)	10 A4	52
GLASNEVIN	GSWR	32 C1	114
Glasnevin Junction ‡	GSWR, MGWR	32 C1	114,115
GLASSAGH HALT	CDRJC	3 A5	94
Glasshouse Crossing	FRRHC	28 B3	14
GLASS MOSS ROAD	BCDR	11 C2	80
Glass Moss Crossing, (Comber No.3)	BCDR	11 C3	80
GLASTHULE (SANDYCOVE &, SANDYCOVE)	DK	23 B1	31
Glebe Crossing, Co Leitrim	CLR	9 A6	97
Glebe Road Crossing, Co Antrim	GNR(I)	11 A3	50
Gleensk Viaduct	GSWR	24 C4	26
GLEN	CVBT	3 D6	103
Glen Crossing (Billa)	GSWR	8 A5	17
GLEN ANNE (LOUGHGILLY)	GNR(I)	10 C5	60
GLEN ANNE	GALT	10 C5	168
Glen Ballynashee Colliery Rly	McTiernan Bros	8 B6	287
Glenagown Crossing	GSWR	25 D1	18
Glenahilty Crossing	GSWR	20 D4	23
GLENARAREEN	DBT	22 D1	119
Glenariff	Glenariff Iron Ore & Harbour Co	5 B5	155
GLENART	DSER	23 A5	31
GLENAVY	GNR(I)	10 D2	65
GLENAGEARY	DK	23 B1	31
Glenageary Siding	DK	23 B1	31
GLENAGALT BRIDGE	TDR	24 D3	109
Glenbane Junction	GSWR	26 D1	8
GLENBEIGH	GSWR	24 D4	26
Glenbeigh Station Gates	GSWR	24 D4	26
GLENBROOK	CBPR	33 F3	99
Glenbrook Station Gates	CBPR	33 F3	99
Glencar Barytes Mine Tramway		8 B3	380
GLENCREW	CVR	10 A3	91
Glenconway Bog Railway	C Tennant Ltd	4 B5	337
Glendonnell Crossing (Garrandarra)	GSWR	28 B3	6
GLENEALY	DSER	23 B4	31
GLENEALY (Old Station)	DSER	23 B4	31
Glenealy Crossing (Ballymanus)	DSER	23 B4	31
GLENFARNE	SLNCR	8 D4	108
Glenfarne (No.12) Station Gates	SLNCR	8 D4	108
Glenfarne Forestry Railway		8 D4	140
Gleniff Quarry	Barium Consolidated	8 B3	203
GLENKEEN	CVR	10 A4	91
Glenlough Crossing	NCC	5 A4	67
GLENMACHAN	BCDR	34 D2	78
Glenmanus Siding	NCC	4 D3	73
GLENMAQUIN	SLR	3 C5	96
GLENMORE, Co Donegal	CDRJC	3 B6	94
Glenmore No.1 Crossing	DSER	28 B3	33
Glenmore Crossing (Rathinure)	DSER	28 B3	33
Glenmore Crossing (No.34), Co Donegal	CDRJC	3 B6	94
GLENMORE, Co Kerry	TDR	24 C3	109
GLENMORE & AYLWARDSTOWN, Co Kilkenny	DSER	28 B3	33
Glenravel Mine	Parkmore Siding	5 B5	336
GLENTIES	CDRJC	2 D6	94
Glenties Station Gates (No.40)	CDRJC	2 D6	94
Glenties Turf Co-op Society Ltd		2 C6	150
Glenties Works		2 C6	150
GLENWICK (CLONDULANE (GLENWICK)	FRRHC	26 D4	14
GLOUNTHAUNE (QUEENSTOWN JUNCTION, COBH JUNCTION)	GSWR	33 F2	16,28
GLYNN, Co Antrim	NCC	5 D6	76
GLYNN, Co Carlow	GSWR	28 C1	3
Glynn Crossing (Ballyling, Co Carlow)	GSWR	28 C1	3
Gogginshill Tunnel	CBSCR	31 C1	85
Goland Crossing	CVR		91
GOLF HALT (LISFANNON GOLF LINKS)	LLSR	3 D3	102
GOLF LINKS HALT – not shown	PT	4 C3	132
GOODYEAR	NIR	10 D3	50
Googannis Crossing (Gougane)	GSWR	26 A4	9
GOOLD'S CROSS (& CASHEL)	GSWR	27 B1	8,29
GORAGHWOOD	GNR(I)	10 C5	50,60
Goraghwood Ballast Quarry	GNR(I)	10 C5	50
GORESBRIDGE	GSWR	22 A6	3
Goresbridge Station Gates	GSWR	22 A6	3
GOREY	DSER	23 A6	31
Gorrell Gates (No.6)	CDRJC	8 C1	93
GORMANSTON	GNR(I)	17 B4	50
Gormanston Aerodrome Railway	WD	17 B4	50
GORT	GSWR	19 D2	17
Gortahorn Crossing	NCC	10 D1	66
Gortafica Crossing	GSWR	19 D3	17
Gortaloughan Halt	GNR(I)	9 B3	49
GORTATLEA	GSWR	25 A3	9,12
Gortatlea Station Gates	GSWR	25 A3	9
Gortatlee Crossing	GSWR	25 B5	11
Gortawarla Crossing	MGWR	13 B1	48
Gortcurreen Crossing	GSWR	25 B1	18
Gortcurreen East Crossing	GSWR	25 B1	18
Gorteade Crossing (O'Kane's)	NCC	4 D6	74
Gorteens Crossing ‡ (29)	IE	28 B3	33
GORTFADA	CLR	15 B1	97
Gortfada Crossing	CLR	15 B1	97
Gortgommon Crossing (Mulally's)	GNR(I)	9 C5	49
Gortin Quarry	Carnlough Lime Co	5 C5	157
Gortinee Siding	MGWR	15 A2	37
Gortmore No.1 Crossing	GSWR	26 A4	9
Gortnaclough Crossing	CBSCR	31 C1	85
GORTNAGALLON	GNR(I)	10 D2	65
Gortnagree Crossing	GSWR	24 B4	26
Gortnaminsha Crossing	GSWR	25 B1	18
Gortnamuck Crossing (Church Road)	CBSCR	30 B1	88
Gortnavogher Crossing	GSWR	19 D3	17
GORTNEE – not shown	GCPBVT	4 D3	113
Gougane Crossing (Googannis)	GSWR	26 A4	9
Gowla Bog	Derryfadda Group, BnM	14 C5	210
Gowla Farm Railway	CSET	14 C5	285
GOWRAN	GSWR	22 A6	2
Gowran Station Gates	GSWR	22 A6	2
Grace Dieu Junction (Waterford) ‡	FRRHC	28 B3	14
Gracefield Colliery	BoW	22 A4	120
GRACEHILL	BR	5 A4	77
Graceys Concrete Products, Tanderagee		10 C4	429
Granaghan Bog	Mountdillon Group, BnM	15 A3	178
Granaries	GSWR	32 D2	114
Grand Canal Street Works & Depot	DK	32 D2	31
Grand Canal Tramway		22 C1	200
GRANGE, Co Kilkenny	GSWR	28 A3	13

L

Porthall Station Gates	GNR(I)	3 D5	49
Porthall Crossing	GNR(I)	3 D5	49
Porthall Lime Kiln Railway		3 D5	238
PORTLAOISE (MARYBOROUGH)	GSWR	21 D3	6,8
Portlaoise Permanent Way Works	CIE	21 D3	6
PORTLAW (FIDDOWN &)	GSWR	28 A3	13
PORTMARNOCK	GNR(I)	17 B6	50
Port Quay (Letterkenny)	SLR	3 C5	96
PORTRUSH	NCC, GCPBVT	4 D3	73,113
Portrush Columner Basalt Co Railway		4 D3	234
Portrush Harbour	NCC, GCPBVT	4 D3	73,113
Portrush Miniature Railways		4 D3	293
PORTRUSH POST OFFICE – not shown	GCPBVT	4 D3	113
PORTSTEWART (TOWN)	NCC	4 C3	132
PORTSTEWART (CROMORE HALT)	NCC	4 D3	73,132
PORTUMNA BRIDGE	PPBR	20 D2	118
Portumna Bridge Quay	PPBR	20 D2	118
Portumna	(unknown contract)	20 D2	340
POULAPHOUCA	DBT	22 D2	119
Poulaphouca Reservoir Scheme		22	228
Powells Crossing (Castle Lambert)	MGWR	14 A6	34
POWERSTOWN PARK	GSWR	27 C2	27
POYNTZPASS	GNR(I)	10 C5	50
Poyntzpass Station Gates	GNR(I)	10 C5	50
Priorstown Crossing	GSWR	27 C2	13
PRITCHARD'S BRIDGE	GNR(I)	10 D3	50
Priority Drilling Co	Turlough Hill Railway	23 A3	355
PROMENADE (PARADE) – not shown	PT	4 C3	132
PROSPECT (BALLYCUMBER)	GSWR	15 B6	4
Prospect Brickworks, Belfast		34 C4	395
Prospect Hill Tunnel	MGWR	13 C6	39
PROUDSTOWN PARK	MGWR	16 C4	46
Proudstown Park Crossing	MGWR	16 C4	46
PUCK ISLAND	TDR	24 C3	109
Punchbowl Loop – not shown	GCPBVT	4 D3	113
Purgatory Crossing	GNR(I)	10 C4	52

Q

Quakers Crossing	GNR(I)	10 C4	52
Quaker's Road Crossing	GSWR	21 B4	23
Quagmire Viaduct	GSWR	25 B4	9
QUARRYVALE	DLT	23 A1	121
Quay Bawn Crossing	GSWR	24 D4	26
QUAY STREET (Dundalk) ‡	DNGR	17 A1	104
QUEEN'S BRIDGE (Belfast)	BCR	34 C3	116
Queen's Bridge Subway	BCR	34 C3	116
QUEEN'S QUAY (Belfast)	BCDR	34 C3	78,79
QUEENSTOWN (COBH)	GSWR	33 F3	28
QUEENSTOWN JUNCTION (COBH JUNCTION, GLOUNTHAUNE)	GSWR	33 F1	16,28
QUILTY	SCR	19 A4	111
Quilty Station Gates	SCR	19 A4	111
Quilty East Crossing	SCR	19 A4	111
QUIN (ARDSOLLUS &)	GSWR	19 D4	17
Quinn's Crossing [R]	CDRJC	3 B6	93
Quoile Bridge	BCDR	11 C4	79

R

RACECOURSE (Downpatrick)	BCDR	11 C5	82
Racrane Crossing [R]	GNR(I)	9 C3	49
RAFFEEN	CBPR	33 E4	99
Raffeen Crossing	CBPR	33 E4	99
Raffeen Quarry Siding	CBPR	33 E4	99
Rafian Crossing (Drumary)	CLR	9 B6	97
Raford Crossing	LALR	14 B6	41
Rahan Peat Works Railway		21 B1	193
Rahans Crossing	MGWR	7 B5	45
RAHENY	GNR(I)	32 E1	50
RAILWAY STREET (ARMAGH)	GNR(I)	10 B4	52,53,54 60
RAMAKET	CVR	10 A4	91
RANDALSTOWN	NCC	10 D1	66
Randalstown Station Gates	NCC	10 D1	66
RANDALSTOWN MILITARY PLATFORM	NCC	10 D1	66

Randalstown Viaduct	NCC	10 D1	66
RANELAGH & RATHMINES (RANELAGH)	DSER	32 C3	30
RAPHOE	SLR	3 C5	96
RASHENNY	CER	4 A2	102
Ratass Crossing	GSWR	25 A2	9
Rath No.1 Crossing	CBSCR	30 C3	85
Rath No.2 Crossing	CBSCR	30 C3	85
Rathaldon Crossing	MGWR	16 C4	46
Rathbaun Crossing	MGWR	7 B6	45
Rathbeg 1 Crossing	GSWR	21 A3	24
Rathbeg 2 Crossing	GSWR	21 A3	24
RATHCOOL	GSWR	25 D4	9
Rathcoole No.1 Crossing	GSWR	25 D4	9
Rathcoole No.2 Crossing	GSWR	25 D4	9
Rathcoole No.3 Crossing	GSWR	25 D4	9
Rathdooney More Crossing	MGWR	8 A5	37
Rathdown Deviation ‡	DSER	23 B2	31
RATHDRUM	DSER	23 A4	31
RATHDRUM – old station	DSER	23 A4	31
Rathdrum No.1 Tunnel	DSER	23 A4	31
Rathdrum No.2 Tunnel	DSER	23 A4	31
Rathdrum No.3 Tunnel	DSER	23 A4	31
Rathduane Crossing	GSWR	25 D4	9
Rathdrum Viaduct (Corballis Viaduct)	DSER	23 A4	31
RATHDUFF	GSWR	26 B5	8
Rathellan Crossing	GSWR	22 B6	2
RATHGAROGUE	DSER	28 C2	33
Rathgarogue No.1 Crossing	DSER	28 C2	33
Rathgarogue No.2 Crossing	DSER	28 C2	33
Rathinure Crossing (Glenmore)	DSER	28 B3	33
RATHKEALE	GSWR	26 A1	18
RATHKENNY	NCC	5 B5	72
Rathkenny Creamery Siding	NCC	5 B5	72
Rathkenny Mines Siding	NCC	5 B5	72
Rathkenny Mines Tramway		5 B5	414
RATHLUIRC (CHARLEVILLE)	GSWR	26 B2	8,25
Rathlyon Crossing	GSWR	22 C5	1
RATHMINES (RANELAGH &, RANELAGH)	DSER	32 C3	30
RATHMORE, (SHINNAGH, SHINNAGH & RATHMORE)	GSWR	25 C4	9
Rathmore Station Gates	GSWR	25 C4	9
Rathmore Crossing	GSWR	25 C4	9
RATHNEW	DSER	23 B4	31
Rathnew Brickworks Tramway		23 B4	382
RATHOWEN (STREETE &)	MGWR	15 D4	37
Rathpatrick Crossing	DSER	28 B3	33
Rathpeacon	GSWR	33 C1	8
Rathregan Crossing	MGWR	16 D6	46
Rathroeen Crossing	MGWR	7 B5	45
Rathscanlon Crossing	GSWR	7 D6	17
Rathumney Crossing	FRRHC	28 C3	14
RATHVILLY	GSWR	22 C4	1
RAVENSDALE	GNR(I) HoH	17	62
Ravenhill Brick & Tile Co Railway		34 D3	310
Rea's Siding (Antrim)	NCC	10 D1	67
Reastown Crossing (Drumare)	NCC	4 D5	74
RECESS	MGWR	12 D4	39
Recess Station Gates	MGWR	12 D4	39
RECESS HOTEL PLATFORM	MGWR	13 A4	39
RED LANE	DBT	22 D2	119
Red Hill Mine Tramway		8 D6	437
REDHILLS	GNR(I)	9 C6	52
RED ROCK	GNR(I) HoH	17	62
Red Tench, North Crossing	GSWR	25 B5	11
Reed Mallick Ltd	Altnahinch Dam Railway	5 A4	317
Reenard Crossing	GSWR	24 B5	26
Reenroe Crossing	CBSCR	30 C1	85
REILLY'S BRIDGE	MGWR	32 B1	34
Reilly's Crossing	MGWR	32 B1	34
Reilly's Rocks Crossing	GNR(I)	10 B4	52
Renny Crossing	GSWR	26 C4	14
Reynolds' Crossing [R]	GNR(I)	10 A2	53
RETREAT, Co Antrim	NCC	5 B4	72
RETREAT HALT, Co Armagh	GNR(I)	10 C4	52
Rhode Power Station	ESB	16 A6	183
Ribbontail Crossing (Geraghty's)	MGWR	16 B6	34
Rice's Road Crossing	CBSCR	31 B1	85

Part Three

ROUTE TABLES

THIS PART of the book amplifies the information displayed on the map pages and presents it in tabular form. It includes the detailed distances between features as well as providing data on the opening and closing dates of lines and stations.

The stations at the beginning and end of the section of line covered in each table are given in its title. This is followed by the initials or name of the owner/operator of that section of line as at 1922, the gauge, and an indication of the point from which the milepost distances are measured. The opening and closing dates of the whole line or its component parts and original company or companies which built the route are then listed. In the case of industrial and private railways, the title will be either the name by which that line is most commonly known, followed by the last known operator, or in some cases the title will be the name of the owning company.

The opening and closing dates of the industrial and private railways will be found in the associated notes. As these railways tend not to have 'official' mileposts, no starting point is given but the lengths of line will be contained in the notes, where known.

The data in the body of the tables is arranged as follows. The first column indicates the position of a feature as shown by the milepost. Next is the distance in miles and chains from the starting point of the table, where known. The distances quoted are the official railway distances, except where stated. These are sometimes at variance to the actual distance, or those given by other railway sources. Distances suffixed by a '?' indicate that distance shown is an approximation. The third column lists the place or feature itself. Passenger stations and halts are printed in capital letters, other features are in upper and lower case type characters. Any additional information about the place or feature appears immediately below that entry. The fourth column shows the opening date, while the fifth column shows whether it is still open, and if not, its date of closure. The sixth column provides a cross-reference to the Atlas, the page on which the feature is located comes first, followed by the grid reference. The final column lists other Route Tables in which the place or feature appears

Closure dates for stations indicate when they lost their passenger services. In many cases stations remained open for goods traffic long after the last passenger train had departed. For example, in Route Table 1, passenger trains between Sallins and Tullow ceased to run in 1947 but the branch remained open for goods traffic until 1959. Thus, to ascertain the closing dates of lines please refer to the information at the beginnning of each table rather than to the entries for individual stations. One odd manifestation of this form of tabulation is that a number of lines appear to have had all the stations closed before the level crossings, bridges, and viaducts. This is of course quite correct, as goods trains would still have to use these features if they were using the line after the end of the passenger service.

Where a siding or short branch strikes off the line being described, this is distinguished from the main route by being displayed within horizontal dotted rules with the distances and place names indented as with normal railway timetable practice. For example, on Route Table 2, the new junctions at Lavistown, opened in 1996 to permit through running from Waterford to Dublin without reversal at Kilkenny, are dealt with in this way.

1 Sallins to Tullow

GSWR / 5ft 3in gauge / mileposts measured from Sallins

Sallins to Colbinstown opened 22-06-1885 by the GSWR.
Colbinstown to Baltinglass opened 01-09-1885 by the GSWR.
Baltinglass to Tullow opened 01-06-1886 by the GSWR.

Passenger services suspended from 24-04-1944 due to fuel shortage.
Passenger services resumed from 10-12-1945.
Passenger services suspended from 27-01-1947.
Goods services suspended from 10-03-1947.

Closed to passengers 27-01-47 by CIE.
Closed to regular goods services 10-03-1947 but monthly livestock specials ran 1947-59.
Closed completely 01-04-1959 by CIE.

MPost Dist.	Miles & Chains	Place / Feature (notes)	Date Opened	Date Closed	Map Grid	Table Ref.
0	0:00	SALLINS & NAAS formerly SALLINS, closed 09-09-1963, reopened as Sallins & Naas 16-05-1994	1846	Open	22 C1	8
1¾	1:54	Boreen Crossing also called Lusk (Oldtown)	1885	1959	22 C2	
2¼	?	NAAS	1885	1959	22 C2	
7¼	?	HARRISTOWN	1885	1959	22 C2	
14	?	DUNLAVIN	1885	1947	22 C3	
17	?	COLBINSTOWN	1885	1947	22 C3	
19¾	?	GRANGE CON	1885	1947	22 C3	
24¼	?	BALTINGLASS	1885	1947	22 C4	
28¼	28:13	Waterstown Crossing	1886	1959	22 C4	
29	?	RATHVILLY	1886	1947	22 C4	
33	32:70	Rathlyon Crossing	1886	1959	22 C5	
34¾	?	TULLOW	1886	1947	22 C5	

2 Cherryville Junction to Kilkenny

GSWR / 5ft 3in gauge / mileposts measured from Dublin Heuston

Cherryville Junction to Carlow opened 04-08-1846 by GSWR.
Carlow to Bagenalstown opened 24-07-1848 by the ISER.
Bagenalstown to Lavistown Junction opened 14-11-1850 by the ISER.
Lavistown Junction to Kilkenny opened 1848 by the WKR.
Lavistown Junction to Kilkenny opened 1870 by the ISER.

Passenger services suspended 24-02-1947 due to fuel shortage.
Passenger services resumed 24-05-1947.

Lavistown Loop opened 25-03-1996 by Iarnród Éireann.

A second parallel line was constructed from Lavistown Junction to Kilkenny by the GSWR in 1867 after a dispute with the WKR, this layout exsisted until 09-06-1979 when CIE re-instated the junction and removed the former GSWR line.

MPost Dist.	Miles & Chains	Place / Feature (notes)	Date Opened	Date Closed	Map Grid	Table Ref.
32½	32:35	Cherryville Junction	1847	Open	22 B2	8
		opened as a junction 1847				
36½	36:46	KILDANGAN	1909	1963	22 A2	
		closed to passengers 01-01-1963				
40¾	40:70	Kilberry	c.1950	1975	22 A3	
		siding for Bord na Móna peat factory				
44¾	44:64	ATHY	1846	Open	22 B3	120
44¾	44:74	Junction for Wolfhill Branch	1918	1965	22 B3	120
		short length in use to Tegral Factory				
47¾	47:50	Grangemellon	?	?	22 B4	
		siding for Beet loading				
51	51:00	MAGENEY	1846	1963	22 B4	
		closed to passengers 01-01-1963				
55	55:13	Carlow Beet Factory Siding	1926	?	22 B5	245
55¾	55:68	CARLOW	1846	Open	22 B5	
57¼	57:18	Blackbog Crossing	1848	Open	22 B5	
58	58:02	Ballybar Crossing	1848	Open	22 B5	
60	60:09	MILFORD	1848	1963	22 B5	
		closed to passengers 01-01-1963				
63½	63:33	Rathellan Crossing	1848	Open	22 B6	
66	66:00	MUINE BHEAG	1848	Open	22 B6	
		formerly Bagenalstown				
66	66:04	Junction for Palace East	1858	1963	22 B6	3
67	67:04	Barrow Bridge	1850	Open	22 A6	
69	69:05	Shankhill Crossing	1850	Open	22 A6	
70½	70:35	Jordanstown Crossing	1850	Open	22 A6	
73¼	73:25	Commons Crossing	1850	Open	22 A6	
		also called Commons Bog Crossing				
74¼	74:16	Gowran Station Gates	1850	Open	22 A6	
74¼	74:17	GOWRAN	1852	1963	22 A6	
		closed to passengers 01-01-1963				
76¾	76:50	Clifden Crossing	1850	Open	22 A6	
		also called Rathgarvan Crossing				
77¾	77:53	Highrath Crossing	1850	Open	21 D6	
78	77.73	Lavistown North Junction	1996	Open	21 D6	
0	0:00	Lavistown North Junction	1996	Open	21 D6	
0½	0:42	Lavistown South Junction	1996	Open	21 D6	6
78½	78:40	Lavistown Crossing	1850	Open	21 D6	
78½	78:46	Lavistown West Junction	1850	Open	21 D6	6
		closed as a Junction 1867 to 09-06-1979				
80¾	80:61	Leggetsrath Crossing	1850	Open	21 D6	
80¾	80:66	KILKENNY	1848	Open	21 D6	6
		ISER platform added in 1850.				
		KILKENNY McDONAGH from 1966				

3 Bagenalstown to Palace East

GSWR / 5ft 3in gauge / mileposts measured from Dublin Heuston

Bagenalstown to Borris opened 20-12-1858 by the BWR.
Borris to Ballywilliam opened 17-03-1862 by the BWR.
Ballywilliam to Palace East opened 26-10-1870 by the WNRWJR.

Bagenalstown to Ballywilliam closed 01-01-1864.
Bagenalstown to Borris re-opened 05-09-1870.
Borris to Ballywilliam re-opened 26-10-1870.
Bagenalstown to Palace East closed 30-09-1873.
Bagenalstown to Palace East re-opened 09-02-1874.

All services suspended from 24-04-1944 to due to wartime fuel shortage.
Goods services resumed from 10-12-1945.
Regular Goods services suspended from 27-01-1947.
Special Goods and Beet traffic continued to closure.

Bagenalstown to Palace East closed to passengers 02-02-1931 by the GSR.
Bagenalstown to Palace East closed to goods 27-01-1947 (except specials) by the GSR.
Bagenalstown to Palace East closed to completely 01-04-1963 by CIE.

MPost Dist.	Miles & Chains	Place / Feature (notes)	Date Opened	Date Closed	Map Grid	Table Ref.
66	66:00	MUINE BHEAG	1858	Open	22 B6	2
		formerly called BAGENALSTOWN				
66¼	66:24	Kilree Crossing	1858	1963	22 A6	
69½	69:45	Kilgreany Crossing	1858	1963	22 A6	
70¾	?	GORESBRIDGE	1870	1931	22 A6	
70¾	70:66	Goresbridge Station Gates	1858	1963	22 B6	
73¾	73:57	Borris Crossing	1858	1963	28 C1	
74	?	BORRIS	1858	1931	28 C1	
?		Viaduct (16 arch)	1862	1963	28 C1	
78½	78:29	Inch Crossing	1862	1963	28 C1	
81¾	?	GLYNN	1874	1875	28 C1	
		opened 09-02-1874, closed 1875				
81¾	81:51	Glynn Crossing	1862	1963	28 C1	
		also called Ballyling Crossing;				
		there was also a Beet Siding here until 1963.				
86	86:10	Ballywilliam No.1 Crossing	1862	1963	28 C2	
86½	?	BALLYWILLIAM	1862	1931	28 C2	
87½	87:40	Ballywilliam No.2 Crossing	1870	1963	28 C2	
89¾	?	Palace East Junction	1887	1963	28 C2	33
		became a Junction in 1887				
90	?	PALACE EAST	1870	1963	28 C2	33
		junction with DSER				

4 Portarlington to Athlone Midland

GSWR / 5ft 3in gauge / mileposts measured from Dublin Heuston

Portarlington to Tullamore opened 02-10-1854 by the GSWR.
Tullamore to Athlone (GSWR) opened 03-10-1859 by the GSWR.
Athlone GSWR to Athlone East Junction opened 09-1860 by the GSWR.

Passenger services suspended 24-02-1947 due to fuel shortage.
Passenger services resumed 24-05-1947.

MPost Dist.	Miles & Chains	Place / Feature (notes)	Date Opened	Date Closed	Map Grid	Table Ref.
41¾	41:50	PORTARLINGTON	1847	Open	22 A2	8
42	41:58	Portarlington Junction	1854	Open	22 A2	8
43¼	43:12	Power Station Junction	1941	1965	21 D2	
0	0:00	Power Station Junction	1941	1965	21 D2	
		also called Clonsast Siding				
1 ?	?	Power Station	1941	1965	21 D2	262
		served Portarlington Power Station				
44¼	44:12	Shanderry No.1 Crossing	1854	Open	21 D2	
45	45:00	Clonyquin Crossing	1854	Open	21 D2	
		also called Shanderry No.2 Crossing				
45¾	45:50	Bord na Móna Bridge	1953	Open	21 D2	192
		line crosses over the Bord na Móna				
		Clonsast System				
50¼	50:24	GEASHILL	1854	1963	21 D2	
52½	52:31	Cloncoher Crossing	1854	Open	21 D1	
		also called Newtown Crossing				
54¾	54:54	Meelegans Crossing	1854	Open	21 C1	
57¼	57:13	TULLAMORE (2nd station)	1859	1865	21 C1	
		opened 03-10-1859, closed 01-10-1865				
57½ ?	?	TULLAMORE (1st station)	1854	1859	21 C1	
		former terminus on spur, closed 03-10-1859				
58	57:71	TULLAMORE (3rd station)	1865	Open	21 C1	
		opened 01-10-1865				
62¾	62:70	Ashfield Crossing	1859	Open	21 C1	
64½	64:38	Streamstown Junction	1863	1962	15 C6	35
		junction for Streamstown				
64½	64:40	CLARA EXCHANGE PLATFORM	1893	1925	15 C6	
		platform near Streamstown Junction				
64½	64:52	Clara Crossing	1859	Open	15 C6	
65	64:64	CLARA	1859	Open	15 C6	35
65¾	65:73	Erry No.1 Crossing	1859	Open	15 C6	
		also called Armstrong No.1 Crossing				

66	65:78	Clara & Banagher Junction	1884	1962	15 C6	5
		junction for Banagher				
66	66:05	Erry No.2 Crossing	1859	Open	15 C6	
		also called Armstrong No.2 Crossing				
66¾	66:55	Clonshanny Crossing	1859	Open	15 B6	
68¼	68:18	BALLYCUMBER	1862	1963	15 B6	
		formerly PROSPECT, re-named 1890				
70¼	70:26	Bellair No.1 Crossing	1859	Open	15 B6	
70½	70:49	Bellair No.2 Crossing	1859	Open	15 B6	
70¾	70:76	Bord na Móna Bridge	c.1980	Open	15 B6	335
		line crosses over the Bord na Móna Bellair System				
72½?	?	Castle Daly siding	?	1878	15 B6	
		siding served Distillery				
72¾	72:64	Clonydonnin passing loop	1974	Open	15 B6	
73¾	73:50	Torrydonnellan Crossing	1859	Open	15 B6	
73¾	73:52	BALLINAHOUN	1862	c.1940	15 B6	
		formerly DOON, renamed 31-08-1862 on				
		becoming a private flag station, although				
		was public for a few months in 1862;				
		also used for Races up the 1940s				
74¼	74:39	Castletown Crossing	1859	Open	15 B6	
77¾	77:69	Bunnahinly No.1 Crossing	1859	Open	15 A6	
78½	78:45	Kilmacuagh No.1 Crossing	1859	Open	15 A6	
78¾	78:71	Kilmacuagh No.2 Crossing	1859	Open	15 A6	
79	79:11	Bunnavalley Crossing	1859	Open	15 A6	
80½	80:37	ATHLONE (GSWR)	1859	Open	15 A5	
		closed 02-03-1925, re-opened 14-01-1985				
80¾	80:64	Athlone East Junction	1860	Open	15 A5	34
		junction with MGWR				
80¾	80:65	Shannon Bridge	1851	Open	15 A5	34
		crosses River Shannon by a three span,				
		centre opening bridge, 181 yards long				
81	81:00	ATHLONE (MGWR)	1851	1985	15 A5	34
		closed 14-01-1985				

5   Clara to Banagher

GSWR / 5ft 3in gauge / mileposts measured from Clara & Banagher Jnc.

Clara to Banagher opened 29-05-1884 by the CBaR.

Goods services suspended from 10-03-1947 due to fuel shortage.
Passenger services suspended 24-02-1947.
Goods services resumed 30-09-1947.

Closed to passengers 24-02-1947 by CIE.
Closed completely 01-01-1963 by CIE.

MPost Dist.	Miles & Chains	Place / Feature (notes)	Date Opened	Date Closed	Map Grid	Table Ref.
1	1:14	CLARA	1859	Open	15 C6	4
0	0:05	Erry No.1 Crossing	1859	Open	15 C6	4
		also called Armstrong No.1				
0	0:00	Clara & Banagher Junction	1884	1963	15 C6	4
		junction for Athlone				
?	?	Bord na Móna Crossing	?	1963	21 B1	362
		flat crossing with Bord na Móna 3ft gauge line				
7¾	7:70	Ballyvlin Crossing	1884	1963	21 B1	
10¼	10:16	FERBANE	1884	1963	21 B1	
12¾	12:76	Ballyshane Crossing	1884	1963	21 A1	
13	?	BELMONT & CLOGHAN	1884	1963	21 A1	
18¾	?	BANAGHER	1884	1963	21 A1	

6   Portlaoise to Waterford

GSWR / 5ft 3in gauge / mileposts measured from Portlaoise

Portlaoise to Abbeyleix opened for goods 01-05-1867 by the KJR.
Portlaoise to Abbeyleix opened for passengers 15-05-1867 by the KJR.
Abbeyleix to Kilkenny opened 01-03-1865 by the KJR.
Kilkenny to Thomastown opened 12-05-1848 by the WKR.
Thomastown to Jerpoint Hill opened 29-05-1850 by the WKR.

Jerpoint Hill to Dunkitt opened 21-05-1853 by the WKR.
Dunkitt to Waterford (Newrath) opened 11-09-1854 by the WLR.
Waterford (Newrath) to Waterford (North) opened 29-08-1864 by the WLR.
Dunkitt to Waterford (North) opened 1864 by the WKR.
Lavistown Loop opened 25-03-1996 by IE.

Passenger services suspended 24-02-1947 due to fuel shortage.
Passenger services resumed 24-05-1947.

Portlaoise to Kilkenny closed to passengers 01-01-1963 by CIE.

Portlaoise to Clonard level crossing was re-opened for Bord na Móna traffic from the milled peat factory at Coolnamona late 09-1965. Part of this section, now out of use, is used to store recovered track panels.

A second parallel line was constructed from Lavistown Junction to Kilkenny by the GSWR in 1867 after a dispute with the WKR, this layout exsisted until 09-06-1979 when CIE re-instated the junction and removed the former GSWR line.

MPost Dist.	Miles & Chains	Place / Feature (notes)	Date Opened	Date Closed	Map Grid	Table Ref.
0	0:00	PORTLAOISE	1847	Open	21 D3	8
		opened as junction in 1867; formerly MARYBOROUGH				
?	?	Permanent Way Works	1974	Open	21 D3	
?	?	Avonmore Co-op Siding	?	Open	21 D3	
0¾	0:51	Conniberry Junction	1885	1963	21 D3	21
		opened as junction; junction for Mountmellick				
0¾	0:57	Conniberry Junction Crossing	1867	Open	21 D3	
1¾	1:71	Togher Crossing	1867	Open	21 D3	
2¾	2:60	Coolnamona	1964 ?	Closed	21 D3	189
		siding served Bord na Móna Factory				
3	3:00	Clonard Crossing	1867	1963	21 D3	
3½	3:31	Clonadadoran Crossing	1867	1963	21 D3	
5	5:08	Colt Crossing	1867	1963	21 D4	
6½	6:46	Corbally Crossing	1867	1963	21 D4	
7¼	7:20	Tonduff Crossing	1867	1963	21 D4	
9½	?	ABBEYLEIX	1865	1963	21 D4	
11¼	11:30	Clonkeen Crossing	1865	1963	21 D4	
11¾	11:57	Brandra Crossing	1865	1963	21 D4	
14½	?	ATTANAGH	1867	1963	21 D5	
		opened 15-05-1867				
14½	14:45	Attanagh Station Gates	1865	1963	21 D5	
17¼	17:22	Smithstown Crossing	1865	1963	21 D5	
		also called Ballyragget Crossing				
17½	?	BALLYRAGGET	1865	1963	21 D5	
18½	18:36	Donaghmore Crossing	1865	1963	21 D5	
21¼	21:15	Clinstown Crossing	1865	1963	21 D5	
24½	?	Castlecomer Junction	1919	1963	21 D6	22
		Dunmore Ballast Pit	?	?	21 D6	
		in use in 1874				
28¼	28:26	KILKENNY	1848	Open	21 D6	2
		junction for Bagenalstown; KILKENNY McDONAGH Station from 1966				
29¼	29:11	Leggetsrath Crossing	1848	Open	21 D6	
		LAVISTOWN	c.1850	1853	21 D6	
30½	30:49	Lavistown West Junction	1850	Open	21 D6	2
		closed as a Junction 1867 to 09-06-1979.				
78½	78:46	Lavistown West Junction	1850	Open	21 D6	
78½	78:40	Lavistown Crossing	1850	Open	21 D6	
77½	77:33	Lavistown North Junction	1996	Open	21 D6	
30¾	30:55	Lavistown Crossing	1848	Open	21 D6	2
0	0:00	Lavistown North Junction	1996	Open	21 D6	
0½	0:45	Lavistown South Junction	1996	Open	21 D6	
31¼	31:09	Lavistown South Junction	1996	Open	21 D6	
33	32:65	DUNBELL	?	?	28 B1	
		possible early flag station				
32½	32:68	Dunbell Crossing	1848	Open	28 B1	
32½	?	Bennett's Bridge Siding	1970	1982	28 B1	
		Dolomite ore loading point				
33¾	33:55	Ballyreddin Crossing	1848	Open	28 B1	
34¼	34:25	BENNETT'S BRIDGE	1848	1963	28 B1	
		closed to passengers 01-01-1963				

37	36:72	NEWHOUSE possible early flag station	?	?	28 B1	
37	36:73	Newhouse Crossing	1848	Open	28 B1	
37¾	37:64	Legan Crossing	1848	Open	28 B1	
39	39:03	THOMASTOWN	1848	Open	28 B1	
39½	39:36	Thomastown Viaduct crosses River Nore, main span 212ft	1850	Open	28 B1	
40¼	40:10	JERPOINT HILL	1850	1853	28 B1	
42¼	42:42	Derrynahinch Crossing	1853	Open	28 B2	
43	43:10	Kiltorcan Crossing	1853	Open	28 B2	
43¼	43:23	BALLYHALE closed to passengers 01-01-1963	1853	1963	28 B2	
43¼	43:40	Ballyhale Station Gates	1853	Open	28 B2	
44½	44:35	Knockwilliam Crossing	1853	Open	28 A2	
45¾	45:64	Castlegannon Crossing	1853	Open	28 A2	
47¼	47:30	Knockmoylan Crossing	1853	Open	28 A2	
51	51:08	Glendonnell Crossing also called Garrandarra Crossing	1853	Open	28 B3	
51½	51:45	Mullinavat Station Gates	1853	Open	28 B3	
51½	51:47	MULLINAVAT closed to passengers 01-01-1963	1853	1963	28 B3	
53½	53:46	Rossinan Crossing	1853	Open	28 B3	
54½	54:39	Ballykeoghan No.1 Crossing	1853	Open	28 B3	
54½	54:45	Ballykeoghan No.2 Crossing	1853	Open	28 B3	
54½	54:51	KILMACOW closed to passengers 01-01-1963	1853	1963	28 B3	
55¾	55:52	Milltown Crossing	1853	Open	28 B3	
56¾	56:60	DUNKITT terminus of WKR until WLR line opened to Waterford in 1854.	1853	1854/5	28 B3	13
57½	57:30	Newrath Junction also called Dunkitt Junction; junction with WLR until 1864	1854	1864	28 B3	13
57¾	57:66	Newrath No.1 Crossing	1854	Open	28 B3	
58¼	?	NEWRATH COMMONS temporary terminus, opened 10-1867, closed 01-04-1868	1867	1868	28 B3	
58¼	58:17	Newrath No.2 Crossing	1854	Open	28 B3	
58¼	58:37	Suir Bridge Junction junction with FRRHC	1854	Open	28 B3	14
59	58:75	WATERFORD (NEWRATH) original WLR Station	1854	1864	28 B3	
59	59:08	WATERFORD (NORTH) PLUNKETT station from 1966	1864	Open	28 B3	33

7 Birdhill to Killaloe

GSWR / 5ft 3in gauge / mileposts measured from Birdhill

Birdhill to Killaloe opened 12-04-1862 by the LCKR.
Killaloe to Killaloe Pier opened to goods by 09-09-1867 by the LCKR.

Closed to passengers 17-07-1931 by the GSR.

Goods services suspended from 24-04-1944 due to fuel shortage, not re-instated.

Closed to goods 24-04-1944 by the GSR.

MPost Dist.	Miles & Chains	Place / Feature (notes)	Date Opened	Date Closed	Map Grid	Table Ref.
0	0:00	BIRDHILL	1860	Open	20 B5	23
0¾	0:64	Coole Crossing	1862	1944	20 B5	
3¼	?	KILLALOE (old station)	1862	1894	20 B5	
3½	?	KILLALOE (new station) new station 34 chains north probably opened 09-07-1894	1894	1931	20 B5	
4	?	Killaloe Pier occasional passenger services in connection with Shannon sailings, 07-1894 to 09-1914	1867	?	20 B5	

8 Dublin Heuston to Cork Kent

GSWR / 5ft 3in gauge / mileposts measured from Dublin Heuston

Dublin to Cherryville Junction opened 04-08-1846 by the GSWR.
Curragh Siding opened 17-04-1856 by the GSWR.
Cherryville Junction to Portlaoise opened 26-06-1847 by the GSWR.
Portlaoise to Ballybrophy opened 01-09-1847 by the GSWR.
Ballybrophy to Thurles opened 13-03-1848 by the GSWR.
Thurles to Limerick Junction opened 03-07-1848 by GSWR.
Limerick Junction to Mallow opened 19-03-1849 by the GSWR.
Mallow to Cork Victoria opened 29-10-1849 by the GSWR.
Cork Victoria to Cork Penrose Quay (temporary terminus) opened 03-12-1855 by GSWR.
Penrose Quay opened 28-07-1856 by the GSWR.
Cork Glanmire Road opened 01-02-1893 by the GSWR.

Clondalkin and Lucan South were closed from 24-04-1944 to 10-12-1945 and from 20-01-1947 due to fuel shortage, they did not re-open.
Passenger services suspended 24-02-1947 due to fuel shortage, except Mallow to Cork.
Limited accommodation available on mail and overnight perishable trains.

Passenger services resumed 24-05-1947.

MPost Dist.	Miles & Chains	Place / Feature (notes)	Date Opened	Date Closed	Map Grid	Table Ref.
0	0:00	DUBLIN HEUSTON KINGSBRIDGE until 1966	1846	Open	32 B2	
0¼ ?	?	Junction to Guinness Brewery	1875	1965	32 B2	131
0¾	0:53	Islandbridge Junction opened as a junction to Glasnevin 1877	1877	Open	32 B2	114
1½	1:43	Inchicore Works Platform platform serving Works; had limited passenger service to North Wall, later Amiens Street from 1901 to 1907	?	?	32 B2	
1¾	1:60	Inchicore Works main GSWR, GSR, CIE and IE Works	1846	Open	32 A3	
3	3:09	CHERRY ORCHARD opened 16-05-1994	1994	Open	23 A1	
4½	4:32	CLONDALKIN closed 20-01-1947, re-opened 16-05-1994	1846	Open	23 A1	
?	?	Baldonnel Siding exchange sidings for Baldonnel Aerodrome Railway	1918	?	22 D1	153
6¾	6:63	LUCAN SOUTH called LUCAN until 1925; closed 20-01-1947	1846	1947	22 D1	
10	10:00	HAZELHATCH AND CELBRIDGE closed 10-11-1947, re-opened 16-05-1994. formerly HAZELHATCH.	1846	Open	22 D1	
13	13:10	STRAFFAN closed 10-11-1947	c.1849	1947	22 D1	
17¾	17:72	SALLINS AND NAAS closed 09-09-1963, re-opened 16-05-1994. formerly SALLINS.	1846	Open	22 C1	1
19	19:02	River Liffey Bridge	1846	Open	22 C1	
25½	25:38	NEWBRIDGE formerly DROICHEAD NUA 1920s to 1994	1846	Open	22 B2	
26¾	26:60	Ballast Pit Junction	?	1973	22 B2	
26¾	?	Newbridge Ballast Pit former Ballast Pit on up side	?	1973	22 B2	
27½	27:40	CURRAGH MAINLINE for Race and Military Specials	1846	Open	22 B2	
?	?	Curragh Stand House Crossing	1856	1977	22 B2	
0½	0:38	CURRAGH RACECOURSE PLATFORM racecourse platforms behind main stand; also used for Military Specials. Closed 07-03-1977	1856	1977	22 B2	
27¾	27:52	Junction from Racecourse line closed 07-03-1977	1856	1977	22 B2	
30	30:00	KILDARE	1846	Open	22 B2	
32½	32:35	Cherryville Junction opened as a junction for Kilkenny 1847	1847	Open	22 B2	2
36¾	36:54	MONASTEREVAN	c.1849	1976	22 A2	
41¾	41:50	PORTARLINGTON junction for Clara and Athlone	1847	Open	22 A2	4
41¾	41:58	Portarlington Junction	1854	Open	22 A2	4
47¾	47:75	Straboe Crossing	1847	Open	21 D3	

MPost Dist.	Miles & Chains	Place / Feature (notes)	Date Opened	Date Closed	Map Grid	Table Ref.
51	?	Odlum's Sidings *private sidings to north of Portlaoise station*	?	?	21 D3	
51	50:72	PORTLAOISE *formerly MARYBOROUGH. Junction for KILKENNY AND MOUNTMELLICK*	1847	Open	21 D3	6,21
53¼	53:22	Bord na Móna Bridge *the 3ft gauge Bord na Móna Coolnamona System railway passes under the line*	1964 ?	Open	21 D3	189
53½	53:38	Clonkeen Crossing	1847	Open	21 D3	
59½	59:32	MOUNTRATH & CASTLETOWN	c.1849	1976	21 C4	
61½	61:50	Cuddagh Crossing	1847	Open	21 C4	
66½	66:52	BALLYBROPHY *formerly BORRIS & ROSCREA, re-named ROSCREA & PARSONSTOWN JUNCTION in 1857; re-named BALLYBROPHY in 1870; junction for Limerick via Nenagh*	1847	Open	21 B4	23
69¼	69:17	Coolowley Crossing *replaced by underpass in 1995*	1848	1995	21 B4	
72	71:76	Kyleshaw Crossing	1848	Open	21 B4	
72½	72:35	Lisduff Station Gates	1848	Open	21 B4	
72½	72:33	LISDUFF *formerly KNOCKAHAW, private station for Lord Castleton.*	1894	1963	21 B4	
72½	?	Lisduff Quarry Sidings *CIE's principal Ballast Quarry*	?	?	21 B4	
78¾	78:60	TEMPLEMORE	1848	Open	21 A5	
86¼	86:35	THURLES	1848	Open	21 A6	27
87¼	87:20	Thurles Beet Factory Siding *sugar beet factory sidings, lifted 1990*	1934	1989	21 A6	263
87¾	87:50	Thurles Junction *former junction for Clonmel*	1880	1967	21 A6	27
95	94:78	GOOLD'S CROSS *GOOLD'S CROSS & CASHEL until 1904*	1850	1976	27 B1	29
95	95:07	Junction for Cashel line	1904	1954	27 B1	29
98¼	98:17	Bishopswood Crossing	1848	Open	27 A1	
99¼	99:11	Dundrum Station Gates	1848	Open	27 A1	
99½	99:39	DUNDRUM	1848	1976	27 A1	
103¾	103:63	Grange Crossing	1848	Open	27 A1	
106¼	106:23	Kyle Crossing *direct curve to Limerick, installed 1967*	1848	Open	26 D1	126
106¾	106:56	Flat Crossing *crossing with Limerick-Waterford line*	1848	Open	26 D1	13
107	107:00	LIMERICK JUNCTION *junction for Limerick and Waterford*	1848	Open	26 D1	13
110	?	Glenbane Junction *not a junction but probably a level crossing, replaced by a bridge*	1849	?	26 D1	
113½	113:34	Emly Station Gates	1849	Open	26 D1	
113½	113:38	EMLY	1879	1963	26 D1	
117	117:05	KNOCKLONG *closed 07-03-1977*	1849	1977	26 C2	
122½	122:36	Fanstown Crossing	1849	Open	26 C2	
124	124:09	KILMALLOCK *closed 07-03-1977*	1849	1977	26 C2	
127	127:03	Thomastown Crossing	1849	Open	26 B2	
128	127:64	Charleville North Junction *junction for Limerick; made a triangle in 1897 with a facing connection to Limerick; facing connection closed in 1906*	1897	1906	26 B2	25
128	128:12	Charleville South Junction *trailing junction from Limerick*	1862	1967	26B2	25
129¼	129:16	CHARLEVILLE *formerly Rathluirc 1920s to 1990*	1849	Open	26 B2	25
130½	130:40	Ballyhay Crossing	1849	Open	26 B2	
131¾	131:63	Newtown Crossing	1849	Open	26 B2	
132	132:00	Ballycoskerry Crossing	1849	Open	26 B3	
134	134:07	Shinanagh Crossing	1849	Open	26 B3	
137¼	137:14	Buttevant Station Gates	1849	Open	26 B3	
137¼	137:16	BUTTEVANT *formerly BUTTEVANT & DONERAILE; closed 07-03-1977*	1849	1977	26 B3	
141	141:06	Two-Pot-House Siding *siding for local goods traffic*	?	?	26 B3	
143½	143:49	Kilnockin No.1 Crossing	1849	Open	26 B4	
144	144:05	Kilnockin No.2 Crossing	1849	Open	26 B4	

MPost Dist.	Miles & Chains	Place / Feature (notes)	Date Opened	Date Closed	Map Grid	Table Ref.
144½	144:37	MALLOW *junction for Killarney and Fermoy*	1849	Open	26 B4	9,14
144¾	144:76	Mallow Viaduct *crosses River Blackwater*	1849	Open	26 B4	
145¼	?	MALLOW SOUTH *temporary station during rebuilding of viaduct*	1922	1923	26 B4	
145¼	145:18	Killarney Junction *junction for Killarney and Tralee*	1853	Open	26 B4	9
148¼	148:18	MOURNE ABBEY	1892	1963	26 B4	
154¼	154:24	RATHDUFF	c.1852	1976	26 B5	
156¼	156:18	Kilmona Crossing *replaced by underbridge on Cork side*	1849	Closed	26 B5	
159¼	159:28	BLARNEY	1850	1963	26 B5	
160¾	?	Monard Viaduct *8 arch masonry viaduct*	1849	Open	33 C1	
161¼	161:31	Rathpeacon *Marshalling Yard, also platform for railway staff 1920s/1930s*	?	?	33 C1	
?	?	ESB Sidings *trailing sidings on Up side*	c.1929	1962	33 C1	
?	?	ESB Sidings *facing sidings on Down side with level crossing towards end. Closed July 1972*	1949	1972	33 C1	
?	?	CORK VICTORIA *locally called BLACKPOOL, terminus from 1849 to 1855 until Cork Tunnel completed*	1849	1855	33 C1	
163	163:16	Kilbarry Sidings	?	?	33 C1	
164¼	164:31	Cork Tunnel *1,355yd Tunnel completed in 1855*	1855	Open	33 C2	
?	?	CORK (Penrose Quay) *temporary terminus in Goods Store from 03-12-1855 to 28-07-1856*	1855	1856	33 D2	
?	?	CORK (PENROSE QUAY) *opened 28-07-1856; called CORK GLANMIRE from 1871*	1856	1893	33 D2	
165½	165:20	CORK GLANMIRE ROAD *KENT station from 1966, opened 01-02-1893. Line continues to Cobh, Youghal and Cork City Railways.*	1893	Open	33 D2	16,89

9   Mallow to Tralee

GSWR / 5ft 3in gauge / mileposts measured from Killarney Junction

Killarney Junction to Millstreet opened 16-04-1853 by the KJR.
Millstreet to Freemount opened 25-05-1853 by the KJR.
Freemount to Killarney opened 15-07-1853 by the KJR.
Tralee Junction to Tralee opened for passengers 18-07-1859 by the TKR.
Tralee Junction to Tralee opened for goods 24-08-1859 by the TKR.
Tralee (LKR) to Tralee (TKR) opened to goods 1883.
Tralee (LKR) to Tralee (TKR) opened to passengers 1901.

Passenger services suspended 24-02-1947 due to fuel shortage.
Passenger services resumed 24-05-1947.

MPost Dist.	Miles & Chains	Place / Feature (notes)	Date Opened	Date Closed	Map Grid	Table Ref.
144½	144:37	MALLOW	1849	Open	26 B4	8,14
144¾	144:76	Mallow Viaduct *crosses River Blackwater*	1849	Open	26 B4	8
145¼	145:18	Killarney Junction *junction to Cork*	1853	Open	26 B4	8
0	0:00	MILEAGE CHANGE *(mileposts measured from Killarney Junction)*				
0¼	0:20	Webb's Mill Siding *private siding, ½ mile long, lifted 1980s*	1863	1964/5	26 B4	
1¼	1:24	Mallow Beet Factory Siding *served Beet Factory, closed c.1974, lifted c.1980 but re-laid into factory 1989/90*	1934	Open	26 B4	246
1¾	1:69	Newberry East Crossing	1853	Open	26 B4	
2½	2:45	Newberry West Crossing	1853	Open	26 B4	
3½	3:33	Drumineen Crossing	1853	Open	26 B4	
3¾	3:64	Mohereen No.1 Crossing	1853	Open	26 A4	

4¼	4:15	Mohereen No.2 Crossing	1853	Open	26 A4	
5½	5:40	LOMBARDSTOWN	c.1855	1963	26 A4	
5½	5:42	Lombardstown Station Gates	1853	Open	26 A4	
6¾	6:67	Gortmore No.1 Crossing	1853	Open	26 A4	
7½	7:34	Gortmore No.2 Crossing	1853	Open	26 A4	
8½	8:37	Curraghrour West Crossing	1853	Open	26 A4	
9	8:73	Googannis Crossing	1853	Open	26 A4	
		also called Gougane Crossing				
9¼	9:27	Knightsfield Crossing	1853	Open	26 A4	
10¾	10:54	BANTEER	1853	Open	26 A4	10
		called KANTURK up to 1889				
10½	10:57	Banteer Station Gates	1853	Open	26 A4	
12	12:03	Garrane Crossing	1853	Open	26 A4	
14	13:78	Ballymore Crossing	1853	Open	25 D4	
		also called Boulamore Crossing				
14¾	14:55	Rathcoole No.1 Crossing	1853	Open	25 D4	
15	14:60	RATHCOOL	1914	1963	25 D4	
15¼	15:20	Rathcoole No.2 Crossing	1853	Open	25 D4	
15½	15:48	Rathcoole No.3 Crossing	1853	Open	25 D4	
16½	16:44	Ballinkeen Crossing	1853	Open	25 D4	
18½	18:34	Doneen Crossing	1853	Open	25 D4	
19	19:00	MILLSTREET	1853	Open	25 D4	
19	19:05	Millstreet Station Gates	1853	Open	25 D4	
22½	22:45	Rathduane Crossing	1853	Open	25 D4	
24½	24:33	Fry Cadbury Siding	?	1980	25 C4	
		sidings and loop for factory, lifted 1980s				
25½	25:37	RATHMORE	1855	Open	25 C4	
		formerly SHINNAGH, later SHINNAGH & RATHMORE				
25½	25:39	Rathmore Station Gates	1853	Open	25 C4	
26¼	26:15	Rathmore Crossing	1853	Open	25 C4	
28	28:05	FREEMOUNT	1853	1853	25 C4	
		temporary station May-July 1853				
28	28:06	Freemount Crossing	1853	Open	25 C4	
30	29:79	Stagmount Crossing	1853	Open	25 C4	
31	?	HEADFORD	1859	1893	25 B4	
31½	31:50	Quagmire Viaduct	1853	Open	25 B4	
32½	32:42	Headford Junction Station Gates	1853	Open	25 B4	
32¾	32:47	HEADFORD JUNCTION	1893	1963	25 B4	11
		junction for Kenmare				
32¾	32:52	Headford Junction	1893	1960	25 B4	11
33¼	33:27	Knockanes Crossing	1853	Open	25 B4	
33¾	33:53	Clohane Crossing	1853	Open	25 B4	
36	35:75	Minish No.1 Crossing	1853	1996	25 B4	
		closed 14-07-1996, replaced by crossing below				
36	36:06	Minish New Crossing	1996	Open	25 B4	
		opened 14-07-1996, replaced above crossing				
36½	36:48	Minish No.2 Crossing	1853	Open	25 B4	
38	38:04	Yellow Quarry Crossing	1853	Open	25 B4	
39¾	39:55	Tralee Junction	1859	Open	25 B4	
39¾	39:55	Killarney Check	1859	?	25 B4	
39¾	39:55	Tralee Junction	1859	Open	25 B4	
39¾	39:69	KILLARNEY	1853	Open	25 B4	
40½	40:35	Killarney Ballast Pit	?	?	25 B4	
40½	40:40	FITZGERALD PLATFORM	?	1976	25 B4	
		served sports stadium				
43½	43:38	Killeen Crossing	1859	Open	25 A4	
45	45:05	Ballyhar Crossing	1859	Open	25 A4	
46	45:77	Ballinelane Crossing	1859	Open	25 A4	
46¾	46:52	BALLYBRACK	1892	1963	25 A3	
46¾	46:57	Ballybrack Station Gates	1859	Open	25 A3	
48¾	48:59	Ballybane Crossing	1859	Open	25 A3	
49¾	49:66	Dromore No.1 Crossing	1859	Open	25 A3	
50¼	50:19	Dromore No.2 Crossing	1859	Open	25 A3	
50½	50:41	Junction from Valentia Harbour	1885	1960	25 A3	26
50½	50:44	FARRANFORE	1859	Open	25 A3	26
50½	50:48	Farranfore Station Gates	1859	Open	25 A3	
54½	54:28	GORTATLEA	1871	1963	25 A3	12
		junction for Castleisland				
54½	54:29	Gortatlea Station Gates	1859	Open	25 A3	
55½	55:48	Ahane No.1 Crossing	1859	Open	25 A3	
56	55:78	Ahane No. 2 Crossing	1859	Open	25 A3	
56¾	56:52	Bealagrellagh Crossing	1859	Open	25 A2	
60½	60:33	Ratass Crossing	1859	Open	25 A2	
61	60:75	Clash West Crossing	1859	Open	25 A2	
61	61:09	Cloonalour Crossing	1859	Open	25 A2	
61½	61:27	TRALEE (TKR)	1859	Open	25 A2	18,20
		TRALEE CASEMENT Station from 1966				
61½	61:38	Edward Street Crossing	1883	1978	25 A2	
61½	61:45	TRALEE (LKR)	1880	1914	25 A2	18,20
		Old Limerick & Kerry Station				

10 Banteer to Newmarket

GSWR / 5ft 3in gauge / mileposts measured from Banteer

Banteer to Newmarket opened 01-04-1889 by the KNR.

All services suspended from 24-04-1944 due to fuel shortage.
Passenger services resumed from 10-12-1945.
All services suspended from 27-01-1947.

Closed completely 27-01-1947 by CIE except for cattle specials and excursions.

Re-opened 01-06-1956 for daily goods train by CIE.

Closed completely 04-02-1963 by CIE.

MPost Dist.	Miles & Chains	Place / Feature (notes)	Date Opened	Date Closed	Map Grid	Table Ref.
0	0:00	BANTEER	1853	Open	26 A4	9
		called KANTURK up to 1889				
0½	0:37	Ahern's Crossing	1889	1963	26 A4	
1	0:73	Blackwater Bridge No.1 Crossing	1889	1963	26 A4	
1	1:09	Blackwater Bridge No.2 Crossing	1889	1963	26 A4	
2¾	2:68	Old Court Crossing	1889	1963	26 A3	
3½	3:34	Kathleen's Lane Crossing	1889	1963	26 A3	
3¾	3:57	Kanturk Station Gates	1889	1963	26 A3	
4	?	KANTURK	1889	1947	26 A3	
5	5:01	Meelhara Crossing	1889	1963	25 D3	
9	?	NEWMARKET	1889	1947	25 D3	

11 Headford Junction to Kenmare

GSWR / 5ft 3in gauge / mileposts measured from Headford Junction

Headford Junction to Kenmare opened 04-09-1893 by the GSWR.

Passenger services suspended 24-02-1947 due to fuel shortage.
Passenger services resumed 24-05-1947.

Line closed completely 01-01-1960 by CIE.

MPost Dist.	Miles & Chains	Place / Feature (notes)	Date Opened	Date Closed	Map Grid	Table Ref.
0	0:00	HEADFORD JUNCTION	1893	1963	25 B4	9
		junction for Tralee				
0	0:05	Headford Junction	1893	1960	25 B4	9
0¾	0:69	Knockhane Crossing	1893	1960	25 B4	
2¼	2:17	Curreal Crossing	1893	1960	25 B5	
4¼	4:14	Islandmore Crossing	1893	1960	25 B5	
5	?	LOO BRIDGE	1893	1960	25 B5	
5¼	5:33	Loo Bridge Station Gates	1893	1960	25 B5	
6¼	6:20	Gortatlee Crossing	1893	1960	25 B5	
8½	8:39	Droomacosh Crossing	1893	1960	25 B5	
10	?	MORLEY'S BRIDGE	1893	1960	25 B5	
10¾	10:59	Red Tench, North Crossing	1893	1960	25 B5	
11¾	11:50	Caher Crossing	1893	1960	25 B5	
12¾	12:61	Church Ground Crossing	1893	1960	25 B5	
13	?	KILGARVAN	1893	1960	25 B5	
13¼	13:20	Kilgarvan Station Gates	1893	1960	25 B5	
14	14:06	Kilpadder Crossing	1893	1960	25 B5	
14½	14:46	Ardtully Crossing	1893	1960	25 A5	
15½	15:36	Clontoo Crossing	1893	1960	25 A5	
16	15:74	Cooragweanish Crossing	1893	1960	25 A5	
18¾	18:51	Peafield Crossing	1893	1960	25 A5	
22	?	KENMARE	1893	1960	25 A5	

12 Gortatlea to Castleisland

GSWR / 5ft 3in gauge / mileposts measured from Gortatlea

Gortatlea to Castleisland opened 30-08-1875 by the CR.

Goods services suspended from 10-03-1947 due to fuel shortage, not re-instated.
Passenger services suspended 24-02-1947.

Closed to passengers 24-02-1947 by CIE.
Closed to regular goods 10-03-1947 by CIE.

Remained open for grain specials, monthly Cattle Fair traffic and annual Knock pilgrimage (although not necessarily run every year).

Re-opened for regular goods 07-01-1957 by CIE.

Closed to completely 10-01-1977 by CIE. Lifting commenced 1988.

MPost Dist.	Miles & Chains	Place / Feature (notes)	Date Opened	Date Closed	Map Grid	Table Ref.
0	0:00	GORTATLEA	1871	1963	25 A3	9
		opened as a junction 1875				
3¼	3:15	Camp Crossing	1875	1977	25 B3	
4¼	?	CASTLEISLAND	1875	1947	25 B3	

13 Limerick to Waterford

GSWR / 5ft 3in gauge / mileposts measured from Limerick

Limerick (new station) to Limerick (old station) opened c.10-1857 by the WLR.
Limerick to Tipperary opened for goods 24-04-1848 by the WLR.
Limerick to Tipperary opened for passengers 09-05-1848 by WLR.
Markets Branch Tramway opened 07-01-1864 by the WLR.
Tipperary to Clonmel opened 01-05-1852 by the WLR.
Clonmel to Fiddown opened 15-04-1853 by the WLR.
Fiddown to Dunkitt opened 23-08-1853 by theWLR.
Dunkitt to Waterford (Newrath) opened 11-09-1854 by the WLR.
Waterford (Newrath) to Waterford (North) opened 29-08-1864 by the WLR.

Passenger services suspended 24-02-1947 due to fuel shortage.
Passenger services resumed 24-05-1947.

Limerick Markets Branch Tramway closed completely c.1950 by CIE.

MPost Dist.	Miles & Chains	Place / Feature (notes)	Date Opened	Date Closed	Map Grid	Table Ref.
0	0:00	LIMERICK	1857	Open	20 A6	17,18
		LIMERICK COLBERT Station from 1966				
0¼	0:25	LIMERICK (old station)	1848	1858	20 A6	17,18
0¼	?	Markets Branch Tramway	1864	c.1940	20 A6	14,17
		Tramway to the Markets Area				
0	0:00	Market Branch Junction	1864	1950	20 A6	
?	?	GSR Bus Depot	1864	1950	20 A6	
?	?	Factory	1864	c.1940	20 A6	
0¾	?	Markets Area	1864	c.1931	20 A6	
0½	0:45	Limerick Check	1859	1963	20 A6	17
		closed 15-06-1963				
0¾	0:70	Ennis Junction	1859	1910	20 A6	17
		former junction for Ennis, line now diverges at Limerick Check; platforms erected near junction for 1863 Munster Fair				
2½	2:45	Garryglass Crossing	1848	Open	20 A6	
4½	4:16	KILLONAN	1848	1963	20 B6	23
		junction for Ballybrophy				
4¼	4:21	Killonan Station Gates	1848	Open	20 B6	23
4¼	4:22	Killonan Junction	1858	Open	20 B6	23
		open as junction; junction removed in 1931 and former double track worked as two separate lines from Limerick, re-instated 1947				
8	7:70	BOHER	c.1849	1963	20 B6	
10½	10:34	Woodfarm Crossing	1848	Open	20 B6	
11½	11:46	DROMKEEN	1852	1976	20 B6	
11½	11:50	Dromkeen Station Gates	1848	Open	20 B6	
12½	12:46	Linfield Crossing	1848	Open	20 B6	
13¾	13:76	PALLAS	1848	1963	20 B6	
15½	15:41	Cross Crossing	1848	Open	26 D1	
18½	18:35	OOLA	1848	1963	26 D1	
20½	20:45	Monard Crossing	1848	Open	26 D1	
21½	21:33	Milltown Crossing	1848	Open	26 D1	126
		direct curve to Dublin				
21¾	21:56	Keane's Points	1848	Open	26 D1	125
		direct curve to Limerick Junction				
?	?	LIMERICK JUNCTION	1880	1880	26 D1	
		temporary platforms erected by WLR opened 20-07-1880, closed shortly afterwards				
22	22:09	LIMERICK JUNCTION	1848	Open	26 D1	
21¾	21:65	Flat Crossing	1848	Open	26 D1	8
		Flat crossing with Dublin-Cork Line				
24¾	24:63	TIPPERARY	1848	Open	27 A1	
24¾	24:66	Tipperary Station Gates	1852	Open	27 A1	
29½	29:42	Bansha Station Gates	1852	Open	27 A2	
29½	29:46	BANSHA	1852	1963	27 A2	
33	33:03	Cappagh Crossing	1852	Open	27 A2	
33¼	?	Cappagh Ballast Pit	?	?	27 A2	
		in use for a short period after opening of line; re-opened in 1864 to handle timber traffic, closed ?				
34	33:77	Toureen Crossing	1852	Open	27 B2	
37¾	37:60	Cahir Abbey Siding	?	?	27 B2	
38¼	38:13	Cahir Viaduct	1852	Open	27 B2	
		crosses River Suir				
38¼	38:26	CAHIR	1852	Open	27 B2	432
43¼	43:19	Nicholastown Crossing	1852	Open	27 B2	
46¾	46:60	Patrick's Well Crossing	1852	Open	27 B2	
48½	48:42	Heywood Crossing	1852	Open	27 C2	
48¾	48:63	Cashel Road Crossing	1852	Open	27 C2	
49	48:75	Burgagerylands Crossing	1852	Open	27 C2	
49¼	49:20	CLONMEL	1852	Open	27 C2	27
49½	49:30	Clonmel Junction	1879	1967	27 C2	27
		junction for Thurles				
53¾	53:66	Ballynevin Crossing	1853	Open	27 C2	
54¼	54:15	Priorstown Crossing	1853	Open	27 C2	
55¼	55:23	Kilsheelan Station Gates	1853	Open	27 C2	
55¼	55:27	KILSHEELAN	1853	1963	27 C2	
58	58:01	Ballindine Crossing	?	Open	27 D3	
63	62:76	Carrick-on-Suir Station Gates	1853	Open	27 D3	
63	63:06	CARRICK-ON-SUIR	1853	Open	27 D3	
63	?	Irish Traction Group Sidings	1992	Open	27 D3	
66¼	66:21	Ardclone Crossing	1853	Open	28 A3	
67¼	67:25	Fiddown Station Gates	1853	Open	28 A3	
67¼	67:28	FIDDOWN & PORTLAW	1853	1963	28 A3	
		terminus between April and August 1853				
68	68:03	Turkistown Crossing	1853	Open	28 A3	
69	69:07	Emil Crossing	1853	Open	28 A3	
70	70:03	GRANGE	1855	1963	28 A3	
70	70:06	Grange Station Gates	1853	Open	28 A3	
71¾	71:70	Ballinacurra Crossing	1853	Open	28 A3	
74½	74:34	Tinlough Crossing	1853	?	28 A3	
75½	75:32	Dunkitt Viaduct	1853	Open	28 B3	
75½	75:44	DUNKITT	1853	1854/5	28 B3	6
		junction for Kilkenny				
75½	75:44	Newrath Junction	1854	1864	28 B3	
		also called Dunkitt Junction				
76	75:78	Newrath No.1 Crossing	1854	Open	28 B3	
76½	76:33	Newrath No.2 Crossing	1854	Open	28 B3	
76½	76:50	Suir Bridge Junction	1854	Open	28 B3	14
		junction for Mallow				
77	77:07	WATERFORD (NEWRATH)	1854	1864	28 B3	14
77¼	77:20	WATERFORD (NORTH)	1864	Open	28 B3	14,33
		WATERFORD PLUNKETT Station from 1966				

14 Mallow to Waterford and Rosslare Harbour

5ft 3in gauge / mileposts measured from Mallow

GSWR – Mallow to Fermoy.
FRRHC – Fermoy to Grace Dieu Junction and Waterford South.
FRRHC – Grace Dieu Junction to Suir Bridge Junction.
GSWR – Suir Bridge Junction to just past New Wharf Junction.
DSER & FRRHC Joint – just past New Wharf Junction to Abbey Junction
FRRHC – Abbey Junction to Rosslare Harbour Pier.
FRRHC – Killinick to Felthouse Junction.

Note: Waterford-Rosslare is still owned by FRRHC and leased/operated by IE

Mallow to Fermoy opened 17-05-1860 by the GSWR.
Fermoy to Lismore opened 01-10-1872 by the FLR.
Lismore to Waterford South opened 12-08-1878 by the WDLR.
Grace Dieu Junction to Suir Bridge Junction opened 30-08-1906 by the FRRHC.
Suir Bridge Junction to Waterford (Newrath) opened 1854 by the WKR.
Waterford (Newrath) to Waterford (North) opened 29-08-1864 by the WLR.
Waterford North to New Wharf Junction opened to goods 26-05-1883 by the WLR.
New Wharf Junction to Abbey Junction opened 15-02-1904 by the DWWR.
Abbey Junction to Felthouse Junction opened 01-08-1906 by the FRRHC.
Killinick Junction to Rosslare Strand opened 30-08-1906 by the FRRHC.
Rosslare Strand to Rosslare Pier opened 24-06-1882 by the WWR.
Rosslare Pier to Rosslare Harbour Pier opened 30-08-1906 by the FRRHC.
Ballinacourty Junction to Ballinacourty opened 03-04-1970 by CIE.

Passenger services suspended 24-02-1947 due to fuel shortage.
Passenger services resumed 24-05-1947.

Mallow to Suir Bridge Junction closed completely 27-03-1967 by the FRRHC.
Grace Dieu Junction to Waterford South closed to passengers 31-01-1908 by the FRRHC.
Grace Dieu Junction to Waterford South closed completely 09-09-1976 by the FRRHC.
Killinick Junction to Felthouse Junction closed to passengers 01-07-1910 by the FRRHC.
Killinick Junction to Felthouse Junction closed completely 28-05-1911 by the FRRHC.
Rosslare Pier to Rosslare Harbour Pier closed to passengers 14-09-1989.

Suir Bridge Junction to Ballinacourty Junction re-opened 03-04-1970 by CIE.

Suir Bridge Junction to Ballinacourty closed 28-07-1982 by CIE.
Ballinacourty to Suir Bridge Junction closed but line remained intact but severed at Suir Bridge Junction, last known train movement was track recording vehicle EM50 on 09-05-1990. Line converted to a siding, and therefore presumed closed, 21-11-1993.
Opening span of Suir Bridge removed and placed adjacent to Waterford-Newrath line 1996.

MPost Dist.	Miles & Chains	Place / Feature (notes)	Date Opened	Date Closed	Map Grid	Table Ref.
0	0:00	MALLOW	1849	Open	26 A4	8
0½	0:39	Leaselands Crossing	1860	1967	26 A4	
3¼	3:13	Lissinasky Crossing	1860	1967	26 A4	
7	7:06	Castletownroche Station Gates	1860	1967	26 C4	
7	?	CASTLETOWNROCHE & KILLAVULLEN	1861	1967	26 C4	
7¾	7:55	Clifford Crossing	1860	1967	26 C4	
8½	8:47	Bridgetown Crossing	1860	1967	26 C4	
9½	?	Kilcummer Viaduct	1860	1967	26 C4	
9¾	9:67	Renny Crossing	1860	1967	26 C4	
11¼	?	BALLYHOOLY	1861	1967	26 C4	
14¼	14:25	Acres Crossing	1860	1967	26 D4	
15¾	15:52	Grange Crossing	1860	1967	26 D4	
16¾	?	FERMOY	1860	1967	26 D4	15
16¾	?	Fermoy F&L Goods Yard	1872	?	26 D4	
		on spur on north of line				
17	?	Carrickabrick Viaduct	1872	1967	26 D4	
		crosses River Blackwater, 100ft high				
18¾	18:50	Carrigatoortane Crossing	1872	1967	26 D4	
19½	19:37	Clondulane Station Gates	1872	1967	26 D4	
19½	?	CLONDULANE	1872	1967	26 D4	
		formerly CLONDULANE (GLENWICK) in early years				
19¾	19:52	Clondulane Crossing	1872	1967	26 D4	
25¾	?	BALLYDUFF	1872	1967	27 A4	
29½	?	TALLOW ROAD	1872	1967	27 A4	
32¼	?	LISMORE	1872	1967	27 B4	
32½	?	LISMORE (WDLR)	1878 ?	1893 ?	27 B4	
		WDLR Platform 200 yards East of FLR Station				
32½	32:33	Ballysaggertbeg No.1 Crossing	1878	1967	27 B4	
32½	32:47	Ballysaggertbeg No.2 Crossing	1878	1967	27 B4	
		also called Deerpark Crossing				
33¼	33:22	Ballyea Crossing	1878	1967	27 B4	
35¼	35:14	Kilbree Crossing	1878	1967	27 B4	
36	35:79	Cappoquin Station Gates	1878	1967	27 B4	
36	?	CAPPOQUIN	1878	1967	27 B4	
37¼	37:20	Affane Crossing	1878	1967	27 B4	
		also called Grenantane Crossing				
38½	38:38	Ballyhane No.1 Crossing	1878	1967	27 B4	
38¾	38:70	Ballyhane No.2 Crossing	1878	1967	27 B4	
39½	39:40	Boherwillan Crossing	1878	1967	27 B4	
40¼	40:20	Cappagh Station Gates	1878	1967	27 C4	
40½	?	CAPPAGH	1878	1967	27 C4	
41	41:00	Cappagh Crossing	1878	1967	27 C4	
42	41:78	Killashal Crossing	1878	1967	27 C4	
42¾	42:50	Ballinacourty Crossing	1878	1967	27 C4	
		also called Knockacullen Crossing				
44	43:78	Ballymacmague No.1 Crossing	1878	1967	27 C4	
44½	44:36	Ballymacmague No.2 Crossing	1878	1967	27 C5	
45½	45:37	Ballinamuck Crossing	1878	1967	27 C5	
46½	?	DUNGARVAN	1878	1967	27 C5	
46½	46:41	Shandon Road Crossing	1878	1967	27 C5	
46¾	46:59	Causeway Crossing	1878	1967	27 C5	
46¾	46:65	Abbeyside Crossing	1878	1967	27 C5	
46¾	46:74	Sarsfield Street Crossing	1878	1967	27 C5	
48	47:78	Ballinacourty	1970	1982	27 C5	
		served Quigley's Magnesite Works				
		Ballinacourty Crossing	1970	1982	27 C5	
48¼	48:28	Clonea No.2 Crossing	1970	1982	27 C5	
48¾	48:58	Clonea No.1 Crossing	1970	1982	27 C5	
49½	49:36	Ballinacourty Junction	1970	1982	27 C5	
48¼	48:24	Barnawee Crossing	1878	1967	27 C5	
		also called Kilminion Crossing				
49	49:07	Ballinrode Crossing	1878	1967	27 C5	
		also called Garrynageragh East Crossing				
49½	49:36	Ballinacourty Junction	1970	1982	27 C5	
		trailing junction				
51¼	51:23	Knock Crossing	1878	1982	27 D5	
52	51:76	Ballyvoyle Viaduct	1878	1982	27 D5	
		8 x 35ft spans				
52¼	52:20	Durrow Tunnel	1878	1982	27 D5	
		417yds long				
53½	53:20	DURROW & STRADBALLY	1878	1967	27 D4	
53½	53:40	Shanacoole Crossing	1878	1982	27 D4	
		also called Durrow Crossing				
55½	55:29	Carrigaree Crossing	1878	1982	27 D4	
56¼	56:10	Ballyvaloona Crossing	1878	1982	27 D4	
57¾	57:55	Currabaha Crossing	1878	1982	27 D4	
59¾	59:75	Kilmacthomas Viaduct	1878	1982	27 D4	
		crosses River Mahon, 8 arch stone viaduct				
?	?	Flavin's Mill Siding	?	?	27 D4	
60	60:07	Kilmacthomas Viaduct	1878	1982	27 D4	
		across Kilmacthomas Town,				
		7 arch stone and steel viaduct				
60¼	60:20	KILMACTHOMAS	1878	1982	27 D4	
62	62:05	Ballybrack No.2 Crossing	1878	1982	27 D4	
63	63:00	Ballybrack No.1 Crossing	1878	1982	27 D4	
63¾	63:58	Greenan Crossing	1878	1982	28 A4	
64½	64:35	Carroll's Cross Station Gates	1878	1982	28 A4	
64½	64:38	CARROLL'S CROSS	1882	1967	28 A4	
		opened 08-1882; deviation works carried out				
		here with station resited, opening 07-11-1909				
64¼	64:13	Ardeenlone Crossing	1878	1982	28 A4	
66¼	66:16	Kildermody Crossing	1878	1982	28 A4	
67	66:78	Kilmagemoge Crossing	1878	1982	28 A4	
69	68:78	KILMEADAN	1878	1967	28 A4	
73¾	73:64	Grace Dieu Junction	1906	1976	28 B3	
73¾		Grace Dieu Junction	1906	1976	28 B3	
75½		WATERFORD (South)	1878	1908	28 B3	
		served Waterford Iron Founders				
		until 1974, closed 05-09-1976				
74¼	74:20	Suir Bridge	1906	1982	28 B3	
		9 span opening bridge, 1205ft long with				
		80ft opening span				
74¾	74:62	Newrath No.2 Crossing	1854	Open	28 B3	
75	75:05	Suir Bridge Junction	1906	1982	28 B3	6,13

75½	75:37	WATERFORD (NEWRATH)	1854	1864	28 B3	
75¾	75:56	WATERFORD (NORTH)	1864	Open	28 B3	6
		rebuilt in 1906; WATERFORD PLUNKETT Station from 1966				
76	75:73	New Wharf Junction	?	?	28 B3	33
		North Wharf siding (34 chains) diverges here				
76	75:73	Mill Lane Crossing	1883	Open	28 B3	
76	76:02	Junction	1904	Open	28 B3	33
		end-on junction between GSWR and DSER / FHHRC joint line				
76	?	R & H Halls Flour Mill Sidings	1883	Open	28 B3	
76¼	76:20	Pier Head Crossing	1904	Open	28 B4	
76¼	76:20	Waterford Abbey Junction	1904	Open	28 B4	33
		DSER / FRRHC joint line ends here				
76½	76:36	Ferry Slip Crossing	1906	Open	28 B4	
76½	?	Bell Ferry Sidings	1969	1993	28 B4	
		opened 16-09-1969				
77	77:04	Clover Meats Siding	1927	1976	28 B4	
78¼	78:15	Gile's Quay Crossing	1906	Open	28 B4	
79¾	79:58	Belview Sidings	1993	Open	28 B4	
		serves Bell Ferry terminal, opened 22-08-1993				
79¾	79:60	Belview No.2 Crossing	1995	Open	28 B4	
79¾	79:68	Belview No.1 Crossing	1993	Open	28 B4	
		opened 16-08-1993				
80¼	80:13	Glasshouse Crossing	1906	Open	28 B3	
81½	81:30	Snow Hill Tunnel – 217yds long	1906	Open	28 B3	
81¾	81:40	Barrow Bridge	1906	Open	28 B3	
		2,131ft 13 span swing bridge is longest bridge in Ireland				
82	81:76	KILMOKEA HALT	1966	1970s	28 B3	
		temporary platform for Great Island Power Station construction in 1960s, closed 1968; re-opened 1970; closed ?				
83¾	83:78	Dunbrody Crossing	1906	Open	28 C3	
84½	84:48	CAMPILE	1906	Open	28 C3	
85¼	85:24	Carrowanree Crossing	1906	Open	28 C3	
87½	87:33	Drillistown Crossing	1906	Open	28 C3	
87½	87:48	Rathumney Crossing	1906	Open	28 C3	
88¼	88:16	Burkestown Crossing	1906	Open	28 C3	
89¼	89:25	BALLYCULLANE	1906	Open	28 C3	
91	91:18	Taylorstown Bridge	1906	Open	28 C4	
93	92:75	Ballylannan Crossing	1906	Open	28 D4	
93¼	93:27	WELLINGTON BRIDGE	1906	Open	28 D4	
93¼	93:34	Wellington Bridge Gates	1906	Open	28 D4	
95	95:01	Kilcavan No.1 Crossing	1906	Open	28 D4	
95¼	95:27	Kilcavan No.2 Crossing	1906	Open	28 D4	
96¾	96:69	Ballyfrory Crossing	1906	Open	28 D4	
98	98:02	DUNCORMICK	1906	1976	28 D4	
99½	99:36	Nicharee Crossing	1906	Open	28 D4	
101	101:00	Muchtown Crossing	1906	Open	28 D4	
103	103:00	Bridgetown Station Gates	1906	Open	29 A4	
103¼	103:16	BRIDGETOWN	1906	Open	29 A4	
105	104:76	Mayglass Crossing	1906	Open	29 A4	
107¾	107:54	KILLINICK	1906	1976	29 A4	
107¾	107:66	Killinick Junction	1906	1911	29 A4	31
		junction for Wexford, also known as Orristown or Assaly Junction				
0	0:00	Killinick Junction	1906	1911	29 A4	31
2	2:10	Felthouse Junction	1906	1911	29 A4	31
		also called Killiane Junction				
110½	110:38	Grange Big Crossing	1906	Open	29 A4	31
110¾	110:62	Junction	1906	Open	29 A4	31
		junction from Wexford				
110¾	110:66	ROSSLARE STRAND	1882	Open	29 A4	31
		formerly Rosslare, renamed 1906				
113	113:04	KILRANE	1882	1970	29 A4	31
		formerly Rosslare Harbour, renamed 1906, closed 12-10-1970				
113¾	113:57	Fishermans Crossing	?	Closed	29 B4	31
113¾	113:63	Ballygeary West Crossing	1989	Open	29 B4	31
?	?	BALLYGEARY	1970	1971	29 B4	31
		temporary wooden platforms, opened 12-10-1970, closed 02-08-1971				
113¾	113:60	ROSSLARE HARBOUR MAINLAND	1971	1989	29 B4	31
		formerly BALLYGEARY, opened 02-08-1971, renamed 27-06-1977				
113¾	113:70	Ballygeary East Crossing	1882	Open	29 B4	31
114	113:76	ROSSLARE EUROPORT	1989	Open	29 B4	31
		opened 14-09-1989 as ROSSLARE HARBOUR, renamed 20-05-1996				
114	114:05	ROSSLARE PIER	1882	1906	29 B4	31
		used for specials until 06-1895 when opened for passengers				
114¼	114:20	ROSSLARE HARBOUR PIER	1906	1989	29 B4	31
		formerly ROSSLARE HARBOUR, renamed 1977; closed 14-09-1989				

15 Fermoy to Mitchelstown

GSWR / 5ft 3in gauge / mileposts measured from Fermoy

Fermoy to Mitchelstown opened 23-03-1891 by the FMR.

All services suspended from 24-04-1944 due to fuel shortage.
Passenger services resumed from 10-12-1945.
Passenger services suspended from 27-01-1947.

Livestock Specials ran from 27-01-1947 to 01-12-1953.

Closed to passengers 27-01-1947 by CIE.
Closed completely 01-12-1953 by CIE.

MPost Dist.	Miles & Chains	Place / Feature (notes)	Date Opened	Date Closed	Map Grid	Table Ref.
0	0:00	FERMOY	1860	1967	26 D4	14
		junction for Mallow				
1	0:78	Gurrane Crossing	1891	1953	26 D4	
1¾	1:63	Bounbawn Crossing	1891	1953	26 D4	
3¾	3:64	Johnstown Crossing	1891	1953	26 D4	
4¼	4:13	Glanworth Station Gates	1891	1953	26 D4	
4½		GLANWORTH	1891	1947	26 D4	
4¾	4:63	Boherash Crossing	1891	1953	26 D4	
6¾	6:56	Ballykennelly Crossing	1891	1953	26 D3	
7¾	7:70	Ballindangan No.1 Crossing	1891	1953	26 D3	
8	?	BALLINDANGAN	1901	1947	26 D3	
		opened 01-04-1901				
8	8:12	Ballindangan Station Gates	1891	1953	26 D3	
8¾	8:54	Flemingstown Crossing	1891	1953	26 D3	
9½	9:46	Curragheen No.1 Crossing	1891	1953	26 D3	
10	10:02	Curragheen No.2 Crossing	1891	1953	26 D3	
11	11:06	Brigown Crossing	1891	1953	26 D3	
11½	?	Brigown Military Platform	1899	?	26 D3	
		to serve Kilworth Camp				
11½	?	Brigown Siding	1898	?	26 D3	
		adjacent to platform with goods store				
11½	11:35	Mitchelstown Crossing	1891	1953	26 D3	
12	?	MITCHELSTOWN	1891	1947	26 D3	

16 Cork to Youghal

GSWR / 5ft 3in gauge / mileposts measured from Dublin Heuston

Bruin Lodge to Tivoli opened for passengers 01-10-1860 as Horse Drawn Tramway, temporary arrangement.
Cork Summerhill to Tivoli opened for passengers 30-12-1861 by the CYR.
Cork Penrose Quay to Grattan Hill Junction opened for goods 12-1868 by the GSWR.
Cork Penrose Quay to Grattan Hill Junction opened for passengers 05-1873 by the GSWR.
Cork Penrose Quay to Grattan Hill Junction opened for mails 01-01-1876 by the GSWR.
Cork Glanmire Road to Water Street Junction opened 01-02-1893 by the GSWR.
Tivoli to Dunkettle opened for passengers 15-09-1860 by the CYR.
Dunkettle to Midleton opened for passengers 10-11-1859 by the CYR.
Midleton to Killeagh opened for passengers 27-02-1860 by the CYR.
Killeagh toYoughal opened for passengers 23-05-1860 by the CYR.
Cork Summerhill to Youghal opened for goods 31-12-1861 by the CYR.

Bruin Lodge to Tivoli closed between 05-1861 and 30-12-1861 while line to Summerhill Station was being built.

Passenger services suspended between Cobh Junction and Youghal from 24-02-1947 due to fuel shortage.

Passenger services resumed 24-05-1947.

Cork Penrose Quay to Grattan Hill Junction closed 01-02-1893 by the GSWR.
Cork Summerhill to Grattan Hill Junction closed to goods 12-1878 by the GSWR.
Cork Summerhill to Water Street closed to passengers 01-02-1893 by the GSWR.
Cork Summerhill to Water Street closed completely in 1927 by the GSR (see note below).
Cobh Junction to Youghal closed to passengers 04-02-1963 by CIE.
Cobh Junction to Youghal closed to goods 02-06-1978 except for Beet traffic which ceased in 1981.

Summerhill line: It is possible that a few trains ran to Summerhill between 1893 and 1896. Between 1896 and 1927 only one train a year (locomotive and van) ran to preserve the legal right of way. A short section to Mahoney's Avenue Bridge was used as a siding until about 1930. Abandoned 1971. Certain features on the Cobh Junction to Youghal Line are shown as open, this is because the line has not yet been officially closed. The last passenger special to Youghal was 1987, to Midleton in 1988.

MPost Dist.	Miles & Chains	Place / Feature (notes)	Date Opened	Date Closed	Map Grid	Table Ref.
165¼	165:20	CORK GLANMIRE ROAD CORK KENT Station from 1966	1893	Open	33 D2	8
0	0:00	CORK CORK GLANMIRE from 1871	1869	1893	33 D2	8
0½	0:38	Grattan Hill Junction original link from Penrose Quay to C&YR	1868	1893	33 D2	
0	0:00	CORK SUMMERHILL former CYR Station, track remained in situ until 1927	1861	1893	33 C2	
?	0:09 ?	BRUIN LODGE temporary station open 01-10-1860 to 05-1861	1860	1861	33 D2	
?	?	Grattan Hill Junction	1869	1893	33 D2	
0½	?	Water Street Junction also called Tivoli Junction	1893	1927	33 D2	
165¾	165:58	Water Street Junction junction to Glanmire Road, also called Tivoli Junction	1893	1927	33 D2	
165¾	165:70	Myrtlehill Crossing	1860	Open	33 D2	
166	166:06	Woodhill No.1 Crossing	1860	Open	33 D2	
166	166:07	Woodhill No.2 Crossing	1860	Open	33 D2	
166¼	166:25	Woodhill No.3 Crossing	1860	Open	33 D2	
166½	166:45	TIVOLI	1860	1931	33 D2	
167	?	Burmah Oil Siding opened 05-03-1973; level crossing at entrance to yard	1973	1990	33 D2	
167	?	Magnesite Siding served Roofchrome Premises; level crossing on leaving main line; out of use from 1982 when Quigley Magnesite factory closed; see below	1969	1982	33 D2	
167	?	Tivoli Container Terminal above siding was extended from about halfway along by 440m to the container compound of Cork Harbour Commissioners, first train on 23-08-1985; remainder of spur lifted 1985.	1985	Open	33 D2	
168	168:00	DUNKETTLE	1859	1966	33 E2	
168½	168:40	North Esk Crossing replaced by bridge 04-09-1990	1859	1990	33 E2	
168¾	?	North Esk Freight Yard opened 05-05-1975	1975	Open	33 E2	
169¾	169:57	Littleisland Station Gates replaced by bridge in 1996	1859	Open	33 E2	
169¾	169:60	LITTLEISLAND	1859	Open	33 E2	
171	171:04	GLOUNTHAUNE formerly QUEENSTOWN JUNCTION, later COBH JUNCTION; re-named GLOUNTHAUNE 07-11-1994	1862	Open	33 F2	28
171¼	171:17	Cobh Junction junction for Cobh	1862	Open	33 F2	28
0	0:00	MILEAGE CHANGE (mileposts measured from Cobh Junction)				
0½	0:30	Killora Crossing	1859	Open	33 F1	
2¾	2:60	CARRIGTWOHILL	1859	1963	26 D6	
4¾	4:65	Ballyrichard Crossing	1859	Open	26 D6	
5¼	5:25	Waterrock Crossing	1859	Open	26 D6	
5¾	5:65	Kennels Crossing	?	Open	22 D6	
6¼	6:17	Midleton Station Gates	1859	Open	26 D6	
6¼	6:18	MIDLETON CYR Works were behind down platform	1859	1963	26 D6	
8	7:75	Roxborough Crossing	1860	Open	26 D6	
11½	11:38	MOGEELY	1860	1963	27 A6	
11½	11:38	Mogeely Station Gates	1860	Open	27 A6	
12½	12:46	Neville's Road Crossing	1860	Open	27 A6	
13¼	13:20	Ballyquirke Crossing	1860	Open	27 A6	
14¼	14:15	KILLEAGH	1860	1963	27 A6	
14¼	14:16	Killeagh Station Gates	1860	Open	27 A6	
15	14:73	Ballymakee Crossing	1860	Open	27 A6	
16¼	16:16	Burgess Crossing	1860	Open	27 A6	
18¾	18:62	Bog Road Crossing	1860	1963	27 B6	
20½	20:63	YOUGHAL	1860	1963	27 B6	

17 Limerick to Sligo

GSWR except, ATECLR – Tuam to Claremorris /
5ft 3in gauge / mileposts measured from Limerick

Ennis Junction to Longpavement opened 26-03-1859 by the LER.
Longpavement to Clarecastle opened 17-01-1859 by the LER.
Clarecastle to Ennis opened 20-06-1859 by the LER.
Ennis to Athenry opened 15-09-1869 by the AEJR.
Athenry to Tuam opened 27-09-1860 by the ATR.
Tuam to Claremorris (South) opened 30-04-1894 by the ATECLR.
Claremorris (South) to Claremorris (Midland) opened 01-10-1895 by the ATECLR.
Claremorris (North Junction) to Collooney Junction opened 01-10-1895 by the WLR.
Collooney Junction to Sligo opened 03-12-1862 by the MGWR.

Passenger services suspended 24-02-1947 due to fuel shortage.
Passenger services resumed 24-05-1947.

Limerick to Claremorris passenger services ceased 05-04-1976 by CIE.
Claremorris to Collooney Junction closed to passengers 17-06-1963, but closed completely on 03-11-1975, track in situ but severed at Collooney Junction. Last known train movement was on 24-09-1988, 052+1460+1935 travelled from Claremorris to Kiltimagh.

Limerick to Ennis passenger services recommenced on Tuesdays and Thursdays only in 1988, Friday and Saturday from 19-02-1993 and full six day service from 16-05-1994.

MPost Dist.	Miles & Chains	Place / Feature (notes)	Date Opened	Date Closed	Map Grid	Table Ref.
0	0:00	LIMERICK LIMERICK COLBERT Station from 1966	1858	Open	20 A6	13,18
0¼	0:25	LIMERICK (old station)	1848	1858	20 A6	13,18
0¼		Markets Branch Tramway see Table 13 for full details	1864	c.1950	20 A6	13,18
0½	0:45	Limerick Check Platform closed 15-06-1963	1859	1963	20 A6	13
0¾	0:70	Ennis Junction junction removed in 1910, lines diverging at Limerick Check Platforms erected near junction for 1863 Munster Fair	1859	1910	20 A6	13
0¾	0:70	Ennis Junction Crossing	1859	Open	20 A6	
1½	1:39	Singland Crossing	1859	Open	20 A6	
2½	2:49	Park Crossing	1859	Open	20 A6	
3½	3:49	River Shannon Bridge	1859	Open	20 A5	
3¾	3:68	Ardnacrusha Siding 1¼ mile siding used to serve Ardnachrusha Power Station. Part of the route was mixed gauge (5'3"/900mm), see Table 188. Re-opened 1975 for a short distance to serve a refuse tip.	1925 ?	1980	20 A5	
3¾	?	Railway Crossing Shannon Hydro-electric railway crossed on the level	1925	1930	20 A5	188
4	3:71	Longpavement Station Gates	1859	Open	20 A5	
4	3:73	LONGPAVEMENT	1859	1963	20 A5	
5¼	5:30	Pass Crossing	1859	Open	20 A5	
6½	6:32	Meelick Crossing	1859	Open	20 A5	
6½	?	MEELICK opened early 1862, closed 30-04-1862	1862	1862	20 A5	
7¾	7:60	Cratloe Woods Crossing	1859	Open	20 A5	
8	7:78	Cratloe Lower Crossing	1859	Open	20 A5	
9¾	9:57	Cratloe Station Gates	1859	Open	20 A5	
9¾	9:60	CRATLOE	1859	1963	19 D5	

11½	11:35	Callura Crossing	1859	Open	19 D5	
13	13:00	SIXMILEBRIDGE	1859	1963	19 D5	
16	16:06	Ballycar 1 Crossing	1859	Open	19 D5	
16½	16:58	BALLYCAR & NEWMARKET	1859	1963	19 D5	
16¾	16:61	Ballycar 2 Crossing	1859	Open	19 D5	
19¾	19:60	ARDSOLLUS & QUIN	1859	1963	19 D4	
20	19:72	Ardsollus Crossing	1859	Open	19 D4	
23	23:00	CLARECASTLE	1859	1963	19 D4	
23¼	23:28	Lower Fergus Bridge	1859	Open	19 D4	
24½	24:51	ENNIS	1859	Open	19 C4	111
		Interchange with West Clare Railway; closed 05-04-1976; re-opened 1988 (see notes at head of table)				
25¼	25:30	Upper Fergus Bridge	1869	Open	19 D4	
26	25:71	Curravorrin Crossing	1869	Open	19 D4	
30¼	30:24	Chipfield Crossing	1869	Open	19 D3	
32½	32:37	CRUSHEEN	1869	1963	19 D3	
33	32:70	Gortafica Crossing	1869	Open	19 D3	
36	36:08	Gortavogher Crossing	1869	Open	19 D3	
36¾	36:56	TUBBER	1869	1963	19 D3	
37¼	37:22	Gurtane Crossing	1869	Open	19 D3	
38¼	38:13	Derra Crossing	1869	Open	19 D3	
41¼	42:25	GORT	1869	1976	19 D2	
43	42:76	Lavalla Crossing	1869	Open	19 D2	
44¼	44:16	Castletown Crossing	1869	Open	20 A2	
44¾	44:58	Kiltartan Crossing	1960s	Open	20 A2	
49	49:00	ARDRAHAN	1869	1976	20 A1	
49	49:03	Ardrahan Crossing	?	Open	20 A1	
50¾	50:64	Caherduff Crossing	1869	Open	20 A1	
55	55:13	CRAUGHWELL	1869	1982	20 A1	
		formerly CRAUGHWELL & LOUGHREA				
55¾	55:60	Craughwell Crossing	?	Open	20 A1	
56½	56:40	Templemartin Crossing	1869	Open	20 A1	
60¼	60:30	Ennis Junction	1869	Open	14 A6	34
		junction with MGWR from Galway				
60½	60:40	Athenry Station Gates	1851	Open	14 A6	34
60½	60:46	ATHENRY	1851	Open	14 A6	34
		also called ATHENRY & ENNIS JUNCTION and ATHENRY & TUAM JUNCTION on platform nameboards				
60¾	60:54	Tuam Junction	1860	Open	14 A6	34
		junction with MGWR to Dublin				
64	63:75	Belville Siding	?	1977	14 A6	
		lifted 08-02-1977				
70	69:76	BALLYGLUNIN	1860	1976	14 A5	
		formerly called BROOK LODGE				
76¼	76:08	TUAM	1860	1976	14 A4	
		Headquarters of Westrail				
0	0:00	MILEAGE CHANGE (mileposts measured from Tuam)				
0	0:02	Tuam Station Gates	1894	Open	14 A4	
0¼	0:18	Galway Road Crossing	1894	Open	14 A4	
1½	1:50	Tuam Sugar Factory	1934	1985	14 A4	253
2½	2:32	Kilbannon Crossing	1894	Open	14 A4	
4	4:03	Castlegrove Road Crossing	1894	Open	13 D4	
		also called Pollacarragune Crossing				
4½	4:37	CASTLEGROVE	1894	1963	13 D4	
4½	4:53	Castlegrove Station Gates	1894	Open	13 D4	
5½	5:46	Brooklawn Crossing	1894	Open	13 D4	
		also called Brooklands Crossing				
6	6:03	Fartamore Crossing	1894	Open	13 D4	
7	7:07	Liskeavy Crossing	1894	Open	19 D4	
8½	8:45	Milltown Station Gates	1894	Open	13 D3	
8½	8:51	MILLTOWN	1894	1963	13 D3	
9¼	9:11	Killerneen Crossing	?	Open	13 D3	
		also called Drim Crossing				
9½	9:39	Drim Crossing	1894	Open	13 D3	
10	10:00	Illaune Crossing	1894	Open	13 D3	
11½	11:49	Cloonrane Crossing	1894	Open	13 D3	
12¼	12:15	Ballindine Road Crossing	1894	Open	13 D3	
12½	12:44	BALLINDINE	1894	1963	13 D3	
12½	12:47	Ballindine Station Gates	1894	Open	13 D3	
13½	13:33	Avenue Crossing	1894	Open	13 D3	
14½	14:40	Garryduff Crossing	?	Open	13 D3	
15¾	15:52	Lisduff Crossing	1894	Open	13 D3	
16¾	16:52	CLAREMORRIS (SOUTH)	1894	1895	13 D3	
		temporary terminus pending extension northwards				
16¾	16:54	Claremorris Station Gates	1895	Open	13 D3	
16¾	?	Claremorris Southern Yard	1894	1979	13 D3	
16¾	16:68	Claremorris South Junction	1895	Open	13 D2	44
		junction with MGWR from Athlone				
17	16:72	CLAREMORRIS	1862	Open	13 D2	43,44
		junction with MGWR from Ballinrobe				
0	0:00	MILEAGE CHANGE (mileposts measured from Claremorris)				
0½	0:16	Claremorris North Junction	1895	1975	13 D2	44
		junction with MGWR to Westport				
1¼	1:27	Lugatemple Crossing	1895	1975	13 D2	
3	3:05	Aghareville Crossing	1895	1975	13 D2	
3¾	3:51	Kilcolman Crossing	1895	1975	13 D2	
4¼	4:25	Ballintaffy Crossing	1895	1975	13 D2	
5¼	5:18	Murneen Crossing	1895	1975	13 D2	
6¼	6:11	Cuiltybo Crossing	1895	1975	13 D2	
8¾	8:51	Ballyglass Crossing	1895	1975	13 D1	
		also called Cordarragh Crossing				
9¼	9:25	Kiltimagh Station Gates	1895	1975	13 D1	
9¾	9:31	KILTIMAGH	1895	1963	13 D1	
		Museum at station, two carriages alongside goods store brought by rail from Claremorris 1988				
9½	9:37	Kiltimagh Station Gates North	1895	1975	13 D1	
11	11:03	Polronahane Crossing	1895	1975	13 D1	
11¾	11:52	Killedan Crossing	1895	1975	13 D1	
12¼	12:25	Treanfohanaun Crossing	1895	1975	13 D1	
13½	13:51	Ballinlag Crossing	1895	1975	13 D1	
14	13:77	Kinaff Crossing	1895	1975	13 D1	
15¼	15:15	Ballinvoher Crossing	1895	1975	13 D1	
16¼	16:15	Esker Crossing	1895	1975	13 D1	
16½	16:45	Lisheenabrone Crossing	1895	1975	13 D1	
17¾	16:79	SWINFORD	1895	1963	13 D1	
22	22:00	Sonnagh Crossing	1895	1975	14 A1	
23¾	23:57	Lowpark Crossing	1895	1975	14 A1	
24	24:10	CHARLESTOWN	1895	1963	7 D6	
24¼	24:13	Charlestown Station Gates	1895	1975	7 D6	
24½	24:40	Bellahy Crossing	1895	1975	7 D6	
25½	25:35	Broher Crossing	1895	1975	7 D6	
27	27:10	Drumbaun South Crossing	1895	1975	7 D6	
27¼	27:36	CURRY	1895	1963	7 D6	
27½	27:44	Drumbaun North Crossing	1895	1975	7 D6	
28¼	28:12	Carrowwilkin South Crossing	1895	1975	7 D6	
28½	28:29	Carrowwilkin North Crossing	1895	1975	7 D6	
30	29:76	Rathscanlon Crossing	1895	1975	7 D6	
30¾	30:59	Tubbercurry Station Gates	1895	1975	7 D6	
31	30:62	TUBBERCURRY	1895	1963	7 D6	
32¼	32:15	Carrawntober Crossing	1895	1975	7 D6	
32¾	32:69	Carrawn Crossing	1895	1975	7 D6	
34	34:00	Lissaneagh Crossing	1895	1975	7 D5	
34¾	34:60	Cloonarara Crossing	1895	1975	7 D5	
36	35:67	CARROWMORE	1895	1963	7 D5	
36	35:70	Carrowmore Station Gates	1895	1975	7 D5	
38	37:71	Carrowloughan South Crossing	1895	1975	7 D5	
38¼	38:20	Carrowloughan North Crossing	1895	1975	7 D5	
39¾	39:58	Shancough Crossing	1895	1975	7 D5	
40¼	40:26	Carrowleam Crossing	1895	1975	7 D5	
41	41:11	Leyny Station Gates	1895	1975	7 D5	
41½	41:14	LEYNY	1895	1963	7 D5	
41½	41:40	Coolaney Crossing	1895	1975	8 A5	
41½	43:41	Billa Crossing	1895	1975	8 A5	
		also called Glen Crossing				
44¾	44:57	Kilnamagh Crossing	1895	1975	8 A5	
45¼	45:13	Ardcotten Crossing	1895	1975	8 A5	
45¾	45:70	COLLOONEY (GSWR)	1895	1963	8 A5	
46	45:75	Junction	1895	1957	8 A5	108
		connection to SLNCR				
0	0:00	Junction	1895	1957	8 A5	108
		this section known as 'Southern Siding'.				
?	?	Junction	1895	1957	8 A5	108
		line from Carrignagat Junction on SLNCR line				
?	?	Owenmore River Bridge	1882	1957	8 A5	108
?	?	Crossing	1882	1957	8 A5	108
0½	0:46	COLLOONEY (SLNCR)	1881	1957	8 A5	108

46¼	46:14	Collooney Junction	1895	1975	8 A5	37,108
		junction for MGWR to Sligo, severed in 1975				
128	128:03	MILEAGE CHANGE (mileposts measured from Dublin Broadstone)				
128¾	128:65	Carrignagat Junction	1882	1923	8 A5	37,108
		junction with SLNCR until 1923				
129¾	129:61	BALLYSODARE	1862	1963	8 A4	37
		junction with SLNCR from 1923 to 1957				
?	?	Pollexfen & Co Siding	1862	?	8 A4	37
		¼ mile siding to flour mill				
134		SLIGO	1862	1863	8 A4	37
		temporary terminus 03-12-1862 to 07-1863				
134¼	134:16	SLIGO	1863	Open	8 A4	37
		opened 07-1863; SLIGO McDIARMADA Station from 1966				

18 Limerick to Tralee

GSWR / 5ft 3in gauge / mileposts measured from Limerick

Limerick (new station) to Limerick (old station) opened c.10-1857 by the WLR.
Limerick to Ballingrane (via Limerick Check and Foynes Junction) opened 12-07-1856 by the LFR.
Cork Direct Curve opened 01-05-1863 by the CLDR.
Ballingrane to Newcastle West opened 01-01-1867 by the RNJR.
Newcastle West to Tralee opened 20-12-1880 by the LKR.
Tralee (LKR) to Tralee (TKR) opened to goods 02-02-1883.
Tralee (LKR) to Tralee (TKR) opened to passengers 1901.

Passenger services suspended 24-02-1947 due to fuel shortage.
Passenger services resumed 24-05-1947.

Limerick Check to Foynes Junction closed to passengers 1910 by the GSWR.
Cork Direct Curve closed to passengers 04-02-1963 by CIE.
Cork Direct Curve closed completely 29-09-1975 by CIE.
Limerick to Tralee (TKR Station) closed to passengers 04-02-1963 by CIE.
Ballingrane Junction to Listowel closed completely 03-11-1975 by CIE.
Listowel to Abberdorny closed completely 10-01-1977 by CIE.
Abbeydorney to Tralee (TKR Station) closed completely 02-06-1978 by CIE.

Track remained in situ after closure until lifting commenced 1988 at the Ballingrane end

MPost Dist.	Miles & Chains	Place / Feature (notes)	Date Opened	Date Closed	Map Grid	Table Ref.
0	0:00	LIMERICK	1857	Open	20 A6	13,17
		LIMERICK COLBERT Station from 1966				
?	?	Cork Direct Curve	1863	1975	20 A6	
		closed 02-10-1975, movements now go via Limerick Check				
?	?	Limerick Station Gates	1856	1975 ?	20 A6	
		removed when Cork Direct Curve closed				
1	1:00	Foynes Junction	1856	Open	20 A6	13,17
		via Cork Direct Curve				
1¼	1:26	Rathbane Crossing	?	Open	20 A6	127
1½	1:62	Rossbrien Crossing	1856	Open	20 A6	127
2	1:78	Cement Factory Junction	1957	1968	20 A6	127
		junction removed 11-08-1968 and replaced with a separate parallel line from Limerick Check				
3	3:11	Dooradoyle Crossing	1856	Open	20 A6	
4¾	4:60	Ashfort Crossing	1856	Open	20 A6	
5¾	5:58	Barnakyle Crossing	1856	Open	20 A6	
6¼	6:16	Greenmount Crossing	1856	Open	20 A6	
6½	6:39	FORT ETNA ROAD	c.1861	1867	20 A6	
		flag station				
6½	6:40	Fort Etna Crossing	1856	Open	20 A6	
7¼	7:26	PATRICKSWELL	1856	1963	20 A6	25
		junction for Charleville, closed to freight 1974				
9¾	9:62	KILGOBBIN HALT	1928	1963	19 D6	
9¾	9:66	Kilgobbin Crossing	1856	Open	19 D6	
10¾	10:61	Ardshanbally Crossing	?	Open	19 D6	
11	11:04	ADARE	1856	1963	19 D6	
		closed to freight 1974				
11	11:04	Adare Station Gates	1856	Open	19 D6	
12	12:00	Kilnockin Crossing	1856	Open	19 D6	
14	14:45	Knockdromin Crossing	1856	Open	19 D6	
17¼	17:20	BALLINGRANE	1856	1963	19 C6	19
		formerly RATHKEALE, renamed BALLINGRANE JUNCTION in 1867, closed to freight 1974				
17¼	17:27	Ballingrane Station Gates	1856	Open	19 C6	19
17¼	17:27	Ballingrane Junction	1856	Open	19 C6	19
		junction for Foynes				
18	17:73	Stoneville Crossing	1867	1975	19 C6	
		also called Ballingrane Crossing				
19¼	19:07	RATHKEALE	1867	1963	25 D1	
24½	24:42	ARDAGH	1867	1963	25 D1	
27¼	27:30	NEWCASTLE WEST	1867	1963	25 D1	
		terminus, reversal necessary				
0	0:00	MILEAGE CHANGE (mileposts measured from Newcastle West)				
1	1:00	Churchtown Crossing	1880	1975	25 D1	
2	2:09	Ashgrove Crossing	1880	1975	25 D1	
2½	2:34	Dromin Crossing	1880	1975	25 D1	
4	3:76	Glenagown Crossing	1880	1975	25 D1	
5¾	5:73	Barnagh Tunnel (110 yds long)	1880	1975	25 D1	
6¼	6:27	BARNAGH	1880	1963	25 D1	
9¼	9:24	Tullagoline Crossing	1880	1975	25 C1	
11	10:67	DEVON ROAD	1880	1963	25 C1	
11¼	11:21	Ballybehy Crossing	1880	1975	25 C1	
14	14:24	ABBEYFEALE	1880	1963	25 C1	
18	18:24	KILMORNA	1880	1963	25 C1	
22¾	22:69	Ballygologue Crossing	1880	1975	25 B1	
		also called Dromin Upper Crossing				
23	23:06	Dowds Crossing	1880	1975	25 B1	
23½	23:47	LISTOWEL	1880	1963	25 B1	92
		interchange with LBR				
23¾	23:61	Craughatussane Crossing	1880	1977	25 B1	
24½	24:44	Gortcurreen East Crossing	1880	1977	25 B1	
25½	25:32	Gortcurreen Crossing	1880	1977	25 B1	
26¼	26:21	Gortnaminsha Crossing	1880	1977	25 B1	
26¾	26:60	Ennismore Crossing	1880	1977	25 B1	
27¼	27:21	County Council Siding	?	?	25 B1	
		siding on Down side used by Kerry CC for road materials				
27¾	27:58	Ballyhorgan Crossing	1880	1977	25 B1	
28	28:07	Ballyhorgan West Crossing	1880	1977	25 B1	
29¼	29:21	Ballintogher Crossing	1880	1977	25 A1	
30	29:78	Lixnaw Station Gates	1880	1977	25 A1	
30	30:07	LIXNAW	1880	1963	25 A1	
32	31:70	Aghacoora Crossing	1880	1977	25 A1	
		also called Knockacoura Crossing				
32¼	32:29	Killaspicktarvin No.1 Crossing	1880	1977	25 A1	
32½	32:48	Killaspicktarvin No.2 Crossing	1880	1977	25 A1	
34¾	34:67	ABBEYDORNEY	1880	1963	25 A1	
34¾	34:69	Abbeydorney Station Gates	1880	1977	25 A1	
35¾	35:52	Knockreagh Crossing	1880	1978	25 A2	
36¼	36:18	Ballynahine Crossing	1880	1978	25 A2	
		also called Ballylahiff Crossing				
37¼	37:22	Turbridbeg Crossing	1880	1978	25 A2	
38	38:11	Ardfert Station Gates	1880	1978	25 A2	
38	38:27	ARDFERT	1880	1963	25 A2	
39	39:10	Liscahane Crossing	1880	1978	25 A2	
41¾	41:42	Point of divergence	1887	1978	25 A2	20
		Fenit line diverges at this point				
42¾	42:46	Gallowsfields Crossing	1880	1978	25 A2	
		also called Gallows Green Crossing				
42¾	42:61	Rock Street Crossing	1883	1978	25 A2	20
43	42:78	Junction with Fenit Line	1887	1978	25 A2	20
		facing junction to Fenit line, reversed in 1914, closed 02-06-1978				
43	43:01	TRALEE (LKR)	1880	1914	25 A2	20
		original Limerick and Kerry Station; Limerick trains extended into TKR station from 01-01-1901, Fenit services used bay in LKR station up to 1914 when junction was reversed to allow direct acces to TKR station				
0	0:00	MILEAGE CHANGE (mileposts measured from Tralee LKR Station)				
0¼	0:07	Edward Street Crossing	1883	1978	25 A2	20
0¼	0:18	TRALEE (TKR)	1859	Open	25 A2	9,20
		TRALEE CASEMENT Station from 1966				

MPost Dist.	Miles & Chains	Place / Feature (notes)	Date Opened	Date Closed	Map Grid	Table Ref.
1½	1:35	Point of divergence Limerick line diverges at this point	1887	1975	25 A2	18
1¾	1:63	Bawnboy Crossing	1887	1978	24 D2	
2¾	2:54	Knockanish No.1 Crossing	1887	1978	24 D2	
3¼	3:20	Knockanish No.2 Crossing	1887	1978	24 D2	
4	3:71	Coolrone Crossing	1887	1978	24 D2	
4¼	4:20	SPA	1887	1934	24 D2	
5	4:73	Ballymacegogue Crossing	1887	1978	24 D2	
6	5:77	Kilfenora Crossing	1887	1978	24 D2	
6¼	6:20	KILFENORA	1887	1934	24 D2	
8	8:00	FENIT	1887	1934	24 D2	206
8½	8:53	Fenit Pier closed c.1941, re-opened 10-1955	1887	1973	24 D2	206

19   Ballingrane to Foynes

GSWR / 5ft 3in gauge / mileposts measured from Limerick

Ballingrane to Askeaton opened 12-05-1857 by the LFR.
Askeaton to Foynes opened 28-04-1858 by the LFR.

Passenger services suspended 24-02-1947 due to fuel shortage.
Passenger services resumed 24-05-1947.

Ballingrane to Foynes closed to passengers 04-02-1963 by CIE.

MPost Dist.	Miles & Chains	Place / Feature (notes)	Date Opened	Date Closed	Map Grid	Table Ref.
17¼	17:20	BALLINGRANE formerly RATHKEALE, renamed BALLINGRANE JUNCTION in 1867; closed to freight 1974	1856	1963	19 C6	18
17¼	17:27	Ballingrane Station Gates	1857	Open	19 C6	18
17¼	17:28	Ballingrane Junction junction for Tralee	1857	Open	19 C6	18
17¾	17:60	Ballingrane No.1 Crossing	1857	Open	19 C6	
18	17:74	Ballingrane No.2 Crossing	1857	Open	19 C6	
20¾	20:69	Askeaton Station Gates	1857	Open	19 C6	
20¾	20:70	ASKEATON closed to Freight 1974	1857	1963	19 C6	
25	25:00	Robertstown Viaduct	1858	Open	19 C6	
26¼	26:18	Oil Company Crossing	?	Open	19 C6	
26¾	26:65	FOYNES freight depot for Oil, Zinc Ore and Barytes.	1858	1963	19 C6	
?	?	FOYNES PIER	1858	Open	19 C6	

20   Tralee to Fenit

GSWR / 5ft 3in gauge / mileposts measured from Tralee

Tralee (LKR) to Tralee (TKR) opened to goods 1883.
Tralee (LKR) to Tralee (TKR) opened to passengers 1901.
Tralee to Fenit opened 05-07-1887 by the TFR.
Fenit to Fenit Pier opened 1887 by the TFPHC.

Tralee to Fenit closed to passengers 31-12-1934 by the GSR.
Fenit to Port of Fenit closed c.1941 by the TFPHC.

Goods services suspended from 24-04-1944 due to fuel shortage.
Goods services resumed from 10-12-1945.
Goods services suspended from 27-01-1947.
Goods services resumed 30-06-1947.

Port of Fenit rail services restored 10-1955 by CIE.
Port of Fenit rail services withdrawn late 1973 by CIE.
Beet traffic over branch ceased 01-1978.
Tralee to Fenit closed completely 02-06-1978 by CIE.

Tralee to Fenit partially refurbished 1983-88 by the GSR Preservation Society, project abandoned 1989.

MPost Dist.	Miles & Chains	Place / Feature (notes)	Date Opened	Date Closed	Map Grid	Table Ref.
0¼	0:18	TRALEE (TKR) TRALEE CASEMENT Station from 1966	1859	Open	25 A2	9,18
0¼	0:07	Edward Street Crossing	1883	1978	25 A2	18
0	0:00	MILEAGE CHANGE (mileposts measured from Tralee LKR Station)				
0	0:00	TRALEE (LKR) old Limerick & Kerry Railway station	1880	1914	25 A2	18
0	0:12	Junction with Limerick Line facing junction with LKR line, junction reversed in 1914 to allow direct running into TKR station, closed 02-06-1978	1887	1978	25 A2	18
0¼	0:16	Rock Street Crossing	1883	1978	25 A2	18
0½	0:31	Gallowsfields Crossing	1883	1978	25 A2	18

21   Portlaoise to Mountmellick

GSWR / 5ft 3in gauge / mileposts measured from Conniberry Junction

Conniberry Junction to Mountmellick opened 02-03-1885 by the CIR.

All services suspended from 24-04-1944 due to fuel shortage.
Passenger services resumed from 10-12-1945.
All services suspended from 27-01-1947.

Beet Specials ran from 1947 to 1963.

Conniberry Junction to Mountmellick closed to passengers 27-01-1947 by CIE.
Conniberry Junction to Mountmellick completely closed 01-01-1963 by CIE.

MPost Dist.	Miles & Chains	Place / Feature (notes)	Date Opened	Date Closed	Map Grid	Table Ref.
0	0:00	PORTLAOISE formerly MARYBOROUGH	1847	Open	21 D3	6,8
0¼	0:13	Junction junction for Cork	1867	Open	21 D3	6,8
		Permanent Way Depot	1974	Open	21 D3	6
0¾	0:51	Conniberry Junction junction for Kilkenny, trains for Mountmellick reversed here. Closed as junction 1963	1885	1963	21 D3	6
0¾	0:57	Conniberry Junction Crossing	1867	Closed	21 D3	6
0	0:00	MILEAGE CHANGE (mileposts measured from Conniberry Junction)				
0¾	0:58	Clonroosk Crossing also called Knockmay Crossing	1885	1963	21 D3	
2¼	2:29	Clonreher Crossing	1885	1963	21 D3	
6½	6:37	Mountmellick Crossing	1885	1963	21 D2	
7½		MOUNTMELLICK	1885	1947	21 D2	

22   Castlecomer Junction to Castlecomer and Deerpark Colliery

Board of Works – worked by GSWR, vested in GSR 01-01-1929 / 5ft 3in gauge / mileposts measured from Castlecomer Junction

Castlecomer Junction to Castlecomer opened for goods 15-09-1919 by the British Government.
Castlecomer Junction to Castlecomer opened for passengers 25-04-1921.
Castlecomer to Deerpark Colliery opened to coal traffic 19-10-1920 by the GSWR.

Castlecomer Junction to Castlecomer closed to passengers 26-01-1931 by the GSR.
Castlecomer Junction to Deerpark Colliery closed completely 01-01-1963 by CIE.

MPost Dist.	Miles & Chains	Place / Feature (notes)	Date Opened	Date Closed	Map Grid	Table Ref.
0	0:00	Castlecomer Junction	1919	1963	21 D6	6
0½	0:35	Ballyragget Road Crossing	1919	1963	21 D6	
1	1:06	The Pike Crossing also called Jenkinstown	1919	1963	21 D6	
1½	1:36	Ballyrafton Crossing	1919	1963	21 D6	
2¼	2:21	Mohill Crossing	1919	1963	21 D5	
3¼ ?	?	CORBETSTOWN opened by July 1922	1922	1931	21 D5	

3½	3:35	Corbetstown Crossing	1919	1963	21 D5	
6¼	6:18	Dysart Crossing	1919	1963	21 D5	
7½	?	CASTLECOMER	1921	1931	21 D5	
		opened 25-04-1921				
7¼	7:59	Workhouse Crossing	1920	1963	21 D5	
8	7:79	Barrack Street Crossing	1920	1963	21 D5	
9½	9:25	Deerpark Crossing	1920	1963	21 D5	
?	?	Deerpark Colliery	1920	1963	21 D5	

23 Ballybrophy to Limerick

GSWR / 5ft 3in gauge / mileposts measured from Ballybrophy

Ballybrophy to Roscrea opened 19-10-1857 by the GSWR.
Roscrea to Nenagh opened 05-10-1863 by the GSWR.
Nenagh to Birdhill opened 01-06-1864 by the GSWR.
Birdhill to Castleconnell opened 23-07-1860 by the LCaR.
Castleconnell to Killonan Junction opened 28-08-1858 by the LCaR.
Killonan to Limerick opened 09-05-1848 by the WLR.

Passenger service suspended between Ballybrophy and Nenagh from 24-02-1947 due to fuel shortage.
Passenger services resumed 24-05-1947.

MPost Dist.	Miles & Chains	Place / Feature (notes)	Date Opened	Date Closed	Map Grid	Table Ref.
0	0:00	BALLYBROPHY	1847	Open	21 B4	8
		formerly BORRIS & ROSCREA, re-named ROSCREA & PARSONSTOWN JUNCTION in 1857, re-named BALLYBROPHY in 1870				
2½	2:46	Shanboe Crossing	1857	Open	21 B4	
3	3:00	Borris-in-Ossory Beet Siding	?	1966	21 B4	
		former Beet loading siding				
5	5:05	Quaker's Road Crossing	1857	Open	21 B4	
6¼	6:14	Ballaghmore 1 Crossing	1857	Open	21 B4	
6¾	6:62	Ballaghmore 2 Crossing	1857	Open	21 B4	
7¼	7:15	Ballaghmore 3 Crossing	1857	Open	21 B4	
9¼	9:25	Ashberry Crossing	1857	Open	21 B3	
10	10:04	ROSCREA	1857	Open	21 A3	24
		junction for Birr, line ran parallel for ½ mile				
10¾	10:67	Point of divergence	1858	1963	21 A3	24
		Birr line diverged at this point				
14¼	14:25	Clonbrennan 1 Crossing	1863	Open	21 A4	
14½	14:45	Clonbrennan 2 Crossing	1863	Open	21 A4	
15¼	15:15	Clonlisk 1 Crossing	1863	Open	21 A4	
15¾	15:65	Clonlisk 2 Crossing	1863	Open	21 A4	
16¼	16:20	Blakefield Crossing	1863	Open	21 A4	
18	18:03	Cooraclaven Crossing	1863	Open	21 A4	
19¼	19:11	Stoneyacre Crossing	1863	Open	20 D4	
20	20:00	CLOUGHJORDAN	1863	Open	20 D4	
21¾	21:55	Bantiss Crossing	1863	Open	20 D4	
22½	22:41	Glenahilty Crossing	1863	Open	20 D4	
29½	29:33	NENAGH	1863	Open	20 C4	
32½	32:42	Moonaroon Crossing	1864	Open	20 C4	
35	35:00	Mogul Crossing	1966	Open	20 C5	
35¼	35:19	Silvermines Junction	1966	1993 ?	20 C5	128
		trailing junction to Silvermines				
36	36:02	SHALLEE	1904	1963	20 C5	
38¼	38:60	Ballinteenoe Crossing	1864	Open	20 B5	
39¼	39:20	Cappadine Crossing	1864	Open	20 B5	
40½	40:47	Cappanaskeady Crossing	1864	Open	20 B5	
40¾	40:70	Kilmastulla Siding	1982	Open	20 B5	
		opened 29-08-1982 as Shale Siding for traffic to Castlemungret Cement Works				
42¼	42:15	Junction for Killaloe	1862	1944	20 B5	7
42½	42:36	BIRDHILL	1860	Open	20 B5	7
43	43:09	Birdhill Crossing	1860	Open	20 B5	
44¼	44:18	Annaholty No.1 Crossing	1860	Open	20 B5	
44½	44:40	Annaholty No.2 Crossing	1860	Open	20 B5	
45	45:09	Coolready Crossing	1860	Open	20 B5	
46¾	46:59	Spa Crossing	1860	Open	20 B5	
47	47:01	Castleconnell Station Gates	1860	Open	20 B5	
47	47:05	CASTLECONNELL	1858	Open	20 B5	
		closed 1963, re-opened 15-05-1989				
47½	47:52	Stradbally Crossing	1858	Open	20 B5	
48¼	48:21	Sallymount Crossing	1858	Open	20 B5	
48¾	48:60	LISNAGRY	1858	1963	20 B6	
		named Nenagh Road until 1878				
48¾	48:62	Lisnagry Station Gates	1858	Open	20 B6	
49	49:00	Lisnagry Crossing	1858	Open	20 B6	
49½	49:40	Richhill Crossing	1858	Open	20 B6	
50¼	50:20	Clyduff Crossing	1858	Open	20 B6	
50½	50:45	Annacotty Crossing	1858	Open	20 B6	
50½	50:46	ANNACOTTY HALT	1858	1963	20 B6	
		formerly GRANGE, re-named ANNACOTTY 01-1859, closed 01-11-1863, re-opened 23-07- 1928				
51¾	51:68	Scart Crossing	1858	Open	20 B6	
52½	52:46	Killonan Junction	1858	Open	20 B6	13
		junction removed in 1931 and former double track worked as two separate lines to Limerick, re-instated 1947, open as junction.				
4¼	4:22	MILEAGE CHANGE (mileposts measured from Limerick)				
4¼	4:21	Killonan Station Gates	1848	Open	20 B6	13
4¼	4:16	KILLONAN	1848	1963	20 B6	13
2½	2:45	Garryglass Crossing	1848	Open	20 B6	
1	0:70	Ennis Junction	1859	Open	20 A6	13,17
		junction for Ennis; special platforms erected 1863 for visitors to the Munster Fair				
0½	0:45	Limerick Check	?	1963	20 A6	13,17
		Ennis line Junction				18
0¼	?	Markets Branch Tramway	1864	c.1950	20 A6	14,17
		see Table 14 for full details				18
0¼	0:25	LIMERICK (old station)	1848	1858	20 A6	13,17 18
0	0:00	LIMERICK	1858	Open	20 A6	13,17
		LIMERICK COLBERT Station from 1966				18

24 Roscrea to Birr

GSWR / 5ft 3in gauge / mileposts measured from Roscrea

Roscrea to Birr opened 08-03-1858 by the RPR.

Goods services suspended from 10-03-1947 due to fuel shortage.
Passenger services suspended 24-02-1947.
Goods services resumed 24-05-1947.
Passenger services resumed 16-06-1947.

Roscrea to Birr closed completely 01-01-1963 by CIE.

MPost Dist.	Miles & Chains	Place / Feature (notes)	Date Opened	Date Closed	Map Grid	Table Ref.
0	0:00	ROSCREA	1857	Open	21 A3	23
		junction for Ballybrophy				
0¾	0:62	Limerick line diverges at this point	1863	Open	21 A3	23
3¼	3:18	Moynure 1 Crossing	1858	1963	21 A3	
3¼	?	Brosna No.2 Siding	?	?	21 A3	
4	3:75	Moynure 2 Crossing	1858	1963	21 A3	
5	5:02	Brosna Station Gates	1858	1963	21 A3	
5½	?	BROSNA HALT	c.1910	1963	21 A3	
		Perry and Sons Brewery Siding	?	?	21 A3	
5¾	5:60	Boveen 1 Crossing	1858	1963	21 A3	
6¼	6:14	Boveen 2 Crossing	1858	1963	21 A3	
7	?	Brosna No.1 Siding	?	?	21 A3	
		also called Sharavogue Siding				
8½	8:36	Rathbeg 1 Crossing	1858	1963	21 A3	
8¾	8:62	Rathbeg 2 Crossing	1858	1963	21 A3	
9¾	9:60	Ballyegan 1 Crossing	1858	1963	21 A3	
10	10:02	Ballyegan 2 Crossing	1858	1963	21 A3	
10	10:07	Ballyegan 3 Crossing	1858	1963	21 A3	
10½	10:32	Clonkelly Crossing	1858	1963	21 A3	
11	11:11	Crinkle Crossing	1858	1963	21 A2	
		also called Lord Ross Road Crossing				
11½ ?	?	Junction with PPBR	1868	1878	21 A2	118
11¾	?	BIRR	1858	1963	21 A2	118
		PARSONSTOWN until 02-1900				

25 Charleville Junction to Patrickswell

GSWR / 5ft 3in gauge / mileposts measured from Charleville Junction

Patrickswell to Rathluirc opened 01-08-1862 by the CLDR.

Closed to passengers 31-12-1934 by the GSR.
Closed completely 27-03-1967 by CIE.

MPost Dist.	Miles & Chains	Place / Feature (notes)	Date Opened	Date Closed	Map Grid	Table Ref.
0	0:00	Charleville Junction	1862	1967	26 B2	8
		junction to Charleville; former triangle northbound connection closed 1906				
4½		BRUREE	1862	1934	26 B2	
8¾	8:50	Rosstemple Station Gates	1862	1967	26 B1	
8¾		ROSSTEMPLE	1865/6	1934	26 B1	
10¼	10:30	Tullaven Crossing	1862	1967	26 B1	
12		CROOM	1862	1934	26 B1	
17½		PATRICKSWELL	1856	1963	20 A6	18
		junction for Limerick				

26 Farranfore to Valentia Harbour

GSWR / 5ft 3in gauge / mileposts measured from Farranfore

Farranfore to Killorglin opened 15-01-1885 by the GSWR.
Killorglin to Valentia Harbour opened 12-08-1893 by the GSWR.

Passenger services suspended 24-02-1947 due to fuel shortage.
Passenger services resumed 24-05-1947.

Farranfore to Valentia Harbour closed 01-02-1960 by CIE.
Remained open for cattle specials until c.08-1960.

MPost Dist.	Miles & Chains	Place / Feature (notes)	Date Opened	Date Closed	Map Grid	Table Ref.
0	0:00	FARRANFORE	1859	Open	25 A3	9
		junction for Mallow				
0½	0:30	Dromore Crossing	1885	1960	25 A3	
1¾	1:57	Molahiffe Station Gates	1885	1960	25 A3	
1¾		MOLAHIFFE	1885	1960	25 A3	
2	2:05	Ballinvarrig Crossing	1885	1960	25 A3	
2½	2:48	Clonmilane Crossing	1885	1960	25 A3	
4¼	4:12	Ballybrack Crossing	1885	1960	25 A3	
4¾	4:52	Rusheen Crossing	1885	1960	25 A3	
6½		CASTLEMAINE	1885	1960	25 A3	
7¾	7:55	Milltown Station Gates	1885	1960	25 A3	
7¾		MILLTOWN	1887	1960	25 A3	
9	9:06	Kilderry Crossing	1885	1960	24 D3	
10¼	10:13	Callanfercy Crossing	1885	1960	24 D3	
10¾	10:65	Steelroe Crossing	1885	1960	24 D3	
?	?	Laune Viaduct	1885	1960	24 D3	
		Bowstring Girder, 3x105ft spans				
12½		KILLORGLIN	1885	1960	24 D3	
12½	12:39	Killorglin Station Gates	1893	1960	24 D3	
14¾	14:60	Muingaphuca Crossing	1893	1960	24 D4	
16	15:69	Caragh Lake Station Gates	1893	1960	24 D4	
16		CARAGH LAKE	1893	1960	24 D4	
17	17:07	Quay Bawn Crossing	1893	1960	24 D4	
18¼		DOOKS	1897	1960	24 D4	
18¼	18:24	Dooks Crossing	1893	1960	24 D4	
		also called Curragheen No.1 Crossing				
18½	18:47	Curragheen No.2 Crossing	1893	1960	24 D4	
19½		GLENBEIGH	1893	1960	24 D4	
19¾	19:70	Glenbeigh Station Gates	1893	1960	24 D4	
20¼	20:20	Rossbeigh Crossing	1893	1960	24 C4	
		also called Kilnabrack Crossing				
21	21:05	Curra Crossing	1893	1960	24 C4	
22½	22:40	Drom Crossing	1893	1960	24 C4	
23	23:10	Coolnaharragill Crossing	1893	1960	24 C4	
23½		MOUNTAIN STAGE	1893	1960	24 C4	
24¼	24:17	Kilkeehagh Crossing	1893	1960	24 C4	
25	25:11	Covered Way	?	1960	24 C4	
		50 yd roof over track to protect from rock falls, not a tunnel				
25¼	25:18	Drung Hill No.1 Tunnel	1893	1960	24 C4	
		120 yds long				
25¼	25:27	Drung Hill No.2 Tunnel	1893	1960	24 C4	
		91 yds long				
29¼	29:20	Knockaneyouloo Crossing	1893	1960	24 C4	
?	?	Gleensk Viaduct	1893	1960	24 C4	
30½	30:45	Kells Station Gates	1893	1960	24 B4	
30½		KELLS	1893	1960	24 B4	
30¾	30:66	Gortnagree Crossing	1893	1960	24 B4	
33¼	33:18	Dooneen Crossing	1893	1960	24 B4	
34½	34:33	Ballydarrig Crossing	1893	1960	24 B4	
34¾	34:55	Killurley Crossing	1893	1960	24 B4	
35	35:02	Cloghanelinaghan Crossing	1893	1960	24 B4	
?	?	Cahirciveen Viaduct	1893	1960	24 B4	
36½	36:42	Cahirciveen Station Gates	1893	1960	24 B5	
36¾		CAHIRCIVEEN	1893	1960	24 B5	
36¾	36:69	Cahirciveen Station Gates	1893	1960	24 B5	
38	37:75	Reenard Crossing	1893	1960	24 B5	
39¼		VALENTIA HARBOUR	1893	1960	24 B5	

27 Thurles to Clonmel

Southern Railway – worked by GSWR
5ft 3in gauge / mileposts measured from Thurles Junction

Thurles Junction to Fethard opened 01-07-1880 by the SR.
Fethard to Clonmel opened 23-06-1879 by the SR.

Goods services suspended from 10-03-1947 due to fuel shortage.
Passenger service suspended 24-02-1947.
Passenger and goods services resumed 24-05-1947.

Thurles to Clonmel closed to passengers 09-09-1963 by CIE.
Thurles to Clonmel closed completely 27-03-1967 by CIE.

Thurles Junction to Powerstown Park lifted 1971, Powerstown Park to Clonmel Junction used as siding, lifted after the rest of the line.

MPost Dist.	Miles & Chains	Place / Feature (notes)	Date Opened	Date Closed	Map Grid	Table Ref.
0	0:00	Thurles Junction	1880	1967	21 A6	8
5½	5:36	Curraheen Crossing	1880	1967	21 A6	
5½		HORSE & JOCKEY	1880	1963	21 A6	
6½	6:36	Lurgoe Crossing	1880	1967	21 A6	
9¼		LAFFAN'S BRIDGE AND KILLENAULE	1880	1963	27 C1	
9½	9:46	Cathaganstown Crossing	1880	1967	27 C1	
		also called Carriganstown Crossing				
10¾	10:53	Buffanagh Crossing	1880	1967	27 C1	
13¼		FARRANALLEEN	1880	1963	27 C1	
16¼		FETHARD	1879	1963	27 C2	
22¾	22:63	Tannersrath Crossing	1879	1967	27 C2	
23¼		POWERSTOWN PARK	1916	?	27 C2	
		served the Racecourse				
25½		Clonmel Junction	1879	1963	27 C2	13
		junction with Waterford-Limerick line				
25¾		CLONMEL	1852	Open	27 C2	13

28 Cobh Junction to Cobh

GSWR / 5ft 3in gauge / mileposts measured from Dublin Heuston

Cobh Junction to Cobh opened 10-03-1862 by the CYR.

MPost Dist.	Miles & Chains	Place / Feature (notes)	Date Opened	Date Closed	Map Grid	Table Ref.
171	171:04	GLOUNTHAUNE	1862	Open	33 F1	16
		originally QUEENSTOWN JUNCTION, renamed COBH JUNCTION, re-named GLOUNTHAUNE 07-11-1994				

171	171:17	Cobh Junction junction for Youghal.	1862	Open	33 F1	16
171½	171:38	Bridge	1862	Open	33 F2	
171¾		Crossing temporary crossing for road building project, to be replaced by bridge	1994	Open	33 F2	
172	172:14	Slatty Viaduct	1862	Open	33 F2	
172¼	172:31	FOTA formerly called FOATY; public from 1864	1862	Open	33 F2	
172¼	172:31	Fota Crossing staggered platforms with an accommodation crossing between them	1862	Open	33 F2	
172¾	172:54	Belvelly Viaduct	1862	Open	33 F2	
		Marino Point Crossing temporary crossing replaced by bridge for Ammonia plant construction and access	1975	1975	33 F2	
173	173:04	Marino Point Junction	1979	Open	33 F2	
173	173:04	Marino Point Junction	1979	Open	33 F2	
		Marino Point siding diverges on down side for Nitrigin Éireann Teoranta, now called Irish Fertiliser Industries	1979	Open	33 F2	
174¼	174:25	CARRIGALOE	1862	Open	33 F3	
175¾	175:57	RUSHBROOKE formerly MONKSTOWN FERRY, renamed 1868/9	1862	Open	33 F3	
175¾	175:58	Rushbrooke Station Gates staggered platforms with an accommodation crossing between them	1862	Open	33 F3	
176¼		QUEENSTOWN (old station) original CYR Station	1862	1868	33 F3	
176½	176:61	COBH formerly QUEENSTOWN	1868	Open	33 F3	

29 Goold's Cross to Cashel

GSWR / 5ft3in gauge / mileposts measured from Goold's Cross

Goold's Cross to Cashel opened 19-12-1904 by the GSWR.

All services suspended from 24-04-1944 due to fuel shortage.
Passenger services resumed from 10-12-1945.
All services suspended from 27-01-1947.

Closed to passengers 27-01-1947 by CIE.
Closed completely 01-09-1954 by CIE.

MPost Dist.	Miles & Chains	Place / Feature (notes)	Date Opened	Date Closed	Map Grid	Table Ref.
0	0:00	GOOLD'S CROSS formerly GOOLD'S CROSS & CASHEL until opening of branch; junction for Dublin	1848	1976	27 B1	8
2¼	2:22	Ardmayle Crossing	1904	1954	27 B1	
3½		ARDMAYLE opened by 07-1907	by 1907	1947	27 B1	
5¼	5:25	Camus Crossing	1904	1954	27 B1	
5¾		CASHEL	1904	1954	27 B1	

30 Dublin Harcourt Street to Bray

DSER / 5ft3in gauge / mileposts measured from Dublin Harcourt Street

Dublin Harcourt Road to Bray opened 10-07-1854 by the DWR.
Dublin Harcourt Street to Harcourt Road opened 07-02-1859 by the DWR.

Dublin Harcourt Street to Shanganagh Junction closed completely 01-01-1959 by CIE.

MPost Dist.	Miles & Chains	Place / Feature (notes)	Date Opened	Date Closed	Map Grid	Table Ref.
0	0:00	DUBLIN HARCOURT STREET had a small goods yard which closed 1925	1859	1959	32 C3	
0¼	0:10	DUBLIN HARCOURT ROAD temporary terminus	1854	1859	32 C3	
?	?	Grand Canal Bridge	1854	1959	32 C3	
1	1:00	RANELAGH formerly RATHMINES & RANELAGH, renamed 1921	1896	1959	32 C3	
1¾	1:60	MILLTOWN	1860	1959	32 C4	
1¼	?	River Dodder Viaduct 9 arch stone viaduct	1854	1959	32 C4	
3	3:00	DUNDRUM	1854	1959	32 C4	
5¼	5:20	STILLORGAN	1854	1959	23 B1	
5½	5:40	Leopardstown Crossing	1854	1959	23 B1	
6	6:10	FOXROCK	1861	1959	23 B1	
?	?	Foxrock Crossing	1854	1959	23 B1	
7¼	7:20	CARRICKMINES	1854	1959	23 B1	
8	8:00	Tulla Crossing	1854	1959	23 B1	
?	?	Bride's Glen Viaduct Stone viaduct	1854	1959	23 B2	
9¾	9:55	SHANKILL	1854	1959	23 B2	
10½	10:42	Shanganagh Junction junction from Westland Row; no 'physical' junction existed between1876 and 1915, during that period a 'third' line continued to a junction just before Bray Station.	1876	1915	23 B2	31
10¾	10:65	Shanganagh Junction later installed junction for Westland Row	1915	1959	23 B2	31
12	12:10	Shanganagh Junction original Junction for Harcourt Street until 1876	1854	1876	23 B2	31
12	12:10	SHANGANAGH JUNCTION exchange platform 23-08-1861 to 07-10-1876	1861	1876	23 B2	31
12¼	12:14	Bray Station Gates	1854	Open	23 B2	31
12¼	12:20	BRAY BRI CHUALANN 1925 to c.1930. BRAY DALY Station from 1966	1854	Open	23 B2	31

31 Dublin Connolly to Rosslare Harbour Pier

5ft3in gauge / mileposts measured from Dublin Westland Row to Shanganagh Junction, thence from Dublin Harcourt Street

4ft8½in gauge Westland Row to Dalkey from 1834 until conversion to 5ft3in gauge from 10-10-1855

CDJR – Dublin Amiens St Jct Station to Dublin Westland Row Station.
DKR – Dublin Westland Row to Dalkey.
DSER – Dalkey to Wexford North.
FRRHC – Wexford North to Rosslare Harbour Pier.
Note: Wexford-Rosslare is still owned by FRRHC and leased/operated by IE.

Dublin Amiens Street to Dublin Westland Row opened 01-05-1891 by the CDJR.
Dublin Westland Row to Dunleary opened 17-12-1834 by the DKR.
Dunleary to Kingstown opened 13-05-1837 by the DKR.
Kingstown to Carlisle Pier opened 23-12-1859 by DKR.
Kingstown to Dalkey (Atmospheric Station) opened 29-03-1844 by the DKR.
Dalkey to Bray opened 10-07-1854 by the DWR.
Bray to Wicklow Town opened 30-10-1855 by the DWR.
Wicklow Junction to Kilcommon (Rathdrum Old Station) opened 20-08-1861 by DWWR.
Rathdrum (old station) to Avoca (Ovoca until 1912) opened 18-07-1863 by the DWWR.
Avoca (Ovoca until 1912) to Enniscorthy opened 16-11-1863 by the DWWR.
Enniscorthy to Wexford (Old station) opened 17-08-1872 by the DWWR.
Wexford (Old station) to Wexfords Goods opened 10-06-1873 by the DWWR.
Wexford (Old station) to Wexford opened 08-1874 by the DWWR.
Wexford to Rosslare Harbour Pier opened 24-06-1882 by the WWR.
Rosslare Pier to Rosslare Harbour Pier opened 30-08-1906 by the FRRHC.

Wexford to Rosslare Pier closed 16-05-1889 (except for a few cattle trains).
Wexford to Kilrane re-opened 06-08-1894.
Kilrane to Rosslare Pier re-opened 1895.

Passenger services suspended 24-02-1947 due to fuel shortage except suburban services to Bray and Greystones.
Passenger services resumed 24-05-1947.

Kinsgtown to Dalkey (Atmospheric Station) closed 12-04-1854 by DKR – Atmospheric line length was 1¾ miles.
Dun Laoghaire Pier Junction to Dun Laoghaire Pier closed fully 11-10-1980 by CIE.
Rosslare Pier to Rosslare Harbour Pier closed to passengers 14-09-1989.

Electrified between Amiens Street and Bray at 1,500V DC overhead, electric service commenced 23-07-1984.

MPost Dist.	Miles & Chains	Place / Feature (notes)	Date Opened	Date Closed	Map Grid	Table Ref.
1	1:12	Junction with GNR(I) Lines	1891	Open	32 C2	50
1	1:01	DUBLIN AMIENS STREET JUNCTION	1891	Open	32 C2	114,
		DUBLIN CONNOLLY Station from 1966				50
0½	0:29	Liffey Viaduct	1891	Open	32 C2	
0¼	0:21	DUBLIN TARA STREET	1891	Open	32 C2	
		formerly TARA STREET & GEORGES QUAY				
0	0:00	DUBLIN WESTLAND ROW	1834	Open	32 C2	
		renamed DUBLIN PEARSE in 1966				
?	0:20 ?	Boston Sidings	c.1877	Open	32 D3	
		carriage sidings				
0¼	0:25	Grand Canal Street Works	1837	1925	32 D2	
		former Works on Up Side				
0¼	0:25	Grand Canal Street Depot	c.1860	1972	32 D2	
		Running Shed (later a PW Depot)				
0½	0:46 ?	BARROW STREET	–	–	32 D2	
		new station, due to open 1998				
1	1:06	Lansdowne Road Station Gates	1834	Open	32 D3	
1	1:10	LANSDOWNE ROAD	1870	Open	32 D3	
		opened 01-07-1870; formerly LANSDOWNE ROAD & BALLSBRIDGE, renamed 1872.				
1¼	?	Ballsbridge Siding	1893	1971	32 D3	
		spur served Royal Dublin Society's Showground				
1½	?	Serpentine Avenue	1834	1839	32 D3	
		DKR Works				
1½	?	SERPENTINE AVENUE	1835	1835	32 D3	
		open during January and February 1835.				
1½	1:32	Serpentine Crossing	1834	Open	32 D3	
1¾	1:50	SANDYMOUNT	1835	Open	32 D3	
		formerly SANDYMOUNT AVENUE, opened 02-1835, closed 10-05-1841, opened 23-07-1860, closed 30-04-1862, opened 03-04-1882, closed 01-10-1901, opened 05-03-1928, closed 13-06-1960, opened 20-06-1960, closed 12-09-1960 and was re-opened 23-07-1984				
1¾	1:52	Sandymount Station Gates	1834	Open	32 D3	
2¼	2:19	Sidney Parade Station Gates	1834	Open	32 D3	
		also spelt Sydney Parade				
2¼	2:22	SIDNEY PARADE	1835	Open	32 D3	
		also spelt SYDNEY PARADE; closed 10-05-1841, opened 05-1862, closed in 1960, opened 1972				
2¾	2:60	MERRION	1835	1935	32 D3	
		opened 01-1835, closed 30-08-1862, opened 03-04-1882, closed 01-10-1901, opened 05-03-1928, closed 07-1929, re-opened 08-1930, closed 09-1935				
2¾	2:60	Merrion Crossing	1834	Open	32 D3	
3¼	3:20	BOOTERSTOWN	1835	Open	32 E4	
		closed in 1960, re-opened 03-03-1975				
3½	3:51	WILLIAMSTOWN	1835	1841	32 E4	
		closed 10-05-1841				
4	4:07	BLACKROCK	1834	Open	32 E4	
?	?	Blackrock Tunnel	1834	Open	32 E4	
		70ft long				
4¾	4:60	SEAPOINT	1863	Open	32 E4	
		formerly SEAPOINT, re-named MONKSTOWN & SEAPOINT in 1964; renamed SEAPOINT 06-1991				
5¼	5:26	SALTHILL & MONKSTOWN	1837	Open	32 F4	
		renamed SALTHILL 1960; closed 1960, re-opened 23-07-1984, renamed SALTHILL & MONKSTOWN 06-1991				
5½	5:43	DUNLEARY	1834	1837	32 F4	
		Original DKR Terminus near to this point				
5¾	5:44	Dunleary Crossing	1837	1983	32 F4	
		also called West Pier Crossing, closed 11-1983 due to electrification.				
?		Coal Quay Crossing	1863	?	32 F4	
?		Mineral Wharf Siding	1863	?	32 F4	
		crossed road to wharf, also called Trader's Wharf and Coal Quay				
?		Victoria Wharf Crossing	1891	1966	32 F4	
?		St Michael's Wharf Siding	1891	1966	32 F4	
		crossed road to wharf, later called Victoria Wharf				
6	6:12	DUN LAOGHAIRE	1837	Open	32 F4	
		originally KINGSTOWN HARBOUR, renamed KINGSTOWN in 1861, renamed DUN LAOGHAIRE in 1921; DUN LAOGHAIRE MALLIN Station from 1966; original terminus behind present down platform				
6¼	6:15	Pier Junction	1859	1980	32 F4	
		junction to Carlisle Pier				
6¼	6:15	Pier Junction	1859	1980	32 F4	
6¼	6:20	Carlisle Pier Crossing	1859	1980	32 F4	
6½	6:33	DUN LAOGHAIRE PIER	1859	1980	32 F4	
		formerly called KINGSTOWN PIER, opened 23-12-1859, closed 11-10-1980				
6¾	6:58	SANDYCOVE & GLASTHULE	1855	Open	23 B1	
		originally KINGSTOWN SANDYCOVE; renamed SANDYCOVE 1861; renamed SANDYCOVE & GLASTHULE 1967; renamed SANDYCOVE in 1970s; currently SANDYCOVE & GLASTHULE FROM 06-1991				
7¼	7:20	GLENAGEARY	1867	Open	23 B1	
		opened 21-08-1867				
7¾	7:55	DALKEY (Atmospheric Station)	1844	1854	23 B1	
		former terminus of the Kingstown-Dalkey atmospheric line				
7¾	7:57	Glenageary Siding	c.1890	1918	23 B1	
		on former atmospheric trackbed				
8	8:05	DALKEY	1854	Open	23 B1	
		resited Station				
8½	8:38	Dalkey Tunnel	1854	Open	23 B1	
		160 yards long				
9	9:00	OBELISK HILL	1855	1858	23 B1	
		opened 06-1855, closed 01-01-1858				
9¾	9:50	KILLINEY (old station)	1858	1882	23 B1	
10	9:74	KILLINEY (new station)	1882	Open	23 B1	
		formerly KILLINEY & BALLYBRACK, renamed 1921				
10¼	10:15	BALLYBRACK (old station)	1854	1857	23 B2	
		old route to Bray diverged here, new route opened 1915				
10¼	10:20	BALLYBRACK (new station)	1857	1882	23 B2	
11	11:00	Fields Crossing	1854	1984	23 B2	
		also called Shanganagh Crossing				
11¼	11:20	SHANKILL	1977	Open	23 B2	
		opened 10-06-1977				
12	11:77	Shanganagh Junction	1876	1915	23 B2	30
		junction for Harcourt Street.; no 'physical' junction existed between 1876 and 1915, during that period a 'third' line continued to a junction just before Bray Station Gates.				
12	12:00	Shanganagh Junction	1915	1959	23 B2	30
		later installed Junction for Harcourt Street				
12	12:10	Shanganagh Junction	1854	1876	23 B2	30
		original Junction for Harcourt Street until 1876				
12	12:10	SHANGANAGH JUNCTION	1861	1876	23 B2	31
		exchange platform 23-08-1861 to 07-10-1876				
10½	10:42	MILEAGE CHANGE (mileposts measured from Dublin Harcourt Street)				
11	11:10	WOODBROOK	1910	1960	23 B2	30
		served adjacent Golf Course, original single Down side platform on third line (1910-1915), later a two platform halt built on deviated lines				
12¼	12:14	Bray Station Gates	1854	Open	23 B2	30
12¼	12:20	BRAY	1854	Open	23 B2	30
		BRI CHUALANN 1925 to c.1930. BRAY DALY Station from 1966				
?	?	Bray Works	1854	1869	23 B2	
		DWR Works				
13	13:10	BRAY COVE HALT	1906	1929	23 B2	
		also called NAYLOR'S COVE HALT; closed 1907, re-opened in 1929 only.				
13¼	?	Worthington's Stone Siding	1873	?	23 B2	
13¾	13:59	Bray Head No.1 Tunnel	1876	Open	23 B2	
		307 yds long, combined length of the two tunnels with a small gap in the middle.				
?	?	Brabazon Tunnel	1855	1876	23 B2	
		replaced by No.1 Tunnel due to erosion				
14	14:10	Quarry Siding	c.1860	?	23 B2	

14¼	14:15	Brandy Hole (No.2) Tunnel	1855	Open	23 B2	
		143 yds long				
?		Former Route	1855	1879	23 B2	
		current route further inland				
14¾	14:53	Cable Rock (No.3) Tunnel	1855	Open	23 B2	
		210 yds long				
?		Former Routes	1855	1917	23 B2	
		original route replaced by the 'Rathdown Deviation' in 1888, replaced by No.4 Tunnel in 1917.				
15	14:69	The Long (No.4) Tunnel	1917	Open	23 B2	
		1,084 yds long, built when line moved inland due to coastal erosion				
16	15:77	Ennis Lane Crossing	1917	Open	23 B2	
		formerly an underbridge				
16¼	16:24	Jubilee Sidings	1918	1921	23 B2	
		on down side, site of creosoting plant; sidings were in use in 1950s for storing 6-wheel carriages awaiting scrapping				
17	17:05	GREYSTONES	1855	Open	23 B2	
		formerly DELGANY, renamed GREYSTONES & DELGANY 1886, renamed GREYSTONES 1914.				
18	?	Line realignment	1970	Open	23 B3	
		line moved inland by 60 ft due to coastal erosion; opened May 1970.				
19	?	Line realignment	1970	Open	23 B3	
		line rejoins original course				
19¾	19:66	KILCOOLE	1856	Open	23 B3	
		closed 30-03-1964, re-opened 09-06-1980; formerly KILCOOL & NEWTOWNMOUNTKENNEDY, re-named KILCOOLE on re-opening				
19¾	19:69	Kilcoole Station Gates	1855	Open	23 B3	
22½	22:35	Newcastle Station Gates	1855	Open	23 B3	
22½	22:38	NEWCASTLE	1856	1964	23 B3	
		closed 30-03-1964				
23¼	23:20	Five Mile Point Crossing	1855	Open	23 B3	
25½	25:43	Killoughter Crossing	1855	Open	23 B3	
25½	25:44	KILLOUGHTER	1856	1867	23 B3	
		closed 01-04-1867				
27¾	27:60	Wicklow Junction	1861	1976	23 B4	
		junction to Wicklow Murrough				
27¾	27:60	Wicklow Junction	1861	1976	23 B4	
		junction removed 30-04-1987				
28½	28:32	WICKLOW MURROUGH	1855	1976	23 B4	171
		closed 12-1893, remained open for goods and excursions; re-opened 10-03-1969 for passengers as MURROUGH Station; closed again 01-11-1976.				
28	27:72	Chemical Yard Crossing	1861	Open	23 B4	
28¼	28:16	Bolarney Crossing	1861	Open	23 B4	
28¼	28:20	WICKLOW	1885	Open	23 B4	
		opened 02-1885				
29½	29:54	RATHNEW	1866	1964	23 B4	
		closed 30-03-1964				
30½	30:37	Brickfields Siding	1896	1930/1	23 B4	382
		trailed off on Up side, crossed road to Brickworks				
30¾	30:60	Ballymerrigan Crossing	1861	Open	23 B4	
32½	32:54	Ballymanus Crossing	1861	Open	23 B4	
		also called Glenealy Crossing				
32½	32:54	GLENEALY (old station)	1861	1866	23 B4	
33¼	33:20	GLENEALY (new station)	1866	1964	23 B4	
		closed 30-03-1964				
33¼	33:40	Ballyfree Crossing	?	Open	23 B4	
35¾	35:60	Kilcommon No.1 Crossing	1861	Open	23 A4	
36¼	36:09	RATHDRUM	1861	1863	23 A4	
		original Rathdrum Station at Kilcommon				
36¼	36:20	Kilcommon No.2 Crossing	1861	Open	23 A4	
37¼	37:15	Corballis Viaduct	1863	Open	23 A4	
		5 arch viaduct				
37¼	37:24	RATHDRUM (new station)	1863	Open	23 A4	
37½	37:47	Rathdrum No.1 Tunnel	1863	Open	23 A4	
		190yds long				
38¼	38:17	Balleece Siding	1901	1937	23 A4	
		Balleece Woods Quarry Co. Closed 02-1937				
39¼	39:13	Rathdrum No.2 Tunnel	1863	Open	23 A4	
		25yds long				
39¼	39:17	Rathdrum No.3 Tunnel	1863	Open	23 A4	
		50yds long				
40¼	40:20	Connorree Siding	1865	1869	23 A5	
41½	41:30	Cronebane	1874	1889	23 A5	
		also known as Tigroney, Copper, Sulphur & Iron loading siding				
42¾	42:66	AVOCA	1863	1964	23 A5	
		called OVOCA until 1912, closed 30-03-1964, except for special excursions				
44½	44:55	Woodenbridge Junction	1865	1953	23 A5	32
		junction for Shillelagh				
44¾	44:62	WOODENBRIDGE	1865	1964	23 A5	32
		formerly WOODENBRIDGE JUNCTION, renamed 1950s; closed 30-03-1964				
44¾	44:65	Woodenbridge Station Gates	1863	Open	23 A5	
46¾	46:62	Shelton Abbey Crossing	1964	Open	23 A5	
46¾	46:68	Shelton Abbey Sidings	1964	Open	23 B5	
		Nitrigin Éireann Teoranta Works, now Irish Fertilizer Industries (IFI), opened 19-01-1964.				
47	47:05	GLENART	18 ?	?	23 B5	
		private platform for Earl of Carysfort				
49	49:04	ARKLOW	1863	Open	23 B5	
50½	50:60	Kish Siding	1886	?	23 B5	265
		siding with loading bank for Parnell Whinstone Quarries				
53½	53:38	INCH	1885	1964	23 A6	
		closed 30-03-1964				
57	56:77	Aske Crossing	1863	Open	23 A6	
57½	57:33	Knockinagh Crossing	1863	Open	23 A6	
59½	59:44	GOREY	1863	Open	23 A6	
65¼	65:29	Tullabeg Crossing	1863	Open	29 B1	
67	67:08	CAMOLIN	1867	1964	29 A1	
		closed 30-03-1964				
70	69:71	FERNS	1863	1977	29 A1	
		closed 07-03-1977 except for excursions				
71½	71:29	Crory Crossing	1863	Open	29 A1	
73¼	73:20	Scarawalsh Ballast Pit	1918	?	29 A1	
77½	77:40	ENNISCORTHY	1863	Open	29 A2	
77¾	77:52	River Slaney Bridge	1872	Open	29 A2	
77¾	77:56	Roache's Siding	c.1879	?	29 A2	
		on Up side before tunnel entrance				
77¾	77:57	Enniscorthy Tunnel	1872	Open	29 A2	
		405yds long				
78½	78:40	St John's Siding	1873	1965	29 A2	
		private siding from Davis's Cornmill				
81	81:03	EDERMINE FERRY	1872	1964	29 A2	
		closed 30-03-1964				
81	81:07	Edermine Ferry Station Gates	1872	Open	29 A2	
83¼	83:30	MACMINE JUNCTION	1873	1964	29 A2	33
		junction for Waterford, closed 30-03-1964				
86¼	86:16	KILLURIN	1872	1964	29 A3	
		closed 30-03-1964				
86¾	86:62	Killurin Tunnel	1872	Open	29 A3	
		89yds long				
87	87:00	Ballast Pit	18 ?	18 ?	29 A3	
?	?	Level Crossing	1994 ?	1995 ?	23 A3	
		temporary crossing during bridge works				
90½	90:25	Ferrycarrig Tunnel	1872	Open	29 A3	
		296yds long				
92¼	92:12	WEXFORD (old station)	1872	1874	29 A3	
		in the Carcur district; closed when new station opened				
92½		Wexford Goods	1873	Open	29 A3	
		Old Station to New was built on the Goods extension				
92¾	92:54	WEXFORD	1874	Open	29 A3	
		named WEXFORD NORTH c.1900 to 1960s. WEXFORD O'HANRAHAN Station from 1966				
92¾	92:67	Junction	1882	Open	29 A3	
		end-on junction with FRRHC. Line runs along Quays to Wexford South				
6¼	6.20	MILEAGE CHANGE (mileposts now measurerd from Rosslare Strand)				
6	6:07	Wexford Station Gates	?	Open	29 A3	
5¾	5:70	Crescent Lift Bridge	1882	Open	29 A3	
		rebuilt as fixed bridge				

5½	5:25	WEXFORD SOUTH formerly SOUTH WEXFORD, renamed by 1904; closed 07-03-1977	c.1886	1977	29 A3	
5¼	5:22	Newlane Crossing	1882	Open	29 A3	
5¼	?	Smith Motor Works Siding	?	?	29 A3	
3½	3:42	Drinagh Siding served Cement Factory	1883	1911	29 A3	214
3¼	3:18	Drinagh Crossing	1882	Open	29 A4	
2	2:02	Felthouse Junction junction to Killinick; also known as Killiane Junction	1906	1911	29 A4	14
0¾	0:61	Factory Crossing	?	Open	29 A4	
0¼	0:21	Slaney Bridge Crossing	?	Open	29 A4	
0	0:04	Junction junction from Waterford	1906	Open	29 A4	14
0	0.00	ROSSLARE STRAND formerly ROSSLARE, renamed 1906	1882	Open	29 A4	14
110¾	110:66	MILEAGE CHANGE (mileposts measured from Mallow via Fermoy)				
113	113:04	KILRANE formerly ROSSLARE HARBOUR; renamed 1906; closed 12-10-1970	1882	1970	29 A4	14
113¾	113:57	Fishermans Crossing	?	Closed	29 B4	14
113¾	113:63	Ballygeary West Crossing	1989	Open	29 B4	14
?	?	BALLYGEARY temporary wooden platforms, opened 12-10-1970, closed 02-08-1971	1970	1971	29 B4	14
113¾	113:60	ROSSLARE HARBOUR MAINLAND formerly BALLYGEARY, opened 02-08-1971, renamed 27-06-1977, closed 14-09-1989	1971	1989	29 B4	14
113¾	113:70	Ballygeary East Crossing	1882	Open	29 B4	14
114	113:76	ROSSLARE EUROPORT opened 14-09-1989 as ROSSLARE HARBOUR, renamed 20-05-1996	1989	Open	29 B4	14
114	114:05	ROSSLARE PIER used for specials until 06-1895 when opened for passengers	1882	1906	29 B4	14
114¼	114:20	ROSSLARE HARBOUR PIER formerly ROSSLARE HARBOUR, renamed 27-06-1977, closed 14-09-1989	1906	1989	29 B4	14

32 Woodenbridge Junction to Shillelagh

DSER / 5ft 3in gauge / mileposts measured from Dublin Harcourt Street

Woodenbridge Junction to Shillelagh opened 22-05-1865 by the DWWR.

All services suspended from 24-04-1944 due to fuel shortage.

Shillelagh to Woodenbridge Junction closed to passengers 24-04-1944 by the GSR.
Shillelagh to Aughrim closed to goods 20-04-1945 by the GSR.
Woodenbridge Junction to Aughrim closed completely 01-05-1953 by CIE.

Branch was closed 24-04-1944 due to the fuel shortage although goods trains still operated as far as Aughrim until 01-05-1953. Although Aughrim to Shillelagh was closed and lifted in 1944, the branch as a whole was not 'officially' closed until 1953.

MPost Dist.	Miles & Chains	Place / Feature (notes)	Date Opened	Date Closed	Map Grid	Table Ref.
44¾	44:62	WOODENBRIDGE JUNCTION junction to Dublin Harcourt Street	1865	1964	23 A5	31
?	?	Level Crossing crossing with Hodgson's Tramway	1865	1870	23 A5	205
49¼	49:25	AUGHRIM	1865	1944	23 A5	
49¼	?	Fogarty's Mill Siding trailed in on Up side	1865	1953	23 A5	
53¾	53:58	BALLINGLEN opened Spring 1875	1875	1944	22 D5	
56	56:54	TINAHELY	1865	1944	22 D5	
59¾	59:52	Coolattin Crossing	1865	1944	22 D5	
61¼	61:16	SHILLELAGH (temporary terminus) 445yds from final terminus	1865	?	22 D6	
61¼	61:20	Shillelagh Crossing	?	1944	22 D6	
61½	61:38	SHILLELAGH opened after 1867	?	1944	22 D6	

33 Macmine Junction to Waterford North

DSER / 5ft 3in gauge / mileposts measured from Dublin Harcourt Street

Macmine Junction to Mackmine opened 01-04-1873 by the WNRWJR.
Mackmine to Palace East opened 26-10-1870 by the WNRWJR.
Palace East to New Ross opened 19-09-1887 by the DWWR.
New Ross to Waterford opened for goods 15-03-1904 by the DWWR.
New Ross to Waterford opened for passengers 27-04-1904 by the DWWR.

Palace East to Macmine Junction closed 30-09-1873.
Palace East to Macmine Junction re-opened 09-02-1874.

Passenger services suspended from 24-04-1944 due to fuel shortage.
Passenger services resumed from 10-12-1945.
Passenger services suspended from 27-01-1947.
Goods services suspended from 10-03-1947.
Goods services resumed 24-05-1947.
Passenger services resumed 16-06-1947.

Macmine Junction to New Ross closed completely 01-04-1963 by CIE.
New Ross to Waterford North closed to passengers 01-04-1963 by CIE.
New Ross to Waterford North closed to daily goods 06-09-1976 by CIE, remains open for fertiliser traffic.

MPost Dist.	Miles & Chains	Place / Feature (notes)	Date Opened	Date Closed	Map Grid	Table Ref.
83¼	83:30	MACMINE JUNCTION opened as junction; junction to Dublin Harcourt Street	1873	1964	29 A2	31
84¼	84:14	MACKMINE closed 01-04-1873	1870	1873	28 D2	
86½	86:34	SPARROWSLAND	1870	1876	28 D2	
86½	86:34	Sparrowsland Siding beet siding on down side at former Sparrowsland station site	?	1963 ?	28 D2	
89¾	89:69	CHAPEL	?	1963	28 D2	
93¾	93:69	PALACE EAST	1870	1963	28 C2	3
94	94:03	Palace East Junction junction to Bagenalstown	1887	1963	28 C2	3
96	95:71	Rathgarogue No.1 Crossing	1887	1963	28 C2	
96½	96:34	Rathgarogue No.2 Crossing	1887	1963	28 C2	
96½	96:55	RATHGAROGUE open by 10-1893	1893	1963	28 C2	
100½	100:35	Mount Elliot Tunnel 748yds long, also called New Ross Tunnel	1887	1963	28 C2	
101	101:02	Barrow Bridge Five span 596ft girder bridge with opening span	1887	1963	28 C2	
102	102:09	NEW ROSS this section still used for fertilizer traffic from the Albatross Factory	1887	1963	28 C3	
102¼	102:14	New Ross Station Gates	1904	Open	28 C3	
102¼	102:23	Rosbercon Crossing also called Staffords Crossing	1904	Open	28 C3	
102½	102:45	Dock Road Crossing	?	Open	28 C3	
103	102:75	Ross Factory Crossing also called Main Road Crossing	?	Open	28 B3	
106¼	106:24	Ballyverneen Crossing	1904	Open	28 B3	
107¼	107:25	Carrigcloney Crossing	1904	Open	28 B3	
107¾	107:62	Glenmore No.1 Crossing	1904	Open	28 B3	
108	108:02	GLENMORE also known as GLENMORE, AYLWARDSTOWN; formerly GLENMORE & AYLWARDSTOWN, renamed in 1921	1904	1963	28 B3	
109¼	109:26	Glenmore Crossing also called Rathinure Crossing	1904	Open	28 B3	
111½	111:31	Curraghmore Crossing	1904	Open	28 B3	
111¾	111:66	Luffney Crossing	1904	Open	28 B3	
112½	112:36	Rathpatrick Crossing	1904	Open	28 B3	
113¾	?	Lousiana Pacific/Coillte Timber Siding proposed siding to open 1997 with one level crossing at Gorteens	–	–	28 B3	
115½	?	Garage Siding used to supply fuel to CIE bus garage	?	Open	28 B3	

115¾	115:57	Waterford Abbey Junction opened as junction; opened as block post in 1904; junction with FRRHC Rosslare Line; joint DSER/FRRHC starts here	1906	Open	28 B4	14
76¼	76:20	MILEAGE CHANGE (mileposts measured from Mallow via Fermoy)				
76¼	76:20	Pier Head Crossing	1906	Open	28 B4	
76		R & H Halls Flour Mill Sidings	1883	Open	28 B3	
76	76:02	Junction end-on junction between GSWR and DSER/FHHRC joint line	1904	Open	28 B3	33
76	75:73	Mill Lane Crossing	1883	Open	28 B3	
76	75:73	New Wharf Junction North Wharf siding (34 chains) diverges here	?	?	28 B3	33
75¾	75:56	WATERFORD (NORTH) DSER used eastern end of station; WATERFORD PLUNKETT Station from 1966	1904	Open	28 B3	14

34 Dublin Broadstone to Galway

MGWR / 5ft 3in gauge / mileposts measured from Dublin Broadstone

Dublin Broadstone to Enfield opened 28-06-1847 by the MGWR.
Enfield to Hill of Down opened 06-12-1847 by the MGWR.
Hill of Down to Mullingar opened 02-10-1848 by the MGWR.
Mullingar to Galway opened 01-08-1851 by the MGWR.

Passenger services to Clonsilla, Lucan (North), Leixlip, Kilcock, Ferns Lock, Moyvalley and Clonhugh suspended from 08-10-1941 to 29-06-1942 due to fuel shortage.
Passenger services suspended 24-02-1947, although limited accommodation available between Dublin and Athlone on overnight perishable trains soon afterwards.
Passenger services resumed 24-05-1947.

Dublin Broadstone to Liffey Junction closed to passengers 18-01-1937 by the GSR.
Dublin Broadstone to Liffey Junction closed to goods 10-07-1944, remained in use for access to locomotive shed.
Dublin Broadstone to Liffey Junction closed completely 08-04-1961, lifted March 1977 by CIE.
Mullingar to Athlone Midland closed to passengers 18-05-1987 by CIE.
Mullingar to Athlone closed to all traffic except specials 02-11-1987 by CIE.

MPost Dist.	Miles & Chains	Place / Feature (notes)	Date Opened	Date Closed	Map Grid	Table Ref.
0	0:00	DUBLIN BROADSTONE closed 18-01-1937	1847	1937	32 C2	
1½	1:33	LIFFEY JUNCTION opened as a junction; platforms provided in 1877; closed as a junction in 1961	1864	1937	32 B1	130
1¾	1:67	BROOMBRIDGE opened 02-07-1990	1990	Open	32 B1	
2	2:06	Reilly's Crossing	1847	Open	32 B1	
2	2:06	REILLY'S BRIDGE race traffic only from 1902-1906 and 1934-1941	1847	1847	32 B1	
3	3:08	ASHTOWN closed 1934; in use as temporary platform for Pope John Paul II's visit 29-09-1979; re-opened 12-01-1982	1902	Open	32 A1	
3	3:10	Ashtown Crossing	1847	Open	32 A1	
3		Todd's Mill Siding	1882	c.1890	32 A1	
4½	4:35	Blanchardstown Crossing Replaced by bridge	1847	1875	17 A6	
4½	4:43	BLANCHARDSTOWN closed 01-01-1934	1847	1934	17 A6	
4¾	4:68	CASTLEKNOCK opened 02-07-1990	1990	Open	17 A6	
5¾	5:56	COOLMINE opened 02-07-1990	1990	Open	17 A6	
5¾	5:60	Coolmines Crossing	1847	Open	17 A6	
6½	6:25	Porterstown Crossing	1847	Open	17 A6	
7	7:07	Clonsilla Station Gates	1847	Open	17 A6	
7	7:08	CLONSILLA junction for Navan from 1862; closed 10-11-1947, re-opened 30-11-1981.	1847	Open	17 A6	46
7¾	7:66	Barberstown Crossing	1847	Open	17 A6	
9	8:72	LUCAN NORTH formerly COLDBLOW & LUCAN	1847	1941	17 A6	
9	?	Shackleton's Mill Siding	?	?	17 A6	
10¼	10:20	LEIXLIP (CONFEY) opened 02-07-1990	1990	Open	16 D6	
11¼	11:20	LEIXLIP LOUISA BRIDGE temporarily closed 10-11-1947 due to fuel shortage, did not re-open but was available for football specials etc.; re-opened 12-1981, formerly LOUISA BRIDGE & LEIXLIP	1847	Open	16 D6	
12¼	12:24	Blakestown Crossing	1847	Open	16 D6	
15	14:72	MAYNOOTH closed 10-11-1947; re-opened 30-11-1981	1847	Open	16 D6	
18	18:00	Branganstown Crossing	1847	Open	16 D6	
18½	18:40	KILCOCK (old station)	1847	1848	16 C6	
18½	18:50 ?	KILCOCK proposed station due to open 1997	–	–	16 C6	
19¼	19:12	KILCOCK (new station) closed 10-11-1947.	1848	1947	16 C6	
21	20:75	FERNS LOCK closed 10-11-1947.	1848	1947	16 C6	
21	20:75	Ferns Lock Crossing	1847	Open	16 C6	
23¼	23:11	Cappagh Crossing	1847	Open	16 C6	
23½	23:45	Kilbrook Crossing	1847	Open	16 C6	
23½	23:45	Kilbrook Ballast Pit	1891	1906	16 C6	
26¼	26:40	ENFIELD closed 10-11-1947; re-opened 16-05-1988	1847	Open	16 C6	36
27¾	27:62	Nesbitt Junction junction for Edenderry, junction removed in 1930 and lines ran parallel from Enfield	1877	1930	16 C6	36
30¼	30:28	MOYVALLEY opened by March 1850	1850	1963	16 B6	
31¼	31:20	Ribbontail Crossing also called Geraghty's Crossing	1847	Open	16 B6	
32¾	32:69	River Boyne Bridge	1847	Open	16 B5	
33	33:05	Ballynabarney No.1 Crossing	1847	Open	16 B5	
33½	33:45	Ballynabarney No.2 Crossing	1847	Open	16 B5	
35¾	35:55	HILL OF DOWN KINNEGAD & BALLIVOR until 1853, later KINNEGAD; closed 10-11-1947 but had re-opened by 03-10-1949	1847	1963	16 B5	
39½	39:40	Concrave Crossing	1848	Open	16 A5	
40	39:74	Annascannon Crossing	1848	Open	16 A5	
40½	40:40	Thomastown Crossing	1848	Open	16 A5	
40¾	40:69	Cushiontown Crossing	1848	Open	16 A5	
41¾	41:58	KILLUCAN closed 10-11-1947.	1848	1947	16 A5	
41¾	41:60	Killucan Station Gates	1848	Open	16 A5	
45¾	45:52	Downs Bog Crossing	1848	Open	16 A5	
47	46:72	Baltrasna Crossing	1848	Open	16 A5	
50¼	50:17	MULLINGAR junction for Sligo	1848	Open	15 D5	37
51¼	51:22	Newbrook Crossing	1851	Open	15 D5	
51½	51:40	NEWBROOK RACECOURSE race traffic only	1902 ?	1929 ?	15 D5	
53½	53:28	Bellmount Crossing also called Ballinca Crossing	1851	Open	15 D5	
56¾	56:70	Ballyhandy Crossing	1851	Open	15 D5	
58¼	58:20	Castletown Station Gates	1851	Open	15 C5	
58¼	58:22	CASTLETOWN	1851	1963	15 C5	
58¼	58:50	Adamstown Crossing also called Killians Crossing	1851	Open	15 C5	
61¾	61:56	STREAMSTOWN junction from 1863 for Clara	1851	1963	15 C6	35
63	62:71	Lisnagree Crossing	1851	Open	15 C6	
64½	64:42	Ballynabarna Crossing	1851	Open	15 C6	
67	67:05	Cappantack Crossing	1851	Open	15 B6	
68½	68:29	Moate Station Gates	1851	Open	15 B6	
68½	68:33	MOATE	1851	1987	15 B6	
69	68:71	Jones' Lake Crossing	1851	Open	15 B6	
69½	69:39	Coughlans Crossing also called Knockdomney Crossing	1851	Open	15 B6	
70¾	70:63	Magheramore Crossing	1851	Open	15 B6	
71½	71:40	Williamstown Crossing	1851	Open	15 B6	
72	72:08	Mount Temple Sidings closed ?; re-opened 1934; served Mount Temple Co-operative Society's premises	1919	Closed	15 B6	

76¼	76:20	Kilnafaddoge Crossing	1851	Open	15 A5	
		also called Cartrontroy Crossing				
77¼	77:29	Moorings Crossing	1851	Open	15 A5	
77¾	77:65	Athlone East Junction	1859	Open	15 A5	4
		opened as junction				
78	77:70	Shannon Bridge	1851	Open	15 A5	
		542ft long, opening span				
78	78:05	ATHLONE	1851	1985	15 A5	
		closed 14-01-1985				
78¼	78:24	Athlone West Junction	1860	Open	15 A5	44
		opened as junction				
79	79:04	Bellaugh Crossing	1851	Open	15 A5	
79¼	79:14	Monksland Ballast Pit	1877	1928	15 A5	
		siding diverged on Up side				
79½	79:42	Monksland Crossing	1851	Open	15 A6	
84¾	84:65	Carrowduff Station Gates	1851	Open	14 D6	
85	84:71	CARROWDUFF	1912	1963	14 D6	
		THOMASTOWN until 1925				
89½	89:45	Clarary Crossing	1851	Open	14 D6	
		also called Clara Bog Crossing				
91¾	91:51	Ballinasloe Station Gates	1851	Open	14 D6	
91¾	91:53	BALLINASLOE	1851	Open	14 D6	
101½	101:38	WOODLAWN	1851	Open	14 B6	
101½	101:41	Woodlawn Station Gates	1851	Open	14 B6	
104½	104:31	Doughcloon Crossing	1851	Open	14 B6	
107¼	107:20	ATTYMON	1890	Open	14 B6	41
		formerly ATTYMON JUNCTION, renamed late 1970s; junction for Loughrea				
108½	108:31	Bord na Móna Crossing	?	Open	14 B6	
110	109:79	Ballyboggan Crossing	1851	Open	14 A6	
112½	112:45	Caherryon Crossing	1851	Open	14 A6	
113½	113:32	Tuam Junction	1860	Open	14 A6	17
		junction to Tuam and Sligo				
113½	113:36	ATHENRY	1851	Open	14 A6	17
		also called ATHENRY & ENNIS JUNCTION and ATHENRY & TUAM JUNCTION on station nameboards				
113½	113:47	Athenry Station Gates	1851	Open	14 A6	
113¾	113:56	Ennis Junction	1869	Open	14 A6	17
		junction for Ennis and Limerick				
114	113:74	Castle Lambert Crossing	1851	Open	14 A6	
		also called Powells Crossing				
115	115:02	Agricultural College Siding	?	?	14 A6	
118¾	118:55	Sullivan's Crossing	1851	Open	13 D6	
120	120:04	Healy's Crossing	1851	Open	13 D6	
120¼	120:23	Frenchfort Crossing	1851	Open	13 D6	
121½	121:30	Oranmore Station Gates	1851	Open	13 D6	
121½	121:32	ORANMORE	1851	1963	13 D6	
122¼	122:14	Garraun Crossing	1851	Open	13 D6	
123½	123:34	Rosshill Crossing	1851	Open	13 D6	
124½	124:47	Morrough Crossing	1851	Open	13 D6	
126¼	126:28	Lough Atalia Viaduct	1851	Open	13 D6	
		240ft long, 4 spans, 1 opening span				
?	?	Galway Docks	1859	1867	13 D6	
		¼ mile Spur on Down side before station, closed 09-1867, declared dangerous				
126½	126:30	Junction for Clifden Branch	1895	1935	13 D6	
126¾	126:53	GALWAY	1851	Open	13 D6	39
		junction for Clifden; GALWAY CEANNT Station from 1966				

35 Streamstown Junction to Clara

MGWR / 5ft 3in gauge / mileposts measured from Dublin Broadstone

Streamstown Junction to Clara opened 01-04-1863 by the MGWR.

Passenger services suspended from 08-10-1941 due to fuel shortage.
Goods services suspended between Horseleap and Streamstown (Horseleap served from Clara) from 15-02-1943 due to fuel shortage.
Goods services suspended between Horseleap and Clara (Horseleap served from Streamstown) from 22-11-1943 due to fuel shortage.
All services suspended between Horseleap and Clara from 24-04-1944.
Goods services resumed from 10-12-1945.
Passenger services resumed from 04-11-1946.
All services suspended from 27-01-1947.
Closed to passengers 27-01-1947 by CIE.
Closed to regular goods 27-01-1947 by CIE.

Occasional Specials from 1947 to 1959, then used for wagon storage 1960 to 1963, last known movement 18-03-1963.

Closed completely 01-07-1965 by CIE, lifted 1966.

From 1863 to 1868 and after 03-1925, Clara trains on arriving at Streamstown Junction, trains would reverse or run round before proceeding back to Clara GSWR Station.

MPost Dist.	Miles & Chains	Place / Feature (notes)	Date Opened	Date Closed	Map Grid	Table Ref.
61¾	61:56	STREAMSTOWN	1851	1963	15 C6	34
61¾	61:74	Junction	1863	1947	15 C6	34
		junction to Athlone				
64¾	64:68	HORSELEAP	1875	1947	15 C6	
		opened July 1875				
66¼	66:20	Kilmalady Crossing	1863	1947	15 C6	
69	69:19	CLARA (MGWR)	1868	1925	15 C6	
		trains used GSWR Station 1863 to 1868; closed 02-03-1925				
69¼	69:23	CLARA EXCHANGE PLATFORM	1893	1925	15 C6	4
69¼	69:24	Streamstown Junction	1863	1947	15 C6	4
		junction with GSWR				
69½	69:35	Clara Crossing	1859	Open	15 C6	4
69½	69:47	CLARA (GSWR)	1859	Open	15 C6	4

36 Enfield to Edenderry

MGWR / 5ft 3in gauge / mileposts measured from Dublin Broadstone

Nesbitt Junction to Edenderry opened 10-04-1877 by the MGWR.

Closed to passengers 01-06-1931 by the GSR.
Closed to goods 01-01-1935 by the GSR but open for livestock specials.
Closed completely 01-04-1963 by CIE.

MPost Dist.	Miles & Chains	Place / Feature (notes)	Date Opened	Date Closed	Map Grid	Table Ref.
26½	26:40	ENFIELD	1847	Open	16 C6	34
		closed 10-11-1947, re-opened 16-05-1988				
27¾	27:62	Nesbitt Junction	1877	1930	16 C6	34
		junction for Mullingar, junction removed in 1930 and lines ran parallel from Enfield				
29½	29:36	Thomastown Crossing	1877	1963	16 B6	
30	30:09	Clonagh Crossing	1877	1963	16 B6	
32	32:10	Mylerstown Crossing	1877	1963	16 B6	
33½	33:32	Knockcor Crossing	1877	1963	16 B6	
		also called Carbury Crossing				
33¾	33:60	CARBURY	1877	1931	16 B6	
		closed to goods 01-04-1963				
36¼	36:14	Kishawanny Crossing	1877	1963	16 B6	
37¼	37:20	EDENDERRY	1877	1931	16 B6	
		closed to goods 01-04-1963				

37 Mullingar to Sligo

MGWR / 5ft 3in gauge / mileposts measured from Dublin Broadstone

Mullingar to Longford opened to passengers 08-11-1855 by the MGWR.
Mullingar to Longford opened for goods 01-11-1856 by the MGWR.
Longford to Sligo temporary terminus opened to passengers 03-12-1862 by the MGWR.
Longford to Sligo temporary terminus opened for goods 17-12-1862 by the MGWR.
Temporary terminus to current terminus opened 07-1863 by MGWR.
Sligo to Sligo Goods opened 17-12-1862 by the MGWR.
Sligo Goods to Sligo Quay (Deep Water Extension) opened 1900 by Sligo Harbour Commissioners.

Passenger services suspended 24-02-1947 due to fuel shortage.
Passenger services resumed 24-05-1947.

MPost Dist.	Miles & Chains	Place / Feature (notes)	Date Opened	Date Closed	Map Grid	Table Ref.
50¼	50:17	MULLINGAR	1848	Open	15 D5	34
		junction for Galway				
50¾	50:49	Canal Crossing	1855	Open	15 D5	
50¾	50:61	Canal Bridge Sidings	?	?	15 D5	
		served cattle loading bank				
52¼	52:15	Culleenmore Crossing	1855	Open	15 D5	
52½	52:33	Levington Crossing	1848	Open	15 D5	
53½	53:40	Lake Crossing	1855	Open	15 D5	
55½	55:40	Woodlands Crossing	1855	Open	15 D5	
56	56:00	Clonhugh Crossing	1855	Open	15 D4	
56¼	56:28	CLONHUGH	1855	1947	15 D4	
		opened as a private station for the Earl of Granard 1855-1858				
57½	57:37	MULTYFARNHAM	1855	1963	15 D4	
57½	57:40	Multyfarnham Station Gates	1855	Open	15 D4	
59¾	59:69	Lackenwood Crossing	1855	Open	15 D4	
61	60:69	INNY JUNCTION	1856	1947	15 D4	38
		CAVAN JUNCTION until 1878; closed to passengers 27-01-1947, as a junction 01-01-1960				
61¼	61:20	Clonkeen No.1 Crossing	1855	Open	15 D4	
61½	61:40	Clonkeen No.2 Crossing	1855	Open	15 D4	
63¼	63:17	Street Station Gates	1855	Open	15 D4	
63¼	63:18	STREET & RATHOWEN	1877	1963	15 D4	
64¾	64:63	Clonwhelan Crossing	1855	Open	15 C4	
67¾	67:52	EDGEWORTHSTOWN	1855	Open	15 C3	
		MOSTRIM (EDGEWORTHSTOWN) 1920s-1970s, MOSTRIM 1970s to 20-05-1995				
68¼	68:29	Ballymahon Crosing	1855	Open	15 C3	
		also called Tinare Crossing				
72¼	72:40	Clonahard Crossing	1855	Open	15 B3	
74¾	74:62	Knockshaw Crossing	1855	Open	15 B3	
75½	75:35	Ardnacassagh Crossing	1855	Open	15 B3	
76¼	76:22	LONGFORD	1855	Open	15 B3	
80	80:05	NEWTOWNFORBES	1863	1963	15 B3	
85¾	85:67	Dromard Crossing	1862	Open	15 B2	
		also called Rooskey Crossing				
87¼	87:25	DROMOD	1862	Open	15 B2	97
		interchange with CLR				
88½	88:30	Furnace Crossing	1862	Open	15 B2	
90	90:00	Gortinee	?	?	15 A2	
		siding which served a brick works c.1885				
92	92:00	River Shannon Bridge	1862	Open	15 A1	
		with opening 'telescopic' span, section drawn back rather than swivelling				
93	93:00	DRUMSNA	1863	1963	15 A1	
97¼	97:21	Kelleher's Crossing	1862	Open	15 A1	
		also called Cortober Crossing				
97¾	97:62	CARRICK-ON-SHANNON	1862	Open	15 A1	
106¼	106:10	Greatmeadow Crossing	1862	Open	14 D1	
106½	106:33	BOYLE	1862	Open	14 D1	
108½	108:42	Tinacarra Crossing	1862	Open	14 D1	
110½	110:35	Stonepark Crossing	1862	Open	14 C1	
112	112:02	Tawran Crossing	1862	Open	14 C1	
		also called Murray's Crossing				
112½	112:40	KILFREE JUNCTION	1874	1963	8 A6	42
		junction for Ballaghaderreen				
114¾	114:56	Seafin Crossing	1862	Open	8 A6	
118½	118:42	Ardree Crossing	1862	Open	8 A6	
119¾	119:60	Woodfield Crossing	1862	Open	8 A6	
120¼	120:15	BALLYMOTE	1862	Open	8 A6	
121¼	121:22	Rathdooney More Crossing	1862	Open	8 A5	
122¼	122:20	Cluid Crossing	1862	Open	8 A5	
122½	122:46	Carrowcushly Crossing	1862	Open	8 A5	
		also called Cloonamanagh Crossing				
123¾	123:53	Carrownree Crossing	1862	Open	8 A5	
127¾	127:56	COLLOONEY	1862	Open	8 A5	
128	128:02	Collooney Junction	1895	1976	8 A5	17
		junction for Limerick				
128¾	128:64	Carrignagat Junction	1875	1930	8 A5	108
		junction for Enniskillen, junction closed 1930 but SLNCR trains then used separate line to/from former junction to Ballysodare 1930-1957				
129¾	129:61	BALLYSODARE	1862	1963	8 A4	
130 ?	?	Pollexfen & Co Siding	1862	?	8 A4	
		½ mile siding to Mill				
134	?	SLIGO (temporary terminus)	1862	1863	8 A4	
		temporary terminus 03-12-1862 to 07-1863				
134	134:07	Junction to Quay Branch	1862	Open	8 A4	
		Quay Branch diverges at this point				
0	0:00	Junction from mainline	1862	Open	8 A4	
0¼	0:21	Oil Siding	1862	Open	8 A4	
?	?	Container Terminal	?	Open	8 A4	
0½	0:41	Level Crossing	1862	Open	8 A4	
0¾	0:61	Gouldings Waste Siding	?	Closed	8 A4	
1	1:01	Sligo Quay	1900	Open	8 A4	
		Cold Chon Siding at end of Quay				
134¼	134:16	SLIGO	1863	Open	8 A4	
		opened 07-1863, SLIGO McDIARMADA from 1966				

38 Inny Junction to Cavan

MGWR / 5'3" gauge / mileposts measured from Dublin Broadstone

Inny Junction to Cavan opened 08-07-1856 by the MGWR.

Passenger services suspended from 24-04-1944 due to fuel shortage.
Passenger services resumed from 10-12-1945.
Passenger services suspended from 27-01-1947.
Goods services suspended from 10-03-1947.
Goods services resumed 03-06-1947.

Closed to passengers 27-01-1947 by CIE.
Closed completely 01-01-1960 by CIE.

MPost Dist.	Miles & Chains	Place / Feature (notes)	Date Opened	Date Closed	Map Grid	Table Ref.
61	60:69	INNY JUNCTION	1856	1947	15 D4	37
		CAVAN JUNCTION until 1878; closed to passengers 27-01-1947, as a junction in 01-01-1960				
61¼	61:15	Derradd Crossing	1856	1960	15 D4	
61¾	61:65	Bottomy Crossing	1856	1960	15 D4	
63¼	63:13	O'Beirne's Crossing	1856	1960	15 D4	
64	63:72	Newman's Crossing	1856	1960	15 D3	
		also called Coolnagan Crossing				
64¼	64:20	Float Station Gates	1856	1960	15 D3	
65	64:75	FLOAT	1856	1947	15 D3	
65½	65:40	Clonmore Crossing	1856	1960	15 D3	
		also called Boyce's Crossing				
67½	67:40	Cooldoney Crossing	1856	1960	15 D3	
68¾	?	Ballywillan Ballast Pit Siding	?	1915	15 D3	
		siding about 1 mile long				
69¼	69:30	Springtown Crossing	1856	1960	15 D3	
70	70:09	BALLYWILLAN	1856	1947	15 D3	
71¾	71:60	Cullaboy Crossing	1856	1960	15 D2	
		also called Loughlin's Crossing				
74½	74:41	Carnagh Crossing	1856	1960	15 D2	
?		Carnagh Siding	1871	1877	15 D2	180
		exchange sidings with Carnagh Tramway				
75½	75:40	Grousehall Crossing	1856	1960	15 D2	
76¼	76:15	DRUMHOWNA	1876	1947	15 D2	
76¼	76:25	Drumhowna Station Gates	1856	1960	15 D2	
76¾	76:55	Drumcor Crossing	1856	1960	15 D2	
77	77:07	Drumcor (Cullen's) Crossing	1856	1960	15 D2	
79½	79:30	Lacken (Upper) Crossing	1856	1960	15 D2	
80¼	80:20	Legaginny Crossing	1856	1960	15 D1	
81½	81:34	CROSSDONEY	1856	1947	15 D1	
82½	82:40	Kevit Upper Crossing	1856	1960	15 D1	
85¾	85:47	CAVAN	1856	1947	15 D1	52
		closed to CIE passengers 14-10-1947, closed to GNRB passenger services 14-10-1957, closed to goods 01-01-1960.				
85¾	85:51	Junction	1862	1960	15 D1	52
		end-on junction with GNR(I) line to Clones				

39 Galway to Clifden

MGWR / 5ft 3in gauge / mileposts measured from Dublin Broadstone

Galway to Oughterard opened 01-01-1895 by the MGWR.
Oughterard to Clifden opened 01-07-1895 by the MGWR.
Shantalla Siding opened 1911 by the the MGWR.

Shantalla Siding closed and lifted 1923 by the MGWR.
Galway to Clifden closed completely 29-04-1935 by GSR.

MPost Dist.	Miles & Chains	Place / Feature (notes)	Date Opened	Date Closed	Map Grid	Table Ref.
126¾	126:53	GALWAY	1851	Open	13 D6	34
		GALWAY CEANNT STATION from 1966				
127 ?	?	Prospect Hill Tunnel	1895	1935	13 C6	
		89yds long				
127¼ ?	?	Corrib Viaduct	1895	1935	13 C6	
		3 x 150ft spans with 21ft Bascule opening span				
127½ ?	?	Siding	?	1935 ?	13 C6	
		trails in on down side				
127¾ ?	?	Junction	1911	1935 ?	13 C6	
0	0:00	Junction	1911	1923	13 C6	
0¼ ?	?	Crossing	1911	1923	13 C6	
		across Newcastle Road				
1¼ ?	?	Crossing	1911	1923	13 C6	
		across Shantallow Road				
1½	?	Shantalla	1911	1923	13 C6	
		siding to Marble & Granite Quarry				
128 ?	?	Crossing	1895	1935	13 C6	
		crosses road to Newcastle Distillery				
132½	132:36	Clooniff Crossing	1895	1935	13 C6	
133¾	133:67	Lodge Road Crossing	1895	1935	13 C6	
134¼	134:28	MOYCULLEN	1895	1935	13 C6	
134¼	?	Moycullen Station Gates	1895	1935	13 C6	
136¼	136:20	Corbally Crossing	1895	1935	13 C5	
136¼	?	Ross Station Gates	1895	1935	13 C5	
138¾	138:61	ROSS	1895	1935	13 C5	
		opened by July 1895				
139½	139:46	Killola Crossing	1895	1935	13 C5	
141½	141:48	Rushveela Crossing	1895	1935	13 C5	
142	142:10	Carrowntubber Crossing	1895	1935	13 B5	
143¼	143:20	OUGHTERARD	1895	1935	13 B5	
143¼	?	Oughterard Station Gates	1895	1935	13 B5	
147	147:05	Leam Crossing	1895	1935	13 B5	
149¾	149:60	Kill Crossing	1895	1935	13 B4	
153½	153:36	MAAM CROSS	1896	1935	13 A4	
153½	?	Maam Cross Station Gates	1895 ?	1935	13 A4	
160¾	160:55	RECESS HOTEL PLATFORM	1902	1922	13 A4	
162¾	162:67	RECESS	1895	1935	12 D4	
162¾		Recess Station Gates	1895	1935	12 D4	
163¾	163:65	Athry Lough Crossing	1895	1935	12 D4	
165½	165:32	Ballinafad Crossing	1895	1935	12 D4	
168¼	168:16	BALLYNAHINCH	1895	1935	12 D4	
		opened November 1895				
168¼	?	Ballynahinch Station Gates	1895	1935	12 D4	
172	172:06	Munga Crossing	1895	1935	12 C4	
174½	?	Clifden Station Gates	1895	1935	12 C4	
174½	174:46	CLIFDEN	1895	1935	12 C4	

40 Crossdoney Junction to Killeshandra

MGWR / 5ft 3in gauge / mileposts measured from Dublin Broadstone

Crossdoney Junction to Killeshandra opened 01-06-1886 by the MGWR

All services suspended from 24-04-1944 due to fuel shortage, regular goods not resumed.
Passenger services resumed from 10-12-1945.
Passenger services suspended 24-02-1947.
Livestock Specials only from 1947 to 01-03-1955.

Closed to Goods 24-04-1944 by GSR.
Closed passengers 27-01-1947 by CIE.

Closed completely 01-03-1955, lifted between April and August 1957.

MPost Dist.	Miles & Chains	Place / Feature (notes)	Date Opened	Date Closed	Map Grid	Table Ref.
81½	81:34	CROSSDONEY JUNCTION	1886	1947	15 D1	38
84	83:70	ARVA ROAD	1886	1947	15 D1	
88½	88:35	KILLESHANDRA	1886	1947	15 D1	

41 Attymon Junction to Loughrea

LALR – worked by MGWR
5ft 3in gauge / Milepost measured from Dublin Broadstone

Attymon Junction to Loughrea opened 01-12-1890 by the LALR.

Passenger services suspended 24-02-1947 due to fuel shortage.
Goods services suspended from 10-03-1947.
Goods services resumed 24-05-1947.
Passenger services resumed 16-06-1947.

Closed completely 03-11-1975 by CIE, lifted 1988.

MPost Dist.	Miles & Chains	Place / Feature (notes)	Date Opened	Date Closed	Map Grid	Table Ref.
107¼	107:20	ATTYMON	1890	1975	14 B6	34
		formerly ATTYMON JUNCTION,				
		renamed late 1970s				
108½	108:43	Killimor Crossing	1890	1975	14 B6	
110	110:00	Raford Crossing	1890	1975	14 B6	
110½	110:40	Killariv Crossing	1890	1975	14 B6	
111¼	111:15	Dunsandle Station Gates	1890	1975	14 B6	
111¼	111:26	DUNSANDLE	1890	1975	14 B6	
112¼	112:14	Toolobaun Crossing	1890	1975	20 B1	
113¾	113:60	Lynchford Crossing	1890	1975	20 B1	
115¾	115:50	Loughrea Crossing	1890	1975	20 B1	
		also called Cosmona Crossing				
116¼	116:15	LOUGHREA	1890	1975	20 B1	

42 Kilfree Junction to Ballaghaderreen

MGWR / 5ft 3in gauge / mileposts measured from Dublin Broadstone

Kilfree Junction to Ballaghaderreen opened 02-11-1874 by the SBJR.

Closed from 01-01-1876 to 24-03-1876.

All services suspended from 27-01-1947 due to fuel shortage.
Passenger and goods services resumed 24-05-1947.

Closed completely 04-02-1963 by CIE.

MPost Dist.	Miles & Chains	Place / Feature (notes)	Date Opened	Date Closed	Map Grid	Table Ref.
112½	112:40	KILFREE JUNCTION	1874	1963	8 A6	37
113	113:00	Mullaghroe Crossing	1874	1963	8 A6	
115	115:00	Falleens Crossing	1874	1963	14 C1	
117¼	117:28	ISLAND ROAD	1909	1963	14 C1	
117¼	117:28	Island Road Station Gates	1874	1963	14 C1	
119	119:01	Edmondstown Station Gates	1874	1963	14 C1	
119¼	119:15	EDMONDSTOWN	1874	1963	14 C1	
120	120:09	Tullaghanrock Crossing	1874	1963	14 C1	
122	122:03	BALLAGHADERREEN	1874	1963	14 B1	

43 Claremorris to Ballinrobe

BCLR – worked by MGWR
5ft 3in gauge / mileposts measured from Dublin Broadstone

Claremorris to Ballinrobe opened 01-11-1892 by the BCLR.

Passenger services suspended 24-02-1947 due to fuel shortage.
Goods services suspended from 10-03-1947.
Passenger and Goods services resumed 24-05-1947.

Closed completely 01-01-1960 by CIE.

MPost Dist.	Miles & Chains	Place / Feature (notes)	Date Opened	Date Closed	Map Grid	Table Ref.
135	134:67	CLAREMORRIS	1892	1960	13 D2	44
135½	135:39	Mayfield Crossing	1892	1960	13 D3	
137	137:12	Belladaff Crossing	1892	1960	13 D3	
138	137:70	Robe River Crossing	1892	1960	13 D3	
140½	140:35	Lissatava Crossing	1892	1960	13 D3	
142	142:05	HOLLYMOUNT	1892	1960	13 D3	
142¼	142:21	Hollymount Station Gates	1892	1960	13 D3	
143¼	143:30	Ballina No.1 Crossing	1892	1960	13 C3	
143½	143:39	Ballina No.2 Crossing	1892	1960	13 C3	
144½	144:30	Carrowmore Crossing	1892	1960	13 C3	
145	144:73	Cregmore Crossing	1892	1960	13 C3	
147½	147:31	BALLINROBE	1892	1960	13 C3	

44 Athlone to Westport Quay

MGWR / 5ft 3in gauge / mileposts measured from Dublin Broadstone

Athlone to Roscommon opened for passengers 13-02-1860 by the GNWR.
Athlone to Roscommon opened for goods 12-03-1861 by the GNWR.
Roscommon to Castlerea opened 15-11-1860 by the GNWR.
Castlerea to Ballyhaunis opened 09-09-1861 by the GNWR.
Ballyhaunis to Claremorris opened 19-05-1862 by the GNWR.
Claremorris to Castlebar opened 17-12-1862 by the GNWR.
Castlebar to Westport opened 29-01-1866 by the GNWR.
Westport to Westport Quay opened for goods 19-11-1873 by the GNWR.
Westport to Westport Quay opened for passengers 01-10-1874 by the GNWR.

Passenger services suspended 24-02-1947 due to fuel shortage.
Passenger services resumed 24-05-1947.

Westport to Westport Quay closed to passengers 16-09-1912 by the MGWR.
Westport to Westport Quay closed to regular goods 01-03-1943 by the GSR.
Westport to Westport Quay closed completely 1977 by CIE.

MPost Dist.	Miles & Chains	Place / Feature (notes)	Date Opened	Date Closed	Map Grid	Table Ref.
78	78:05	ATHLONE	1851	1985	15 A5	
78¼	78:24	Athlone West Junction junction for Galway	1860	Open	15 A5	34
81		Hill O'Berries Ballast Pit	?	?	15 A5	
81	80:73	Hill O'Berries Crossing also called Wood O'Berries or Barrymore	1860	Open	15 A5	
81¼	81:23	Hodson's Bay Crossing	1860	Open	15 A5	
84	83:79	Kiltoom Crossing	1860	Open	15 A5	
84	84:00	KILTOOM closed from 01-11-1860 to 08-1880	1860	1963	15 A5	
85¾	85:63	Glanduff Crossing	?	Open	15 A5	
87½	87:25	NINE MILE BRIDGE also called ST JOHN'S WELL, pilgrims to a Holy Well once a year	?	?	15 A4	
88¼	88:20	Lecarrow Ballast Pit extensive trackwork on Quarry floor junction removed 21-03-1989	1910	1989	15 A4	
88¾	88:66	Culleen Crossing	1860	Open	15 A4	
90	89:77	Knockcroghery Station Gates	1860	Open	15 A4	
90	90:00	KNOCKCROGHERY	1860	1963	15 A4	
91¾	91:58	Curry Crossing	1860	Open	14 D4	
93	92:71	BALLYMURRY	1860	1963	14 D4	
93	92:73	Ballymurry Crossing	1860	Open	14 D4	
95½	95:41	Slevin Crossing also called Ballymartin Crossing	1860	Open	14 D4	
96¼	96:19	ROSCOMMON	1860	Open	14 D4	
96¼	96:22	Roscommon Station Gates	1860	Open	14 D4	
99	98:79	Fuerty Crossing	1860	Open	14 D4	
101¾	101:73	DONAMON	1860	1963	14 D3	
102¼	102:28	Ballymacfrane Crossing	1860	Open	14 C3	
103	103:01	Stanleys No.1 Crossing also called Island No.1 Crossing	1860	Open	14 C3	
103¼	103:18	Stanleys No.2 Crossing also called Island No.2 Crossing	1860	Open	14 C3	
103¾	103:57	Stanleys No.3 Crossing also called Island No.3 Crossing	1860	Open	14 C3	
104	103:65	Stanleys No.4 Crossing also called Island No.4 Crossing	1860	Open	14 C3	
106	105:71	Bellacagher Crossing closed and realigned due to road improvements	1860	1966	14 C3	
106	106:03	Bellacagher Crossing replaced old crossing	1966	Open	14 C3	
106¾	106:66	Corrastoona Crossing	1860	Open	14 C3	
107¾	107:55	BALLYMOE opened 01-03-1861	1861	1963	14 C3	
109	109:01	Frenchlawn Crossing	1860	Open	14 C3	
110¼	110:25	Adragoole Crossing	1860	Open	14 C3	
112	111:70	Longford Crossing	1860	Open	14 C3	
112¾	112:53	CASTLEREA	1860	Open	14 C2	
112¾	112:61	Castlerea Station Gates	1861	Open	14 C2	
113¾	113:61	Arm No.1 Crossing also called Meyers No.1 Crossing	1861	Open	14 C2	
114	114:06	Arm No.2 Crossing also called Meyers No.2 Crossing	1861	Open	14 C2	
?		Ballast Pits	c.1891	?	14 C2	
114¾	114:60	Clonkeen Crossing	1861	Open	14 C2	
116¼	116:25	Clooncanra Crossing	1861	Open	14 B2	
118¾	118:60	BALLINLOUGH opened 01-01-1880	1880	1963	14 B2	
119½	119:31	Willsborough Crossing	1861	Open	14 B2	
?		Ballast Pit served by long siding from Ballinlough	?	?	14 B2	
120¼	120:18	Carrick Crossing	1861	Open	14 B2	
122	121:76	Kiltybo Crossing	1861	Open	14 B2	
122½	122:41	Cooloughra Crossing	1861	Open	14 B2	
123¾	123:73	Ballast Pit	?	?	14 B2	
124¼	124:02	BALLYHAUNIS	1861	Open	14 A2	
?		Hannon's Siding	?	?	14 A2	
?		Fahey's Siding	?	?	14 A2	
125	125:18	Hazelhill Crossing	1862	Open	14 A2	
126¼	126:19	Holywell Crossing	1862	Open	14 A2	
128¾	128:58	BEKAN opened 01-01-1909	1909	1963	14 A2	
131	131:00	Garryredmond Crossing also called Cloondin Crossing	1862	Open	14 A2	
134½	134:18	Clare Crossing also called Cloonconner Crossing	1862	Open	13 D2	
134¾	134:76	Claremorris South Junction junction for Athenry	1895	Open	13 D2	17
135	135:00	CLAREMORRIS	1862	Open	13 D2	17,43
135	135:06	Junction for Ballinrobe line	1892	1960	13 D2	43
135	135:16	Claremorris North Junction junction for Sligo	1895	1975	13 D2	17
135½	135:32	Fordes Crossing	1862	Open	13 D2	
136¼	136:17	Streamstown Crossing	1862	Open	13 D2	
137¾	137:51	Cloonboy Crossing	1862	Open	13 D2	
138½	138:49	Mossbrook Crossing	1862	Open	13 D2	
142½	142:35	BALLA	1862	1963	13 D2	
144¼	144:12	Carrontubber Crossing	1862	Open	13 C2	
144½	144:36	Smuttanagh Crossing	1862	Open	13 C2	
144¾	144:63	Bellcaragh Crossing also called Lisnolan Crossing	1862	Open	13 C2	
146	145:70	Manulla Junction	1868	Open	13 C1	

146	145:76	MANULLA JUNCTION closed 1963, re-opened 07-11-1988; junction for Ballina, exchange platform only, no road access	1868	Open	13 C1	45
150	149:74	CASTLEBAR	1862	Open	13 C1	
151¾	151:52	Knockaphunta Crossing	1862	Open	13 C1	
153¼	153:14	Derrycoosh Crossing	1866	Open	13 C1	
154	153:70	Cloonkeen Crossing	1862	Open	13 C1	
154¾	154:69	Greenhill Crossing	1866	Open	13 B1	
155½	155:39	ISLANDEADY possible flag station opened here c.1866, later station opened 05-1914, closed 17-06-1963	1914	1963	13 B1	
155½	155:42	Islandeady Station Gates	1866	Open	13 B1	
157¾	157:59	Rockfield Crossing	1866	Open	13 B2	
161¼	161:11	WESTPORT junction for Achill	1866	Open	13 B2	48
163	162:67	WESTPORT QUAY	1874	1912	13 B2	
163	163:00	Westport Quay Crossing	1873	1977	13 A2	
?	?	Westport Quay	1873	1977	13 A2	

45 Manulla Junction to Ballina and Killala

MGWR / 5ft 3in gauge / mileposts measured from Dublin Broadstone

Manulla Junction to Foxford opened 01-05-1868 by the GNWR.
Foxford to Ballina opened 19-05-1873 by the GNWR.
Ballina to Killala opened 02-01-1893 by the MGWR.

Ballina to Killala closed to passengers 01-10-1931 by GSR.
Ballina to Killala closed to goods 02-07-1934 by GSR.

Passenger services suspended 24-02-1947 due to fuel shortage.
Passenger services resumed 24-05-1947.

MPost Dist.	Miles & Chains	Place / Feature (notes)	Date Opened	Date Closed	Map Grid	Table Ref.
146	145:70	Manulla Junction	1868	Open	13 C1	44
146	145:76	MANULLA JUNCTION closed 1963, re-opened 07-11-1988; junction for Westport	1868	Open	13 C1	44
146¾	146:63	Barrackland Crossing	1868	Open	13 C1	
148½	148:47	Keelogues Crossing	1868	Open	13 C1	
149¾	149:63	Ballygommon Crossing	1868	Open	13 C1	
150¾	150:30	BALLYVARY opened 19-06-1894	1894	1963	13 D1	
150¾	150:60	Ballyvary Station Gates	1868	Open	13 D1	
151¼	151:16	Corraun Crossing	1868	Open	13 D1	
152¾	152:65	Strade Crossing also called Knockshanbally Crossing	1868	Open	13 D1	
152¾	?	Strade Ballast Pit	?	?	13 D1	
154	153:70	Darragh Crossing	1868	Open	13 D1	
155½	155:34	Pollagh Crossing	1868	Open	13 D1	
156	156:00	River Moy Bridge	1868	Open	7 B6	
156½	156:40	Corlummin Crossing	1868	Open	7 B6	
157¼	157:12	Foxford Station Gates	1868	Open	7 B6	
157¼	157:14	FOXFORD closed 1963, re-opened 07-11-1988	1868	Open	7 B6	
160¼	160:24	Lisaniska Crossing	1873	Open	7 B6	
161	161:07	Rathbaun Crossing	1873	Open	7 B6	
162	161:72	Shanclogh Crossing	1873	Open	7 B6	
165	165:10	Rahan's Crossing	1873	Open	7 B5	
165½	165:50	Behybaun Crossing	1873	Open	7 B5	
166½	166:21	BALLINA	1873	Open	7 B5	
166½	166:45	Ballina Station Gates	1873	Open	7 B5	
166¾	166:69	Crossmolina Siding spur now used for Oil deliveries to Bus Garage and Wood traffic	1873	Open	7 B5	
166½	166:47	Workhouse Crossing	1893	1934	7 B5	
168½	168:47	Culleens Crossing	1893	1934	7 B5	
169¾	169:51	Rathroeen Crossing	1893	1934	7 B5	
169¾	169:52	Coonealcaraun Crossing	1893	1934	7 B5	
171½	171:47	Knockalough Crossing	1893	1934	7 B4	
173½	173:48	Moyne Crossing	1893	1934	7 B4	
174¼	174:30	KILLALA	1893	1931	7 B4	

46 Clonsilla to Kingscourt

MGWR / 5ft 3in gauge / mileposts measured from Dublin Broadstone

Clonsilla to Navan (old station) opened 29-08-1862 by the DMR.
Navan (old station) to Navan Junction opened 15-12-1862 by the DMR.
Navan Junction to Kilmainham Wood opened 01-11-1872 by the NKR.
Kilmainham Wood to Kingscourt opened 01-11-1875 by the NKR.

Passenger services suspended from 08-10-1941 due to fuel shortage.
Passenger services resumed from 12-07-1943.
Passenger services suspended from 24-04-1944.
Passenger services resumed from 10-12-1945.
Passenger services suspended from 27-01-1947, not resumed.
Goods services suspended from 10-03-1947.
Goods services resumed 30-06-1947.

Clonsilla to Kingscourt closed to passengers 27-01-1947 by CIE.
Clonsilla to Navan closed completely 01-04-1963 by CIE.

MPost Dist.	Miles & Chains	Place / Feature (notes)	Date Opened	Date Closed	Map Grid	Table Ref.
7	7:08	CLONSILLA closed 10-11-1947, reopened 30-11-1981	1847	Open	17 A6	34
8½	8:40	Hilltown Crossing	1862	1963	17 A6	
10½	10:32	DUNBOYNE	1862	1947	16 D6	
12¾	12:52	FAIRYHOUSE BRIDGE originally race traffic only, regular advertised passenger service 1927-1931. Race traffic only 1931- c.1940	1881 ?	1931	16 D6	
15¾	15:60	Rathregan Crossing	1862	1963	16 D6	
16	15:72	BATTERSTOWN opened July 1863	1863	1947	16 D6	
19	18:73	DRUMREE	1862	1947	16 D5	
24¼	24:20	KILMESSAN JUNCTION junction for Athboy	1862	1947	16 D5	47
		Boyne Viaduct	1862	1947	16 D5	
27¼	27:25	BECTIVE	1862	1947	16 D4	
30¼		NAVAN (temporary terminus)	1862	1869	16 D4	
30½	30:42	NAVAN JUNCTION closed 27-01-1947	1869	1947	16 D4	57
30½	30:52	Navan East Junction junction with GNR(I) from Drogheda	1862	1963	16 D4	57
30½	30:56	Commons Road Crossing also called Poorhouse Crossing	1853	Open	16 C4	57
31	30:77	Navan West Junction junction with GNR(I) to Oldcastle; junction taken out of use in 1911 with two parallel lines running from Navan Junction Station and diverging at this point; junction reinstated as Tara Mines Junction 29-06-1977; also known as Nevinstown Junction, Kingscourt Junction, latterly Tara Mines Junction	1872	Open	16 C4	57
31¼	31:29	Moathill Crossing	1872	Open	16 C4	
32	31:75	Nevinstown Crossing	1872	Open	16 C4	
32¼	32:29	Rathaldon Crossing	1872	Open	16 C4	
33	32:73	Proudstown Park Crossing	1872	Open	16 C4	
33	33:00	PROUDSTOWN PARK race traffic only	1914	1939	16 C4	
33¼	33:20	Simonstown Crossing	1872	Open	16 C4	
34½	34:32	GIBBSTOWN	1872	1947	16 C4	
34½	34:40	Gibbstown Station Crossing	1872	Open	16 C4	
37	37:00	Wilkinstown Station Gates	1872	Open	16 C3	
37	37:00	WILKINSTOWN	1872	1947	16 C3	
37½	37:40	Lower Wilkinstown Crossing	1872	Open	16 C3	
38	38:00	Knightstown Crossing	1872	Open	16 C3	
38¾	38:60	Legga Crossing	1872	Open	16 C3	
40	39:70	CASTLETOWN HALT opened 01-12-1927.	1927	1935	16 C3	
40	39:73	Castletown Upper Crossing	1872	Open	16 C3	
40½	40:40	Castletown Lower Crossing	1872	Open	16 C3	
42¾	42:60	Spiddal Crossing	1872	Open	16 C3	

MPost Dist.	Miles & Chains	Place / Feature (notes)	Date Opened	Date Closed	Map Grid
43¼	43:23	NOBBER	1872	1947	16 C3
46¼	46:09	Kilmainham Wood Station Gates	1872	Open	16 C2
46¼	46:12	KILMAINHAM WOOD	1872	1947	16 C2
47½	47:40	Poles Crossing also called Lisnagrew	1875	Open	16 C2
48	47:75	Gypsum Siding served Gypsum Industries Ltd	1939	?	16 C2
49½	49:34	Enniskean Crossing	1875	Open	16 C2
50	?	Thompson's Siding served the Kingscourt Brick Company	?	?	16 C2
50¼	50:20	Kingscourt Crossing also called Corgarry Crossing	1875	Open	16 C2
50½	50:45	KINGSCOURT	1875	1947	16 C2

47 Kilmessan to Athboy

MGWR / 5ft 3in gauge / mileposts measured form Dublin Broadstone

Kilmessan to Trim opened for Goods 15-12-1863 by the DMR.
Trim to Athboy opened for Goods 21-01-1864 by the DMR.
Kilmessan to Athboy opened to Passengers 26-02-1864 by the DMR.

Passenger services suspended from 08-10-1941 due to fuel shortage.
Passenger services resumed from 10-12-1945.
Passenger services suspended from 27-01-1947.
Regular Goods services suspended from 10-03-1947.

Weekly livestock train continued to 1953. Used for wagon storage, lifted from 08-1958.

Kilmessan to Athboy closed to passengers 27-01-1947 by CIE.
Kilmessan to Athboy closed completely 15-01-1954 by CIE.

MPost Dist.	Miles & Chains	Place / Feature (notes)	Date Opened	Date Closed	Map Grid	Table Ref.
24¼	24:20	KILMESSAN JUNCTION	1864	1947	16 D5	46
25¾	25:60	Knockstown Crossing	1864	1954	16 C5	
29¾	29:61	TRIM	1864	1947	16 C5	
36½	36:32	ATHBOY	1864	1947	16 B4	

48 Westport to Achill

MGWR / 5ft 3in gauge / mileposts measured from Dublin Broadstone

Westport to Newport opened 01-02-1894 by the MGWR.
Newport to Mallaranny opened 16-07-1894 by the MGWR.
Mallaranny to Achill opened 13-05-1895 by the Board of Works (Achill Extension Rly).
Newport Deviation opened 07-03-1896 by the MGWR.

Westport to Achill closed to passengers 01-01-1935 by the GSR.
Re-opened 20-04-1936 due to road construction in the Achill area but finally closed as below.
Westport to Achill closed completely 01-10-1937 by the GSR.

MPost Dist.	Miles & Chains	Place / Feature (notes)	Date Opened	Date Closed	Map Grid	Table Ref.
160¾	160:74	WESTPORT	1866	Open	13 B2	44
?		Viaduct	1894	1937	13 B1	
161¾	161:65	Deerpark East Crossing	1894	1937	13 B1	
162¼	162:23	Attireesh Crossing	1894	1937	13 B1	
164¼	164:20	Cross Crossing also called Buckfield Crossing	1894	1937	13 B1	
164¼	164:30	Buckfield Crossing	1894	1937	13 B1	
165¼	165:31	Clooneen Crossing	1894	1937	13 B1	
165¾	165:68	Knocknaboley Crossing also called Kilmeena Crossing	1894	1937	13 B1	
166¼	166:28	Gortawarla Crossing	1894	1937	13 B1	
166¾	166:51	Corragaun Crossing	1894	1937	13 B1	
168¼		Tunnel 88yds long tunnel built as part of a 35 chain diversion from the original route	1896	1937	13 B1	
168½		Newport Tunnel 133yds long	1894	1937	13 B1	
168¾		Newport Viaduct 7 arch stone viaduct	1894	1937	13 B1	
168¾	168:69	NEWPORT	1894	1937	13 B1	
171¼	171:24	Doontrusk Crossing	1894	1937	13 A1	
171¾	171:73	Derrycooldrim Crossing	1894	1937	13 A1	
172½	?	Carrowsallagh Bridge Petrol Railcar stopping place for mail bags only from 11-1911 to 01-1916	1911	1916	13 A1	
173½	173:41	Knocknabreaga Crossing	1894	1937	13 A1	
174¼	174:26	Roskeen Crossing	1894	1937	13 A1	
177¼	177:24	Rosturk Crossing Petrol Railcar stopping place for mail bags only from 11-1911 to 01-1916	1894	1937	13 A1	
178¾		Mallaranny Ballast Pit	?	?	6 C6	
179¼		MALLARANNY (temporary station) temporary terminus from 16-07-1894 to 13-05-1895, replaced by a new station	1894	1895	6 B6	
179½	179:32	MALLARANNY	1895	1937	6 B6	
183¾	183:62	Tonregee East Crossing Petrol Railcar stopping place for mail bags only from 11-1911 to 01-1916	1895	1937	6 B6	
184¼	?	Tonregee Fish Siding	?	?	6 B6	
184¾	184:56	Tonregee West Crossing	1895	1937	6 B6	
186¾	186:61	Pollranny Crossing	1895	1937	6 B6	
187½	187:46	ACHILL	1895	1937	6 B6	

49 Dundalk Barrack Street to Londonderry Foyle Road

GNR(I) / 5ft 3in gauge / mileposts measured from Dundalk Barrack St.

Dundalk Barrack Street to Castleblayney opened 15-02-1849 by the DER.
Dundalk Junction (old station) to Dundalk West Junction opened 15-02-1849 by the DER.
Castleblayney to Ballybay opened 17-07-1854 by the DER.
Ballybay to Newbliss opened 14-08-1855 by the DER.
Newbliss to Lisnaskea opened 07-07-1858 by the DER.
Lisnaskea to Lisbellaw opened 16-08-1858 by the DER.
Lisbellaw to Enniskillen opened 15-02-1859 by the DER.
Enniskillen to Dromore Road opened 19-08-1854 by the LEnR.
Dromore Road to Fintona Junction opened 16-01-1854 by the LEnR.
Fintona to Omagh opened 15-06-1853 by the LEnR.
Omagh to Newtonstewart opened 13-09-1852 by the LEnR.
Newtonstewart to Strabane opened 09-05-1852 by the LEnR.
Strabane to Londonderry (Cow Market) opened 19-04-1847 by the LEnR.
Londonderry (Cow Market) to Londonderry Foyle Road opened 18-04-1850 by the LEnR.

Windmill Road Junction to Dundalk West Junction closed to passengers 01-01-1952 by the GNR(I).
Windmill Road Junction to Dundalk Barrack Street closed completely c.1955 by the GNRB.
Dundalk Barrack Street to Dundalk East Junction closed 31-12-1995 by IE.
Dundalk East Junction to West Junction closed completely 01-01-1952 by the GNR(I).
Dundalk Junction to West Junction closed 01-01-1960 by CIE.
Dundalk Junction to Clones closed to passengers 14-10-1957 by the GNRB.
Dundalk Junction to Clones closed completely 01-01-1960 by CIE.
Clones to Omagh closed completely 01-10-1957 by the GNRB.
Fintona to Fintona Junction closed 01-10-1957 by the GNRB.
Omagh to Londonderry Foyle Road closed 15-02-1965 by the UTA.

Londonderry Foyle Road southwards being re-opened as a 3'0" gauge preserved railway by the Foyle Valley Railway. Circa 2½ miles open in 1997.

MPost Dist.	Miles & Chains	Place / Feature (notes)	Date Opened	Date Closed	Map Grid	Table Ref.
0½	0:36	DUNDALK QUAY STREET	1873	1952	17 A1	104
0½		Quay Street Station Gates	1873	c.1955	17 A1	104
0¼	0:11	Windmill Road Junction end-on junction with DNGR	1873	c.1955	17 A1	104
		Windmill Road Crossing replaced by bridge c.1880	1873	c.1880	17 A1	104

0¼	0:20	Barrack Street Goods Yard	1849	1995	17 A1	104
		closed 31-12-1995				
0¼	0:20	Dundalk Barrack Street	–	–	17 A1	104
		no passenger train known to have used this station				
0	0:00	Junction	1873	c.1955	17 A1	104
		junction with Quay Street Line				
0	0:00	Junction	1873	c.1955	17 A1	104
		junction from Barrack Street				
?	?	Pork Factory Siding	?	?	17 A1	
		facing siding on down side, served Lunham's Pork Factory				
1		East Junction	1849	1960	17 A1	50
1¼		Square Crossing	1849	1960	17 A1	50
0	0:00	DUNDALK JUNCTION	1893	Open	17 A1	50
		CLARKE STATION from 1966				
?	?	Central Junction	1849	1960	17 A1	50
?	?	DUNDALK JUNCTION (DBJR)	1849	1893	17 A1	50
		DER platforms adjacent to DBJR station				
0½	0:36	West Junction	1849	1960	17 A1	
1½	1:34	West Junction	1849	1960	17 A1	
3		Carrickallen Crossing	1849	1960	17 A1	
		also a railcar stop, 1935 to 1940s				
4		KELLYBRIDGE HALT	c.1924	1957	17 A1	
7¼		INNISKEEN	1849	1960	16 D1	55
		junction for the Carrickmacross branch				
7¾		Lannatt Crossing	1849	1960	16 D1	
		also a railcar stop, 1935 to 1940s				
9½		BLACKSTAFF HALT	1927	1957	16 D1	
		opened 15-08-1927				
9½		Blackstaff Station Gates	?	1960	16 D1	
12		CULLOVILLE	1849	1957	10 B6	
14		Drumgoose Crossing	1849	1960	10 B6	
		also a railcar stop, 1935 to 1940s				
15½		Annadrumman Crossing	1849	1960	10 B6	
		also a railcar stop, 1935 to 1940s				
16		Carragartha Crossing	1849	1960	10 B6	
		also a railcar stop, 1935 to 1940s				
18		Castleblayney Station Gates	1849	1960	10 B6	
18		CASTLEBLAYNEY	1849	1957	10 B6	
21½		Doohamlet Siding	?	?	10 A6	
		in use c.1939				
21½		Doohamlet Crossing	1854	1960	10 A6	
		also a railcar stop, 1935 to 1940s				
24¼		Knocknamaddy Crossing	1854	1960	10 A6	
		also a railcar stop, 1935 to 1940s				
24¾		BALLYBAY	1854	1957	10 A6	64
26¼		Shantonagh Junction	1860	1960	10 A6	64
		junction for Cootehill. The railcar stop, spelt Shantona Junction, in use 1935 to 1940s				
28½		Lislynchahon Crossing	1855	1960	10 A6	
		also a railcar stop, 1935 to 1940s				
29½		Monaghan Road Station Gates	1855	1960	9 D6	
29½		MONAGHAN ROAD	1859	1957	9 D6	
		opened by 01-03-1859				
31½		Killygraggy No.1 Crossing	1855	1960	9 D6	
32		Killygraggy No.2 Crossing	1855	1960	9 D6	
		Railcar Stop, 1935 to 1940s				
33		Dromate Crossing	1855	1960	9 D5	
		also a railcar stop, 1935 to 1940s				
34		Drumshannon Crossing	1855	1960	9 D5	
		also a railcar stop, 1935 to 1940s				
35		NEWBLISS	1855	1957	9 D5	
38½		Laeger Crossing	1858	1960	9 D5	
		also a railcar stop, 1935 to 1940s				
?		Clones East Junction	1863	1960	9 C5	52
		junction with Armagh line				
39½		Clones Station Gates	1858	1960	9 C5	52
39½		CLONES	1858	1960	9 C5	52
		Cavan and Enniskillen line run parallel for ¾ mile				
40		Carn Crossing	1858	1960	9 C5	52
40¼		Cavan line diverges here	1862	1960	9 C5	52
40½		Clonedergole Crossing	1858	1957	9 C5	
41		Clonmaulin Crossing	1858	1957	9 C5	
		also a railcar stop, 1935 to 1940s				
42		Carrigans Crossing	1858	1957	9 C5	

42½		Kilroot Crossing	1858	1957	9 C5	
43		Legnacaffry Crossing	1858	1957	9 C5	
43½		Kilready Crossing	1858	1957	9 C5	
44½		Gortgommon Crossing	1858	1957	9 C5	
		at Newtownbutler station, locally called Mulally's				
44½		NEWTOWNBUTLER	1858	1957	9 C5	
44½		Aghagay Crossing	1858	1957	9 C5	
		locally called McLaughlin's				
46½		Lisnanock Crossing	1858	1957	9 C5	
		also a railcar stop, 1935 to 1940s				
		Locally called Gribben's				
48		Sallaghy Crossing	1858	1957	9 B5	
		also a railcar stop, 1935 to 01-10-1957				
48¼		Keady Crossing	1858	1957	9 B5	
		also a railcar stop, 1935 to 1940s				
49¼		Aughalurcher Crossing	1858	1957	9 B5	
		also a railcar stop, 1935 to 1940s				
49¾		Killynamph Crossing	1858	1957	9 B5	
		also a railcar stop, 1935 to 1940s				
50¼		Castlebalfour Crossing	1858	1957	9 B5	
		also a railcar stop, 1935 to 1940s				
50¾		Barnhill Crossing	1858	1957	9 B5	
		also a railcar stop, 1935 to 1940s, locally called Murphy's				
51¼		LISNASKEA	1858	1957	9 B5	
51¼		Drumhaw Crossing	1858	1957	9 B5	
		at Lisnaskea station, locally called Symington's				
52¼		Lisnagole Crossing	1858	1957	9 B4	
		also a railcar stop, 1935 to 1940s				
52¾		Aughnaskew Crossing	1858	1957	9 B4	
		also a railcar stop, 1935 to 1940s				
		locally called Armstrong's				
53¾		Drumgoon Crossing	1858	1957	9 B4	
		at Maguiresbridge station				
53¾		MAGUIRESBRIDGE	1859	1957	9 B4	91
		opened by 01-03-1859				
54		Kilnashambally Crossing	1858	1957	9 B4	
		also a railcar stop, 1935 to 1940s				
54¾		Coolane Crossing	1858	1957	9 B4	
		also a railcar stop, 1935 to 1940s,				
		locally called Whitley's				
57		LISBELLAW	1858	1957	9 B4	
60		Ballylucas Crossing	1859	1957	9 B4	
		also a railcar stop, 1935 to 01-10-1957,.				
		also locally called Whitley's				
62		ENNISKILLEN (DER station)	1860	1957	9 B4	108
		opened 1860 to replace LEnR station				
62¼		ENNISKILLEN (LEnR station)	1854	1860	9 A4	
		closed when new DER station opened				
62½		Drumclay Crossing	1854	1957	9 A4	
		also a railcar stop, 1935 to 1940s				
64½		GORTALOUGHAN HALT	1940	1957	9 B3	
65¾		Drumcullion Crossing	1854	1957	9 B3	
65¾		DRUMCULLION HALT	1940s	1940s	9 B3	
		unadvertised halt during 1940s servicing workers at the Seaplane Base on Lower Lough Erne				
66½		Drumsonnis Crossing	1854	1957	9 B3	
		also a railcar stop, 1935 to 1940s				
67½		BALLINAMALLARD	1854	1957	9 B3	
70		BUNDORAN JUNCTION	1854	1957	9 B3	58
		formerly LOWTHERSTOWN ROAD (1854-61), IRVINESTOWN (1861-63), IRVINESTOWN ROAD (1863-66)				
?	?	Bundoran 'South' junction	1866	1957	9 B3	58
?	?	Bundoran 'East' junction	1894	1957	9 B3	58
70½		Loughterush Crossing	1854	1957	9 B3	
		also a railcar stop, 1935 to 1940s				
71½		TRILLICK	1854	1957	9 B3	
		closed for a period by INWR				
71½		Trillick Station Gates	1854	1957	9 B3	
73¼		Shanmullagh Crossing	1854	1957	9 B3	
		also a railcar stop, 1935 to 01-10-1957				
74¼		Galbally Crossing	1854	1957	9 B3	
		also a railcar stop, 1935 to 1940s				
75¼		DROMORE ROAD	1854	1957	9 B3	
77¼		Lissaneden Crossing	1854	1957	9 C3	
		also a railcar stop, 1935 to 1940s				

MPost/Dist.	Miles & Chains	Place / Feature (notes)	Date Opened	Date Closed	Map Grid	Table Ref.
80¾		Racrane Crossing also a railcar stop, 1935 to 1940s	1854	1957	9 C3	
0	0:00	FINTONA branch horse-worked 1854-1957	1853	1957	9 C3	
0¾	0:55	FINTONA JUNCTION	1854	1957	9 C3	
81		FINTONA JUNCTION	1854	1957	9 C3	
82¼		Togher Crossing also a railcar stop, 1935 to 1940s	1853	1957	9 C2	
83		Kiltamnagh Crossing also a railcar stop, 1935 to 1940s	1853	1957	9 C2	
83½		Edergole Upper Crossing also a railcar stop, 1935 to 1940s	1853	1957	9 C2	
86¾		Culmore Crossing also a railcar stop, 1935 to 1940s	1853	1957	9 C2	
87¾		OMAGH (new station) at junction with Portadown line	1863	1965	9 C2	53
88 ?		OMAGH (old station) closed when new station opened at junction	1852	1863	9 C2	
88¼		Mullaghmena Crossing	1852	1965	9 C2	
89¼		Drumquin Crossing	1852	1965	9 C2	
?		Nestlé Milk Factory Siding	?	1965	9 C2	
89¾		Conneywarren Crossing	1852	1965	9 C1	
90¾		Tully Crossing	1852	1965	9 C1	
91¼		MOUNTJOY HALT open 1852-59, 1870-78, 1928-35	1852	1935	9 C1	
91¾		Tattyraconnaghty Crossing	1852	1965	9 C1	
92		Castletown Crossing	1852	1965	9 C1	
92¼		Bradford's Bridge crosses River Strule	1852	1965	9 C1	
94		Blackrock Bridge crosses River Strule	1852	1965	9 C1	
96½		Moyle Bridge crosses River Strule	1852	1965	9 C1	
96¾		Moyle Crossing	1852	1965	9 C1	
97¼		NEWTOWNSTEWART	1852	1965	9 C1	
100¾		Mulvin Bridge crosses River Mourne	1852	1965	3 D6	
101¼		Victoria Bridge Station Gates	1852	1965	3 D6	
101¾		VICTORIA BRIDGE curving bay platform serving CVBT	1852	1965	3 D6	103
102 ?		Breen Bridge crosses River Mourne	1852	1965	3 D6	
102¼ ?		TRAFALGAR private station	?	?	3 D6	
102½		Camus Bridge crosses River Mourne	1852	1965	3 D6	
103½		SION MILLS a siding also served a Flax Mill	1852	1965	3 D6	
103½		Sion Mills Station Gates	1852	1965	3 D6	
106		Clady Crossing	1852	1965	3 D6	
106¼		Finn Valley Junction opened as Junction, disconnected 15-07-1894 due to regauging the FVR to 3'0"	1863	1894	3 D6	93
106¾		Strabane Station Gates	1852	1965	3 D6	
106¾		STRABANE DR/CDRJC station adjacent, connected by footbridge	1847	1965	3 D6	93,96
107¼		Greenbrae Crossing	1847	1965	3 D6	
109¾		Hoffmans Lime Kilns Siding	1874	?	3 D5	238
109¾		PORTHALL	1848	1965	3 D5	
109¾		Porthall Station Gates	1847	1965	3 D5	
110¾		Porthall Crossing	1847	1965	3 D5	
111½		CARRICKMORE remained as a flag station/market days platform 1853-1861	1847	1853	3 D5	
111¾		Carrickmore Crossing	1847	1965	3 D5	
114		ST JOHNSTON	1847	1965	3 D5	
114		St Johnston Station Gates	1847	1965	3 D5	
115¾		CARRIGANS	1847	1965	3 D5	
120¾		LONDONDERRY COW MARKET	1847	1850	3 D5	135
		LONDONDERRY (GALLOWS STRAND) temporary terminus, later became Goods Depot	?	?	3 D4	
121½		LONDONDERRY FOYLE ROAD called FOYLE ROAD by 1904	1850	1965	3 D4	

50 Dublin Amiens Street to Belfast Great Victoria Street & Ardee Branch

GNR(I) / 5ft 3in gauge / mileposts measured from Dublin Connolly

6ft 2in gauge from Belfast Great Victoria St to Portadown until 05-1847

Dublin Amiens Street to Dublin (temporary terminus) opened 29-11-1844 by the DDR.
Dublin (temporary terminus) to Drogheda opened 26-05-1844 by the DDR.
Ossory Road Junction opened 09-04-1973 by CIE.
Ossory Road Junction to Suburban Junction opened 09-08-1981 by CIE.
East Wall Junction to Church Road Junction opened 01-12-1877 by the GNR(I).
Drogheda to Newfoundwell via temporary wooden viaduct opened 11-05-1853 by the DBJR.
Drogheda to Newfoundwell via permanent viaduct opened 05-04-1855 by the DBJR.
Drogheda Cement Branch opened 04-1938 by the GNR(I).
Newfoundwell to Dundalk opened 15-02-1849 by the DBJR.
Dundalk South Junction to Dundalk East Junction opened 1874 by the DBJR.
Dromin Junction to Ardee opened 01-08-1896 by the DBJR.
Dundalk to Wellington Inn opened 31-07-1850 by the DBJR.
Wellington Inn to Mullaghglass opened 10-06-1852 by the DBJR.
Mullaghglass to Portadown opened 06-01-1852 by the DBJR.
Portadown to Seagoe opened 12-09-1842 by the UR.
Seagoe to Lurgan opened 31-01-1842 by the UR.
Lurgan to Lisburn opened 18-11-1841 by the UR.
Lisburn to Belfast Great Victoria Street opened 12-08-1839 by the UR.

Ossory Road Junction closed 1981 by CIE.
East Wall Junction to Church Road Junction closed to passengers 17-01-1921 by GNR(I).
Dromin Junction to Ardee closed to passengers 03-06-1934 by the GNR(I).
Dromin Junction to Ardee closed to goods 03-11-1975 by CIE.
Dundalk South Junction to Dundalk East Junction closed 31-03-1995 by IE.
Belfast Central Junction to Great Victoria Street Closed 26-04-1976 by NIR.

Belfast Central Junction to Great Victoria Street re-opened 30-09-1995 by NIR.

Electrified between Connolly and Howth Junction at 1,500V DC overhead, electric service commenced 23-07-1984.

MPost Dist.	Miles & Chains	Place / Feature (notes)	Date Opened	Date Closed	Map Grid	Table Ref.
0	0:00	DUBLIN AMIENS STREET opened 29-11-1844, DUBLIN CONNOLLY from 1966	1844	Open	32 C2	
0	0:00	AMIENS STREET JUNCTION Station	1891	Open	32 C2	31
	0:05	Amiens Street Junction junction with Newcomen Bridge lines	1892	Open	32 C2	115
	0:07	Junction with North Strand Line junction with North Strand Road Junction lines	1906	Open	32 C2	114
0¼	0:11	Junction with GNR(I)	1891	Open	32 C2	
0¼	0:21	Junction with Loop Line	1891	Open	32 D2	31
?	?	Ossory Road Junction opened 09-04-1973 by CIE to connect former GNR(I) lines to the Link Line; removed 1981 as part of electrification remodelling; new crossover installed nearer station	1973	1981	32 D2	114
0	0:00	Ossory Road Junction new Double track junction opened 09-08-1981 from Link Line to GNR(I) Lines	1981	Open	32 D2	114
?	?	Suburban Junction Connection on GNR(I) Lines opened 09-08-1981	1981	Open	32 D2	
		Suburban Junction connection from Link Line	1981	Open	32 D2	114
0¼		DUBLIN (temporary terminus) open 05-1844 to 11-1844	1844	1844	32 D2	
0	:00	Church Road Junction (West)	1877	Open	32 D2	114
0½	0:40	East Wall Junction section called 'Drogheda Curve'	1877	Open	32 D2	
1	0:57	East Wall Junction	1877	Open	32 D2	
1	1:00	Fairview Depot with staff halt on main lines, rendered redundant by new Clontarf Road Station	?	1997	32 D2	

1¼	1:26 ?	CLONTARF ROAD	1997	Open	32 D2	
		opened 01-09-1997				
1¾	1:53	CLONTARF	1844	1956	32 D2	
		closed 1850 weekdays, 1852 Sundays, re-opened 1898, closed again 03-09-1956				
2 ?		KILLESTER	1845	1847	32 D1	
		Dublin & Drogheda Railway station				
2¼	2:31	KILLESTER	1923	Open	32 D1	
		opened by the GNR(I)				
3	3:00	HARMONSTOWN	1957	Open	32 E1	
		opened 07-01-1957				
3¾	3:57	RAHENY	1844	Open	32 E1	
4½	4:40	KILBARRACK	1969	Open	17 B6	
4¾	4:58	Howth Junction	1846	Open	17 B6	51
4¾	4:64	HOWTH JUNCTION	1846	Open	17 B6	51
		formerly called 'JUNCTION' until 1912				
5¼	5:22	BALDOYLE	1844	1846	17 B6	
		closed when Howth line opened				
6¾	6:56	PORTMARNOCK	1844	Open	17 B6	
9	9:00	MALAHIDE	1844	Open	17 B6	
9¼	9:14	Malahide Viaduct	1844	Open	17 B6	
11½	11:35	DONABATE	1844	Open	17 B6	
12½	12:36	Rogerstown Viaduct	1844	Open	17 B5	
14	13:74	RUSH & LUSK	1844	Open	17 B5	
16	16:01	BALDUNGAN	1845	1847	17 B5	
		closed 01-04-1847				
17¼	17:19	SKERRIES GOLF CLUB HALT	1927	1967	17 B5	
		opened 07-1927, closed 18-09-1967				
18	17:77	SKERRIES	1844	Open	17 B5	
		DDR Ballast Pit behind Goods Shed				
20¼	20:13	Ardgillan Crossing	1844	Open	17 B5	
20½	?	ARDGILLAN	1844	?	17 B5	
		private station for Taylor family				
21½	21:47	Balbriggan Viaduct	1844	Open	17 B5	
21¾	21:60	BALBRIGGAN	1844	Open	17 B4	318
24	23:59	Delvin Viaduct	1844	Open	17 B4	
24	24:00	GORMANSTON	1845	Open	17 B4	
25¾	25:63	MOSNEY	1948	Open	17 B4	
		formerly called BUTLIN'S (MOSNEY), fully advertised from 02-06-1958				
27	26:78	Nanny Viaduct	1844	Open	17 B4	
27	27:13	LAYTOWN	1844	Open	17 B4	
		named LAYTOWN & BETTYSTOWN 1913 to 19 ??				
28½	28:47	BETTYSTOWN	1844	1847	17 B4	
		closed 10-1847				
31¼	31:41	Point of Deviation	1855	1855	17 A4	

31¼		Point of Deviation	1855	1855	17 A4	
?		Buckie's Sidings	?	Open ?	17 A4	
		on site of original station				
31½		DROGHEDA (old station)	1844	1855	17 A4	

31½	31:47	Junction	1850	Open	17 A4	57
		junction for Navan				
31¾	31:60	DROGHEDA	1855	Open	17 A4	
		DROGHEDA MacBRIDE Station from 1966				
32	32:00	Boyne Viaduct	1853	Open	17 A4	
		temporary viaduct open 11-05-1853, main viaduct opened 05-04-1855				
32¼	32:20	Newfoundwell Viaduct	1853	Open	17 A4	
32½	32:45	NEWFOUNDWELL	1849	1855	17 A4	
		original D&BJR terminus, closed 05-04-1855				
32½	32:48	Cement Branch Junction	1938	Open	17 A4	
		trails in on Up line only				

0	0:00	Cement Branch Junction	1938	Open	17 A4	
0¼	0:19	Ballast Depot Sidings	1938	Open	17 A4	
0½	0:39	Newfoundwell Crossing	1938	Open	17 A4	
0¾	0:65	Newtown Crossing	1938	Open	17 A4	
0¾	0:71	Oil Terminal Sidings	1938	Open	17 A4	
1	1:08	IE Boundary Fence	1938	Open	17 A4	
	?	Level Crossing	1938	Open	17 A4	
1	?	Boyne Road Cement Factory	1938	Open	17 A4	
		Premier Periclase Cement Works				

32½		Greenbatter Crossing	1849	?	17 A3	
41¾	41:56	DUNLEER	1851	1984	17 A3	
		closed 06-09-1976, re-opened 11-06-1979, closed 26-11-1984				
43½	43:51	DROMIN JUNCTION	1896	1955	17 A2	56
		closed as junction 31-10-1975				

0	0:00	DROMIN JUNCTION	1896	1955	17 A2	50
		closed as junction 31-10-1975				
5	4:66	ARDEE	1896	1934	16 D2	
		closed for goods 31-10-1975				

47¼	47:16	CASTLEBELLINGHAM	1851	1976	17 A2	
		Closed 06-09-1976				
49¼	49:14	Dromiskin Crossing	1849	Open	17 A2	
49½	49:50	Commons Crossing	1849	Open	17 A2	
53½	53:40	Dundalk South Junction	1874	1995	17 A1	49

53½	53:40	Dundalk South Junction	1874	1995	17 A1	
0	0:00	MILEAGE CHANGE (mileposts measured from Dundalk Sth Junction)				
0½	0:36	Dundalk East Junction	c.1874	1995	17 A1	49
0½	1:38	Dundalk Barrack Street	–	–	17 A1	49
		no passenger trains known to have used this station				
1½	1:38	Barrack Street Goods	1849	1995	17 A1	49
		closed 31-03-1995				

53½		Dundalk Works	1881	1958	17 A1	
		GNR(I) Works on down side				
53½		Cambricville Brewery Siding	?	?	17 A1	418
		served Macardle Moore Brewery				
53¾	53:68	Dundalk Square Crossing	1849	1960	17 A1	49
		removed 07-1954				
54	53:76	DUNDALK JUNCTION (DBJR)	1849	1893	17 A1	49
		original DBJR station in 'V'				
54	54:10	Dundalk Central Junction	1849	1960	17 A1	49
54¼	54:30	DUNDALK	1893	Open	17 A1	
		formerly DUNDALK JUNCTION, CLARKE STATION from 1966				
54¼		Harp Brewery Sidings	1972 ?	Open	17 A1	
		facing sidings on Up line serving Brewery				
55	55:00	Manisty's Siding	?	c.1920	17 A1	
		facing siding on down side serving brickworks				
58	57:78	MOUNT PLEASANT	1850	by 1887	17 A1	
		named PLASTER 1850-1851, MOUNT PLEASANT & JONESBOROUGH 1851-1855; closed 30-11-1865, re-opened later, finally closed by 1887				
58	58:00	Mount Pleasant Station Gates	1850	Open	17 A1	
59½	59:48	Border	1922	Open	10 C6	
		border of Éire and Northern Ireland				
60½	60:45	Faughal Upper Crossing	1850	Open	10 C6	
		also called Faughaleitra Crossing				
62½	62:40	ADAVOYLE	1892	1933	10 C6	
63	63:09	Meigh Crossing	1850	1985	10 C6	
64¼		WELLINGTON INN	1850	1852	10 C6	
69¼	69:20	NEWRY	1855	Open	10 C5	
		formerly NEWRY, later MONAGHAN ROAD, later NEWRY MAIN LINE, later BESSBROOK, closed 1942, re-opened 14-05-1984 as NEWRY				
69½	69:40	Craigmore Viaduct	1852	Open	10 C5	
		18 arch masonary viaduct, 140ft high				
70¾	70:52	NEWRY ARMAGH ROAD	1852	c.1856	10 C5	
		MULLAGHGLASS until 1854				
71¾	71:63	Junction from Warrenpoint	1854	1965	10 C5	60
71¾	71:71	GORAGHWOOD	1854	1965	10 C5	60
71¾		Church Lane Crossing	1852	?	10 C5	
?	?	Goraghwood Ballast Quarry	1911	?	10 C5	
		opened February 1911; adjacent to station				
72¼	72:18 ?	Warrenpoint-Armagh line overbridge	1864	1955	10 C5	60
73½	73:43	Knockarney Crossing	1852	Open	10 C5	
		also a railcar stop, 1935 to 04-01-1965				
76	76:05	Augheranter Crossing	1852	Open	10 C5	
		also a railcar stop, open 1935 closed by 06-1955				
77	76:70	Poyntzpass Station Crossing	1852	Open	10 C5	
77	76:73	POYNTZPASS	1852	Open	10 C5	
		closed 04-01-1965, re-opened 14-05-1984				
78	78:05	Acton Crossing	1852	Open	10 C4	
		also a railcar stop, 1935 to ?				
79¼		Crozier's Crossing	1852	?	10 C4	
79½	79:47	SCARVA	1852	Open	10 C4	59
		closed 04-01-1965, re-opened 14-05-1984				
79¾	79:69	Junction for Banbridge line	1859	1955	10 C4	59

82	82:00	TANDERAGEE	1852	1965	10 C4	
		originally MADDEN BRIDGE, later TANDERAGEE & GILFORD, called TANDERAGEE from 1894				
84½	84:50	Adam's Crossing	1852	Open	10 C4	
86	86:07	Tavanagh Crossing	1852	Open	10 C4	
87¼	87:15	Portadown Junction	1852	1965	10 C3	52,53
87¼	87:24	PORTADOWN (2nd station)	1848	1863	10 C3	
87¼	87:24	PORTADOWN (4th station)	1970	Open	10 C3	
		opened 05-10-1970, almost on same site as 2nd station, as PORTADOWN (CRAIGAVON WEST), renamed PORTADOWN in 1971				
87½	87:45	River Bann Bridge	1848	Open	10 C3	
87¾	87:55	PORTADOWN (3rd station)	1863	1970	10 C3	
		opened 01-07-1863 alongside 1st station, closed 05-10-1970				
87¾	87:55	PORTADOWN (1st station)	1842	1848	10 C3	
		original UR terminus				
88½	88:48	SEAGOE	1842	1842	10 C3	
		original UR temporary terminus				
88½	88:48	Seagoe Crossing	1842	?	10 C3	
88¾	88:52	Collen's Brickworks Siding	?	?	10 C3	
		trailing access from up main only				
88¾	88:62	Kernan Crossing	1842	?	10 C3	
89½	89:39	Drumnagoon Crossing	1842	?	10 C3	
90½	90:51	Boilie Crossing	1842	?	10 C3	
91½	91:35	GOODYEAR	1970	1983	10 C3	
		served local tyre factory, opened 31-08-1970, closed 30-10-1983				
91¾	91:35	Ballinamoney Crossing	1842	?	10 C3	
?	?	CRAIGAVON CENTRAL	–	–	10 C3	
		proposed station, never built				
92½	92:48	William Street Crossing	1842	Open	10 C3	
		Lurgan Station Gates				
92½	92:53	LURGAN	1841	Open	10 C3	
		called LURGAN (CRAIGAVON EAST) from 29-06-1970 to 1971				
92¾	92:78	Dougher Crossing	1841	?	10 C3	
93	93:00	Lake Street Crossing	1841	Open	10 C3	
93¼	92:31	Bell's Row Crossing	1841	Open	10 C3	
94¾	94:67	Kilmore Crossing	1841	1985	10 C3	
		Right of Way extinguished				
95½	95:40	PRITCHARD'S BRIDGE	1842	1844	10 C3	
96¼		McKinley's Crossing	1841	?	10 C3	
97¼	97:29	Drumbane Crossing	1841	Open	10 C3	
98	98:00	Moira Station Gates	1841	Open	10 C3	
98	98:03	MOIRA	1841	Open	10 C3	
98¾	98:60	Trummery Crossing	1841	Open	10 C3	
100	100:02	Damhead South Crossing	1841	Open	11 A3	
100	100:03	DAMHEAD	1935	1973	11 A3	
		closed 02-07-1973				
100	100:03	THE DAMHEAD	1842	1844	11 A3	
		UR 'Signal Station'; same site as Damhead Station				
101½	101:11	Broomhedge Crossing	1841	?	11 A3	
101½	101:13	BROOMHEDGE	1935	1953	11 A3	
102½	102:40	Maze Station Gates	1841	Open	11 A3	
102½	102:44	MAZE	1895	1974	11 A3	
		called MAZE PLATFORM at opening; trains ceased to call from 01-07-1974				
102¾	102:60	Lissue Crossing	1841	Open	11 A3	
103¼	103:35	Knockmore Junction	1863	1977	11 A3	61,65
		closed 30-05-1977, junction now at Lisburn				
103½		Knockmore Junction Stn Gates	1841	?	11 A3	
103¾		KNOCKMORE JUNCTION HALT	1932	1946	11 A3	
		opened 23-10-1932, closed 1933/4, re-opened 1945, closed 1946.				
104	104:00	KNOCKMORE	1974	Open	11 A3	
		opened 01-07-1974 as KNOCKMORE				
105	105:04	LISBURN	1839	Open	11 A3	
105		Lisburn Station Gates	1841	1877	11 A3	
		replaced by bridge when station rebuilt				
106	106:01	HILDEN HALT	1907	Open	11 A3	
106½	106:45	LAMBEG	1877	Open	11 A3	
		opened 01-09-1877				
107		Ballast Pit Crossing	1839	?	11 A3	
107½	107:40	DERRIAGHY HALT	1907	Open	11 A3	
		closed 1953, reopened in 1956				
108¼	108:22	Meeting House Lane Crossing	1839	Open	11 A3	
		Pedestrian Crossing				
108½	108:30	Glebe Road Crossing	1839	Open	11 A3	
108½	108:37 ?	Dunmurry Station Gates	1839	?	11 A3	
		replaced by bridge				
108½	108:40	DUNMURRY	1839	Open	11 A3	
109 ?		Finaghy Sidings	?	?	34 B4	
109½	109:37 ?	Finaghy Station Gates	1839	1912	34 B4	
		replaced by bridge				
109½	109:40	FINAGHY HALT	1907	Open	34 B4	
110¼	110:24	BALMORAL	c.1858	Open	34 B4	
		closed for a period until 1863				
110¼ ?		Royal Ulster Agricultural Society Sidings	?	?	34 B4	
		served R.U.A.S. at Balmoral				
110½ ?		Rail Welding Plant Sidings	?	?	34 B4	
		serve rail welding plant at Lislea Drive				
111¼		Adelaide Yard	1909	?	34 C4	
111¼		Adelaide Locomotive Depot	1911	1966	34 C4	
		opened 03-1911, closed 11-1966, now a goods depot opened 06-1972				
111¼	111:15	ADELAIDE	1897	Open	34 C4	
		formerly ADELAIDE & WINDSOR, re-named 07-1936				
111¾	?	Tate's Avenue Crossing	1839	1926	34 C3	
		replaced by bridge				
112	112:00	Central Junction	1875	Open	34 C3	116
		closed 31-07-1965, re-opened 26-04-1976; formerly Ulster Junction				
112	112:00	ULSTER JUNCTION	1878	1885	34 C3	116
		opened 05-08-1878, closed 30-11-1885; exchange platforms; also called BELFAST CENTRAL JUNCTION				
?	?	Grosvenor Road Goods Depot	1874 ?	1965	34 C3	
		line diverged at Central Junction to Goods Depot				
112¼	112:17	Westlink Junction	1994	Open	34 C3	116
112¼	?	Durham Street Crossing	1839	1863	34 C3	
		replaced by the 'Boyne Bridge'				
112½	112:44	BELFAST GREAT VICTORIA STREET (new station)	1995	Open	34 C3	
		opened 30-09-95				
112½	112:50	BELFAST GREAT VICTORIA STREET (old station)	1839	1976	34 C3	
		closed 26-04-1976; called BELFAST 1839 to 1854, BELFAST VICTORIA STREET 1854 to 1856 and BELFAST GREAT VICTORIA STREET 1856 to 1976				

51 Howth Junction to Howth

GNR(I) / 5ft 3in gauge / mileposts measured from Howth Junction

Howth Junction to Howth (temporary station) opened 30-07-1846 by the DDR.
Howth (temporary station) to Howth opened 30-05-1847 by the DDR.

Electrified at 1,500V DC Overhead, electric service commenced 23-07-1984.

MPost Dist.	Miles & Chains	Place / Feature (notes)	Date Opened	Date Closed	Map Grid	Table Ref.
0	0:00	Howth Junction	1846	Open	17 B6	50
0	0:07	HOWTH JUNCTION	1846	Open	17 B6	50
		called JUNCTION until 1912				
1	0:69	BAYSIDE	1973	Open	17 B6	
		opened 11-06-1973				
1¼	1:30	Baldoyle Road Crossing	1846	Open	17 B6	
		also called Kilbarrack Crossing				
1¾	1:56	Sutton Station Gates	1846	Open	17 B6	
1¾	1:60	SUTTON	1846	Open	17 B6	
		formely SUTTON & BALDOYLE and BALDOYLE & SUTTON				
1¾	?	Cosh Siding	?	?	17 B6	
2	1:73	Cosh Crossing	1847	Open	17 B6	
		also called Cush Crossing				
2¾	?	HOWTH	1846	1847	17 B6	
		temporary terminus				
3	3:00	Claremont Crossing	1847	Open	17 B6	
3½	3:40	HOWTH	1847	Open	17 C6	

52 Portadown to Cavan

GNR(I) / 5ft 3in gauge / mileposts measured from Portadown

Portadown to Armagh opened 01-03-1848 by the UR.
Armagh to Monaghan (old station) opened 25-05-1858 by the UR.
Monaghan (old station) to Clones opened 02-03-1863 by the UR.
Clones to Cavan opened 07-04-1862 by the CCER.

Portadown to Glaslough closed to passengers 01-10-1957 by the GNRB.
Portadown to Brownstown Siding closed completely 04-01-1965 by the UTA.
Brownstown Siding to Glaslough closed completely 01-10-1957 by the GNRB.
Glaslough to Cavan closed to passengers 14-10-1957 by the GNRB.
Glaslough to Monaghan closed completely 02-06-1958 by the GNRB.
Monaghan to Cavan closed completely 01-01-1960 by CIE.

MPost Dist.	Miles & Chains	Place / Feature (notes)	Date Opened	Date Closed	Map Grid	Table Ref.
0	0:00	PORTADOWN	1848	Open	10 C3	50,53
0¼	0:09	Portadown Junction	1848	1965	10 C3	50,53
1		Brownstown Crossing	1848	1965	10 C4	
1		Brownstown Siding	1942	1965	10 C4	
		siding for Metal Box Co factory				
2		Dobbin's Crossing	1848	1957	10 C4	
2½		Purgatory Crossing	1848	1957	10 C4	
6¼		RICHHILL	1848	1957	10 C4	
6¼		Richhill Station Gates	1848	1957	10 C4	
7½		Quakers Crossing	1848	1957	10 C4	
		at Retreat Halt				
7½		RETREAT HALT	1936	1957	10 C4	
		no platform				
9½		Reilly's Rocks Crossing	1848	1957	10 B4	
?		Junction with Markethill line	1865	1933	10 B4	60
10¾		Asylum Siding	?	?	10 B4	60
		served Asylum via wagon turntable				
10¾		ARMAGH	1848	1957	10 B4	54,60
		known as ARMAGH RAILWAY STREET in 1910s/1920s				
10¾		Mill Siding	?	?	10 B4	54
		served Mill via wagon turntable				
10¾		Armagh Station Gates	1858	1957	10 B4	54
10¾		Junction with Keady line	1909	1957	10 B4	54
11¼		Desert Crossing	1858	1957	10 B4	
15¼		KILLYLEA	1859	1957	10 B4	
17¾		TYNAN	1858	1957	10 A4	91
		formerly TYNAN, CALEDON & MIDDLETOWN, from 1858-1880 then TYNAN & CALEDON				
21¾		Glaslough Station Gates	1858	1957	10 A4	
21¾		GLASLOUGH	1858	1957	10 A4	
22¾		Scott's Crossing	1858	1958	10 A4	
24¾		Faulkland Crossing	1858	1958	10 A5	
25¾		Eden Island Crossing	1858	1958	10 A5	
27¼		MONAGHAN (old station)	1858	1863	10 A5	
27½		MONAGHAN (new station)	1863	1957	9 D5	
33¼		SMITHBOROUGH	1863	1957	9 D5	
?		Clones East Junction	1858	1960	9 C5	49
		junction with Dundalk line				
39½		Clones Station Gates	1858	1960	9 C5	49
39¼		CLONES	1858	1957	9 C5	49
		Enniskillen and Cavan lines run parallel for ¾ mile				
39¾		Carn Crossing	1858	1960	9 C5	49
40		Enniskillen line diverges here	1858	1957	9 C5	49
41¼		Derrygoas No.1 Crossing	1862	1960	9 C5	
41¾		Derrygoas No.2 Crossing	1862	1960	9 C5	
42½		Clonagore Crossing	1862	1960	9 C5	
44½		Annaghraw Crossing	1862	1960	9 C6	
46¼		REDHILLS	1872	1957	9 C6	
		opened c.1872				
48		Mullanavarogue Crossing	1862	1960	9 C6	
48¼		BALLYHAISE	1862	1957	9 C6	63
		formerly BELTURBET JUNCTION, renamed 1885				
49¾		Drumharid Crossing	1862	1960	9 C6	
52		Ballymackinroe Crossing	1862	1960	15 D1	
52¾		LORETO COLLEGE HALT	1930	1957	15 D1	
52¾		Coolboyoge Crossing	1862	1960	15 D1	
54¾		Junction	1862	1960	15 D1	38
		end-on junction with MGWR				
54¾		CAVAN	1856	1957	15 D1	38
		MGWR Station, served by passenger services from Inny Junction from 1856 to 1947				

53 Portadown to Omagh

GNR(I) / 5ft 3in gauge / mileposts measured from Portadown

Portadown to Dungannon (old station) opened 05-04-1858 by the PDOR.
Dungannon (old Station) to Omagh opened 02-09-1861 by the PDOR.
Omagh Market Branch opened 06-1862 by the PDOR.

Portadown to Omagh closed completely 15-02-1965 by the UTA.

MPost Dist.	Miles & Chains	Place / Feature (notes)	Date Opened	Date Closed	Map Grid	Table Ref.
0		PORTADOWN	1848	Open	10 C3	50,52
0½		Portadown Junction	1852	1965	10 C3	50,52
		junction to Omagh from July 1858				
?		PORTADOWN (temporary station)	1858	1858	10 C3	
		open from 05-04-1858 to 04-07-1858				
2¼		Annakeera Crossing	1858	1965	10 C3	
		also a railcar stop, 1936-7 to 01-10-1957				
2¾		Selshion Crossing	1858	1965	10 C3	
6¾		ANNAGHMORE	1858	1965	10 B3	
7		Derrycoose Crossing	1858	1965	10 B3	
		also a railcar stop, 1936-7 to 01-10-1957				
9¼		VERNERSBRIDGE	1858	1950s	10 B3	
		formerly VERNER Station, renamed 12-1858				
9½		Blackwater Viaduct	1858	1965	10 B3	
		crosses River Blackwater				
10¾		TREW & MOY	1858	1965	10 B3	
13¾		Shaw's Crossing	1858	1965	10 B3	
		also a railcar stop, 1936-7 to 01-10-1957				
14		DUNGANNON (old station)	1858	1861	10 B3	
14½		Dungannon Tunnel	1861	1965	10 B3	
		814yds long				
15		Dickson's Siding	1865	?	10 B3	
		trails in on Down side, disconnected before 1965				
15		DUNGANNON	1861	1965	10 B3	56
15		Dungannon Goods Yard	?	?	10 B3	56
		yard sidings diverge on up side				
15½		Dungannon Junction Crossing	1861	1965	10 B3	56
		also a railcar stop, 1936-7 to 02-06-1958				
15½		Dungannon Junction	1879	1965	10 B3	56
17¾		DONAGHMORE	1861	1965	10 A2	
18¾		Mullafurtherland Crossing	1861	1965	10 A2	
		also a railcar stop, 1936-7 to 13-06-1960				
20¼		Reynold's Crossing	1861	1965	10 A2	
		also a railcar stop, 1936-7 to 13-06-1960				
20¾		Brimmage's	1861	1965	10 A2	
		also a railcar stop, 1936-7 to 13-06-1960				
24		POMEROY	1861	1965	10 A2	
29		County Council Siding	?	?	9 D2	
		trailing siding on up side				
29		CARRICKMORE	1861	1959	9 D2	
29¼ ?		Peat Moss Siding	?	?	9 D2	430
		may have served the Irish Peat Development Company bog at Carrickmore pre-c.1914; post c.1914 it was used as a refuge siding				
30¾		Rollingford Crossing	1861	1965	9 D2	
		also a railcar stop, 1936-7 to 13-06-1960				
32¾		SIXMILECROSS	1862	1965	9 D2	
32¾		Sixmilecross Station Gates	1861	1965	9 D2	

34¼	BERAGH	1861	1965	9 D2	
36¼	Tattykeeran Crossing	1861	1965	9 D2	
	also a railcar stop, 1936-7 to 13-06-1960				
38¼	Edenderry Crossing	1861	1965	9 C2	
	also a railcar stop, 1936-7 to 13-06-1960				
38¾	Garvaghy No.1 Crossing	1861	1965	9 C2	
	also a railcar stop 1936-1937 to 13-06-1960				
39¼	Garvaghy No.2 Crossing	1861	1965	9 C2	
	also a railcar stop 1936-1937 to 13-06-1960				
41	Market Branch Junction	1862	1965	9 C2	
	platform for railway staff				
0	Market Branch Junction	1862	1965	9 C2	
0½	Goods Station	1862	1965	9 C2	
41¾	OMAGH	1863	1965	9 C2	49
	joint INWR/PDOR station at junction				

54   Armagh to Castleblayney

GNR(I) / 5ft 3in gauge / mileposts measured from Armagh (Rly Street)

Armagh to Keady opened to goods 1908 by the CKAR.
Armagh to Keady opened to passengers 31-05-1909 by the CKAR.
Keady to Castleblayney opened 10-11-1910 by the CKAR.

Keady to Castleblayney closed completely 02-04-1923 by the GNR(I).
Armagh to Keady closed to passengers 01-01-1932 by the GNR(I).
Armagh to Keady closed completely 01-10-1957 by the GNRB.

MPost Dist.	Miles & Chains	Place / Feature (notes)	Date Opened	Date Closed	Map Grid	Table Ref.
0		ARMAGH	1848	1957	10 B4	52,60
		called ARMAGH RAILWAY STREET in 1910s/1920s				
0		Mill Siding	?	?	10 B4	52
		served Mill by wagon turntable				
0		Armagh Station Gates	1858	1957	10 B4	
0		Junction with Clones line	1909	1957	10 B4	
1		IRISH STREET HALT	1909	1932	10 B4	
2½		McCrum's Siding	1909	?	10 B4	
		served McCrum, Watson & Mercer Linen Mill				
2½		MILFORD	1909	1957	10 B4	
		opened by 10-1909				
3¼		Ballyards Viaduct	1909	1957	10 B4	
		7 arch, six stone and 1 plate girder				
3¾		Ballyards Crossing	1909	1957	10 B5	
3¾		BALLYARDS HALT	c.1910	1932	10 B5	
		opened by 02-1910				
3¾		Montgomery's Siding	?	?	10 B5	
		served Montgomery's Linen Mill				
5½		Tassagh Viaduct	1909	1957	10 B5	
		11 arch viaduct, 570ft long				
6½		TASSAGH HALT	1911	1932	10 B5	
		opened by 08-1911				
7¼		Bachelor's Walk Crossing	1909	1957	10 B5	
7½		Annvale Siding	?	?	10 B5	
		served William Kirk & Co Linen Mill				
8		KEADY	1909	1932	10 B5	
8		Keady Viaduct	1910	1923	10 B5	
		6 arch concrete viaduct				
8¾		Newholland Siding	c.1910	?	10 B5	
		Armagh County Council quarry siding				
12		CARNAGH	1911	1923	10 B5	
		opened by 10-1911				
14		Kane's Rocks Crossing	1910	1923	10 B6	
14¼		CREAGHANROE	1910	1923	10 B6	
14¼		Creaghanroe Station Gates	1910	1923	10 B6	
15		Corrintra Crossing	1910	1923	10 B6	
15½		Killycracken Crossing	1910	1923	10 B6	
18¼		CASTLEBLAYNEY	1849	1960	10 B6	49
		connection to Dundalk-Clones line was via a siding				

55   Inniskeen to Carrickmacross

GNR(I) / 5ft 3in gauge / mileposts measured from Inniskeen

Inishkeen to Carrickmacross opened 31-07-1886 by the GNR(I).

Passenger services suspended 10-03-1947 due to fuel shortage.

Inishkeen to Carrickmacross closed to passengers 10-03-1947 by the GNR(I).
Inishkeen to Carrickmacross closed completely 01-01-1960 by CIE.

MPost Dist.	Miles & Chains	Place / Feature (notes)	Date Opened	Date Closed	Map Grid	Table Ref.
0		INNISKEEN	1849	1959	16 D1	49
0½		Mucker Crossing	1886	1959	16 D1	
3½		ESSEXFORD	1887/8	1925	16 D1	
		closed 1922, re-opened 1925				
4½		Kennellybane Crossing	1886	1959	16 D1	
5		Annacroft Crossing	1886	1959	16 D1	
6½		CARRICKMACROSS	1886	1947	16 D1	

56   Dungannon to Cookstown

GNR(I) / 5ft 3in gauge / mileposts measured from Dungannon

Dungannon to Cookstown opened 28-07-1879 by the DCR.

Dungannon to Cookstown closed to passengers 16-01-1956 by the GNRB.
Cookstown to Coalisland closed completely 05-01-1959 by the UTA.
Coalisland to Dungannon closed completely 04-01-1965 by the UTA.

MPost Dist.	Miles & Chains	Place / Feature (notes)	Date Opened	Date Closed	Map Grid	Table Ref.
0		DUNGANNON	1861	1965	10 B3	53
0½		Dungannon Junction Crossing	1861	1965	10 B3	53
		also a railcar stop, 1936-7 to 02-06-1958				
0½		Dungannon Junction	1879	1965	10 B3	53
?		Carlin Road Brickworks Siding	?	?	10 B3	
?		Dungannon Brickworks Siding	?	?	10 B3	167
		also called Tyrone Brickworks				
2		Old Engine Crossing	1879	1965	10 B3	
		also a railcar stop, closed c.01-1942				
2		Congo Siding	?	?	10 B3	
		used for tar wagons for road surfacing by Tyrone County Council				
?		Derry's Brickyard Siding	?	?	10 B2	
5½		COALISLAND	1879	1956	10 B2	
?		'Wee Wall' Sand Siding	?	?	10 B2	
?		Byrne's Sand Siding	?	?	10 B2	
		also known as 'Big Wall' sand siding				
?		Annagher Colliery Siding	?	?	10 B2	
		trails in on down side				
6		Annagher Crossing	1879	1959	10 B2	
		also a railcar stop, closed c.01-1942				
7		Lisnastrain Crossing	1879	1959	10 B2	
		also a railcar stop, closed c.01-1942				
8½		STEWARTSTOWN	1879	1956	10 B2	
?		Grange Crossing	1879	1959	10 B2	
		replaced by a bridge by 1900; also a railcar stop; closed c.01-1942; known as Grange Halt				
?		KILLYMOON GOLF LINKS	?	?	10 B2	
		shown as 'open' in 1945 working timetable				
?		Pork Factory Siding	?	?	10 B2	
14½		Junction	1879	1959	10 B2	66
		junction with NCC line from Magherafelt				
14½		COOKSTOWN	1879	1956	10 B2	66

57 Drogheda to Oldcastle

GNR(I) / 5ft 3in gauge / mileposts measured from junction south of Drogheda

Drogheda to Navan (old station) opened 15-02-1850 by the DDR.
Navan(old station) to Kells opened 11-07-1853 by the DDR.
Kells to Oldcastle opened 17-03-1863 by the DDR.

Drogheda to Oldcastle closed to passengers 14-04-1958 by the GNRB.
Navan to Oldcastle closed completely 30-03-1961 by CIE.

Nevinstown Junction to Tara mines re-opened 29-06-1977 by CIE.

MPost Dist.	Miles & Chains	Place / Feature (notes)	Date Opened	Date Closed	Map Grid	Table Ref.
0¼	0:10	DROGHEDA	1855	Open	17 A4	50
		renamed DROGHEDA MacBRIDE Station from 1966				
0	0:00	Junction for Navan line	1850	Open	17 A4	50
2¾	2:60	Platin Cement Factory	1972	Open	17 A4	
4¾	4:65	DULEEK	1850	1958	17 A4	
		opened by 09-1850				
8¼	8:40	LOUGHER HALT	1940	1958	16 D4	
11¾	11:50	Beauparc Station Gates	1850	Open	16 D4	
11¾	11:54	BEAUPARC	1850	1958	16 D4	
		opened by 09-1850				
16¼	16:20	Factory Crossing	1850	Open	16 D4	
		also a railcar stop 1940 to 14-04-1958				
16½ ?	16:52	NAVAN (old station)	1850	1864	16 D4	
		original DDR Terminus				
16¾	16:54	Navan Viaduct	1853	Open	16 D4	
17	16:75	NAVAN	1864	1958	16 D4	
		replaced DDR station				
17	17:00	Navan Station Gates	1853	Open	16 D4	
17¼	17:20	NAVAN JUNCTION	1869	1947	16 D4	46
		closed 27-01-1947, GNR trains not shown to call from c.1941 to 1946				
17¼	17:30	Navan East Junction	1862	Open	16 D4	46
17½	17:34	Commons Road Crossing	1853	Open	16 C4	46
		also called Poorhouse Crossing				
17½	17:55	Navan West Junction	1853	Open	16 C4	46
		junction with MGWR to Kingscourt; taken out of use in 1911 with two parallel lines running from Navan Junction Station and diverging at this point; junction reinstated as Tara Mines Junction 29-06-1977; also known as Nevinstown Junction, Kingscourt Junction and latterly Tara Mines Junction				
18	18:02	Tara Mines	1977	Open	16 C4	
		first train 29-06-1977				
18¾		Newgate Crossing	1853	1961	16 C4	
		also a railcar stop, opened 1940 closed by 1956				
20		Ardbraccan Crossing	1853	1961	16 C4	
		also a railcar stop, opened 1940 closed by 1956				
21½		Castlemartin Crossing	1853	1961	16 C4	
		also a railcar stop opened 1940 closed by 1956				
22¼		Phoenixtown Crossing	1853	1961	16 C4	
		also a railcar stop opened 1940 closed by 1956				
23	23:01	BALLYBEG	c.1856	1958	16 C4	
		known as BALLYBEG CROSSING from 1865/6 to 1899				
23		Ballybeg Station Gates	1853	1961	16 C4	
26¾		KELLS	1853	1958	16 C3	
26¾		Kells Station Gates	1863	1961	16 C3	
33¼		VIRGINIA ROAD	1863	1958	16 B3	
39½		OLDCASTLE	1863	1958	16 A3	

58 Bundoran Junction to Bundoran

GNR(I) / 5ft 3in gauge / mileposts measured from Bundoran Junction

Bundoran Junction to Bundoran opened 13-06-1866 by the EBSR.

Bundoran Junction to Bundoran closed completely 01-10-1957 by the GNRB.

MPost Dist.	Miles & Chains	Place / Feature (notes)	Date Opened	Date Closed	Map Grid	Table Ref.
0		BUNDORAN JUNCTION	1854	1957	9 B3	49
		Bundoran 'South' Junction	1866	1957	9 B3	49
0		Bundoran 'East' Junction	1894	1957	9 B3	49
		Bundoran 'West' Junction	1894	1957	9 B3	
		Bundoran 'West' Junction	1894	1957	9 B3	
		Tague's Crossing	1866	1957	9 B3	
		also a railcar stop, 09-1934 to 1-10-1957, also called Teague's Crossing				
3½		IRVINESTOWN	1866	1957	9 B3	
?		Johnston's Crossing	1866	1957	9 B3	
		also a railcar stop 09-1934 closed by 1956				
?		Castlearchdale Crossing	1866	1957	9 A3	
		also a railcar stop 09-1934 closed by 1956				
6¼		DRUMADRAVY – private station	?	?	9 A3	
?		Crowe's Crossing	1866	1957	9 A2	
		also a railcar stop, 09-1934 closed by 1956				
9¾		KESH	1866	1957	9 A2	
9¾		Kesh Station Gates	1866	1957	9 A2	
15		PETTIGO	1866	1957	9 A2	
17		Letter	?	?	8 D2	
		stopping place, railcar stopped to load or unload mailbags from nearby Post Office.				
21¾		Leggs Crossing	?	?	8 D2	
		stopping place, railcar stopped to load or unload mailbags from nearby Post Office.				
22¼		CASTLECALDWELL (old station)	1866	1870	8 D2	
		near the site of Legg's Crossing; in use up to 08-1870 when replaced by new station				
22¾		CASTLECALDWELL (new station)	1870	1957	8 D2	
		opened 08-1870				
23		MAGHERAMENAGH CASTLE	?	?	8 D2	
		private platform				
27½		Belleek Pottery Siding	?	?	8 C2	
27½		BELLEEK	1866	1957	8 C2	
29½		Fortwilliam Crossing	1866	1957	8 C2	
30½		Camlin Crossing	1866	1957	8 C2	
31½		BALLYSHANNON	1866	1957	8 C2	
35¼		BUNDORAN	1866	1957	8 B2	

59 Scarva to Banbridge

GNR(I) / 5ft 3in gauge / mileposts measured from Scarva

Scarva to Banbridge opened 23-03-1859 by the BJR.
Banbridge to Banbridge (BLBR station) opened 10-1863 by the BJR.

Branch closed due to railway strike 31-01-1933, re-opened with Railcar service and five railcar stopping places 15-10-1934.

Scarva to Banbridge closed 02-05-1955 by the GNRB.

MPost Dist.	Miles & Chains	Place / Feature (notes)	Date Opened	Date Closed	Map Grid	Table Ref.
0		SCARVA	1859	Open	10 C4	50
1¼		Martin's Bridge	1859	1955	10 D4	
		also a railcar stop 1937/8 to 02-05-1955				
2		Kernon Crossing	1859	1955	10 D4	
		also a railcar stop 1953 to 02-05-1955				
3⅜		Drumhork Crossing	1859	1955	10 D4	
		also a railcar stop 1934 to 02-05-1955				
3⅞		Uprichards Crossing	1859	1955	10 D4	
		also a railcar stop 1934 to 1946				
4		LAURENCETOWN	1859	1955	10 D4	
4¼		Chapel Row Crossing	1859	1955	10 D4	
		also a railcar stop 1934 to 1940; remained available during war mainly for American troops; finally 'closed' 1945				
4½		Hazelbank Crossing	1859	1955	10 D4	
		also a railcar stop 1934 to 02-05-1955				

5		LENADERG	1904	1955	10 D4	
		opened 01-1904, closed 06-1904 to 07-1912				
5		Lenaderg Crossing	1859	1955	10 D4	
5 ?		Geohegan's Foundry Siding	?	?	10 D4	
		served Foundry				
?		SMYTH'S SIDING	1904	?	10 D4	
		passenger halt only from c.1904 to 1929 ?				
6¼		Millmount Crossing	1859	1955	10 D4	
		also a railcar stop 1934 to 02-05-1955				
6¼		Cowdy's Siding – served Mill	?	?	10 D4	
?		Banbridge (BJR station)	1859	1863	10 D4	
		closed when connection into BLBR station opened 10-1863				
6¾		BANBRIDGE (BLBR station)	1863	1956	10 D4	61

60 Warrenpoint to Armagh (Railway Street)

GNR(I) / 5ft 3in gauge / mileposts measured from Warrenpoint

Warrenpoint to Newry Kilmorey Street opened for goods 16-06-1849 by the NWRR.
Warrenpoint to Newry Kilmorey Street opened to passengers 28-05-1849 by the NWRR.
Newry Kilmorey Street Junction to Newry Dublin Bridge opened 02-09-1861 by NWRR.
Newry Dublin Bridge to Newry Edward Street opened 02-09-1861 by the TNCR.
Albert Basin to Newry Edward Street opened to goods 04-01-1865 by the NER, see Table 105 for full details.
Newry Edward Street to Goraghwood opened 07-01-1854 by the NER.
Goraghwood to Armagh (temporary station) opened 25-08-1864 by the NAR.
Armagh (temporary station) to Armagh (Railway Street) opened 13-02-1865 by the NAR.

Newry Kilmorey Street to Kilmorey Street Junction closed to passengers 02-09-1861 by the NWRR.
Newry Kilmorey Street to Kilmorey Street Junction closed completely c.1900 by GNR(I).
Goraghwood to Armagh closed to passengers 01-02-1933 by the GNR(I).
Markethill to Armagh closed to goods 01-02-1933 by the GNR(I).
Markethill to Goraghwood closed to completely 02-05-1955 by the the GNRB.
Goraghwood to Warrenpoint closed completely 04-01-1965 by the UTA.

MPost Dist.	Miles & Chains	Place / Feature (notes)	Date Opened	Date Closed	Map Grid	Table Ref.
0	0:00	WARRENPOINT (old station)	1849	1891	10 D6	122
0	0:07	WARRENPOINT (new station)	1891	1965	10 D6	122
?		Reed's Siding	?	?	10 D6	
		served Reed's Corrugated Casings Ltd				
?		Dow-Mac Siding	?	?	10 D6	
		served concrete sleeper plant				
1¼	1:30	NARROW WATER HALT	1849	1958/9	10 D6	
1¼		Level Crossing	1849	1965	10 D6	
		road crossed line to Ferry Pier				
2¼		GREEN ISLAND	1849	1850	10 D6	
		opened c.09-1849, closed c.07-1850				
5¾	5:70	Kilmorey Street Junction	1861	c.1900	10 D6	
0	0:00	Kilmorey Street Junction	1861	c.1900	10 D6	
0¼	0:10	NEWRY KILMOREY STREET	1849	1861	10 D6	
		in use for goods until c.1900				
6		Lockington's Siding	?	?	10 D6	
		served S. Lockington & Sons, Coal Importers				
6	6:26	NEWRY DUBLIN BRIDGE	1861	1965	10 D6	
6		Dublin Bridge Station Gates	1861	1965	10 D6	
6		Butter Crane Crossing	1861	1965	10 D6	
6¼	6:48	King Street Junction	1861	1965	10 D6	105
6¼		King Street Crossing	1854	1965	10 D6	105
6½		Monaghan Street Crossing	1854	1965	10 D6	105
6¾		Edward Street Station Crossing	1854	1965	10 D6	105
6¾	6:78	NEWRY EDWARD STREET	1854	1965	10 D6	105
		Fleming's Brickworks Siding	?	?	10 D6	
7¼		Pig Hall Crossing	1854	1965	10 D6	
		also called Brickie Loanin or Calwell's Crossing				
11¼		Greenfield's Crossing	1854	1965	10 D5	
10¼	10:26 ?	Junction with Dublin Line	1854	1965	10 C5	50
10¼	10:28	GORAGHWOOD	1854	1965	10 C5	50
10¾ ?		Dublin-Belfast line underbridge	1864	1955	10 C5	50
		dates are for when bridge was in use				
?		Lissummon Tunnel	1864	1955	10 C5	
		1,759 yards long, longest tunnel in Ireland				
14		BALLYDOUGHERTY HALT	1912	1933	10 C5	
		Loughgilly Tunnel	1864	1955	10 C5	
		365 yards long				
15½		LOUGHGILLY (old station)	1864	1897	10 C5	
16	16:13	GLEN ANNE	1897	1933	10 C5	168
		named LOUGHGILLY until 1924				
18¾		Markethill Station Gates	1864	1955	10 C5	
18¾		MARKETHILL	1864	1933	10 C5	
22¾		HAMILTONSBAWN	1864	1933	10 C4	
25		Derry's Crossing	1864	1933	10 B4	
26½		ARMAGH (temporary Station)	1864	1865	10 B4	
		at Drummondmore, closed 13-02-1865				
27¼		Junction with Portadown line	1865	1933	10 B4	52
?		ARMAGH (N&A station)	1875	c.1879	10 B4	
		opened 01-04-1875, adjoining but nominally separate to south east of UR station				
27½		Asylum Siding	?	?	10 B4	52,54
		served Asylum by wagon turntable				
27½		ARMAGH (UR station)	1848	1957	10 B4	52,54
		known as ARMAGH RAILWAY STREET in 1910s/1920s				

61 Knockmore Junction to Castlewellan and Newcastle

GNR(I) – Knockmore Junction to Castlewellan
BCDR – Castlewellan to Newcastle

5ft 3in gauge / mileposts measured from Knockmore Junction

Knockmore Junction to Banbridge opened to passengers 13-07-1863 by the BLBR.
Knockmore Junction to Banbridge opened to goods 12-09-1863 by the BLBR.
Banbridge to Ballyroney opened 14-12-1880 by the GNR(I).
Ballyroney to Castlewellan opened 24-03-1906 by the GNR(I).
Castlewellan to Newcastle opened 24-03-1906 by the BCDR.

Castlewellan to Newcastle closed 02-05-1955 by the UTA.
Banbridge to Castlewellan closed 02-05-1955 by the GNRB.
Knockmore Junction to Banbridge closed to passengers 30-04-1956 by the GNRB.
Newforge Siding to Banbridge closed completely 30-04-1956 by the GNRB.
Knockmore Junction to Newforge Siding closed 02-1965 by the UTA.

MPost Dist.	Miles & Chains	Place / Feature (notes)	Date Opened	Date Closed	Map Grid	Table Ref.
0		Knockmore Junction	1863	1965	11 A3	50,65
		closed as junction to Newforge Siding				
0¼		Newforge Siding	1939	1965	11 A3	
		served 'Burnhouse' Rendering Factory				
?		CANAL BRIDGE	?	?	11 A3	
		stopping point for Maze racegoer's certainly in BLBR days				
1¾		NEWPORT HALT	1942	1956	11 A3	
2¾		HILLSBOROUGH	1863	1956	11 A3	
3		Hillsborough Crossing	1863	1956	11 A3	
4¾		BALLYGOWAN HALT	1929	1956	11 A3	
6¾		MAGHERABEG	1929	1956	11 A4	
8¼		DROMORE	1863	1956	11 A4	
?		Dromore Viaduct	1863	1956	11 A4	
		7 arch stone viaduct across River Lagan				
10¼		ASHFIELD	1930/1	1956	10 D4	
11½		MULLAFERNAGHAN	1863	1956	10 D4	
15		BANBRIDGE	1863	1956	10 D4	59
16½		Kennedy's Crossing	1880	1955	10 D4	
18		Ballievy Siding	?	?	10 D4	
18¼		CORBET	1882	1955	10 D4	
20		POLAND'S BRIDGE	1932	1955	10 D4	
		no platform.				
22		KATESBRIDGE	1880	1955	10 D5	
24		BALLYRONEY	1880	1955	11 A5	
26		DRUMADONALD	1933	1955	11 A5	
		no platform				

27¾		BALLYWARD	1906	1955	11 A5	
29¼		LEITRIM	1906	1955	11 A5	
30¾		SAVAGE'S BRIDGE	1932	1955	11 A5	
33¼		CASTLEWELLAN	1906	1955	11 B5	
		joint BCDR/GNR(I) station				
35		Junction with BCDR Line	1906	1955	11 B5	
37¼		NEWCASTLE	1869	1955	11 B5	79
		BCDR station				

62   Hill of Howth Tramway

GNR(I) / 5ft 3in gauge

Sutton to Hill of Howth opened 17-06-1901 by the GNR(I).
Hill of Howth to Howth opened 01-08-1901 by the GNR(I).

Services suspended 12-06-1944 due to fuel shortage.
Sevices resumed 25-09-1944.

Sutton to Howth closed completely 01-06-1959 by CIE.

Electrified with 550 V DC overhead trolley system.

MPost Dist.	Miles & Chains	Place / Feature (notes)	Date Opened	Date Closed	Map Grid	Table Ref.
0		SUTTON STATION	1901	1959	17	51
		Sutton tramcar shed connected to mainline in 1951				
–		SUTTON CROSS	1901	1959	17	
–		MARINE HOTEL – request stop	1901	1959	17	
		formerly called STRAND HOTEL				
–		CHURCH ROAD – request stop	1901	1959	17	
		formerly called SAXE LANE (or SAX, or SACKS LANE)				
–		STRAND ROAD	1901	1959	17	
–		HOWTH DEMESNE	1901	1959	17	
–		ST FINTAN'S CEMETERY– request stop	1901	1959	17	
–		ST FINTAN'S	1901	1959	17	
–		ST FINTAN'S ROAD – request stop	1901	1959	17	
–		BARREN HILL	1901	1959	17	
–		RED ROCK – request stop	1901	1959	17	
–		SOMALI VILLAGE – request stop	1901	1959	17	
		also called BELLINGHAM'S				
–		CEANCHOR ROAD – request stop	1901	1959	17	
–		BAILY POST OFFICE	1901	1959	17	
–		EARLSCLIFFE – request stop	1901	1959	17	
–		MAXWELL'S CORNER (private stop)	1901	1959	17	
–		CONVENT GATE – request stop	1901	1959	17	
–		STELLA MARIS	1901	1959	17	
		formerly called BAY VIEW or BAILY VIEW				
–		RAVENSDALE – request stop	1901	1959	17	
–		TWEEDY'S LANE – request stop	1901	1959	17	
–		HILL OF HOWTH	1901	1959	17	
		formerly called HOWTH SUMMIT, renamed 1912				
–		KITESTOWN ROAD – request stop	1901	1959	17	
		formerly called BAKER'S LANE				
–		GREY'S LANE – request stop	1901	1959	17	
–		DUNGRIFFEN ROAD	1901	1959	17	
–		BALKILL ROAD – request stop	1901	1959	17	
		also called BALGLASS				
–		ISLAND VIEW – request stop	1901	1959	17	
–		'KOREA'	c.1950s	1959	17	
		unofficial stopping place				
5¼		HOWTH STATION	1901	1959	17	
		connection to mainline				

63   Ballyhaise to Belturbet

GNR(I) / 5ft 3in gauge / mileposts measured from Ballyhaise

Ballyhaise to Belturbet opened 29-06-1885 by the GNR(I).

Passenger services suspended 10-03-1947 due to fuel shortage.
Passenger services resumed 02-06-1947.

Ballyhaise to Belturbet closed to passengers 14-10-1957 by the GNRB.
Ballyhaise to Belturbet closed completely 01-04-1959 by CIE.

MPost Dist.	Miles & Chains	Place / Feature (notes)	Date Opened	Date Closed	Map Grid	Table Ref.
0		BALLYHAISE	1862	1957	9 C6	52
		formerly BELTURBET JUNCTION				
4		Black Bog Crossing	1885	1959	9 B6	
4¼		BELTURBET	1885	1959	9 B6	97
		Cavan & Leitrim trains used a bay platform from 1887 to 1959				

64   Shantonagh Junction to Cootehill

GNR(I) / 5ft 3in gauge / mileposts measured from Shantonagh Junction

Shantonagh Junction to Cootehill opened 18-10-1860 by the DER.

Passenger services suspended 10-03-1947 due to fuel shortage.

Shantonagh Junction to Cootehill closed to passengers 10-03-1947 by the GNR(I).
Shantonagh Junction to Cootehill closed 20-06-1955 by the GNR(I).

MPost Dist.	Miles & Chains	Place / Feature (notes)	Date Opened	Date Closed	Map Grid	Table Ref.
0		Shantonagh Junction	1860	1955	10 A6	49
3½		ROCKCORRY	1860	1947	9 D6	
?		Cootehill Viaduct	1860	1955	9 D6	
7½		COOTEHILL	1860	1947	9 D6	

65   Knockmore Junction to Antrim

GNR(I) / 5ft 3in gauge / mileposts measured from Knockmore Junction

Knockmore Junction to Antrim opened 13-11-1871 by the DAJR.
Aldergrove Aerodrome siding opened c.1916 by the War Department.
Siding Junction to Gortnagallon opened for goods and workmen's trains 05-1942 by the War Department.

Aldergrove Aerodrome siding closed c.1918, lifted early 1930s.
Siding Junction to Gortnagallon, no trains after 10-1945, junction removed 11-04-1948, lifted 1950.
Knockmore Junction to Antrim closed to passengers 12-09-1960 by the UTA.

Knockmore Junction to Antrim re-opened to local passenger traffic 28-01-1974 by NIR and for through Belfast-Londonderry trains 23-01-1978.

MPost Dist.	Miles & Chains	Place / Feature (notes)	Date Opened	Date Closed	Map Grid	Table Ref.
0	0:00	Knockmore Junction	1871	1977	11 A3	50
		closed 30-05-1977, junction now at Lisburn				
1¾	1:63	BROOKMOUNT	1871	1960	11 A3	
3	3:00	BROOKHILL HALT	c.1933	1960	11 A3	
		platform from 1936				
3¾	3:66	Frazer's Crossing	1871	Open	11 A3	
4¼	4:22	MEETING HOUSE HALT	1939	1960	10 D3	
		no platform, closed 12-09-1960				
5¼	5:26	BALLINDERRY	1871	Open	10 D3	
		closed 1960, reopened 28-01-1974				
6½	6:45	LEGATIRIFF HALT	1936	1960	10 D3	
8½	8:50	GLENAVY	1871	Open	10 D2	
		closed 1960, reopened 28-01-1974				
11	10:72	CRUMLIN	1871	Open	10 D2	
		closed 1960, reopened 28-01-1974				
11	11:04	Crumlin Viaduct	1871	Open	10 D2	
11½	11:25	Crumlin Linen Mill Siding	1874	?	10 D2	
		opened 10-1874				
0		Siding Junction	1942	1945	10 D2	
2¼		Gortnagallon	1942	1945	10 D2	
		served wartime aircraft factory				
12	12:01	Siding Junction	1942	1947	10 D2	
13¼	13:16	ALDERGROVE	1871	1960	10 D2	
13½		Junction	c.1916	c.1918	10 D2	

0		Junction	c.1916	c.1918	10 D2	
3		Aldergrove Aerodrome	c.1916	c.1918	10 D2	
		built in latter part of 1914-18 war, disused upon completion of aerodrome				
15¾	15:51	MILLAR'S BRIDGE HALT	1938	1960	10 A1	
		no platform, closed 12-09-1960				
18¼	18:30	Junction with NCC line	1871	Open	10 A1	67
18½	18:40	ANTRIM	1848	Open	10 A1	67
		bay platform at NCC Station				

66   Cookstown Junction to Cookstown

NCC / 5ft 3in gauge / mileposts measured from
Belfast York Road via Greenisland

Cookstown Junction to Randalstown opened 12-04-1848 by the BBR.
Randalstown to Cookstown opened 10-11-1856 by the BBR.

Cookstown Junction to Cookstown closed to passengers 28-08-1950 by the UTA.
Magherafelt to Cookstown closed to goods 02-05-1955 by the UTA.
Cookstown Junction to Magherafelt closed to goods 05-10-1959 by the UTA.

MPost Dist.	Miles & Chains	Place / Feature (notes)	Date Opened	Date Closed	Map Grid	Table Ref.
25		DRUMSOUGH	1848	1976	10 D1	67
		formerly DRUMSOUGH, renamed COOKSTOWN JUNCTION 11-1856, reverted to DRUMSOUGH 26-04-1976, closed 18-10-1976				
25		Drumsough Station Gates	1848	1959	10 D1	67
		formerly called Cookstown Junction Station Gates, also crosses Ballymena line				
?		Londonderry line diverged here	1848	Open	10 D1	67
25¼ ?		Millar's Crossing	1848	1959	10 D1	
25¼ ?		Shannonstown Siding	?	?	10 D1	
		facing siding diverged on up side, 457 yds long				
26 ?		Ballygrooby Crossing	1848	1959	10 D1	
		RANDALSTOWN (old station)	1848	1856	10 D1	
27		Randalstown Station Gates	1848	1856	10 D1	
27		RANDALSTOWN (new station)	1856	1950	10 D1	
		Randalstown Viaduct	1856	1959	10 D1	
		8 span masonry viaduct across River Maine				
27½		RANDALSTOWN MILITARY PLATFORM	1914	?	10 D1	
28 ?		Gortahorn Crossing	1856	1959	10 D1	
32½		Staffordstown Station Gates	?	1959	10 D1	
32½		STAFFORDSTOWN (new station)	1902	1950	10 D1	
33		STAFFORDSTOWN (old station)	1857/8	1864	10 D1	
		closed 03-1864				
		Neeson's Crossing	1856	1959	10 C1	
34		McKeever's Crossing	1856	1959	10 C1	
35¾		Porter's Crossing	1856	1959	10 C1	
36		Toalstown Crossing	1856	1959	10 C1	
		also known as McKay's Crossing				
36¼		TOOME BRIDGE	1856	1950	10 C1	
		also known as TOOME at various times				
36¼		Toome Bridge Station Gates	1856	1959	10 C1	
0		TOOME BRIDGE			10 C1	
?		Toome Quays Siding			10 C1	
		Carlisle Bridge	1856	1959	10 C1	
		lattice girder bridge, centre opening span crossing the River Bann				
36½ ?		Doyle's Crossing	1856	1959	10 C1	
37½		Ward's Crossing	1856	1959	10 C1	
		also known as The Creagh Crossing				
38		Annahorish Crossing	1856	1959	10 C1	
		also known as Molloy's Crossing				
40		Moyola Viaduct	1856	1959	10 C1	
		across the Moyola River				
40 ?		Nestlé Creamery Siding	1947	1959	10 C1	
40½		Castledawson Station Gates	1856	1959	10 C1	
		sometimes called McKeever's Crossing				
40½		CASTLEDAWSON	1856	1950	10 C1	
42½		Magherafelt Station Gates	1856	1959	10 C1	

42¾	MAGHERAFELT	1856	1950	10 C1	69,74
	Derry Central line runs parallel for ½ mile				
43¼	Deehan's Crossing	1856	1955	10 B1	
	adjacent to Hatton's Crossing on Derry Central				
43¼	Point of Divergence	1856	1959	10 B1	
	Derry Central line diverges at this point				
43½ ?	Cookstown U.D.C. Quarry Siding	?	?	10 B1	
43¾	Draperstown Junction	1883	1950	10 B1	69
	closed as Junction				
46¼ ?	Carmean Lime Siding	1943	1955	10 B1	
	lime loading siding diverging on down side				
46½	Carmean Lane Crossing	1856	1955	10 B1	
47¾ ?	Lismoney USA Medical Depot	1942	?	10 B1	264
	opened 07-1942, diverged on Up side, continued for ? mile to depot, one level crossing on siding				
49¼	MONEYMORE	1856	1950	10 B1	
53 ?	Ballyforlea Crossing	1856	1959	10 B1	
53½ ?	Cookstown Lime Co Siding	?	?	10 B2	439
	private siding off north of goods yard				
53¾	Junction	1879	1959	10 B2	56
	with GNR(I) line from Dungannon				
53¾	COOKSTOWN	1856	1950	10 B2	56
?	Union Street Crossing	?	?	10 B2	
?	Cookstown Market Yard	?	?	10 B2	

67   Belfast York Road to Londonderry Waterside

NCC / 5ft 3in gauge
mileposts measured from Belfast York Road via Greenisland
Loop Line mileposts measured from Bleach Green Junction

Belfast York Road to Ballymena via Greenisland opened 12-04-1848 by the BBR.
Bleach Green Junction to Monkstown Junction opened 22-01-1934 by the NCC.
Ballymena to Coleraine (Northbrook) opened 04-12-1855 by the BBCPJR.
Coleraine (Northbrook) to junction via 1st Bann Bridge opened 19-11-1860 by the BLJR.
Coleraine (Northbrook) to junction via 2nd Bann Bridge opened 21-03-1924 by the NCC.
Coleraine Harbour Junction to Harbour opened 01-01-1892 by CHC.
Coleraine (Waterside) to Limavady Junction opened 18-07-1853 by the LCR.
Limavady Junction to Londonderry (Waterside) opened 29-12-1852 by the LCR.
Londonderry (Waterside) to Londonderry opened 24-02-1980 by NIR.

Bleach Green Junction to Antrim closed 22-01-1978 except for special traffic by NIR.
Monkstown Junction to Greenisland closed 01-10-1963 by the UTA.
Coleraine Harbour Branch closed 30-09-1966 by the UTA.

Bleach Green to Antrim re-opened to passengers 16-06-1980 by NIR.
Bleach Green to Antrim closed to passengers 23-02-1981 by NIR.

Note: The NCC operated a Railcar Service between Londonderry and Coleraine which would stop at certain Level Crossings upon request from 1936 to 11-1939.

MPost Dist.	Miles & Chains	Place / Feature (notes)	Date Opened	Date Closed	Map Grid	Table Ref.
0	0:00	BELFAST YORK ROAD	1848	1992	34 C2	
		called YORK ROAD from 1854; closed 17-10-1992				
0	0:00	York Road Works	1992	Open	34 C2	
		on site of former York Road Station				
0	0:00	BELFAST YORKGATE	1992	Open	34 C2	
		opened 17-10-1992				
0¼	0:18	York Road South Junction	1994	Open	34 C2	
		junction to York Road Works				
0¾	0:49	York Road North Junction	1994	Open	34 C2	117
		junction to Crossharbour line				
0¾	0:49	York Road North Junction	1994	Open	34 C2	117
		junction to York Road Works, temporary connection provided in yard area from 1992-1994				
?	?	Dufferin Dock Junction	1855	1969	34 C2	129
		junction to BHC line				
?	?	Duncrue Street Works	1950	1966	34 C2	
0¾ ?	0:60 ?	Fortwilliam Carriage Sidings	1996	Open	34 C2	
		carriage sidings on Up side				

1¾	1:60	Fortwilliam Sidings temporary spoil sidings, also known as Port Arthur Sidings; third line laid on the seaward side of line from Greencastle to Fortwilliam for motorway construction; opened 11-11-1966, closed 02-05-1970	1966	1970	34 C2	
2½	2:35	GREENCASTLE opened by 03-1849; originally called WHITEHOUSE, re-named 1849 or 1850; closed 01-06-1916	1849	1916	34 C1	
3	2:70	Whitehouse Siding at old station site	?	?	34 C1	
3	2:70	WHITEHOUSE (old station) closed 06-1906	1861	1906	34 C1	
3¼	3:20	WHITEHOUSE (new station) opened 06-1906, closed 20-09-1954	1906	1954	34 C1	
3¾	3:57	Shore Road Tunnel 83 yds long	1848	Open	11 B2	
4¼	4:24	WHITEABBEY	1848	Open	11 B2	
4¾	4:56	Bleach Green Junction	1934	Open	11 B2	76
4¾	4:56	Bleach Green Junction 'Loop Line'	1934	Open	11 B1	76
4¼	4:68	Bleach Green Viaduct 630ft long, 70ft high concrete viaduct	1934	Open	11 B1	
6	6:05	Monkstown Junction	1934	1963	11 B1	76
6	6:07	MONKSTOWN (new station) see entry below for details	1934	1981	11 B1	76
8¾	8:46	Monkstown Junction	1934	1963	11 B1	76
8¾	?	Monkstown Halt Crossing replaced by Bridge in 1934	?	1933	11 B1	76
8¾	?	MONKSTOWN HALT (old station) on old alignment; closed 28-05-1933	1905	1933	11 B1	76
8¾	8:48	MONKSTOWN HALT (new station) opened 22-01-1934 on new alignment; closed c.1959, re-opened 04-09-1967, closed 23-01-1978, re-opened 01-09-1980, closed 23-02-1981.	1934	1981	11 B1	76
?	?	Level Crossing replaced by Bridge in 1934	1848	1933	11 B1	
?	?	Level Crossing replaced by Bridge in 1934	1848	1933	11 B1	
9½	?	MOSSLEY (old station) opened c.09-1899, station closed 01-11-1931 for 'loop line' building	1899	1931	11 B1	
9½	9:44	MOSSLEY (new station) closed 20-09-1954, re-opened 01-09-1980, closed 23-02-1981	1934	1981	11 B1	
10¾	?	Ballyclare Junction No.1 Gates replaced by a Motorway bridge	1848	c.1966	11 B1	
10¾	10:60	BALLYCLARE JUNCTION formerly BALLYNURE ROAD, renamed 03-11-1884; closed 08-1875, re-opened 01-06-1877, closed 04-12-1961	by 1850	1961	11 B1	75
11¼	11:15	Kingsmoss No.1 Crossing also called Ballyclare Junction No.2	1848	Open	11 B1	75
11½	11:30	Kingsmoss No.2 Crossing also called Ballyclare Junction No.3	1848	Open	11 B1	75
11¾	11:50	Kingsbog Junction	1884	1950	11 B1	75
11¾	11:59	Kingsbog Crossing	1848	Open	11 B1	
12	12:06	BALLYROBERT HALT closed 01-1920	1905	1920	11 A1	
13¼	13:22	DOAGH formerly BALLYPALLADY, re-named BALLYCLARE & DOAGH 10-1858, renamed DOAGH 03-11-1884; closed 29-06-1970.	1848	1970	11 A1	
14¾	14:67	Ballymartin Crossing	1848	Open	11 A1	
16¼	16:26	TEMPLEPATRICK closed 20-09-1954, re-opened 01-09-1980, closed 23-02-1981	by 1850	1981	11 A1	
17¼	17:27	Kilmakee No.2 Crossing opened 31-10-1977 due to road improvements. Now called Kilmakee	1977	Open	11 A1	
17¼	17:38	Kilmakee No.1 Crossing	1848	Closed	11 A1	
18½	18:37	DUNADRY closed 20-09-1954	1848	1954	11 A1	
20	19:68	MUCKAMORE HALT closed 06-05-1963	1905	1963	11 A1	
20	?	Muckamore Works Siding siding with wagon turntables giving access to branch crossing Six Mile Water to York Street Spinning Co Ltd Works	?	?	11 A1	
20	?	Gravel Pit Siding trailed into Up line	?	?	11 A1	
21¾	21:55	Junction junction with GNR(I) from Knockmore	1871	Open	10 D1	65
21¾	?	Rea's Siding from NCC goods yard across a lane to Works	?	?	10 D1	
21¾	?	Showground Siding from NCC goods yard	?	?	10 D1	
21¾	21:65	ANTRIM	1848	Open	10 D1	65
21¾	21:68	Antrim Station Gates	1848	Open	10 D1	
22½	22:38	Asylum Siding long siding to Mental Hospital	?	1965	10 D1	
22½	22:44	Spring Farm Crossing	1848	Open	10 D1	
23	23:06	Niblock Crossing	1848	Open	10 D1	
23¼	23:10	ORIEL LODGE RACECOURSE also called NIBLOCK CROSSING RACECOURSE PLATFORM	1935	1948	10 D1	
23¾	23:68	Carngranny Crossing	1848	Open	10 D1	
24½	?	Warrick's Crossing removed by M2 motorway overbridge	1848	c.1970	10 D1	
25	24:75	DRUMSOUGH originally DRUMSOUGH JUNCTION, renamed COOKSTOWN JUNCTION 11-1856, reverted to DRUMSOUGH 26-04-1976; closed 18-10-1976	1848	1976	10 D1	66
25	24:79	Cookstown Junction Station Gates now called Drumsough Crossing, also crosses Cookstown Line	1848	Open	10 D1	66
?		Cookstown line diverges here	1848	1959	10 D1	66
25½	25:31	Skegeneah Crossing	1848	?	10 D1	
26¾	26:60	Aughalish Crossing	1848	Open	10 D1	
27½	27:45	Magherabeg Loop passing loop opened when line singled	1990	Open	10 D1	
28¾	28:67	Kellswater South Crossing	1848	Open	5 A6	
29¼	29:16	KELLSWATER closed 15-03-1971	1876	1971	5 A6	
29¼	29:20	Kellswater North Crossing	1848	Open	5 A6	
30¼ ?	?	ANDRAID flag station, Wednesdays & Fridays only	c. 1848	1850	5 A6	
31¼	30:57	Slaght Crossing	1848	Open	5 A6	
32¾	32:50	Spencestown Crossing accommodation crossing	1848	Open	5 A6	
32¾	?	Timber Yard Siding on Up side at Harryville	?	?	5 A6	
32¾	?	Saw Mill Siding on Up side at Harryville	?	?	5 A6	
32¾	32:63	BALLYMENA closed to passengers 04-12-1855, remained in use as goods depot	1848	1855	5 A6	
32¾	?	Linen Mill Siding connection by wagon turntable and street tramway from goods depot to Braid River Weaving Mill	?	?	5 A6	
33½	33:40	BALLYMENA	1855	Open	5 A6	70,72
33½	?	Brewery Siding extension of loco shed headshunt to Brewery	?	?	5 A6	
35	34:71	Galgorm Crossing	1855	Open	5 A6	
36	36:08	Cullybackey No.1 Crossing	1855	Open	5 A6	
36¼	36:20	Cullybackey No.2 Crossing	1855	Open	5 A6	
36½	36:38	CULLYBACKEY closed 09-1856, re-opened 01-03-1865, closed 18-10-1976, re-opened 28-06-1982	1856	Open	5 A6	
36½	36:38	Cullybackey Crossing	1855	Open	5 A6	
37½	37:36	Broughdone Crossing	1855	Open	5 A6	
38	37:75	Andersons Crossing	?	Open	5 A6	
38½	38:40	Dromona Creamery Siding	?	?	5 A5	
41¼	41:14	Glarryford Crossing	1855	Open	5 A5	
41¼	41:17	GLARRYFORD closed 02-07-1973	1856	1973	5 A5	
43½	43:28	Killagan Crossing	1855	Open	5 A5	
43½	43:33	KILLAGAN formerly Bellaghy, re-named 01-1876; closed 02-07-1973	1855	1973	5 A5	

45¼	45:27	Ballymacoldrick No.1 Crossing	1855	Open	5 A5	
45½	45:45	Ballymacoldrick No.2 Crossing	1855	Open	5 A5	
46	46:08	Dunloy Crossing	1855	Open	5 A5	
46	46:12	DUNLOY	1856	1976	5 A5	
		closed 18-10-1976				
47	47:04	Galdanagh Crossing	1855	Open	5 A5	
47½	47:47	Artiferral Crossing	1855	Open	5 A5	
49¾	49:61	Glenlough Crossing	1855	?	5 A4	
50	50:00	Ballyboyland Ballast Pit	?	1957	5 A4	
50¼		Ballyboyland Loop	1958	1967	5 A4	
		passing loop				
50¾	50:49	Ballyboyland Crossing	1855	Open	5 A4	
53½	53:36	BALLYMONEY	1855	Open	4 D4	
54½	54:40	Coldagh Crossing	1855	Open	4 D4	
55½	55:45	Balnamore Crossing	1855	Open	4 D4	
56½		MACFIN (old station)	1856	1867	4 D4	
57	56:72	Macfin Crossing	1855	Open	4 D4	
57	57:05	MACFIN (new station)	1880	1954	4 D4	74
		opened 19-02-1880, closed 20-09-1954, junction with Derry Central Railway				
58¾	58:66	Damhead North Crossing	1855	Open	4 D4	
61¾	?	Coleraine Crossing	1855	1882	4 D4	
		removed when station rebuilt in 1882				
61¾	?	Henry's Siding	?	?	4 D4	
		on east side of station accessed from yard				
61¾	61:60	COLERAINE	1855	Open	4 D4	73
		called COLERAINE (NORTHBROOK) from 1855 to 1861				
61¾	61:61	Coleraine Station Gates	1855	Open	4 D4	73
61¾	61:62	Junction	1860	1963	4 D4	73
		also junction for Portrush				
0	0:00	Junction	1860	1963	4 D4	
?	?	Harbour Junction	1882	1966 ?	4 D4	
		unused from 1963				
0	0	Harbour Junction	1892	1966	4 D4	
		unused from 1963				
?	?	Private Siding	?	?	4 D4	
		trails in on left immediately after junction				
0½	0:31	Coleraine Harbour	1892	1966	4 D4	
		unused from 1963				
?	?	Bann Bridge (old)	1860	1924	4 D4	
		435ft long, 30 spans, wood,centre opening span				
0¾	0:51	Junction	1860	1924	4 C3	
62¼	62:20	River Bann Bridge (new)	1924	Open	4 D3	
		opened 21-03-1924, 800ft long, 11 span				
?	?	Junction	1924	1924	4 C3	
		closed as junction				
62	?	COLERAINE WATERSIDE	1853	1861	4 D4	
62½	?	Junction	1860	1924	4 C3	
62½	62:32	Junction from Waterside	1860	1924	4 C3	
65	65:12	Grangemore Crossing	1855	Open	4 C3	
65¾	66:30 ?	BARMOUTH	1855	1856	4 C3	
		flag station				
66½	66:35	Barmouth Crossing	1853	Open	4 C3	
67½	67:40	Castlerock Crossing	1853	Open	4 C3	
67½	67:40	CASTLEROCK	1853	Open	4 C3	
67¾	67:69	Castlerock Tunnel	1853	Open	4 C3	
		668 yards long				
68¼	68:25	Downhill Tunnel	1853	Open	4 C3	
		307 yards long				
69	68:75	DOWNHILL	1853	1976	4 C3	
		summer only service from 03-09-1973; closed 18-10-1976				
70½		UMBRA	1855 ?	1861 ?	4 C3	
		possible flag station ?				
70½	70:50	Umbra Crossing	1853	Open	4 C3	
71¼	71:30	Woodtown Crossing	1853	Open	4 C3	
72	71:74	Magilligan Crossing	1853	Open	4 B3	
72	71:76	MAGILLIGAN	1853	Closed	4 C3	134
		junction for Magilligan Point Branch; the station closed 18-10-1976, re-opened 16-06-1980, closed again in the 1980s				
73	72:74	Clooney Crossing	1853	Open	4 B3	
73¾	73:53	Duncrun East Crossing	1853	Open	4 B3	
74	73:70	Duncrun West Crossing	1853	Open	4 B3	
75	74:74	Bellarena Crossing	1853	Open	4 B4	
75	74:76	BELLARENA	1853	Open	4 B4	
		closed 18-10-1976, reopened 28-06-1982				
76	76:09	Carrowreagh Crossing	1853	Open	4 B4	
77	77:00	Roe Bridge	1852	Open	4 B4	
		renewed 1948, 480ft long				
78¼	79:18	Myroe Crossing	1853	Open	4 B4	
79¼	79:55	LIMAVADY JUNCTION	1853	1976	4 B4	68
		opened 07-1853, known as 'JUNCTION'. Shown as NEWTOWN JUNCTION 1861 to 1875 and as LIMAVADY JUNCTION from 1876 onwards; closed 18-10-1976				
80½	80:49	Ballykelly Siding	c.1940	?	4 B4	
		installed during WW2 for military use				
81	81:03	Ballykelly Crossing	1943	Closed	4 B4	
		opened 09-1943, airfield runway crossed tracks				
81¼ ?		DRENNAN'S FARM	1942 ?	Closed	4 B4	
		open from 12-04-1942, WW2 military halt				
81¾	81:51	BALLYKELLY	1853	1954	4 B4	
		opened 02-1853, closed 20-09-1954				
82¾	82:52	CARRICHUE	1853	1954	4 B4	
		opened 02-1853, named CARRICKHUGH until 1875/6, closed 20-09-1954				
84	84:76	FAUGHANVALE	1855	1859	4 A4	
87	86:77	Donnybrewer Crossing	1855	Open	4 A4	
87	87:06	Donnybrewer Siding	?	?	4 A4	
		used for Eglinton Aerodrome traffic				
87 ?		LONGFIELD	1942 ?	Closed	4 A4	
		open from 12-04-1942, WW2 military halt				
87¾	87:58	EGLINTON	1853	1973	4 A4	
		opened 02-1853, formerly WILLSBOROUGH, renamed MUFF in 09-1853, renamed EGLINTON in 01-1854; closed 1861 by BNCR, re-opened 1875 by BNCR; closed 02-07-1973				
87¾	87:60	Eglinton Crossing	1852	Open	4 A4	
89	88:70	Lock Crossing	1852	Open	4 A4	
89¾	89:60 ?	Faughan Bridge	1852	Open	4 B4	
		renewed 1937, 355ft, 11 spans				
90	90:00	Du Pont Crossing	?	Open	4 A4	
90¼	90:20	Coolkeeragh Siding	?	?	4 B4	
		industrial siding				
90½	90:32	CULMORE	1854	1973	4 A4	
		closed 02-07-1973				
90¾		Lisahally Siding	?	?	4 A4	
		serving Lisahally Manure Works				
?	?	Naval Base siding,	?	?	–	
		location unknown				
90¾	90:65	Lisahally Crossing	1852	Open	4 A4	
90¾	90:68	LISAHALLY	1942 ?	Closed	4 A4	147
		open from 12-04-1942, WW2 military halt				
95¼	95:20	LONDONDERRY WATERSIDE (old stn)	1852	1980	3 D4	135
		closed 24-02-1980				
95½	95:32	LONDONDERRY (new station)	1980	Open	3 D4	
		opened 24-02-1980, 200yds west of old station				

68 Limavady Junction to Dungiven

NCC / 5ft 3in gauge / mileposts measured from Limavady Junction

LCR opened to Limavady, goods in 10-1852, passenegers 29-12-1852.
The line was extended to Coleraine from the point which became known as Limavady Junction in 1853.
Limavady to Dungiven opened 04-07-1883 by the LDR.

Limavady to Dungiven closed to passengers 01-01-1933 by the NCC.
Limavady to Dungiven closed to goods 03-07-1950 by the UTA.
Limavady Junction to Limavady closed to passengers 03-07-1950 by the UTA.
Limavady Junction to Limavady closed to goods 02-05-1955 by the UTA.

MPost Dist.	Miles & Chains	Place / Feature (notes)	Date Opened	Date Closed	Map Grid	Table Ref.
0		LIMAVADY JUNCTION	1853	1976	4 B4	67
		opened 07-1853, known as 'JUNCTION'; shown as NEWTOWN JUNCTION 1861 to 1875 and as LIMAVADY JUNCTION from 1876 onwards; closed 18-10-1976				

0¾	BROIGHTER	1853	1950	4 B4
	opened 02-1853, not advertised 1920s to 01-06-1934			
0¾	Broighter Station Gates	?	1955	4 B4
3¼	LIMAVADY	1852	1950	4 B4
	called NEWTOWNLIMAVADY until 1870			
?	Sand Pit Siding	?	?	4 B4
5¾	ARDMORE	1883	1933	4 B4
8¼	Drumsurn Station Gates	1883	1950	4 B5
8¼	DRUMSURN	1883	1933	4 B5
10½	DERRYORK	1883	1933	4 B5
12¼	Level Crossing	1883	1950	4 B5
13½	DUNGIVEN	1883	1933	4 B5

69   Magherafelt to Draperstown

NCC / 5ft 3in gauge / mileposts measured from Magherafelt

Draperstown Junction to Draperstown opened to passengers 20-07-1883 by the DrR.
Draperstown Junction to Draperstown opened to goods 08-10-1883 by the DrR.

Draperstown Junction to Draperstown closed to passengers 01-10-1930 by the NCC.
Draperstown Junction to Draperstown closed completely 03-07-1950 by the UTA.

MPost Dist.	Miles & Chains	Place / Feature (notes)	Date Opened	Date Closed	Map Grid	Table Ref.
0		MAGHERAFELT	1856	1950	10 C1	66,74
0		Junction with Macfin line	1880	1959	10 B1	66,74
		ran parallel with Derry Central line for ½ mile				
0½ ?		Deehan's Crossing	1856	1959	10 C1	
		adjacent to Hatton's Crossing				
0½ ?		Point of Divergence	1856	1959	10 C1	74
		Derry Central line diverges at this point				
1¼		Draperstown Junction	1883	1950	10 B1	66
1¾		McCready's Crossing	1883	1950	10 B1	
1¾		Motor Transport Depot Siding	c.1942	c.1945	10 B1	
		¾ mile siding served US Army Motor Transport Depot at Luney Camp				
2		Walls' Crossing	1883	1950	10 B1	
3		DESERTMARTIN	1883	1930	10 B1	
4½		Donnelly's Crossing	1883	1950	10 B1	
7¼ ?		Serjeant's Crossing	1883	1950	4 C6	
8		DRAPERSTOWN	1883	1930	4 C6	

70   Larne Harbour to Ballymena

NCC / 3ft gauge / mileposts measured from Larne Harbour

Larne Harbour to Ballyclare Junction opened for goods 01-09-1877 by the BLR.
Larne Harbour to Ballyclare Junction opened to passengers 24-08-1878 by the BLR.
Ballyclare Junction to Ballymena Harryville opened for goods 01-06-1878 by the BLR.
Ballyclare Junction to Ballymena Harryville opened to passengers 24-08-1878 by the BLR.
Ballymena Harryville to Ballymena opened 22-09-1880 by the BLR.

Larne Harbour to Larne closed to passengers 01-06-1932 by the NCC.
Ballymena to Larne closed to passengers 01-02-1933 by the NCC.
Ballymena to Ballyboley Junction closed completely 02-06-1940 by the NCC.
Larne Harbour to Ballyboley Junction closed completely 03-07-1950 by the UTA.

MPost Dist.	Miles & Chains	Place / Feature (notes)	Date Opened	Date Closed	Map Grid	Table Ref.
		LARNE HARBOUR	1877	c.1890	5 D6	76
0	0:00	LARNE HARBOUR	c.1890	1932	5 D6	76
		one platform at Broad gauge station				
?		British Aluminium Works	1900	1950	5 D6	211
		factory closed 1960				
?		Curran Road Crossing	1877	1933	5 D6	
		replaced by Olderfleet Road overbridge				
1		LARNE	1878	1933	5 D6	76
?		Millbrook Bank Siding	1878	?	5 C6	
3¾		Ballyrickard Siding	1878	?	5 C6	
		siding to Ballyrickard Quarry				
4		Kilwaughter Crossing	1877	1950	5 C6	

4	KILWAUGHTER HALT	1885	1933	5 C6	
	closed 03-1888 to 01-1908				
4	Kilwaughter Siding	1885	1950	5 C6	
6¼	Headwood Crossing	1877	1950	5 C6	
6¼	HEADWOOD	1882	1933	5 C6	
	opened 01-06-1882?; originally BALLYGOWAN, but called HEADWOOD by 10-1882				
6¾	Moss Bridge Siding	1882	1890 ?	5 C6	
	served Shane's Hill Mines				
7¾	BALLYBOLEY JUNCTION	1888	1933	5 C6	71
	formerly BALLYCLARE JUNCTION, renamed 1889				
10	BALLYEASTON HALT	1880	1933	5 C6	
	formerly BALLYEASTON BRIDGE, closed 01-06-1882, re-opened as BALLYEASTON HALT in 1911				
12	BALLYNASHEE	1879	1933	5 C6	
15½	COLLIN HALT	1887	1933	5 B6	
	trains stopped on market days from 1883, or earlier				
17½	MOORFIELDS	1878	1933	5 B6	
	opened 14-12-1878				
?	Tawnybrack Siding	1878	?	5 B6	
	also called Kirk Siding and Tannybrake Siding				
20½	KELLS	1878	1933	5 B6	315
	2'6" gauge line from Dinsmore factory				
23	McQuiston's Siding	1878	?	5 A6	
	served Brickworks				
24¾	Gas Company Siding	?	?	5 A6	
24¾	BALLYMENA HARRYVILLE	1878	1916	5 A6	
	closed to passengers 01-01-1890 but remained in use for goods except for 06.15am morning departure each day until 09-1916				
25¼	BALLYMENA	1880	1933	5 A6	67,72
	Harryville-Ballymena section known as the High Level line				

71   Ballyboley Junction to Doagh

NCC / 3ft gauge / mileposts measured from Larne Harbour

Ballyclare Junction to Ballyclare opened for goods 01-09-1877 by the BLR.
Ballyclare Junction to Ballyclare opened for passengers 24-08-1878 by the BLR.
Ballyclare to Doagh opened for goods 08-02-1884 by the BLR.
Ballyclare to Doagh opened for passengers 01-05-1884 by the BLR.

Ballyboley Junction to Doagh closed to passengers 01-10-1930 by the NCC.
Ballyclare Paper Mill to Doagh closed completely 15-06-1944 by the NCC.
Ballyboley Junction to Ballyclare Paper Mill closed completely 03-07-1950 by the UTA.

MPost Dist.	Miles	Place / Feature (notes)	Date Opened	Date Closed	Map Grid	Table Ref.
7¾	0	BALLYBOLEY JUNCTION	1878	1933	5 C6	70
		originally BALLYCLARE JUNCTION, renamed 1889				
9½	1¾	BALLYNURE	1879	1930	11 B1	
		opened by 05-1879				
11½	3¾	Coal Siding	?	?	11 B1	
		private siding to coal merchant in main street parallel to station				
11½	3¾	BALLYCLARE	1878	1930	11 B1	
12	4¼	Ballyclare Paper Mill Siding	1878	1950	11 B1	
13½	5¾	DOAGH	1884	1930	11 A1	

72   Ballymena to Retreat

NCC / 3ft gauge / mileposts measured from Ballymena

Ballymena to Cargan opened for iron ore 26-03-1875 by the BCRBR.
Ballymena to Cargan opened for goods 01-07-1875 by the BCRBR.
Cargan to Parkmore opened for goods 01-01-1876 by the BCRBR.
Parkmore to Retreat opened for goods 08-10-1876 by the BCRBR.
Ballymena to Knockanally opened for passengers 05-04-1886 by the BNCR.
Knockanally to Parkmore opened for passengers 27-08-1888 by the BNCR.

Ballymena to Parkmore closed to passengers 01-10-1930 by the NCC.
Rathkenny Creamery Siding to Retreat closed completely 10-04-1937 by the NCC.
Ballymena to Rathkenny Creamery Siding closed completely 02-06-1940 by the NCC.

MPost Dist.	Miles & Chains	Place / Feature (notes)	Date Opened	Date Closed	Map Grid	Table Ref.
0	0:00	BALLYMENA	1886	Open	5 A6	67,70
2¾		BALLYGARVEY / advertised from 08-1887	1887	1930	5 A6	
2¾		Ballygarvey Crossing	1875	1940	5 A6	
4		BALLYCLOUGHAN	1886	1930	5 B5	
4		Ballycloughan Crossing	1875	1940	5 B5	
6		RATHKENNY	1886	1930	5 B5	
0	0:00	Rathkenny / line worked by Antrim Iron Ore Company, / joined Rathkenny Mines mineral line			5 B5	414
?		Rathkenny Mine Siding	1876	?	5 B5	
?		Rathkenny Creamery Siding	1905	1940	5 B5	
6¾		CLOUGH ROAD	1886	1930	5 B5	
7¼		Islandtown Crossing	1875	1937	5 B5	
8¼		MARTINSTOWN / formerly KNOCKANALLY, renamed 04-1920	1886	1930	5 B5	
0	0:00	Martinstown / known as 'Bleagh Branch'	?	?	5 B5	
?		Mount Cashel Iron Ore Mines / reopened and extended 1916-1919, / owned by Mount Cashel Mine Co	?	?	5 B5	
?		Evishnablay Mine.				
9¾		Crossing	1875	1937	5 B5	
9¾		CROSS ROADS / formerly CARROWCOWAN, renamed by 07-1889; / had siding for Carrowcowan Ironstone Mine	1888	1930	5 B5	
11¼		CARGAN	1893/4	1930	5 B5	153
0	0:00	CARGAN / branch built by Antrim Iron Ore Co	?	?	5 B5	153
0¼		Crossing	?	?	5 B5	
?		British Aluminium Cargan Bauxite Mine; / later cut back to ¼ mile			5 B5	
1¾		Dungonnell Mines	?	?	5 B5	
0	0:00	CARGAN / opened 02-1877	1877	?	5 B5	
0¼ ?		Legagrane Inclined Plane / rope worked incline	1877	?	5 B5	
2		Crommelin Mines	1877	?	5 B5	
12½		Evishacrow Siding / opened 01-01-1876, served Evishacrow Mine, / Chambers Mine and Binvore Burn; about 1 mile long.	1876	?	5 B5	
13½		PARKMORE / transfer with 2'0" gauge Parkmore Siding	1888	1930	5 B5	336
?		Essathohan Siding / highest point on an Irish railway at 1,045ft	?	?	5 B4	
16¼		Retreat	1876	1937	5 B4	

73 Coleraine to Portrush Harbour

NCC / 5ft 3in gauge / mileposts measured from Belfast York Road via Greenisland

Coleraine to Portrush opened 04-12-1855 by the BBCPJR.
Portrush to Portrush Harbour opened 06-1866 by the BNCR.

Portrush to Portrush Harbour closed 1949 by the UTA.
Coleraine to Portrush closed to goods circa 1954 by the UTA.

MPost Dist.	Miles & Chains	Place / Feature (notes)	Date Opened	Date Closed	Map Grid	Table Ref.
61¾	61:60	COLERAINE / called COLERAINE (NORTHBROOK) from 1855 to 1861	1855	Open	4 D4	67
61¾	61:61	Coleraine Station Gates	1855	Open	4 D4	67
?	?	Junction to Londonderry / via old Bann Bridge	1860	1924	4 D4	67
61¾	61:62	Junction to Londonderry / via new Bann Bridge	1924	Open	4 D3	67
62	62:02	Artillery Road Crossing / also called Millburn or Calf Lane Crossing	1855	Open	4 D3	
63	63:00	UNIVERSITY	1968	Open	4 D3	
65	64:74	Cromore Crossing	1855	Open	4 D3	
65	65:00	CROMORE / formerly PORTSTEWART, closed 09-09-1963, / re-opened and renamed CROMORE 10-03-1969, closed 16-05-1988. / Portstewart Tramway started from station yard.	c.1856	1988	4 D3	132
67	67:03	Glenmanus Siding / used for Stone Traffic	1929	1966	4 D3	
67	67:20	DHU VARREN / station opened 10-02-1969, built on part / of the Glenmanus Siding site	1969	Open	4 D3	
67½	67:60	PORTRUSH	1855	Open	4 D3	
68¼		Portrush Harbour / mixed gauge with GCPBVT 1883-1895	1866	1949	4 D3	113

74 Magherafelt to Macfin Junction

NCC / 5ft 3in gauge / mileposts measured from Magherafelt

Magherafelt to Macfin Junction opened 19-02-1880 by the DCeR.

Magherafelt to Macfin Junction closed to passengers 28-08-1950 by the UTA.
Kilrea to Macfin Junction closed to goods 28-08-1950 by the UTA.
Magherafelt to Kilrea closed to goods 05-10-1959 by the UTA.

MPost Dist.	Miles & Chains	Place / Feature (notes)	Date Opened	Date Closed	Map Grid	Table Ref.
0		MAGHERAFELT	1880	1959	10 C1	66,69
0		Junction with Cookstown line / ran parallel with Cookstown line for ½ mile	1883	1959	10 B1	66,69
0½		Hatton's Crossing / adjacent to Deehan's Crossing	1856	1959	10 C1	66,69
0½		Point of Divergence / Cookstown line diverges at this point	1880	199	10 C1	66,69
3		Bowman's Crossing	1880	1959	4 D6	
4		KNOCKLOUGHRIM	1880	1959	4 D6	
4¼		McGrath's Crossing	1880	1959	4 D6	
7¼		MAGHERA	1880	1959	4 C6	
9½		UPPERLANDS	1880	1959	4 D6	
9½		Siding / to William Clarke's Linen Mill, about 1½ miles / long with a level crossing near Upperlands, / terminated in factory premises with various sidings; / line is crossed by the narrow gauge Horse tramway.	1894	1959		148
10½		McCaw's Crossing	1880	1959	4 D6	
10¾		Gorteade Crossing / also called O'Kane's Crossing	1880	1959	4 D6	
13		TAMLAGHT HALT / had cast concrete shelter with date cast on / shelter as 1916, possibly one of the earliest uses / of cast concrete in an Irish railway structure	1914	1950	4 D6	
13		Tamlaght Halt Gates	?	1959	4 D6	
14¾		Drumagarner Crossing / also called Hutchinson's Crossing	1880	1959	4 D5	
15¾		KILREA	1880	1959	4 D5	
16¾		Reastown Crossing / also called Drumare Crossing	1880	1950	4 D5	
18½		Trinaltinagh Crossing	1880	1950	4 D5	
21½		GARVAGH	1880	1950	4 C5	
23¾		MONEYCARRIE HALT / closed c.1905 to 1908	1888	1950	4 C5	
24¾		Ardreagh Crossing / also called Clinton's Crossing	1880	1950	4 D4	
25½		AGHADOWEY	1880	1950	4 D4	
26¾		Culcrow Crossing / also called Lagan's Crossing	1880	1950	4 D4	
27¾		CURRAGH BRIDGE HALT	1908	1950	4 D4	
28¾		Macfin Bridge / lattice girder with opening span	1880	1950	4 D4	
29¼		MACFIN / opened and closed as junction	1880	1950	4 D4	67

75   Ballyclare Junction to Ballyclare

NCC / 5ft 3in gauge / mileposts measured from Belfast York Road via Greenisland

Kingsbog Junction to Ballyclare opened 03-11-1884 by the BNCR.

Kingsbog Junction to Ballyclare closed to passengers 01-01-1938 by the NCC.
Kingsbog Junction to Ballyclare closed to goods 02-05-1938 by the NCC.
Line re-opened for wartime goods traffic in 1940.
Line remained open for Race Specials until 1950.
Line closed completely 03-07-1950 by the UTA.

There were at least two military sidings in the branch, locations not known, both removed by 1950

MPost Dist.	Miles & Chains	Place / Feature (notes)	Date Opened	Date Closed	Map Grid	Table Ref.
10¾	10:60	BALLYCLARE JUNCTION closed as junction, formerly named BALLYNURE ROAD until 03-11-1884	1848	1950	11 B1	67
11¼	11:15	Kingsmoss No.1 Crossing also called Ballyclare Junction No.2	1848	Open	11 B1	67
11½	11:30	Kingsmoss No.2 Crossing also called Ballyclare Junction No.3	1848	Open	11 B1	67
11¾	11:60	Kingsbog Junction opened and closed as junction	1884	1950	11 B1	67
12		KINGS MOSS HALT	1926	1938	11 B1	
12¾		LISNALINCHY	1885	1938	11 B1	
13¼		LISNALINCHY RACECOURSE race days only	1934	1950	11 B1	
15¼		BALLYCLARE	1884	1938	11 B1	

76   Whiteabbey to Larne Harbour

NCC / 5ft 3in gauge / mileposts measured from Belfast York Road

Whiteabbey to Carrickfergus (old station) opened 12-04-1848 by the BBR.
Monkstown to Carrickfergus Junction opened 12-04-1848 by the BBR.
Carrickfergus to Larne Harbour opened 01-10-1862 by the CLaR.
Carrickfergus Harbour Junction to Carrickfergus Harbour opened 01-01-1887 by the CHJR, using old BBR line to 1848 terminus station.

No service between Larne and Larne Harbour 01-01-1864 to 01-07-1872.
Carrickfergus Harbour Junction Railway closed 1957 by the UTA.
Monkstown Junction to Greenisland closed to passengers 09-09-1961 by the UTA.
Monkstown Junction to Greenisland closed 01-10-1963 by the UTA.

MPost Dist.	Miles & Chains	Place / Feature (notes)	Date Opened	Date Closed	Map Grid	Table Ref.
4¼	4:24	WHITEABBEY	1848	Open	11 B2	67
4¾	4:56	Bleach Green Junction	1934	Open	11 B2	67
4¾	4:61	Bleach Green Halt Crossing replaced by bridge	?	1934	11 B2	
4¾	4:65	BLEACH GREEN HALT opened 04-1925, closed 23-10-1932, re-opened 22-01-1934 on new site, closed 09-05-1977	1925	1977	11 B2	
4¾	4:63	Henderson's Mill Siding trailing siding off down line with level crossing near entrance to Mill	?	1966	11 B1	
5½	5:28	JORDANSTOWN NI POLYTECHNIC added to name 1974	by 1853	Open	11 B1	
5½	5:35	Jordanstown Crossing	1848	Open	11 B1	
8¾		MONKSTOWN HALT (old station) on old alignment; closed 28-05-1933	1905	1933	11 B1	76
8¾	8:46	MONKSTOWN HALT (new station) opened 22-01-1934 on new alignment, closed c.1959, re-opened 04-09-1967, closed 23-01-1978, re-opened 01-09-1980, closed 23-02-1981.	1934	1981	11 B1	76
8¾	?	Monkstown Halt Crossing replaced by Bridge	?	1933	11 B1	76

6¾	6:56	GREENISLAND Monkstown to Greenisland section known as 'the back line'	1848	Open	11 B1	
6¾	6:56	GREENISLAND formerly CARRICKFERGUS JUNCTION, renamed 10-1893	1848	Open	11 B1	
7¾	7:67	Trooperslane Crossing	1848	Open	11 B1	
7¾	7:72	TROOPERSLANE	by 1850	Open	11 B1	
7¾		Belfast Mining Company siding exchange siding for Duncrue Salt Mine Tramway	by 1865	?	11 B1	213
8½	8:50	Courtauld's Siding Extensive internal system	1946	1967	11 B1	152
8¾	8:60	MOUNT HALT opened 04-1925, closed 01-10-1930, re-opened by 01-07-1946 as COURTAULDS' PLATFORM, re-named MOUNT by 07-10-1946, closed 08-05-1972	1925	1972	11 B1	
9	9:10	Carrickfergus Harbour Junction	1887	1957	11 B1	
0	0:00	Carrickfergus Harbour Junc	1887	1957	11 B1	
?		Minorca Siding served Salt Works	?	?	11 C1	
		CARRICKFERGUS (old station)	1848	1862	11 B1	
1⅛		Carrickfergus Harbour	1887	1957	11 C1	
?		Salt Works Siding accessed by headshunt from pier	?	by 1957	11 C1	
?		Carrickfergus West Pier 6 furlongs, 15 chains, 23yds to West Pier	1887	1957	11 C1	
9¼	9:18	Salt Mines Siding	?	?	11 B1	
9¼	9:20	CLIPPERSTOWN opened 04-1925	1925	Open	11 B1	
9¼?	?	Woodburn Junction end-on junction between BNCR & CLaR	1862	Open	11 B1	
?	?	John Kelly's Siding served Albert Brickworks off up goods yard headshunt; removed by 09-1953.		by 1953	11 B1	344
9½	9:45	CARRICKFERGUS (new station)	1862	Open	11 B1	
10	10:03	BARN HALT opened 04-1925, closed 01-06-1931, re-opened c.1942, closed 09-05-1977	1925	1977	11 C1	
10½	10:38	DOWNSHIRE opened 04-1925 as DOWNSHIRE PARK, renamed DOWNSHIRE c.1979	1925	Open	11 C1	
11	11:03	EDEN HALT opened 04-1925, closed 09-05-1977	1925	1977	11 C1	
11¼	11:11	Level Crossing temporary crossing for contractors lorries building power station	1977	1977	11 C1	
11½	11:43	KILROOT closed 09-05-1977	1862	1977	11 C1	
?	?	Briggs Loop passing loop prior to doubling of line	?	1929	11 C1	
?	?	Ballast Pit Siding	?	?	11 C1	
13¾	13:70	WHITEHEAD (1st station) opened 01-05-1863	1863	1864	11 C1	
14	?	WHITEHEAD (2nd station) opened 01-06-1864	1864	1877	11 C1	
14	14:16	Whitehead Tunnel 145yds long on Down line only; Up line avoiding tunnel opened 06-10-1929, singled between MP12½ and MP14½ in 1994; Down line now running line	1862	Open	11 C1	
14¾	14:55	WHITEHEAD (3rd station) opened 06-1877	1877	Open	11 C1	
14¾	14:62	Whitehead Station Gates pedestrian crossing	?	Open	11 C1	
?	?	WHITEHEAD EXCURSION STATION opened 10-07-1907; since 1966 the main depot of the Railway Preservation Society of Ireland, station open for train rides during the summer	1907	Open	11 C1	
16½	16:40	BALLYCARRY	1862	Open	11 C1	
19½	19:28	Magheramorne Loop passing loop; temporary spoil sidings for motorway construction. Opened 11-11-1966, closed 02-05-1970	?	Open	11 C1	
19¾	19:60	MAGHERAMORNE formerly BALLYLIG, renamed 07-1863	1862	Open	5 D6	

MPost Dist.	Miles & Chains	Place / Feature (notes)	Date Opened	Date Closed	Map Grid	Table Ref.
19¾	?	Cement Works Siding siding to Cement Works adjacent to station	?	?	5 D6	
21¾	21:48	GLYNN opened 01-10-1864	1864	Open	5 D6	
23	23:00	Howden Brothers Sidings sidings either side of line, one called Bank Siding the other called Stone Siding	?	?	5 D6	243
23¼	23:20	LARNE closed 23-06-1974 due to deviation	1862	1974	5 D6	
23¼	23:29	LARNE TOWN opened 23-06-1974 on deviation	1974	Open	5 D6	70
24	24:00	LARNE HARBOUR narrow gauge passenger trains from 1890 to 1932; after 1932, two broad gauge platforms	c.1890	Open	5 D6	70
24		LARNE HARBOUR no passenger service 01-01-1864 to 01-07-1872	1862	c.1890	5 D6	

77 Ballymoney to Ballycastle

BR / 3ft gauge / mileposts measured from Ballymoney

Ballymoney to Ballycastle opened 18-10-1880 by the BR.
Ballymoney to Ballycastle closed 24-03-1924 by the BR.
Ballymoney to Ballycastle re-opened 11-08-1924 by the NCC.

Ballymoney to Ballycastle closed completely 03-07-1950 by the UTA, abandoned 31-08-1953

MPost Dist.	Miles & Chains	Place / Feature (notes)	Date Opened	Date Closed	Map Grid	Table Ref.
0		BALLYMONEY	1880	1950	4 D4	67
4½		DERVOCK	1880	1950	5 A4	
6¾		STRANOCUM	1880	1950	5 A4	
8¼		GRACEHILL opened December 1890	1890	1950	5 A4	
10¼		ARMOY	1880	1950	5 A4	
11		Balleeny Siding for local lime and agricultural traffic	1881	1895	5 A4	
13		CAPECASTLE opened February 1882	1882	1950	5 A3	
13		Capecastle Tunnel – 66 yards long	1880	1950	5 A3	
15		Ballast Pit Siding	1897	1950	5 B3	
16		Tow Viaduct – 4 arch stone viaduct	1880	1950	5 B3	
16¼		Nicholl's Sawmill Siding siding running down steep bank to John Nicholl's Sawmill adjacent to Tow Viaduct	c.1925	1940	5 B3	
16¼		BALLYCASTLE	1880	1950	5 B3	

78 Belfast Queen's Quay to Bangor

BCDR / 5ft3in gauge / mileposts originally measured from Belfast Queen's Quay

Belfast Queen's Quay to Holywood opened 02-08-1848 by the BCDR.
Holywood to Bangor opened 18-05-1865 by the BHBR.

Belfast Queen's Quay to Ballymacarrett Junction closed to passengers 12-04-1976 by NIR.

Line was re-mileposted in c.1980-1 following re-opening of Belfast Central Railway and continues GNR(I) sequence from Dublin Amiens Street, new distances shown in brackets.

MPost Dist.	Miles & Chains	Place / Feature (notes)	Date Opened	Date Closed	Map Grid	Table Ref.
0	0:00	BELFAST QUEEN'S QUAY (BCDR) called QUEEN'S QUAY from 1854	1848	1976	34 C3	79
0	0:00	BELFAST QUEENS QUAY (BHBR) became part of BCDR station on merger in 1884	1859	1976	34 C3	79
0	0:00	Central Services Depot closed 28-11-1994	1976	1994	34 C3	79
0½ (114¼)	0:40 (114:27)	Ballymacarrett Junction junction with BCR, BHC and Downpatrick line, opened 09-08-1874; closed as a junction with the Downpatrick line 24-04-1950; closed as a junction with BHC and BCH 31-07-1965; re-opened as a junction with the BCR 12-04-1976; finally closed as a junction to the Central Services Depot 28-11-1994.	1874	1994	34 D3	79, 116
0¾ (114¾)	0:71 (114:58)	BALLYMACARRETT HALT closed 09-05-1977	1905	1977	34 D3	
1¼ (115¼)	1:24 (115:12)	VICTORIA PARK HALT closed 01-02-1988	1905	1988	34 D3	
1¾ (115¾)		Sydenham Level Crossing accommodation crossing at Up end of platforms connected public road to part finished Sydenham Bypass, adjacent to Airport and RNAS Station. Signalled for 'military use' 16-08-1940 and maintained for public use after WW2 until bypass completed late 1950s	?	1950s	34 D2	
1¾ (115¾)	1:70 (115:47)	SYDENHAM formerly BALLYMISERT, renamed 1856	1851	Open	34 D2	
2¼ (116)	2:21 (115:78)	Petroleum Board Siding opened 02-1942; out of use after WW2, connection maintained for several years, connection removed early 1950s	1942	c.1945	34 D2	
2¼ (116)	2:30 (116:06)	GLENMACHAN opened 01-11-1861	1861	1866	34 D2	
2½ (116¼)	2:53 (116:55)	TILLYSBURN HALT no road access; opened 10-1880, closed 02-05-1931, re-opened 23-05-1941	1880	1945	34 E2	
2¾ (116½)	2:75 (116:77)	TILLYSBURN opened 01-11-1848, closed 09-1874 to 05-1877	1848/9	c.1878	34 E2	
3¾ (117½)	3:36 (117:40)	Ministry of Defence (MoD) Crossing accommodation crossing	?	Open	34 E2	
4 (117¾)	3:64 (117:68)	KINNEGAR HALT closed 1930s, re-opened by 05-1943, closed 11-11-1957	1905	1957	34 E1	
4¼ (118¼)	4:16 (118:18)	Kinnegar Ordnance Siding opened 18-11-1940 to service adjacent Ordnance Depot; connection removed 10-1953 but MoD maintained trackwork and gate for many years	1940	1953	34 E1	
4½ (118¼)		Holywood Gasworks Siding siding served Gasworks, removed when down line realigned nearer Gasworks wall; coal was unloaded through shutes from Down Main at night!	?	c.1886	34 E1	
4½ (118¼)	4:37 (118:39)	HOLYWOOD	1865	Open	34 E1	
4½ (118¼)		HOLYWOOD original terminus	1848	1865	34 E1	
?	?	Route Diversion line resited a short way seaward; diversion opened 28-03-1971	1971	Open	34 E1	
5½ (119¼)	5:27 (119:19)	MARINO closed 11-11-1957, re-opened 04-01-1960	1868/9	Open	34 F1	
6 (119¾)	6:03 (119:70)	CULTRA closed 11-11-1957, reopened 03-07-1978	1865	Open	34 F1	
6¼ (120¼)	6:24 (120:11)	Cultra Siding trailing siding to Ulster Folk and Transport Museum	1987	Open	34 F1	
6¾ (120½)	6:45 (120:16)	CRAIGAVAD closed 11-11-1957, re-opened 04-01-1960, closed again 12-06-1961	1865	1961	11 B2	
7¾ (121½)	7:57 (121:38)	SEAHILL opened 04-04-1966	1966	Open	11 C2	
9 (122¾)	9:00 (122:65)	HELEN'S BAY formerly CLANDEBOYE, renamed 08-1885	1865	Open	11 C2	
9¾ (123½)	9:62 (123:48)	Crawfordsburn Viaduct 5 arch stone viaduct	1865	Open	11 C2	
9¾ (123½)	9:63 (123:49)	CRAWFORDSBURN opened 13-09-1965, formerly CRAWFORDSBURN HOSPITAL	1965	Open	11 C2	
10½ (124¼)	10:40 (124:26)	CARNALEA opened 01-06-1877	1877	Open	11 C2	
11¼ (125)	11:20 (125:03)	BANGOR WEST	1928	Open	11 C2	
12¼ (126)	12:20 (126:06)	BANGOR	1865	Open	11 C2	

79   Belfast Queen's Quay to Newcastle and Castlewellan

BCDR / 5ft 3in gauge / mileposts measured from Belfast Queen's Quay

Belfast Queen's Quay to Comber opened 06-05-1850 by the BCDR.
Comber to Ballynahinch Junction opened 10-09-1858 by the BCDR.
Ballynahinch Junction to Downpatrick opened 23-03-1859 by the BCDR.
Downpatrick to Newcastle opened 25-03-1869 by the DDNR.
Downpatrick Loop opened 24-09-1892 by the BCDR.
Newcastle to Castlewellan opened 24-03-1906 by the BCDR.

Ballymacarrett Junction to Comber closed completely 24-04-1950 by the UTA.
Comber to Newcastle closed completely 16-01-1950 by the UTA.
Newcastle to Castlewellan closed 02-05-1955 by the UTA.
Belfast Queen's Quay to Ballymacarrett Junction closed to passengers 11-04-1976 by NIR.

Downpatrick to Downpatrick Loop platform and South Junction re-opened 07-05-1990,
South Junction to Magnus' Grave opened Easter 1995 by the Dowpatrick and Ardglass
Railway, now called the Downpatrick Steam Railway.

MPost Dist.	Miles & Chains	Place / Feature (notes)	Date Opened	Date Closed	Map Grid	Table Ref.
0	0:00	BELFAST QUEEN'S QUAY (BCDR) called QUEEN'S QUAY from 1854	1848	1976	34 C3	79
0	0:00	BELFAST QUEENS QUAY (BHBR) became part of BCDR station on merger in 1884	1859	1976	34 C3	79
0	0:00	Central Services Depot closed 28-11-1994	1976	1994	34 C3	78
0¼	0:40	Ballymacarrett Junction junction with BCR, BHC and Downpatrick line, opened 09-08-1874; closed as a junction with the Downpatrick line 24-04-1950; closed as a junction with BHC and BCH 31-07-1965; re-opened as a junction with the BCR 12-04-1976; finally closed as a junction to the Central Services Depot 28-11-1994.	1874	1994	34 D3	78, 116
0½	0:45	FRASER STREET HALT Up platform only	1928	1950	34 D3	
1	?	Connswater Bridge 3 arch stone bridge	1850	1950	34 D3	
1¼	1:40	BLOOMFIELD	1879	1950	34 D3	
1¼	1:43	Bloomfield Station Gates	1850	1950	34 D3	
1¼	?	Stone Yard Siding on Down side, used by Chas. Ritchie, later R & J Pierce	1893	1926	34 D3	
2	?	Neill's Hill Sand Siding opened 06-1877, closed 06-1907	1877	1907	34 E3	
2	2:25	NEILL'S HILL	1890	1950	34 E3	
2	2:29	Neill's Hill Station Gates	1850	1950	34 E3	
2¾	2:56	Knock Station Gates	1850	1950	34 E3	
2¾	2:60	KNOCK opened late 1850; called KNOCK & BELMONT from 1865/6 to 1888/9	1850	1950	34 E3	
?	?	Monk & Co Siding quarry siding opened 01-1864	1864	?	34 E3	
?	?	Brown, Kent & Smith's Siding quarry siding opened 05-1865	1865	?	34 E3	
?	?	Thos. Dixon & Son's Siding quarry siding opened 10-1889	1889	1919?	34 F3	
5	4:78	DUNDONALD	1850	1950	34 F3	
5½	?	HENRYVILLE HALT temporary station during Tourist Trophy Car Race weeks Aug/Sept 1928-1936; possibly a private halt earlier	1928	1936	11 C3	
5½	5:35	Henryville Crossing	1850	1950	11 C3	
8	8:00	COMBER	1850	1950	11 C3	80
8	?	Andrews' Mill Sidings Board Minutes of 20-04-1863 state in working order except for stop block	1863	1950	11 C3	
8½	8:30	Comber Mainline Crossing also called Carr's Lane and Maxwell's Court Crossing	1858	1950	11 C3	
10¾	?	Dufferin No.1 Quarry Siding trailed on down side, also called Magheracouse Quarry	1885	1929	11 B3	
11¼	?	Dufferin No.2 Quarry Siding facing siding on down side	1899	1921	11 B3	
11¼	11:30	Chas Ritchie's Quarry Siding trailed on up side	1891	1906	11 B3	
11½	?	Robb's Quarry Siding facing siding on up side	1872	1942	11 B3	
11½	11:50	Francis Ritchie's Quarry Siding facing siding on up side	1872	1880	11 B3	
11¾	?	Gill's Siding trailed in up side, loading dock only	1895	1924	11 B3	
12	12:02	Ballygowan Station Gates	1858	1950	11 B3	
12	12:03	BALLYGOWAN	1858	1950	11 B3	
12¼?	?	Walker's Siding on Up side	c.1858	c.1863	11 B3	
13¾	13:60	SHEPHARD'S BRIDGE HALT	1930	1950	11 B3	
15¼	15:25	SAINTFIELD	1858	1950	11 B3	
15¼	15:27	Saintfield Station Gates	1858	1950	11 B3	
17¾	17:53	BALLYNAHINCH JUNCTION	1859	1950	11 B4	81
20¼	?	Crossgar Depot Siding Admiralty Depot; opened 06-1942, closed 06-1945	1942	1945	11 B4	
21½	21:12	CROSSGAR	1859	1950	11 B4	
23¾	23:60	KING'S BRIDGE HALT	1929	1942	11 C4	
25½	?	Quoile Bridge 503ft timber and iron bridge, rebuilt 10-1929 with embankment replacing timber spans and two 66ft steel girder spans on concrete piers	1859	1950	11 C4	
26¼	26:15	Downpatrick North Junction	1892	1950	11 C4	
26¼	26:15	Downpatrick North Junction	1892	1950	11 C4	
26¾	26:68	DOWNPATRICK closed 1950, reopened 1990 by DAR	1859	Open	11 C4	
26½	26:44	Downpatrick South Junction closed 1950, re-opened 1990 by DAR	1892	Open	11 C4	
26¼	26:30	DOWNPATRICK LOOP PLATFORM direct 'loop' built 1892; no road access, closed 1950, platform re-opened 1990 by DAR to a point just north of main line platform	1892	Open	11 C5	82
26¼	26:44	Downpatrick South Junction closed 1950, re-opened 1990 by DAR	1893	Open	11 C4	
26¾	26:64	MAGNUS'S GRAVE new station opened Easter 1995 by DAR	1995	Open	11 C5	
		Ardglass Junction	1892	1950	11 C5	82
30½	30:40	TULLYMURRY (old station)	1871	1896	11 B5	
30½	30:73	TULLYMURRY (new station)	1896	1950	11 B5	
32	32:10	BALLYKINLAR HALT served Army camp; not advertised to public	1914	1950	11 B5	
32¼	?	Ardilea Ballast Pit opened 10-1886, removed 01-1894 after long disuse	1886	by 1894	11 B5	
34¼	34:27	DUNDRUM	1869	1950	11 B5	
34¼	?	East Downshire Steamship Siding sidings ran down to Quay from goods yard	1869	1950	11 B5	
34¼	34:28	Dundrum Station Gates	1869	1950	11 B5	
34½	34:32	North of Ireland Produce Siding trailing siding on Up side	1915	1924	11 B5	
41¾	41:74	CASTLEWELLAN joint BCDR/GNR(I) station	1906	1955	11 B5	61
41¾	?	Murland's Mill Siding siding off goods yard headshunt	1906	1950	11 B5	61
39½	38:30	Junction with Downpatrick line	1906	1950	11 B5	61
36½	37:70	Junction with Castlewellan line	1906	1950	11 B5	61
38	38:10	NEWCASTLE closed 1950 to UTA trains, 1955 to GNR(I)	1869	1955	11 B5	61

80   Comber to Donaghadee

BCDR / 5ft 3in gauge / mileposts measured from Belfast Queen's Quay

Comber to Newtownards (Church Street) opened 06-05-1850 by the BCDR.
Newtownards (Church Street) to Donaghadee opened 03-06-1861 by the the BCDR.
Donaghadee Station to Donaghadee Harbour opened 03-1870 by the BCDR.

Donaghadee Station to Donaghadee Harbour closed officially 24-04-1950.
Comber to Donaghadee closed 24-04-1950 by the UTA.

MPost Dist.	Miles & Chains	Place / Feature (notes)	Date Opened	Date Closed	Map Grid	Table Ref.
8	8:00	COMBER	1850	1950	11 C3	79
8¾	8:53	Comber No.1 Crossing	1850	1950	11 C3	
		also called Killinchy Road Crossing, platform opened here 1851 for 'Quarterly Fair Days' but did not last long				
9½	9:33	Comber No.2 Crossing	1850	1950	11 C3	
		also called Cherryvalley Crossing				
9½	9:33	GLASS MOSS ROAD	1928	1936	11 C3	
		temporary station during Tourist Trophy Car Race weeks in August/September 1928-1936; platforms either side of Comber No.2 Crossing.				
9¾	9:59	Comber No.3 Crossing	1850	1950	11 C3	
		also called Glass Moss Crossing.				
10	10:05	Comber No.4 Crossing	1850	1950	11 C3	
		also called Orr's Road Crossing				
12	?	Scrabo Stone Siding	1851	1927	11 C3	279
		facing siding on down side				
12	?	Ulster Print Works Siding	1927	1950	11 C3	
		facing siding on Up side				
12¾	12:70	NEWTOWNARDS (CHURCH STREET)	1850	1861	11 C2	
		terminus off Church Street				
13½	13:33	NEWTOWNARDS (new station)	1861	1950	11 C2	
15¼	?	Drumhirk Ballast Quarry Siding	1904	1942	11 C2	
		opened 07-1904, closed 03-1942				
15¾	15:50	CONLIG	1861	1873	11 C2	
16½	16:46	Balloo Crossing	1861	1950	11 C2	
17¾	17:50	BALLYGRAINEY	1861	1950	11 C2	
		formerly GROOMSPORT & BANGOR, re-named GROOMSPORT ROAD, later re-named BALLYGRAINEY				
19½	19:36	BALLYFOTHERLY	c.1863	c.1876	11 D2	
		two Saturday trains only, later Wednesdays and Fridays and Saturdays only				
19½	19:46	Ballyfotherly Crossing	1861	1950	11 D2	
20¼	?	Hogstown Ballast Pit Siding	1876	1904	11 D2	
		trailed on down side, opened 06-1876, closed 03-1904				
21¾	21:55	MILLISLE ROAD HALT	1928	1950	11 D2	
22	22:20	DONAGHADEE	1861	1950	11 D2	
22½		Donaghadee Harbour Siding	1870	1950	11 D2	
		opened 03-1870, out of use from the 1930s but closed officially 24-04-1950				

81 Ballynahinch Junction to Ballynahinch

BCDR / 5ft3in gauge / mileposts measured from Belfast Queen's Quay

Ballynahinch Junction to Ballynahinch opened 10-09-1858 by the BCDR.

Ballynahinch Junction to Ballynahinch closed 16-01-1950 by the UTA.

MPost Dist.	Miles & Chains	Place / Feature (notes)	Date Opened	Date Closed	Map Grid	Table Ref.
17¾	17:53	BALLYNAHINCH JUNCTION	1859	1950	11 B4	79
19¼	19:20	CREEVYARGON HALT	1930	1950	11 B4	
21¼	21:20	BALLYNAHINCH	1858	1950	11 B4	

82 Downpatrick to Ardglass

BCDR / 5ft3in gauge / mileposts measured from Belfast Queen's Quay

Downpatrick to Ardglass opened for goods 27-05-1892 by the DKALR.
Ardglass to Ardglass Harbour opened for goods 31-05-1892 by the DKALR.
Downpatrick to Ardglass Harbour opened for Passengers 08-07-1892 by the DKALR.

Ardglass to Ardglass Harbour closed by 1932.
Downpatrick to Ardglass closed 16-01-1950 by the UTA.

Downpatrick to Downpatrick Loop platform and South Junction re-opened 07-05-1990, South Junction to Magnus' Grave opened Easter 1995 by the Dowpatrick and Ardglass Railway (DAR), now called the Downpatrick Steam Railway.

MPost Dist.	Miles & Chains	Place / Feature (notes)	Date Opened	Date Closed	Map Grid	Table Ref.
26¾	26:68	DOWNPATRICK	1859	Open	11 C4	79
		closed 1950, re-opened 1990 by DAR				
26¼	26:30	DOWNPATRICK LOOP PLATFORM	1893	Open	11 C5	79
		closed 1950, re-opened 1990 by DAR				
26½	26:44	Downpatrick South Junction	1893	Open	11 C4	79
		closed 1950, re-opened 1990 by DAR				
26¾	26:64	MAGNUS'S GRAVE	1995	Open	11 C4	79
		opened Easter 1995 by DAR				
		Ardglass Junction	1892	1950	11 C5	79
28	28:05	RACE COURSE PLATFORM	1893	1950	11 C5	
		first used 08-03-1893, race days only				
28¾	28:56	Vianstown Crossing	1892	1950	11 C5	
29¼	29:21	Marshalstown Crossing	1892	1950	11 C5	
30	29:77	Ballynoe Station Gates	1892	1950	11 C5	
30	30:02	BALLYNOE	1892	1950	11 C5	
31	31:09	Starkey's Crossing	1892	1950	11 C5	
		also called Whighamstown and Conianstown Crossing				
29¼	32:00	BRIGHT HALT	1925	1950	11 C5	
32	32:00	Bright Halt Gates	1892	1950	11 C5	
33¼	33:15	Killough Brickworks Siding	1914	1950	11 C5	
33¾	33:65	KILLOUGH	1892	1950	11 C5	
33¾	33:68	Killough Station Gates	1892	1950	11 C5	
33¾	33:70 ?	Killough Ballast Pit Siding	1892	?	11 C5	
34¼	34:20	CONEY ISLAND HALT	1934	?	11 C5	
		1942/3 working timetables state 'trains not to call'				
?	?	Viaduct	1892	1950	11 C5	
35	35:19	ARDGLASS	1892	1950	11 C5	
35½		Ardglass Harbour	1892	1920s	11 C5	

83 Cork to Coachford

CMLR / 3ft gauge / mileposts measured from Cork Western Road

Cork Western Road to Coachford Junction opened 08-08-1887 by the CMLR.
Coachford Junction to Coachford opened 19-03-1888 by the CMLR.

Cork to Coachford closed completely 31-12-1934 by the GSR.

MPost Dist.	Miles & Chains	Place / Feature (notes)	Date Opened	Date Closed	Map Grid	Table Ref.
0	0:00	CORK WESTERN ROAD	1887	1934	33 C2	
0¾		GAOL CROSS	by 1895	1898	33 C2	
		roadside stopping place, hand signals to driver to stop train; closed 1898 when electric tramway opened - see Table 162				
1	1:02	VICTORIA	1887	1934	33 C2	
2		EXHIBITION HALT	1932	1932	33 B2	217
		temporary station for Exhibition, May-Oct only				
3½	3:37	CARRIGROHANE	1887	1934	33 B2	
3¾	3:72	LEEMOUNT	1887	1934	33 A2	
4¾	4:72	HEALY'S BRIDGE	1887	1934	33 A2	
6¼	6:25	COACHFORD JUNCTION	1888	1934	33 A1	84
		open as junction; referred to in very early days as Blarney Junction				
6¼		Crossing	1888	1934	26 B6	
7¾	7:62	CLOGHROE	1888	1934	26 B6	
9½	9:39	GURTEEN	1888	1934	26 B6	
9½		Crossing	1888	1934	26 B6	
11¼	11:19	DRIPSEY	1888	1934	26 A6	
11¼		Crossing	1888	1934	26 A6	
12½	12:38	KILMURRY	1888	1934	26 A6	
12¾	12:61	Myshall Ballast Pit	1899 ?	1934 ?	26 A6	
12¾		Crossing	1888	1934	26 A6	
14¼		Crossing	1888	1934	26 A6	
14¼	14:15	PEAKE	1888	1934	26 A6	
15½	15:47	COACHFORD	1888	1934	26 A6	

84   Coachford Junction to Donoughmore and Blarney

CMLR / 3ft gauge / mileposts measured from Cork Western Road

Coachford Junction to Blarney opened 08-08-1887 by the CMLR.
St Anne's to Donoughmore opened 06-05-1893 by the DELR.

Coachford Junction to Donoughmore and Blarney closed completely 31-12-1934 by the GSR.

MPost Dist.	Miles & Chains	Place / Feature (notes)	Date Opened	Date Closed	Map Grid	Table Ref.
6¼	6:25	COACHFORD JUNCTION open as junction; referred to in very early days as BLARNEY JUNCTION	1888	1934	33 A1	83
6¼		Crossing	1887	1934	33 A1	
6¾	6:73	TOWER BRIDGE	1887	1934	33 A1	
7¼	7:25	ST ANNE'S also spelt ST ANN'S	1887	1934	33 A1	
	7:31	Donoughmore Junction open as junction	1893	1934	33 A1	
	7:31	Donoughmore Junction open as junction	1893	1934	33 A1	
8½	8:55	BLARNEY	1887	1934	33 B1	
7½		Crossing	1893	1934	33 A1	
8¼		Crossing	1893	1934	33 A1	
8¾		BURNT MILL	by 1895	1934	33 A1	
?		GURTH	c.1897	?	26 B5	
11¼		FOX'S BRIDGE	1893	1934	26 B5	
11¼		Crossing	1893	1934	26 B5	
12¼		KNOCKANE	by 1895	1934	26 B5	
12¼		Crossing	1893	1934	26 B5	
14¼		FIRMOUNT	1893	1934	26 B5	
14¼		Crossing	1893	1934	26 B5	
15¾		DONOUGHMORE	1893	1934	26 A5	

85   Cork Albert Quay to Baltimore

5ft 3in gauge / mileposts measured from Albert Quay
CCR – Ford Motor Company and Victoria Quay to Cork Albert Quay
CBSCR – Cork Albert Quay to Skibbereen
BER – Skibbereen to Baltimore Pier

Ballinhassig to Bandon (Low level) opened 30-06-1849 by the CBR.
Cork Albert Quay to Ballinhassig opened 08-12-1851 by the CBR.
Bandon (WCoR) to Dunmanway (old station) opened 12-06-1866 by the WCoR.
Dunmanway (old station) to Skibbereen opened 21-07-1877 by the IVR.
Skibbereen to Baltimore opened 02-05-1893 by the BER.
Cork Victoria Quay to Albert Quay opened to goods 01-01-1912 by the CCR.
Baltimore to Baltimore Pier opened 1917 by the BER.
Ford Motor Company to Victoria Quay opened c.1920 by the CCR.

Passenger services suspended 24-02-1947 due to fuel shortage.
Goods service suspended from Skibbereen to Baltimore from 10-03-1947.
Goods service resumed from Skibbereen to Baltimore from 24-05-1947.
Passenger services resumed 24-05-1947.

Cork Albert Quay to Baltimore closed 01-04-1961 by CIE. Clearance trains on 01-04-1961 and 02-04-1961

MPost Dist.	Miles & Chains	Place / Feature (notes)	Date Opened	Date Closed	Map Grid	Table Ref.
0	0:00	CORK ALBERT QUAY	1851	1961	33 D2	89
0¼	0:14	Junction from Glanmire Road Cork City Railway joins at this point	1912	1976	32 D2	
	?	Ford Motor Company	c.1920	1962 ?	33 D2	
	0:45	Victoria Quay last train ran October 1965	1912	1965 ?	33 D2	
	?	Cork Milling Co Siding virtually on the site of the CBPR Victoria Road Station	1936	1962	33 D2	
	?	Albert Street Cutting	1912	1965	33 D2	
	0:00	Junction with CBSCR joined on east side of station	1912	1965	32 D2	
0¼	0:16	Junction from Victoria Quay	1912	1965	32 D2	
?		Crossing replaced by bridge	1851	1911	33 D2	
?		Old Blackpool Road Tunnel very short, about 50 feet long	1851	1961	33 D2	
1		Ballyphehane Junction formerly Macroom Junction; junction with CMDR, closed in 1879; re-instated as a siding connection from 1918 to 1921 by the Government, and re-named Macroom Junction; re-instated and opened 02-03-1925, closed by CIE in 01-12-1953	1866	1879	33 D2	106
1½		Ballyphehane Viaduct replaced by embankment circa 1860	1851	c.1860	33 D2	
5		Chetwynd Viaduct 90ft high, 4x110ft spans; framework and piers survive	1851	1961	33 B3	
5¼	5:22	Castlewhite Crossing	1851	1961	33 B3	
8½		WATERFALL opened Summer 1852	1852	1961	33 B4	
9¼	9:26	Gogginshill Tunnel 906 yds long, also called Ballinhassig Tunnel	1851	1961	31 C1	
10		BALLINHASSIG aerial ropeway to Ballinphelic Brickworks opened 1901, closed 1913, 3½ miles long	1849	1961	31 C1	
?	?	Half-Way Viaduct stone viaduct (still intact)	1849	1961	31 C1	
12¼	12:19	Gortnaclough Crossing	1849	1961	31 C1	
13¼		KINSALE JUNCTION named 'JUNCTION' until 1888, re-named CROSSBARRY in 1938; Killeady Quarry unloading point	1863	1961	31 B1	86, 212
13¾	13:53	Killeen Crossing	1849	1961	31 B1	
?	?	Crossbarry Siding re-named Ballyhandly Siding 1937	?	?		
14	13:73	Lissnagroom Crossing	1849	1961	31 B1	
14¼	14:27	Lisiniskey Crossing	1849	1961	31 B1	
15	14:73	Dunkereen Crossing	1849	1961	31 B1	
15¼	15:25	Crosses Crossing	1849	1961	31 B1	
15½		UPTON originally BRINNY, re-named UPTON & BRINNY in 1852; re-named UPTON & INNISHANNON ROAD 1871, renamed UPTON	1849	1961	31 B1	
15¾	15:65	Rockfort Crossing	1849	1961	31 B1	
16¾	16:65	Kilpatrick Tunnel 133yds long, also called Innishannon Tunnel	1849	1961	31 B1	
?	?	Innishannon Viaduct centre pier and ironwork gone	1849	1961	31 B1	
?	?	INNISHANNON station repositioned further south after 1856?; closed 1871, re-opened c.1874; also called CURRANURE & INNISHANNON ROAD	1849	1891	31 B1	
19¼ ?		Allman's Tramway 880yds long, crossed road on level then entered distillery	1876	1930	31 B1	
19½		West Cork Junction end-on junction with West Cork Railway	1866	1961	31 B1	
?	?	BANDON at 'West Cork Junction', opened by Cork & Bandon Rly as an interchange with the West Cork Railway	1866	1870	31 B1	
?	?	Beamish Siding diverges on Up side; crossed River Bandon, served bottling plant	1912	1956	31 B1	
20		BANDON 'Low Level', used for goods until final closure	1849	1894	31 B1	
20		BANDON 'High Level', built to replace previous stations	1894	1961	31 B1	

?	?	BANDON	1866	1874	31 B1	
		West Cork Railway, closed and replaced by BANDON 'WEST'				
20¼	20:31	Chapel Crossing	1866	1961	31 B1	
?	?	St Patrick's Churchyard 'Tunnel'	1866	1961	31 B1	
		under St Patricks Churchyard				
20½		BANDON 'WEST',	1874	1880	31 B1	
		West Cork Railway, near St Patrick's Church				
20¾	20:50	Rice's Road Crossing	1866	1961	31 B1	
21¼	21:29	Castlebernard Crossing	1866	1961	31 B1	
21¾		CASTLE BERNARD	1873	1891	31 B1	
		private platform for Lord Bandon's Estate,				
		used by Lord Bandon from 1866;				
		open for goods until 1961				
24		CLONAKILTY JUNCTION	1866	1961	31 A1	87
		possibly a military or other special platform				
		(not advertised) named GAGGIN, until opening				
		of Clonakilty Branch in 1886				
24¼		Gaggin Viaduct	1866	c.1879	31 A1	
		replaced by embankment				
27¾		DESERT	1867	1961	31 A1	
?	?	Desert Mill Siding	1875 ?	?	31 A1	
		300ft siding at right angles to line on Up side				
29½		ENNISKEAN	1866	1891	31 A1	
29¾	29:58	Enniskeane Crossing	1866	1961	31 A1	
30		BALLINEEN & ENNISKEANE	1891	1961	31 A1	
		replaced the separate stations				
30		Ballineen Ballast Pit	?	?	31 A1	
		trailed in on Down side				
30½		BALLINEEN	1866	1891	31 A1	
34¼		MANCH PLATFORM	c.1869	1891	30 D1	
		used after closure for race traffic				
34¾	34:62	Nedinagh Crossing	1866	1961	30 D1	
36¼	36:23	Ballyboy Crossing	1866	1961	30 D1	
36¾	36:55	Milleenananig Crossing	1866	1961	30 D1	
?		DUNMANWAY (1st station)	1866	1877 ?	30 D1	
		temporary station				
37¾		DUNMANWAY (2nd station)	1877 ?	1961	30 D1	
38	37:73	Dunmanway Station Gates	1877	1961	30 D1	
38		Atkins Mill Siding	?	1961	30 D1	
		trailed in on up side				
38½	38:42	Kilbarry Crossing	1877	1961	30 D1	
39½	39:34	Cloonties No.1 Crossing	1877	1961	30 D1	
40	40:01	Cloonties No.2 Crossing	1877	1961	30 D1	
42	41:75	Garranes Crossing	1877	1961	30 D1	
42	42:19	Knockbue Station Gates	1877	1961	30 C1	
42		Knockbue	1878	1935	30 C1	
45	44:77	Derrynagree Crossing	1877	1961	30 C1	
45	45:05	Dromdaleague Crossing	1877	1961	30 C1	
45½		DRIMOLEAGUE (2nd station)	1899	1961	30 C1	88
45¾		DRIMOLEAGUE (1st station)	1877	1899	30 C1	88
		junction for Bantry				
45¾	45:62	Drimoleague Station Gates	1877	1961	30 C1	
46½	46:40	Garranes South Crossing	1877	1961	30 C1	
48½	48:45	Reenroe Crossing	1877	1961	30 C1	
49		MADORE	by 1878	1961	30 C2	
49¼	49:24	Madore Station Gates	1877	1961	30 C2	
50	49:77	Cooragannive Crossing	1877	1961	30 C2	
53¾	53:70	Back of Town Crossing	1877	1961	30 C2	
53¾		SKIBBEREEN	1877	1961	30 C2	
54	53:71	Street Crossing	1893	1961	30 C2	
54½	54:34	Coronea No.1 Crossing	1893	1961	30 C2	
54¾	54:55	Coronea No.2 Crossing	1893	1961	30 C2	
55¼	55:25	Mallavonea Crossing	1893	1961	30 C3	
56¼	56:22	Bunlick Crossing	1893	1961	30 C3	
57¼	57:26	Creagh No.1 Crossing	1893	1961	30 C3	
57¾	57:60	Creagh No.2 Crossing	1893	1961	30 C3	
57¾		CREAGH	1893	1961	30 C3	
58½	58:36	Lackaghane Crossing	1893	1961	30 C3	
59½	59:37	Rath No.1 Crossing	1893	1961	30 C3	
59¾	59:52	Rath No.2 Crossing	1893	1961	30 C3	
60½	60:40	Church Strand Crossing	1893	1961	30 B3	
61¼	61:12	School Crossing	1893	1961	30 B3	
61¾		BALTIMORE	1893	1961	30 B3	
62		Baltimore Pier	1917	1961	30 B3	
		opened Summer 1917				

86 Kinsale Junction to Kinsale

CBSCR / 5ft 3in gauge / mileposts measured from Kinsale Junction

Opened 27-06-1863 by the CKJR.

Closed 01-09-1931 by the GSR, lifted by mid-1934, not legally abandoned until 1962 !

MPost Dist.	Miles & Chains	Place / Feature (notes)	Date Opened	Date Closed	Map Grid	Table Ref.
0		KINSALE JUNCTION	1863	1961	31 B1	85
		named 'JUNCTION' until 1888,				
		re-named CROSSBARRY in 1938				
4		BALLYMARTLE	1864	1931	31 C1	
		opened by 04-1864				
8		FARRANGALWAY	1863	1931	31 C1	
		now owned by enthusiast, including ¾ mile of trackbed				
		Farrangalway Viaduct	1863	1931	31 C1	
11		KINSALE	1863	1931	31 C1	

87 Clonakilty Junction to Clonakilty

CBSCR / 5ft 3in gauge / mileposts measured from Cork Albert Quay

Opened 28-08-1886 by the CExR.

Passenger services suspended 24-02-1947 due to fuel shortage.
Goods services suspended 10-03-1947.
All services resumed 23-06-1947.

Closed 01-04-1961 by CIE, lifted 1962.

MPost Dist.	Miles & Chains	Place / Feature (notes)	Date Opened	Date Closed	Map Grid	Table Ref.
24		CLONAKILTY JUNCTION	1866	1961	31 A1	85
		named GAGGIN until opening of branch				
26	26:10	Cashelmore Crossing	1886	1961	31 A1	
28¾	28:50	Ahalisky Crossing	1886	1961	31 A2	
29¼		BALLINASCARTHY	1886	1961	31 A2	90
		junction for Courtmacsherry				
31		Shannonvale Horse Tramway	1887	1961	31 A2	
		opened March 1887, about ½ mile long to Cork Milling Company's				
		flour mill, private siding; horse worked until 31-03-1961				
31¼		Argadeen Viaduct	1886	1961	31 A2	
		also called Shannonvale Viaduct				
32½	32:45	County Home Crossing	1886	1961	31 A2	
33		CLONAKILTY	1886	1961	31 A2	

88 Drimoleague Junction to Bantry

CBSCR / 5ft 3in gauge / mileposts measured from Cork Albert Quay

Drimoleague to Bantry (old 'Hilltop' terminus) opened for goods 01-07-1881 by the CBR.
Drimoleague to Bantry (old 'Hilltop' terminus) opened for passengers 04-07-1881 by CBR.
Bantry (old 'Hilltop' terminus) to Bantry Town opened for passengers and goods 22-10-1892 by the BBER.
Bantry Town to Bantry Pier opened for goods 22-10-1892 by the BBER.
Bantry Town to Bantry Pier opened to passengers from c.06-1909 by the CBSCR.

Bantry Town to Bantry Pier closed to passengers c.09-1937 by the GSR.

Passenger services suspended 24-02-1947 due to fuel shortage.
Passenger services resumed 24-05-1947.

Bantry Town to Bantry Pier closed to goods 1949 by CIE.
Drimoleague to Bantry closed 01-04-1961 by CIE.

MPost Dist.	Miles & Chains	Place / Feature (notes)	Date Opened	Date Closed	Map Grid	Table Ref.
45½		DRIMOLEAGUE (2nd station)	1899	1961	30 C1	85
45¾		DRIMOLEAGUE (1st station)	1877	1899	30 C1	85
		junction for Baltimore				
45¾	45:70	Drimoleague Station Gates	1881	1961	30 C1	

46½	46:31	Bog No.1 Crossing	1881	1961	30 C1	
47	46:75	Bog No.2 Crossing	1881	1961	30 C2	
48	48:08	Inchingerig Crossing	1881	1961	30 C2	
49½	49:66	Aughaville Station Gates	1881	1961	30 C2	
49½		AUGHAVILLE	1886	1961	30 C2	
		closed 03-1891 to 05-1904				
52		DURRUS ROAD	1881	1961	30 B1	
52	52:30	Durrus Road Station Gates	1881	1961	30 C2	
54¼	54:26	Keilnascarta Crossing	1881	1961	30 B1	
?	?	Stevens Barytes Siding	1907	c.1920	30 B1	
		trailed on down side				
57¼		BANTRY	1881	1892	30 B1	
		original HILL TOP terminus, closed 22-10-1892				
57¾	57:60	Gortnamuck Crossing	1892	1961	30 B1	
		also called Church Road Crossing				
58	57:75	Old Barrack Road Crossing	1892	1961	30 B1	
57¾		BANTRY TOWN	1892	1961	30 B1	
58	58:01	Bantry Station Gates	1892	1961	30 B1	
58½	58:36	Bantry Pier Station Gates	1892	1949 ?	30 B1	
583⁄4		BANTRY PIER	1892	1949	30 B1	
		passenger trains to Pier station c.06-1909 to c.09-1937				

89 Cork City Railways

CCR / 5ft3in gauge

Opened to Goods 01-01-1912 by the CCR.
Opened to passengers June 1914 for that Summer service only.

Closed completely 12-04-1976 by CIE.

Started at west side of Glanmire Road Station, ran along Alfred Street and turned southwards through Clyde Cutting. A facing junction took a siding eastwards along St Patrick's Quay. The line then crossed the Brian Boru Bridge and came to a trailing junction with the siding from Anderson's Quay from the east. A little farther on, a facing junction to Lapp's Quay diverged eastwards. The line then crossed the Clontarf Bridge and ran along Deane Street and joined the CBSCR on the west side of Albert Quay Station.

MPost Dist.	Miles & Chains	Place / Feature (notes)	Date Opened	Date Closed	Map Grid	Table Ref.
0¼	0:15	CORK GLANMIRE ROAD	1912	Open	33 D2	8
0	0:00	Junction with GSWR	1912	1976	33 D2	8
		point at which CCR diverges from GSWR				
?	?	Clyde Cutting	1912	1976	33 D2	
0¼	0:22	St Patrick's Quay Siding	1912	1939	33 D2	
		facing Junction to 3 chain long siding				
?	?	Brian Boru Bridge	1912	1976	33 C2	
		232ft long Scherzer Rolling lift bridge,				
		rebuilt as fixed bridge 1980				
0¼	0:30	Anderson's Quay Siding	1912	1963 ?	33 C2	
		last recorded train January 1963;				
		trailing junction to 3 chain long siding				
0½	0:35	Lapp's Quay Siding	1912	1946	33 C2	
		facing Junction to 3 chain long siding				
?	?	Clontarf Bridge	1912	1976	33 C2	
		197ft long Scherzer Rolling lift bridge				
		rebuilt as fixed bridge 1980				
?	?	Level Crossing with Cork Tramways	1912	1931	33 C2	162
0¾	0:57	CORK ALBERT QUAY	1912	1976	33 C2	85

90 Ballinascarthy to Courtmacsherry

BTJLR / TCELR / 5ft3in gauge / mileposts measured from Ballinascarthy

Ballinascarthy to Timoleague opened 20-12-1890 by the BTJLR.
Timoleague to Courtmacsherry opened 23(?)-5-1891 by the TCELR.
Courtmacsherry to Courtmacsherry Pier opened 1893 by the TCELR.

Passenger services suspended 24-02-1947 due to fuel shortage.
Goods services suspended 10-03-1947.
Goods service resumed 01-10-1947.

Closed to passengers 24-02-1947. Excursions ran in the 1950s.

Closed completely 01-04-1961 by CIE.

MPost Dist.	Miles & Chains	Place / Feature (notes)	Date Opened	Date Closed	Map Grid	Table Ref.
0	0:00	BALLINASCARTHY	1886	1961	31 A2	87
0¼	0:18	Ballinascarthy Crossing	1890	1961	31 A2	
1¾	1:68	Monteen Crossing	1890	1961	31 A2	
3		SKEAF	1890	1947	31 A2	
5		Ummera Ballast Pit Siding	1890	?	31 B2	
?		Inchy Bridge	1890	1961	31 B2	
		1 span iron bridge across River Argadeen				
4¼	4:23	Inchy Bridge Crossing	1890	1961	31 B2	
6	5:76	Timoleague Station Gates	1890	1961	31 B2	
6		TIMOLEAGUE	1890	1947	31 B2	
6	6:06	Timoleague Station Gates	1891	1961	31 B2	
		from Timoleague to Courtmacsherry the line ran as				
		a roadside tramway for most of the way				
9		COURTMACSHERRY	1891	1947	31 B2	
?		Courtmacsherry Pier	1893	1961	31 B2	

91 Tynan to Maguiresbridge

CVR / 3ft gauge / Distances measured from Tynan

Tynan to Maguiresbridge opened 02-05-1887 by the CVT.

Closed completely 01-01-1942 by the CVR.

MPost Dist.	Miles & Chains	Place / Feature (notes)	Date Opened	Date Closed	Map Grid	Table Ref.
0	0:00	TYNAN	1887	1942	10 A4	52
		used bay platform at GNR(I) station				
0¼	0:33	Lemnagore Crossing	1887	1942	10 A4	
		tramway joins road at this point				
1	1:00 ?	CALEDON	1887	1942	10 A4	
		no platform, stopped in main street				
1¾	1:48 ?	KILSAMPSON	1887	1942	10 A4	
		roadside stopping place				
3	3:00	RAMAKET	1887	1942	10 A4	
3		Level Crossing	1887	1942	10 A4	
4¼	4:24 ?	EMYVALE ROAD	1887	1942	10 A4	
		called CURLAGH or CURLOUGH before c.1914				
4½		Level Crossing	1887	1942	10 A4	
5¼	5:16 ?	CUMBER	1887	1942	10 A4	
		roadside stopping place				
6	6:16 ?	GLENKEEN	1887	1942 ?	10 A4	
		roadside stopping place				
7	7:00 ?	CRILLY	1887	1942	10 A4	
		platform, siding and cattle pen				
7		Level Crossing	1887	1942	10 A4	
8 ?		Level Crossing	1887	1942	10 A3	
8¼	8:16 ?	GLENCREW	1887	1942	10 A3	
8½	8:30	Tramway leaves road at this point	1887	1942	10 A3	
9½	9:42	Level Crossing	1887	1942	10 A3	
		crosses Aughnacloy-Dungannon road				
9½	9:40 ?	AUGHNACLOY	1887	1942	10 A3	
10 ?		Line rejoins road	1887	1942	10 A3	
10½		Level Crossing	1887	1942	10 A3	
10½	10:40 ?	STORMHILL	1887	1889	10 A3	
11¾		Level Crossing	1887	1942	10 A3	
11¾	11:56 ?	TULLYVAR	1887	1942	10 A3	
11¾		Quarry Siding	c.1915	?	10 A3	
		County Council Quarry, later owned by Hadden				
12¼	12:17	Level Crossing	1887	1942	10 A3	
		crosses and leaves road				
12½	12:65	Dempsey's Crossing	1887	1942	10 A3	
		officially Tullywinney Crossing				
13¼		McCann's Crossing	1887	1942	9 D3	
		tramway crosses road into station				
13½	13:48 ?	BALLYGAWLEY	1887	1942	9 D3	
		tramway leaves road after station				
13¾ ?		Quarry Siding	1915	1942	9 D3	
14½		Lisdoart Ballast Pit Siding	1887 ?	by 1912	9 D3	
		also known as Mrs Barret's Pit; out of use by 1912				

14½	14:32	Level Crossing	1887	1942	9 D3	
		tramway rejoins road				
14½	14:32 ?	LISDOART	1887	1942	9 D3	
15		tramway leaves road	1887	1942	9 D3	
15½	15:40 ?	ANNAGHILLA	1887	1942	9 D3	
		also crosses a secondary road				
16¾		Tramway rejoins road	1887	1942	9 D3	
16¾	16:56 ?	ROUGHAN	1887	1942	9 D3	
18½ ?	18:28	Level Crossing	1887	1942	9 D3	
		tramway crosses crossroads				
18½	18:32 ?	AUGHER	1887	1942	9 D3	
19 ?		Level Crossing	1887	1942	9 D3	
19¼	19:16	FARRANETRA	1887	1942 ?	9 D3	
		also called SUMMER HILL				
19¼		Line leaves road	1887	1942	9 D3	
		tramway crosses several roads				
		by gated crossings				
19¾	19:71	Level Crossing	1887	1942	9 D3	
		crosses minor road into station				
20	20:00 ?	CLOGHER	1887	1942	9 D3	
20		Level Crossing	1887	1942	9 D3	
		crosses minor road leaving station				
20¼		Ballymagowan Crossing	1887	1942	9 D3	
21	21:23	Level Crossing	1887	1942	9 D3	
21	21:23 ?	CARRYCLOGHER	1887	1942	9 D3	
		at level crossing				
22	22:00 ?	Line rejoins road	1887	1942	9 D3	
22	22:00 ?	FINDERMORE	1887	1942	9 D3	
		stopping place at above point				
22		Level Crossing	1887	1942	9 D3	
22¼		Level Crossing	1887	1942	9 D3	
23½	23:24 ?	BALLAGH	1887	1942	9 D3	
23¾		Level Crossing	1887	1942	9 D3	
25¼	25:16	KILTERMON	1887	1942	9 C4	
25¼		Level Crossing	1887	1942	9 C4	
26½	26:48 ?	BALLYVADDEN	1887	1942	9 C4	
		opened 11-1887				
?		Ballyvadden Ballast Pit Siding	?	?	9 C4	
27½	27:40 ?	FIVEMILETOWN	1887	1942	9 C4	
		tramway leaves road on approach to station				
28½	28:32 ?	CRANBROOKE	1887	1942	9 C4	
29	28:64	TATTYNUCKLE	1890	1897	9 C4	
		opened 08-04-1890,				
		omitted from timetables from 15-04-1897				
29½	29:32 ?	CORRYLONGFORD	1887	1942	9 C4	
29½	29:50	Level Crossing	1887	1942	9 C4	
		crosses minor road				
30¼	30:07 ?	Level Crossing	1887	1942	9 C4	
		tramway rejoins road,				
		gates replaced by cattle grids in 1913				
30¼	30:16 ?	KILLARBRAN	1887	1942	9 C4	
30¼ ?		Tramway leaves road	1887	1942	9 C4	
31¼	31:05 ?	CLARAGHY	1926	1942 ?	9 C4	
		at level crossing				
31½	31:32 ?	COLEBROOKE	1887	1926	9 C4	
31½	31:45	Tramway rejoins road	1887	1942	9 C4	
31¾	31:48	Derryloman Crossing	1887	1942	9 C4	
31¾	31:48	STONEPARKCROSS	1926	1942	9 C4	
		at above crossing				
32		Level Crossing	1887	1942	9 C4	
32½	32:64 ?	SKEOG	1887	1942	9 C4	
		opened 11-1887				
32¾		Line crosses and leaves road	1887	1942	9 C4	
33½ ?	33:16	Level Crossing	1887	1942	9 C4	
		line crosses road to station				
33½	33:40	BROOKEBOROUGH	1887	1942	9 C4	
33½ ?	33:45	Line rejoins road	1887	1942	9 C4	
34¼ ?		Line leaves road	1887	1942	9 C4	
34¾		Level Crossing	1887	1942	9 B4	
		crosses minor road				
34¾	34:56 ?	AGHAVEA	1887	1942	9 B4	
		stopping place at above crossing				
34 ?		Level Crossing	1887	1942	9 B4	
		crosses minor road				
36 ?	36:05	Tramway rejoins road	1887	1942	9 B4	
36½	36:40	MAGUIRESBRIDGE FAIR GREEN	1887	1942	9 B4	

		formerly MAGUIRESBRIDGE TOWN,				
		renamed by 1907				
36½ ?		Level Crossing	1887	1942	9 B4	
		line leaves road				
37		Level Crossing	1887	1942	9 B4	
		adjacent to GNR(I) Drumgoon Crossing				
37	37:03	Maguiresbridge	1887	1942	9 B4	49
		formerly Maguiresbridge Station,				
		renamed by 1907				

92 Listowel to Ballybunion

LBR / Monorail (Lartigue System)

Listowel to Ballybunion and Sand Pits opened 05-03-1888 by the LBR.

Although officially opened 05-03-1888, the line had carried 15,000 tons of 'ballast' for seven weeks previously.

Closed completely 14-10-1924 by the LBR.

MPost Dist.	Miles & Chains	Place / Feature (notes)	Date Opened	Date Closed	Map Grid	Table Ref.
0		LISTOWEL	1888	1924	25 B1	18
4¾		LISSELTON	1888	1924	25 B1	
		formerly Liselton				
7		FRANCIS ROAD	?	1924	18 D6	
		opened ?, closed 06-1901, re-opened 04-1912				
9¼		BALLYBUNION	1888	1924	18 D6	
?		Level Crossing	1888	1924	18 D6	
?		Sand Pits	1888	1924	18 D6	

There are thought to have been 11 level crossings in total, but the locations are unknown. Some were the 'drawbridge' type, others were the moveable track type. There is also a reference to Newmans Cross Station, but again no location or verification has been established.

93 Londonderry Victoria Road to Killybegs

3ft gauge / mileposts measured from Strabane
5ft 3in gauge / FVR, regauged 16-07-1894
NCC – Londonderry to Strabane
CDRJC – Strabane to Killybegs

Londonderry Victoria Road to Strabane (DR station) opened for goods 01-08-1900 by the DR.
Londonderry Victoria Road to Strabane (DR station) opened for passengers 06-08-1900 by the DR.
Strabane (INWR station) to Stranorlar opened 07-09-1863 by the FVR.
Strabane (DR station) to Finn Valley Junction opened 16-07-1894 by the DR
Stranorlar to Druminin opened 25-04-1882 by the WDR.
Druminin to Donegal opened 01-09-1889 by the WDR.
Donegal to Killybegs opened 18-08-1893 by the DR.

Londonderry Victoria Road to Strabane closed completely 01-01-1955 by the NCC.
Strabane to Stranorlar closed to passengers 01-01-1960 by the CDRJC.
Strabane to Stranorlar closed to goods 25-01-1960 by CDRJC.
Stranorlar to Killybegs closed completely 01-01-1960 by the CDRJC.

MPost Dist.	Miles & Chains	Place / Feature (notes)	Date Opened	Date Closed	Map Grid	Table Ref.
14½		LONDONDERRY VICTORIA ROAD	1900	1955	3 D5	135
11¾		NEW BUILDINGS	1900	1955	3 D5	
9½		DESERTONE HALT	1908	1955	3 D5	
8¼		CULLION	1900	1955	3 D5	
6¼		DONEMANA	1900	1955	3 D5	
4½		BALLYHEATHER HALT	1902	1955	3 D5	
2¾	2:57	BALLYMAGORRY	1900	1955	3 D5	
0	00:00	STRABANE (DR Station)	1894	1960	3 D6	
		opened 16-07-1894				
0¼		Lifford Road Overbridge	1894	1960	3 D6	
0¼		River Mourne Bridge	1894	1960	3 D6	

0	0:00	Strabane (INWR station)	1847	1894	3 D6	49
		Donegal Railway ceased to use it 16-07-1894				
0¼		Finn Valley Junction	1863	1894	3 D6	49
		disconnected due to re-gauging on 16-07-1894				
0¾	0:60	Finn Valley Junction	1863	1894	3 D6	49
		junction with INWR / GNR;				
		disconnected due to re-gauging				
		on 16-07-1894				
2		Urney Bridge	1863	1960	3 C6	
		crossed River Finn				
	44:24	CLADY	1863	1960	3 C6	
6		CASTLEFINN	1863	1960	3 C6	
8		Liscooly Station Gates				
		(Schoales, No.1 Gates)	1863	1960	3 C6	
8		LISCOOLY	1863	1960	3 C6	
9¾		KILLYGORDON	1863	1960	3 C6	
12		CAVAN HALT	1931	1960	3 B6	
12½ ?		COUNTY HOME GATE	1944	1956 ?	3 B6	
		railcar stop				
13		TOWN BRIDGE HALT	1934	c.1950	3 B6	
13¾		STRANORLAR	1863	1960	3 B6	94
		junction for Glenties				
14 ?		River Finn Viaduct	1882	1960	3 B6	
16		MEENGLAS HALT	1891	1960	3 B6	
		closed c.08-1918 and re-opened c.1936				
16¼		Quinn's Crossing	1882	1960	3 B6	
		also a railcar stop from 1944				
19		Lough Gates	1882	1960	3 B6	
		also a railcar stop from 1944				
21½		DERG BRIDGE HALT	1912	1960	3 B6	
		opened 02-12-1912				
25½		BARNESMORE HALT	1891	1960	8 D1	
		formerly BARRACK BRIDGE HALT				
26		Dunnion's Crossing	1889	1960	8 D1	
		also a railcar stop from 1938				
27½		LOUGH ESKE	1882	1960	8 D1	
		named DRUMININ until 1889				
27½		Lough Eske Station Gates (No.2)	1889	1960	8 D1	
28		Townawilly Crossing	1889	1956	8 D1	
		also a railcar stop from 1938				
28½ ?		HARVEY'S HILL	1944	1944	8 C1	
		railcar stop in 1944;				
		possible location at Harvey's Brae				
29		McNamee Gates (No.3)	1889	1960	8 D1	
29 ?		McClanaghy Gates (No.4)	1889	1960	8 D1	
29½		CLAR BRIDGE HALT	1891	1960	8 D1	
		formerly CLAR				
29¾ ?		McHugh Gates (No.5)	1889	1960	8 C1	
30½ ?		Gorrell Gates (No.6)	1889	1960	8 C1	
31½		DONEGAL	1889	1960	8 C1	95
		junction for Ballyshannon				
31½		Donegal Station Gates (No.7)	1893	1960	8 C1	
31¾ ?		DRIMARK HILL	1944	1956 ?	8 C1	
		railcar stop from 1944				
32¼ ?		McDaid Gates (No.8)	1893	1960	8 C1	
33 ?		McGroarty Gates (No.9)	1893	1960	8 C1	
32¾ ?		Bogle Gates (No.10)	1893	1960	8 C1	
33½		KILLYMARD HALT	c.1895	1956	8 C1	
		closed c.08-1918 and re-opened c.1936,				
		closed 1956 then 'special occasions'				
		only after 1956				
33¾ ?		Keeney Gates (No.11)	1893	1960	8 C1	
35¼ ?		Meehan Gates (No.12)	1893	1960	8 C1	
35½		MOUNTCHARLES	1893	1960	8 C1	
37 ?		Freeburn Gates (No.13)	1893	1960	8 C1	
37¼		DOORIN ROAD HALT	1893	1960	8 C1	
		made a halt in 1921				
37¼		Doorin Road Station Gates (No. 14)	1893	1960	8 C1	
37½ ?		Keeney Gates (No.15)	1893	1960	8 C1	
38¾		MULLANBOY HALT	1931	1960	8 C1	
38¾		Mullanboy Station Gates (No.16, Rose)	1893	1960	8 C1	
39 ?		Scott Gates (No.17)	1893	1960	8 C1	
39½ ?		INVER CHURCH (at crossing below)	1936	1960	8 C1	
		railcar stop from 1936				
39½ ?		Conaghan Gates (No.18)	1893	1960	8 C1	
39¾		INVER	1893	1960	8 C1	
40 ?		Cannon Gates (No.19)	1893	1960	8 B1	
40¾ ?		Battles Gates (No.20)	1893	1960	8 B1	
		railcar stop from 1936				
41½ ?		Meehan Gates (No.21)	1893	1960	8 B1	
41½		PORT	1893	1960	8 B1	
42¾ ?		Rose's Gates (No.22)	1893	1960	8 B1	
		railcar stop in 1956				
43¾		DUNKINEELY	1893	1960	8 B1	
43¾		Dunkineely Stn Gates (No.23)	1893	1960	8 B1	
44 ?		Lappin Gates (No.24)	1893	1960	8 B1	
44¼ ?		McMenamin Gates (No.25)	1893	1960	8 B1	
44¾		SPAMOUNT	1944	1960	8 B1	
		railcar stop from 1944				
45½ ?		McGroarty Gates (No.26)	1893	1960	8 B1	
		formerly called Kenny Gates				
46		Bruckless Station Gates (No.26A)	1893	1960	8 B1	
46		BRUCKLESS	1893	1960	8 B1	
47¾ ?		McMenamin Gates (No.27)	1893	1960	8 B1	
48¼		ARDARA ROAD	1893	1960	8 B1	
48¼		Ardara Road Station (Gillespie)				
		Gates (No.28)	1893	1960	8 B1	
48½ ?		McGinley Gates (No.29)	1893	1960	8 B1	
48¾ ?		Hegarty's Gates (No.30)	1893	1960	8 B1	
		also a railcar stop from 1936				
50½		KILLYBEGS	1893	1960	8 B1	
50¾ ?		Killybegs Pier	1893	?	8 B1	

94 Stranorlar to Glenties

CDRJC / 3ft gauge / mileposts measured from Stranorlar

Stranorlar to Glenties opened 03-06-1895 by the DR.

Stranorlar to Glenties closed to passengers 15-12-1947 by the CDRJC.
Stranorlar to Glenties closed to regular goods 15-12-1947 by the CDRJC.
Occasional turf and stock trains ran up to 19-09-1949.
Stranorlar to Glenties closed completely 10-03-1952 by the CDRJC.

Part of the line fron Fintown to un-named temporary terminus was re-opened 03-06-1995 by CTGL.

MPost Dist.	Miles & Chains	Place / Feature (notes)	Date Opened	Date Closed	Map Grid	Table Ref.
0		STRANORLAR	1895	1952	3 B6	93
0¼ ?		River Finn Bridge	1882	1960	3 B6	
0½		BALLYBOFEY	1895	1947	3 B6	
0½		Ballybofey Station (No.31)	1895	1952	3 B6	
0¾ ?		McConnell Gates (No.32)	1895	1952	3 B6	
		also called Gallinagh's Gates,				
		and a railcar stop 1944-47.				
1½ ?		BALLINDOON BRIDGE	1944	1947	3 B6	
		railcar stop 1944-47				
2¼ ?		McBride Gates (No.33)	1895	1952	3 B6	
		also called Double Gates,				
		and a railcar stop 1944-47				
4		GLENMORE	1895	1947	3 B6	
4		Glenmore Station (No.34) Gates	1895	1952	3 B6	
6¾		CLOGHAN	1895	1947	3 B6	
9		ELATAGH HALT	1930	1947	3 A6	
		opened 07-1930				
10		CRONADUN BRIDGE	1944	1947	3 A5	
		railcar stop 1944-47				
11½		GLASSAGH HALT	1937	1947	3 A5	
		opened 03-1937				
13¾		BALLINAMORE	1895	1947	3 A5	
13¾		Ballinamore Station Gates				
		(No.35, Doherty)	1895	1952	3 A5	
14¾		S. Doherty's Gates (No.36)	1895	1952	3 A5	
		also a railcar stop 1944-47				
16		FINTOWN	1895	Open	3 A5	
		closed 1947, re-opened 03-06-1995				
16¾ ?		CTGL PLATFORM	1995	1996	2 D5	
		un-named CTGL platform; removed mid-1996				

MPost Dist.	Place / Feature (notes)	Date Opened	Date Closed	Map Grid
18½	Ballast Pit also a railcar stop 1944-47	?	1952	2 D5
20 ?	Brennan's or Herron (No.37) Gates also a railcar stop 1944-47	1895	1952	2 D6
21	SHALLOGANS HALT	c.1903	1947	2 D6
22¾	McMonagle's Gates (No.38) also a railcar stop 1944-47	1895	1952	2 D6
23¾ ?	McNelis Gates (No.39)	1895	1952	2 D6
24	Glenties Station (No.40)	1895	1952	2 D6
24	GLENTIES	1895	1947	2 D6

95 Donegal to Ballyshannon

CDRJC / 3ft gauge./ mileposts measured from Strabane

Donegal to Ballyshannon opened for goods 02-09-1905 by the DR.
Donegal to Ballyshannon opened for passengers 21-09-1905 by the DR.

Donegal to Ballyshannon closed completely 01-01-1960 by the CDRJC.

MPost Dist.	Miles & Chains	Place / Feature (notes)	Date Opened	Date Closed	Map Grid	Table Ref.
31½		DONEGAL	1905	1960	8 C1	93
32		HOSPITAL HALT	1935	c.1950	8 C1	
33		DRUMBAR HALT	1906	1960	8 C1	
34 ?		McHugh's Gates (No.41) railcar stop from 1938	1905	1960	8 C1	
34½ ?		Monaghan Gates (No.42)	1905	1960	8 C1	
34¾		LAGHEY	1905	1960	8 C1	
35¾ ?		Conaghan Gates (No.43)	1905	1960	8 C1	
36½		BRIDGETOWN	1905	1960	8 C1	
36½		Bridgetown Station Gates (No.44, Gallagher)	1905	1960	8 C1	
37		DRUMHORRY BRIDGE railcar stop from 1942	1942	1960	8 C1	
38½		BALLINTRA	1905	1960	8 C2	
39½		DROMORE HALT later a railcar stop	1930	1960	8 C2	
40½		DORRIAN'S BRIDGE railcar stop from 1940	1940	1960	8 C2	
41¾		ROSSNOWLAGH	1905	1960	8 C2	
42		FRIARY HALT opened 01-03-1953	1953	1960	8 C2	
42¼ ?		McAree Gates (No.45)	1905	1960	8 C2	
42½		COOLMORE HALT	1929	1960	8 C2	
43½ ?		Corker (McCann's) Crossing railcar stop from 1940	1905	1960	8 C2	
44¼		CREEVY HALT opened 01-08-1911	1911	1960	8 C2	
44¼		Creevy Halt Gates,	1905	1960	8 C2	
44½ ?		McIntyre (No.46)	1905	1960	8 C2	
45¾ ?		Gillen's (Kildoney) Crossing railcar stop from 1942	1905	1960	8 C2	
46¼ ?		Culleton Gates (No.47)	1905	1960	8 C2	
47		BALLYSHANNON	1905	1960	8 C2	

96 Strabane to Letterkenny

SLR – worked by the CDRJC
3ft gauge / mileposts measured from Strabane

Strabane to Letterkenny opened 01-01-1909 by the SLR.

Strabane to Letterkenny closed completely 01-01-1960 by the SLR.

MPost Dist.	Miles & Chains	Place / Feature (notes)	Date Opened	Date Closed	Map Grid	Table Ref.
0	0:00	STRABANE	1894	1960	3 D6	93
1	0:41	LIFFORD HALT	1909	1960	3 C6	
2¾		BALLINDRAIT	1909	1960	3 C6	

MPost Dist.	Miles & Chains	Place / Feature (notes)	Date Opened	Date Closed	Map Grid	Table Ref.
3 ?		O'Brien (No.48) Gates	1909	1960	3 C6	
3¼ ?		Devenny (No.49) Gates	1909	1960	3 C6	
3¾ ?		Donnelly (No.50) Gates	1909	1960	3 C6	
4¾		COOLAGHY HALT	1909	1960	3 C5	
6½		RAPHOE	1909	1960	3 C5	
?		Kearns (No.51) Gates	1909	1960	3 C5	
7¼ ?		Chembers (No.52) Gates	1909	1960	3 C5	
?		Linney's (No.53) Gates railcar stop from 1936	1909	1960	3 C5	
9		CONVOY	1909	1960	3 C5	
?		Mulrine (No.54) Gates	1909	1960	3 C5	
?		Ayton's (No.56) Gates railcar stop from 1936; formerly Kelly, later Cannon, later Vance Gates	1909	1960	3 C5	
11		CORNAGILLAGH HALT opened 01-08-1911	1911	1960	3 C5	
?		Gillen (No.55) Gates	1909	1960	3 C5	
13¾		GLENMAQUIN	1909	1960	3 C5	
14½ ?		Doherty (No.57) Gates	1909	1960	3 C5	
15¼ ?		Parke (No.58) Gates	1909	1960	3 C5	
16 ?		Maguire (No.59) Gates	1909	1960	3 C5	
16¾ ?		Martin (No.60) Gates	1909	1960	3 C5	
17¼ ?		Killen's (No.61) Gate Signal railcar stop from 1944; Killen's Gate Signal appeared on tickets	1909	1960	3 C5	
17¾ ?		Baird's (No.62) Gates railcar stop in 1944	1909	1960	3 C5	
19		Quay Siding siding to Quayside	?	?	3 C5	
19¼		LETTERKENNY siding connection to LLSR Station	1909	1960	3 B5	101

97 Belturbet to Dromod

CLR / 3ft gauge / mileposts measured from Dromod

Opened for goods 17-10-1887 by the CLRLRTC.
Opened to passengers 24-10-1887 by the CLRLRTC.

Passenger services suspended 24-02-1947 due to fuel shortage.
Passenger services resumed 24-05-1947.

Closed completely 01-04-1959 by CIE.

Dromod to near Clooncolry Level Crossing re-opened by the Cavan & Leitrim Railway Company Limited on 27-05-1995.

MPost Dist.	Miles & Chains	Place / Feature (notes)	Date Opened	Date Closed	Map Grid	Table Ref.
33¾		BELTURBET interchange with GNR(I)	1887	1959	9 B6	52
33¾	33:57	Straheglin Crossing	1887	1959	9 B6	
?		Erne Bridge 4 arch viaduct	1887	1959	9 B6	
?		Staghall Bridge	1887	1959	9 B6	
32½	32:43	Drumacon Crossing accommodation crossing	1887	1959	9 B6	
32	31:77	Rafian Crossing also called Drumary Crossing	1887	1959	9 B6	
30¾	30:60	Carrowfarnaghan Crossing	1887	1959	9 B6	
30½	30:32	Tomkin Road Station Gates also known as Drumrush Gates	1887	1959	9 B6	
30½		TOMKIN ROAD	1887	1959	9 B6	
29½		KILLYWILLY Belturbet market train ordered to stop May-June 1888	1888	1888	9 B6	
29½	29:49	Ardue Crossing also called Killywilly Crossing	1887	1959	9 B6	
28	28:01	Cavanagh Crossing	1887	1959	9 B6	
27½		BALLYCONNELL	1887	1959	9 B6	
27½	27:31	Ballyconnell Station Gates	1887	1959	9 B6	
24¾	24:68	Ballyheady Station Gates accommodation crossing	1887	1959	9 A6	

MPost Dist.	Miles & Chains	Place / Feature (notes)	Date Opened	Date Closed	Map Grid	Table Ref.
24¾		BALLYHEADY	1887	1959	9 A6	
?	?	Ballyheady Ballast Pit	1887	1959	9 A6	161
24½	24:40	Killycluggin Crossing	1887	1959	9 A6	
		also called Currin Crossing				
23	23:07	Bawnboy Road Station Gates	1887	1959	9 A6	
		Cloneary Gates				
23		BAWNBOY ROAD & TEMPLEPORT	1887	1959	9 A6	
22¼	22:22	Killymoriarity Crossing	1887	1959	9 A6	
		accommodation crossing				
21½		KILLYRAN	1888	1959	9 A6	
21¼	21:16	Killyran Station Gates	1887	1959	9 A6	
20¼	20:16	Glebe Crossing	1887	1959	9 A6	
		accommodation crossing				
19½		GARADICE	1887	1959	9 A6	
17½	17:50	Corgar Crossing	1887	1959	9 A6	
		Orange demonstration specials				
		stopped here				
16¾		Kildorough water tank	1887	1959	8 D6	
16¼		BALLINAMORE	1887	1959	8 D6	98
		junction for Arigna				
16¼	16:15	Cannaboe Crossing	1887	1959	8 D6	
16	15:73	Tully No.1 Crossing	1887	1959	8 D6	
15¾	15:50	Tully No.2 Crossing	1887	1959	8 D6	
		also called Cornacreeck Crossing				
14¾		Ballinamore & Ballyconnell				
		Canal Bridge	1887	1959	8 D6	
14¼		LAWDERDALE	1887	1959	8 D6	
14¼	14:25	Lawderdale Station Gates	1887	1959	8 D6	
		Drumraine Glebe				
12¾		FENAGH	1887	1959	8 D6	
12¾	12:66	Fenagh Station Gates	1887	1959	8 D6	
		also called Ardagh Gates				
12½	12:40	Drumharkan Crossing	1887	1959	15 B1	
11¼	11:29	Dunavinally Crossing	1887	1959	15 B1	
		also called Sallyfield Crossing				
10½	10:37	Annaghderry Crossing	1887	1959	15 B1	
		also called Adoon Crossing				
10¼		ADOON	1887	1959	15 B1	
10	10:05	Adoon Station Gates	1887	1959	15 B1	
7½		ROSHARRY (2nd station)	1901	1920	15 B1	
7½	7:42	Aghakilfaughna Crossing	1887	1959	15 B1	
7		ROSHARRY (1st station)	1888	1901	15 B1	
7	7:09	Gortfada Crossing	1887	1959	15 B1	
6	5:69	Hill Street Crossing	1887	1959	15 B1	
		also called Mohill Crossing				
	5:56	Mohill Station Gates	1887	1959	15 B1	
		also called Coolabaun Gates				
5¾		MOHILL	1887	1959	15 B1	
5	4:68	Clooncahir Crossing	1887	1959	15 B2	
		accommodation crossing; trains stopped here				
		on demand for the Reverend J G Digges MA,				
		a Director of the CLR from 1892 until the				
		takeover by the GSR, who lived nearby.				
2½	2:40	Dereen Station Gates	1887	1959	15 B2	
2½		DEREEN	1887	1959	15 B2	
2	1:67	Cooracramp Crossing	1887	1959	15 B2	
0½	0:40	Clooncolry Crossing	1887	1959	15 B2	
0	0:00	DROMOD	1887	Open	15 B2	37
		closed 1959, re-opened 27-05-1995				
		by the new Cavan & Leitrim Railway Co Ltd;				
		transfer sidings for goods, livestock and				
		minerals to MGWR line				

98   Ballinamore to Arigna and Aughabehy

CLR – Ballinamore to Arigna
AVR – Arigna to Aughabehy
3ft gauge / mileposts measured from Ballinamore

Ballinamore to Arigna opened 02-05-1888 by the CLRLRTC.
Arigna to Aughabehy opened 02-06-1920 by the Board of Works.

Arigna Valley Railway owned by the Government until 1929 when it was leased to the

GSR. Worked initially by the CLR and subsequently after 1925 by the GSR.
Derreenavoggy to Aughabehy closed completely 1930 by the GSR.

Passenger services suspended 24-02-1947 due to fuel shortage.
Passenger services resumed 24-05-1947.

Ballinamore to Derreenavoggy closed completely 01-04-1959 by CIE.

MPost Dist.	Miles & Chains	Place / Feature (notes)	Date Opened	Date Closed	Map Grid	Table Ref.
0	0:00	BALLINAMORE	1887	1959	8 D6	97
		junction for Dromod				
0¼	0:27	Tully No.1 Crossing	1887	1959	8 D6	97
0½	0:37	Main Street Crossing	1887	1959	8 D6	
1¼		Stradermot Quarry Siding	1916	1925	8 D6	
		ballast quarry				
3	3:05	Ballyduff Crossing	1887	1959	8 D6	
3		BALLYDUFF	1887	1959	8 D6	
		roadside running commenced here				
3¾		Dromkeen Wood Siding	1918	1919	8 D6	
		permanent way siding				
5¾		CORNABRONE	1887	1959	8 D6	
		roadside stopping place				
6½		Aughacashlaun Ballast Siding	1896	1952	8 D6	
		contractors siding from 1887 to 1895				
7½		ANNADALE	1887	1959	8 D6	
		roadside stopping place				
8		DRINEY	1887	1959	8 D6	
		served by excursions only				
8½	8:56	Kiltubrid Crossing	1887	1959	8 D6	
8¾		KILTUBRID	1887	1959	8 D6	
9		Crossing	1887	1959	8 D6	
10¼		CREAGH	1887	1959	8 C6	
		roadside stopping place				
12¼		DRUMSHANBO	1887	1959	8 C6	
?		Carrignabrack Crossing	1887	1959	8 C6	
?		Crossing	1887	1959	8 C6	
?		Lough Allen Canal Bridge	1887	1959	8 C6	
13¼	13:32	Mahanagh Crossing	1887	1959	8 C6	
?		Shannon Bridge	1887	1959	8 C6	
		single span girder				
14¾		ARIGNA	1887	1959	8 C6	
14¾	14:61	Aghafin Crossing	1920	1959	8 C6	
		also called Bodorragha Crossing				
	16:15	Level Crossing	1920	18959	8 C6	
		ungated crossing across Arigna Village-Keadue Road				
16¼	16:17	Derreenavoggy Sidings	1920	1959	8 C6	
		also called Chapel Loading Bank or Iron Works Sidings				
16½	16:29	Derreenavoggy Crossing	1920	1959	8 C6	
		no gates, crosses Mount Allen road; line runs on old tramway trackbed from about here				
16½		Level Crossing	1920	1930	8 C6	
		crosses the Rover road				
18¾	18:78	Aughabehy	1920	1930	8 C6	142
		Arigna Mining Co				

99   Cork to Crosshaven

CBPR / mileposts measured from Cork Albert Street
5ft 3in gauge – Cork Victoria Road and Cork Albert Street to Passage
        Cork Albert Street to Passage re-gauged to 3ft 29-10-1900
3ft 0in gauge – Passage to Crosshaven

Cork Victoria Road to Passage opened 08-06-1850 by the CBPR.
Cork Albert Street to Marina opened 06-02-1873 by the CBPR.
Passage to Monkstown opened 01-08-1902 by the CBPR.
Monkstown to Carrigaline opened 15-06-1903 by the CBPR.
Carrigaline to Crosshaven opened 01-06-1904 by the CBPR.

Cork Victoria Road to Marina closed 06-02-1873 by the CBPR.

Monkstown to Crosshaven closed 01-06-1932 by the GSR.
Cork Albert Street to Monkstown closed 12-09-1932 by the GSR.

Ballinure and Bessboro' were very close and used a portable platform moved between the locations as required.

MPost Dist.	Miles & Chains	Place / Feature (notes)	Date Opened	Date Closed	Map Grid	Table Ref.
0	0:00	CORK ALBERT STREET	1873	1932	33 D2	
?	?	CITY PARK (see footnote) 'stop by signal only'; closed Autumn 1889	c.1888	1889	33 D2	
?	?	SHOW GROUND HALT (see footnote) for special events, especially fixtures in late June	c.1910	1932 ?	33 D2	
?	?	CORK VICTORIA ROAD called 'CITY PARK' locally	1850	1873	33 D2	
?	?	Point of deviation (Marina)	1873	1873	33 D2	
1½	1:44	Point of Deviation (Marina)	1873	1873	33 D2	
2	2:02	BLACKROCK	1850	1932	33 D2	
		BALLINURE halt for Coursing Fixtures at Lakelands	1909	c.1920s	33 D2	
?	?	BESSBORO' private halt for Pike family in narrow gauge days; later used for excursions to grounds for the blind, and children's parties	?	?	33 E2	
?	?	Douglas Viaduct 3 span viaduct	1850	1932	33 E2	
4	3:61	ROCHESTOWN originally DOUGLAS, renamed by 1856	1850	1932	33 E2	
?	?	Hop Island Crossing	1850	1932	33 E2	
?	?	PASSAGE (old station) terminus	1850	1902	33 F3	
6½	6:32	PASSAGE (new station) through station	1902	1932	33 F3	
?	?	Passage Crossing crossing was actually 75yds long	1902	1932	33 F3	
?	?	Passage Tunnel 535 yards long	1902	1932	33 F3	
7	7:12	GLENBROOK	1902	1932	33 F3	
?	?	Glenbrook Station Gates	1902	1932	33 F3	
?	?	Monkstown Station Gates	1902	1932	33 F3	
8	8:12	MONKSTOWN	1902	1932	33 F3	
?	?	Raffeen Station Gates	1903	1932	33 E4	
9¾	9:53	RAFFEEN	1903	1932	33 E4	
		Raffeen quarry siding	c.1908	?	33 E4	
11½	11:49	CARRIGALINE	1903	1932	31 D1	
?	?	Owenboy Bridge 2 span girder bridge 140ft long	1904	1932	31 D1	
15		Hoddersfield Halt used for School and other parties	1912	c.1920s	31 D1	
?	?	Crosshaven Viaduct 4 span girder bridge 300ft long	1904	1932	31 D1	
16	16:07	CROSSHAVEN	1904	1932	31 D1	

Note: City Park (broad gauge days) and Show Ground Halt (narrow gauge days) may have been on the same or similar site.

100   Waterford Manor to Tramore

WTR / 5ft 3in gauge / mileposts measured from Waterford Manor

Waterford Manor to Tramore opened 07-09-1853 by the WTR.

Waterford Manor to Tramore closed 01-01-1961 by CIE.

MPost Dist.	Miles & Chains	Place / Feature (notes)	Date Opened	Date Closed	Map Grid	Table Ref.
0	0:00	WATERFORD MANOR	1853	1961	28 B4	
0¼	0:12	Bath Street Crossing	1853	1961	28 B4	
2		Level Crossing replaced by bridge	1853	?	28 B4	
7¼	7:20	TRAMORE	1853	1961	28 B4	

101   Londonderry Middle Quay to Burtonport

LLSR – Londonderry to Letterkenny
LBER – Letterkenny to Burtonport
3ft 0in gauge – Tooban Junction to Burtonport
5ft 3in gauge – Londonderry to Farland Point
    Londonderry to Tooban Junction re-gauged to 3'0"
    04 to 05-04-1885
mileposts measured from Londonderry Graving Dock

Londonderry Graving Dock to Farland Point (broad gauge) opened 31-12-1863 by the LLSR.

Tooban Junction to Farland Point (broad gauge) closed 06-1866 by the LLSR.
Tooban Junction to Farland Point (broad gauge) lifted 1877.

Tooban Junction to Burt Junction opened 30-06-1883 by the LLSR.
Burt Junction to Letterkenny opened 30-06-1883 by the LR.
Letterkenny to Burtonport opened 09-03-1903 by the LBER.

Passenger services ran along the LPHC mixed gauge system between Graving Dock and Middle Quay from 01-01-1869 to 03-01-1885 and 01-07-1885 to 01-01-1888.

Tooban Junction to Burtonport closed to passengers 03-07-1940 by the LLSR.
Letterkenny to Burtonport closed to goods 03-07-1940 by the LLSR.

Letterkenny to Gweedore goods service resumed 03-02-1941 by the LLSR.
Letterkenny to Gweedore passenger accommodation provided on trains from 03-1942 by the LLSR.

Letterkenny to Gweedore closed 06-01-1947 by the LLSR, (specials continued to 06-1947).
Tooban Junction to Letterkenny closed completely 01-07-1953 by the LLSR.
Londonderry Graving Dock to Tooban Junction closed completely 09-08-1953 by LLSR.

MPost Dist.	Miles & Chains	Place / Feature (notes)	Date Opened	Date Closed	Map Grid	Table Ref.
1		LONDONDERRY MIDDLE QUAY LPHC line, services used this terminus until 01-06-1888	1863	1888	3 D4	135
0	0:00	LONDONDERRY GRAVING DOCK	1863	1953	3 D4	135
0¼		Pennyburn Crossing	1863	1953	3 D4	
0¼	0:20	Pennyburn Halt not a public halt, though it had nameboard	1863	1888	3 D4	
2		No.1 Gates	1863	1953	3 D4	
2	1:78	GALLAGH ROAD may have closed for periods	1863	1953	3 D4	
2		No.2 Gates	1863	1953	3 D4	
2¾	2:53	HARRITY'S ROAD	1864	1864	3 D4	
4	3:58	BRIDGE END	1863	1953	3 D4	
4		No.3 Gates	1863	1953	3 D4	
5	5:14	BURNFOOT closed 1866 to 1873, except for monthly Fair Days and Sessions Days, when it re-opened as a normal stopping place again	1864	1953	3 D4	
6¼	6:20	TOOBAN JUNCTION formerly called 'JUNCTION' closed 07-1866, re-opened 1883 as BURNFOOT JUNCTION, re-named TOOBAN JUNCTION 1920	1864	1953	3 D4	102
?	?	Inch Causeway this causeway later carried the 2'0" gauge Board of Works line which was used to maintain the causeway	–	–	3 D4	324
7½	7:40	TRADY	1863	1866	3 D4	
8½		Burt Junction point at which the Letterkenny Railway continued from the LLSR and the former broad gauge line to Farland Point diverged	–	–	3 D4	
8½		Burt Junction	–	–	3 D4	
8¾	8:70	Farland Point	1863	1866	3 D4	
9¼	9:22	CARROWEN	1883	1953	3 D4	
13	12:73	NEWTONCUNNINGHAM formerly NEWTOWNCUNNINGHAM	1883	1953	3 C4	
16¾		Sallybrook Station Gates	1883	1953	3 C5	

16¾	16:57	SALLYBROOK opened c.05-1885	1885	1953	3 C5	
18½	18:44	MANORCUNNINGHAM	1883	1953	3 C5	
20½	20:45	PLUCK opened c.12-1883	1883	1953	3 C5	
24¾	24:60	LETTERKENNY adjacent to CDRJC station; siding connection to CDRJC line	1883	1953	3 B5	96
24¾		No.1 Gates	1903 ?	1947 ?	3 B5	
25½	25:40	OLD TOWN	1903	1947	3 B5	
28½	28:49	NEWMILLS	1903	1947	3 B5	
30	30:01	FOXHALL	1903	1947	3 B5	
30½		No.2 Gates	1903	1947	3 B5	
31¼		No.3 Gates	1903	1947	3 B5	
33½		Churchill Station Gates	1903	1947	3 B4	
33½	33:43	CHURCHHILL	1903	1947	3 B4	
35¼		No.4 Gates	1903	1947	3 B4	
36		No.5 Gates	1903	1847	3 B4	
37	37:12	KILMACRENAN	1903	1947	3 B4	
38		No.6 Gates	1903	1947	3 B4	
38½		No.7 Gates	1903	1947	3 B4	
39¾		No.8 Gates	1903	1947	3 B4	
39¾	39:50	BARNES HALT	1927	1940	3 B4	
41		Barnes Gap Viaduct 3 x 60ft spans, 60ft high	1903	1947	3 B4	
42½		Owencarrow Viaduct 380yds long, 30ft high	1903	1947	3 B4	
44¼		No.9 Gates	1903	1947	3 B3	
44½		No.10 Gates	1903	1947	3 B3	
45½	45:32	CREESLOUGH	1903	1947	3 B3	
46½		Faymore Viaduct 3 span girder, 50ft high	1903	1947	3 B3	
46½	46:46	DUNFANAGHY ROAD	1903	1947	3 B3	
47¾		No.11 Gates	1903	1947	3 A3	
48¼		No.12 Gates	1903	1947	3 A3	
51½		No.13 Gates	1903	1947	3 A3	
53½	53:37	FALCARRAGH	1903	1947	3 A3	
53½		Falcarragh Station Gates	1903	1947	3 A3	
55		No.14 Gates	1903	1947	3 A3	
56¾	56:59	CASHELNAGORE	1903	1947	3 A3	
59		No.15 Gates	1903	1947	2 D4	
60		No.16 Gates	1903	1947	2 D4	
63¾	63:66	GWEEDORE	1903	1947	2 D4	
64		No.17 Gates	1903	1940	2 D4	
64½		No.18 Gates	1903	1940	2 D4	
66	65:79	CROLLY	1903	1940	2 D4	
66½		No.19 Gates	1903	1947	2 D4	
70		No.20 Gates	1903	1940	2 D4	
71½	71:40	KINCASSLAGH ROAD	1913	1940	2 D4	
71½		No.21 Gates	1903	1940	2 D4	
72¼		No.22 Gates	1903	1940	2 C4	
73	72:73	DUNGLOE formerly LOUGHMEELA, DUNGLOE ROAD (LOUGHMEELA), DUNGLOE (LOUGHMEELA), finally just DUNGLOE	1903	1940	2 C4	
73½		No.23 Gates	1903	1940	2 C4	
74		No.24 Gates	1903	1940	2 C4	
74½	74:36	BURTONPORT	1903	1940	2 C4	
?		Quay	1903	1940 ?	2 C4	

102　　Tooban Junction to Cardonagh

LLSR / 3ft gauge – Buncrana to Carndonagh
5ft 3in gauge – Tooban Junction to Buncrana and Fahan Pier,
regauged to 3ft on 28-03-1885
mileposts measured from Londonderry Graving Dock

Tooban Junction to Buncrana and Fahan Pier opened 08-09-1864 by the LLSR.
Buncrana to Carndonagh opened 01-07-1901 by the LLSR.
Buncrana to Carndonagh closed completely 02-12-1935 by the LLSR.
Londonderry Graving Dock to Buncrana closed to passengers 06-09-1948 by the LLSR.
Londonderry Graving Dock to Buncrana closed completely 10-08-1953 by the LLSR.

NOTE: Limited passenger accommodation provided on goods trains to Buncrana until
final closure. Excursion traffic to Buncrana continued until final closure.

MPost Dist.	Miles & Chains	Place / Feature (notes)	Date Opened	Date Closed	Map Grid	Table Ref.
6¼	6:20	TOOBAN JUNCTION formerly called JUNCTION, closed 07-1866, re-opened 1883 as BURNFOOT JUNCTION, re-named TOOBAN JUNCTION in 1920	1864	1953	3 D4	101
7	7:06	INCH ROAD	1864	1953	3 D4	
7¾	7:54	LAMBERTON'S HALT	c.1927	1948	3 D4	
9¼	9:17	FAHAN	1864	1953	3 D4	
0		Fahan Pier	1868	1920	3 D4	
0¼		Junction	1868	1920	3 D4	
		Junction	1868	1920	3 D4	
10½	10:40	BEACH HALT	c.1939	c.1948	3 D3	
11	11:00	LISFANNON GOLF LINKS formerly GOLF HALT, re-named 1922	1892	1948	3 D3	
12¼	12:15	BUNCRANA	1864	1953	3 D3	
12¼		Buncrana Station Gates	1901 ?	1953 ?	3 D3	
13		No.1 Gates	1901	1935	3 D3	
13¾		No.2 Gates	1901	1935	3 D3	
14	14:11	BALLYMAGAN	1901	1935	3 D3	
15¾	15:65	KINNEGO HALT	c.1930	1935	3 D3	
15¾	15:65	No.3 Gates	1901	1935	3 D3	
18	17:70	DRUMFRIES	1901	1935	3 D3	
19¼		No.4 Gates	1901	1935	3 D3	
19¼		Cochrane's Siding	?	1935	3 D3	
20½		Meendoran Bridge	1901	1935	3 D2	
21½	21:40	No.5 Gates	1901	1935	3 D2	
21½	21:40	MEENDORAN HALT	c.1930	1935	3 D2	
22		No.6 Gates	1901	1935	3 D2	
22¼		No.7 Gates	1901	1935	3 D2	
23	23:00	CLONMANY	1901	1935	3 D2	
23½		No.8 Gates	1901	1935	3 D2	
23¾		No.9 Gates	1901	1935	3 D2	
24½	24:32	BALLYLIFFIN	1901	1935	3 D2	
25½		No.10 Gates	1901	1935	3 D2	
26¼	26:14	RASHENNY	1901	1935	4 A2	
27½		No.11 Gates	1901	1935	4 A2	
28	28:00	CARNDOAGH HALT	c.1930	1935	4 A2	
28		No.12 Gates	1901	1935	4 A2	
28¼		No.13 Gates	1901	1935	4 A2	
28¾		No.14 Gates	1901	1935	4 A2	
29¾		No.15 Gates	1901	1935	4 A2	
30½	30:29	CARNDONAGH	1901	1935	4 A2	

103　　Castlederg to Victoria Bridge

CVBT / 3ft gauge / mileposts measured from Castlederg

Opened 11-07-1884 by the CVBT.

Closed 17-04-1933 by the CVBT.

Last journeys were on Monday 30-01-1933: a strike commenced on Tuesday 31-01-1933
lasting to Friday 07-04-1933; trams never resumed after the strike and at a meeting held
on 30-09-1933 it was decided to wind up the company.

MPost Dist.	Miles & Chains	Place / Feature (notes)	Date Opened	Date Closed	Map Grid	Table Ref.
		Castlederg Marketplace	?	?	9 B1	
0		CASTLEDERG	1884	1933	9 B1	
1½		SPAMOUNT	1884	1933	9 B1	
3		CREW	1884	1933	9 B1	
4½		FYFIN	1884	1933	9 B1	
5¼		STONEWALLS roadside stopping place	?	?	9 C1	
6		GLEN roadside stopping place	?	?	3 D6	
7		VICTORIA BRIDGE curving bay platform at GNR(I) station	1884	1933	3 D6	49

104 Dundalk to Greenore

DNGR / 5ft 3in gauge / mileposts measured from Windmill Road

Windmill Road Junction to Greenore opened 01-05-1873 by the DGR.

Dundalk Quay Street to Greenore closed 01-01-1952 by the DNGR.
Windmill Road Junction to St Georges Quay closed c.1955 by the Ministry of Industry and Commerce.

MPost Dist.	Miles & Chains	Place / Feature (notes)	Date Opened	Date Closed	Map Grid	Table Ref.
0¼	0:25	Windmill Road Junction end-on junction with the INWR	1873	c.1955	17 A1	49
0		Quay Street Station Gates	1873	c.1955	17 A1	
0	0:00	DUNDALK QUAY STREET	1873	1952	17 A1	
?		St Georges Quay	1873	c.1955	17 A1	
0¾		Castletown Viaduct 22 span lattice girder viaduct	1873	1952	17 A1	
1		Ballymascanlon Viaduct 22 span iron girder viaduct	1873	1952	17 A1	
2¼		BELLURGAN POINT HALT opened 07-07-1935	1935	1952	17 A1	
3¾	3:48	BELLURGAN	1873	1952	17 B1	
5		ANNALOUGHAN HALT opened 07-07-1935	1935	1952	17 B1	
?		Riverstown Viaduct also called Piedmont Bridge	1873	1952	17 B1	
?		Riverstown Siding served Cooley Industrial Alcohol Factory	1938	?	17 B1	
6		GYLES QUAY HALT opened 07-07-1935	1935	1952	17 B1	
8¾	8:62	BUSH	1873	1952	17 B1	
10¼		CROSSALANEY HALT opened 07-07-1935	1935	1952	17 B1	
12¼	12:23	Junction with Newry Line	1876	1952	17 B1	105
12½	12:46	GREENORE	1873	1952	17 B1	105

105 Greenore to Newry Edward Street

DNGR / 5ft 3in gauge / mileposts measured from Greenore

Greenore to Newry Bridge Street opened 01-08-1876 by the DNGR.
Newry Bridge Street to Canal Branch Junction opened for goods 01-02-1877 by the DNGR.
Newry Bridge Street to Canal Branch Junction opened to passengers 01-07-1880 by the DNGR.
Albert Basin to King Street Junction opened 1854 by the NER.
Canal Branch Junction to King Street Junction opened to passengers 01-07-1880 by the GNR(I).

Greenore to Newry Bridge Street to closed 01-01-1952 by the DNGR.
Albert Basin to King Street Junction closed 04-01-1965 by the UTA.
King Street Junction to Newry Edward Street closed 04-01-1965 by the UTA.

MPost Dist.	Miles & Chains	Place / Feature (notes)	Date Opened	Date Closed	Map Grid	Table Ref.
0	0:00	GREENORE	1873	1952	17 B1	104
0¼	0:23	Junction with Dundalk Line	1876	1952	17 B1	104
2½		Dunstable's Crossing railcar stop, opened 1935	1935	1952	17 B1	
2¾	2:52	CARLINGFORD	1876	1952	17 B1	
5¾		White's Crossing railcar stop, opened 1935	1935	1952	17 B1	
?		Essmore Bridge also called McCann's Bridge	1876	1952	10 D6	
7¼		Omeath Station Gates road crossed line to Ferry Pier	1876	1952	10 D6	
7¼	7:25	OMEATH	1876	1952	10 D6	
14	13:77	NEWRY BRIDGE STREET terminus for DNGR trains 1876 to 1880, closed 10-08-1882, re-opened 04-1884	1876	1952	10 D6	
14	14:00	Junction with NAR	1877	1952	10 D6	
14		Bridge Street Crossing	1877	1952	10 D6	
14	13:69	Albert Basin	1854	1965	10 D6	
?		Canal Branch Junction open as a junction	1877	by 1907	10 D6	
?		Canal Branch Junction opened as a junction; junction removed at a later date (by 1907) and moved to King Street Junction, the two lines then ran parallel and diverged at the site of Canal Branch Junction.	1877	by 1907	10 D6	60
?		Fisher's Sawmill Siding	?	?	10 D6	60
14¼	14:21	King Street Junction opened as a junction	1861	1965	10 D6	60
14½		King Street Crossing	1854	1965	10 D6	
14¾		Monaghan Street Crossing	1854	1965	10 D6	
14¾		Edward Street Station Crossing	1854	1965	10 D6	
14¾	14:51	NEWRY EDWARD STREET	1854	1965	10 D6	60

106 Cork Capwell to Macroom

CMDR / 5ft 3in gauge / mileposts measured from Macroom Junction

Macroom Junction to Macroom opened 12-05-1866 by the CMDR.
Cork Capwell to Macroom Junction opened 27-09-1879 by the CMDR.

Cork Capwell to Ballyphehane Junction closed to passengers 02-03-1925 by the GSR.
Macroom Junction to Macroom closed to passengers 01-07-1935 by the GSR.

Cork Capwell to Ballyphehane Junction closed to goods 1946 by CIE (see note below).
Macroom Junction to Macroom closed completely 01-12-1953 by CIE, last train 10-11-1953, lifted 1954/5.

Capwell 'Siding': up to June 1925, Capwell was used for shunting and storage of wagons. From 06-1925 to 1941 one train a year ran to preserve the legal right of way. From 1941 to 1945, weekly workings of fuel tank wagons went to Capwell which was then used as a bus garage. Line was lifted on 1946, although some track remained buried in weeds until 1962 when the line was legally abandoned.

MPost Dist.	Miles & Chains	Place / Feature (notes)	Date Opened	Date Closed	Map Grid	Table Ref.
0¾		CORK CAPWELL opened 27-09-1879, trains previously used Albert Quay Station of CBSCR; Capwell closed to passengers 28-02-1925, passenger services diverted to Albert Quay from 02-03-1925 by the GSR	1879	1925	33 C2	
0	0:00	Macroom Junction formerly Ballyphehane Junction; disconnected 1879, the connection to the CBSCR was re-instated as a siding in 04-1918 at the insistence of the Government; re-instated as a direct junction 02-03-1925 by the GSR, closed 01-12-1953 by CIE; in use for demolition trains until 1954/5; lifted 27-11-1955.	1866	1953	33 C2	85
2½		BISHOPSTOWN not shown in public timetables after 11-1920; probably 'stop as required'	1912	1927	33 C3	
5½		BALLINCOLLIG	1866	1953	33 A2	
6	5:71	Ballincollig Station Gates	1866	1953	33 A2	
8¼	8:25	Grange Crossing	1866	1953	26 B6	
8½		KILUMNEY	1866	1953	26 B6	
8¾	8:56	Kilumney Station Gates	1866	1953	26 B6	
		Kilumney Ballast Pit	?	?	26 B6	
9	8:67	Ballast Crossing	1866	1953	26 B6	
11	11:00	Kilcrea Crossing	1866	1953	26 A6	
11¾		KILCREA	1866	1953	26 A6	
12	12:06	Kilcrea Station Gates	1866	1953	26 A6	
14½	14:29	Coolmucky Crossing	1866	1953	26 A6	
15¾		CROOKSTOWN ROAD the name 'CROOKSTOWN & RYECOURT' appears on some 1" OS Maps, but not found in any timetables	1866	1953	26 A6	
16	16:00	Crookstown Station Gates	1866	1953	26 A6	
19		DOONISKEY	1866	1953	26 A6	
19½	19:28	Dooniskey Station Gates	1866	1953	26 A6	
23½	23:52	Macroom Station Gates	1866	1953	25 D6	
23½		MACROOM	1866	1953	25 D6	

107 Skibbereen to Schull

SSR / 3ft gauge / mileposts measured from Skibbereen
(see note at bottom of table)

Skibbereen to Schull opened 09-09-1886 by the WCLRTC.
Schull to Schull Pier opened 01-10-1893 by the SSR.

Schull Harbour Extension closed 1930s, part lifted in 1941.
All services suspended 24-04-1944 due to fuel shortage.

Passenger services resumed 10-12-1945.
Passenger services suspended 27-01-1947.

Closed completely 27-01-1947 by CIE.

MPost Dist.	Miles & Chains	Place / Feature (notes)	Date Opened	Date Closed	Map Grid	Table Ref.
0	0:00	SKIBBEREEN	1886	1947	30 C2	85
3		NEWCOURT	1886	1947	30 C2	
		no Facilities, roadside halt				
	2:67	Newcourt Crossing	1886	1947	30 C2	
4		CHURCH CROSS	1886	1947	30 C2	
	5:39.	Hollyhill Crossing	1886	1947	30 B2	
6		HOLLYHILL	1886	1947	30 B2	
	5:75	Kilcoe No.1 Crossing	1886	1947	30 B2	
7		KILCOE	1886	1947	30 B2	
	6:46	Kilcoe No.2 Crossing	1886	1947	30 B2	
7½ ?		CROOKED BRIDGE	?	?	30 B2	
		possibly a halt in early days				
	7:37	Ardura Crossing	1886	1947	30 B2	
	8:65	Skeaghanore Crossing	1886	1947	30 B2	
		also called Driscoll's				
10		BALLYDEHOB	1886	1947	30 B2	
?		Ballydehob Viaduct	1886	1947	30 B2	
		12 arch stone viaduct				
	9:61	Shanavagh No.1 Crossing	1886	1947	30 B2	
		also called Sullivan's				
	10:28	Shanavagh No.2 Crossing	1886	1947	30 B2	
		also called Connor's				
	10:36	Shanavagh No.3 Crossing	1886	1947	30 B2	
		also called Connor's				
	12:45	Woodlands Crossing	1886	1947	30 B2	
13		WOODLANDS	1886	1947	30 B2	
		no facilities, roadside halt				
?		Junction	1893	1947	30 A2	
?		Junction	1893	1947	30 A2	
	14:23	Schull Station Gates	1886	1947	30 A2	
15		SCHULL	1886	1947	30 A2	
14½	14:37	Pier Extension Crossing	1893	1930s	30 A3	
?		Crossing	1893	1930s	30 A3	
?		Schull Pier	1893	1930s	30 A3	

Milepost distances obtained from CIE Working Timetable whereas level crossing distances obtained from Working Timetable Appendix.

108 Enniskillen to Carrignagat Junction

SLNCR / 5ft3in gauge / mileposts measured from Enniskillen
(See note at bottom of table)

Enniskillen to Belcoo opened for goods 12-02-1879 by the SLNCR.
Enniskillen to Belcoo opened for passengers 18-03-1879 by the SLNCR.
Belcoo to Glenfarne opened 01-01-1880 by the SLNCR.
Glenfarne to Manorhamilton opened 01-12-1880 by the SLNCR.
Manorhamilton to Collooney (SLNCR) opened 01-09-1881 by the SLNCR.
Collooney to Carrignagat Junction opened 07-11-1882 by the SLNCR.
Collooney (SLNCR) to Collooney (WLR) opened 01-10-1895 by the WLR.

Collooney (SLNCR) to Collooney (GSWR) closed 1944 by the GSR.
Enniskillen to Ballysodare closed completely 01-10-1957 by the SLNCR.

MPost Dist.	Miles & Chains	Place / Feature (notes)	Date Opened	Date Closed	Map Grid	Table Ref.
0	0:00	ENNISKILLEN	1883	1957	9 A4	49
		junction with GNR(I) – SLNCR used a bay platform at the GNR(I) Station				
?		ENNISKILLEN	1879	1883	9 A4	
		temporary terminus – SLNCR platform				
1		Weir's Bridge	1879	1957	9 A4	
		also called Killyhevlin Bridge, 467ft Girder bridge				
2		Lisgoole (No.1) Crossing	1879	1957	9 A4	
		crosses the Belturbet Road				
2½		No.2 Crossing	1879	1957	9 A4	
4		Mullaghy (No.3) Crossing	1879	1957	9 A4	
		crosses Swanlibar Road				
4		MULLAGHY	1886/7	by 1918	9 A4	
5¼		FLORENCECOURT	1879	1957	9 A4	
5¼		Florencecourt Stn (No.4) Gates	1879	1957	9 A4	
5¾		No.5 Crossing	1879	1957	9 A4	
		crosses Brockagh Road				
8¼		ABOHILL	1886	1957	9 A4	
12		BELCOO & BLACKLION	1879	1957	8 D4	
		formerly BELCOO, renamed 1908				
12		Belcoo Station (No.6) Gates	1879	1957	8 D4	
12½		Border Bridge	1880	1957	8 D4	
		85ft long, across MacNean River				
14¼		Killycarney (No.7) Crossing	1880	1957	8 D4	
		crosses Enniskillen to Manorhamilton Road,				
14¾		Killycarney (No.8) Crossing	1880	1957	8 D4	
15		Thornhill (No.9) Crossing	1880	1957	8 D4	
		crosses Dowra Road				
15½		Roo (No.10) Crossing	1880	1957	8 D4	
16¼		Correvan (No.11) Crossing	1880	1957	8 D4	
		Crosses Enniskillen to Manorhamilton Road				
16¾		Annagh (No.11A) Crossing	1880	1957	8 D4	
17¼		Glenfarne (No.12) Station Gates	1880	1957	8 D4	
17¼		GLENFARNE	1880	1957	8 D4	140
		transfer with Glenfarne Forestry Railway				
17½		Glenfarne River Bridge – 36ft long	1880	1957	8 D4	
20½		Cornacloy (No.13) Crossing	1880	1957	8 C4	
		crosses Kilmakerrill Church Road				
21¼		Kilmakerrill (No.14) Crossing	1880	1957	8 C4	
21¼		KILMAKERRILL	1929	1957	8 C4	
		Halt opened 28-07-1929				
22¾		Lissinagroagh (No.15) Crossing	1880	1957	8 C4	
23¾		Cherrybrook (No.16) Crossing	1880	1957	8 C4	
24¾		Manorhamilton Stn (No.17) Gates	1880	1957	8 C4	
24¾		MANORHAMILTON	1880	1957	8 C4	
		Locomotive Works				
29½		LISGORMAN	1887	1957	8 B4	
		closed from 1917 to 1940; no platform when re-opened				
32¼		Cleen (No.18) Crossing	1881	1957	8 B4	
		Bellanamore Bridge/Dromahair Creamery				
33¼		DROMAHAIR	1881	1957	8 B4	
33¼		Dromahair Station(No.19) Gates	1881	1957	8 B4	
34		Edergole (No.20) Crossing	1881	1957	8 B4	
34¼		Derrybrisk (No.21) Crossing	1881	1957	8 B4	
35¼		Toberanania (No.22) Crossing	1881	1957	8 B5	
36		Altvelid (No.23) Crossing	1881	1957	8 B5	
36¼		Kingsfort (No.24) Crossing	1881	1957	8 B5	
		Ballintogher Station Gates				
36¼	36:23	BALLINTOGHER	by 1883	1957	8 B5	
37		Woodfield (No.25) Crossing	1881	1957	8 B5	
38¼		Kilross (No.26) Crossing	1881	1957	8 B5	
39¼		Castle Dargan (No.27) Crossing	1881	1957	8 A5	
39¾		BALLYGAWLEY	1887 ?	1957	8 A5	
		exact opening date uncertain				
40½		Unshin River Bridge	1881	1957	8 A5	
		69ft, 2 span girder				
41½	41:27	COLLOONEY	1881	1957	8 A5	
41½		Collooney Station (No.28) Gates	1881	1957	8 A5	
41½		Owenmore River Bridge	1882	1957	8 A5	
		106ft single span				

41½		Junction junction with WLR and successors	1895	1957	8 A5	17
0	0.00	Junction section known as the 'Southern Siding', used for wagon storage only after 1944	1895	1957	8 A5	17
	0:51	COLLOONEY GSWR	1895	1957	8 A5	17
42¾	42:50	Carrignagat Junction junction with MGWR. Physical junction removed by GSR on 07-09-1930 and operated as independent tracks to Ballysodare.	1882	1930	8 A5	37

Notes: The 0 Milepost is assumed to be at the junction of GNR(I) / SLNCR property in Enniskillen Goods yard, this could account for the 'Route Mileage' being 42m 50c as opposed to the 'Official Returns' of 43m 12c.

Certain mileages and crossing names in the table have been compiled from field notes taken in the 1950s as no official records are thought to survive or have been located.

109 Tralee to Dingle

TDR / 3ft gauge / mileposts measured from Tralee

Tralee to Dingle opened 01-04-1891 by the TDR.
Glenagalt deviation (72 chains) opened 07-1910 by the TDR.
Lispole deviation (? chains) opened 1909.

Tralee to Dingle closed to passengers 17-04-1939 by the GSR.
Dingle to Dingle Harbour closed 1930s by the GSR.

Goods service suspended 10-03-1947 due to fuel shortage.

Closed to goods 10-03-1947 by CIE except for monthly livestock trains.

Tralee to Dingle closed completely 01-07-1953 by CIE.

Tralee Ballyard to Blennerville re-opened 10-07-1993 as tourist railway by the TDSR.

MPost Dist.	Miles & Chains	New Mls & Chns	Place / Feature (notes)	Date Opened	Date Closed	Map Grid	Table Ref.
–			Tralee GSWR Yard freight only interchange with broad gauge	1891	1953	25 A2	9
0	0:00		TRALEE	1891	1939	25 A2	
0¼	0:14		Rock Street Crossing	1891	1953	25 A2	
0½	0:29		Pembroke Street Crossing	1891	1953	25 A2	
0¾	0:58		Strand Street Crossing	1891	1953	25 A2	
1	0:75		Basin No.1 Crossing	1891	1953	25 A2	
1¼			BASIN	1891	1920s	25 A2	
		0:00	TRALEE BALLYARD	1993	Open	25 A2	
1	1:01	0:09	Basin No.2 Crossing closed 1953, re-opened 1993	1891	Open	25 A2	
		1.28	Junction to Depot	1993	Open	25 A2	
		1.28	Junction to Depot	1993	Open	25 A2	
		?	Level Crossing	1993	Open	25 A2	
		?	TDSR Depot	1993	Open	25 A2	
2¼	2:21	1:33	BLENNERVILLE closed 1939, re-opened 1993	1891	Open	25 A2	
2¼	2:29		Blennerville Crossing no gates	1891	1953	25 A2	
?	?		TONEVANE opened by 05-1895, no platform, called TONEVANE CROSS up to c.10-1898	by 1895	c.1908	24 D2	
6			CURRAHEEN	1891	1939	24 D2	
7¾			DERRYMORE	1891 ?	1939	24 D2	
10			CASTLEGREGORY JUNCTION closed as junction; formerly CAMP JUNCTION, re-named 1895	1891	1939	24 D2	110
?			Curraduff Viaduct original viaduct on a 3 chain radius and incline	1891	1908	24 D2	
?			Curraduff Bridge built on a deviation to ease curve of above viaduct	1908	1953	24 D2	
11¾			CAMP	1914	1939	24 D2	
12½	12:48		Skirlough Crossing	1891	1953	24 D2	
14			GLENAGALT BRIDGE opened by 05-1895	by 1895	1939	24 D3	
16			GLENMORE	1897	1939	24 C3	
17½			EMALOUGH	1891 ?	1939	24 C3	
20¾			ANNASCAUL	1891	1939	24 C3	
20½	20:48		Annascaul Station Gates	1891	1953	24 C3	
21½	21:52		Ballinclare Crossing	1891	1953	24 C3	
22½	22:51		Ballinacourty Crossing	1891	1953	24 C3	
23			BALLINASARE	1897/8	1939	24 C3	
?			PUCK ISLAND no platform	1897	1902	24 C3	
24¾			GARRYNADUR	by 1895	1939	24 C3	
?			Lispole Viaduct	1891	1953	24 B3	
26¾			LISPOLE	1891	1939	24 B3	
27¾			BALLINASTEENIG	by 1895	1939	24 B3	
31¾			DINGLE	1891	1939	24 B3	
31¼	31:17		Dingle Station Gates	1891	1939	24 B3	
?			DINGLE PIER station nameboard simply read 'PIER'	1891	1930s	24 B3	
32¼			Dingle Harbour	1891	1930s	24 B3	

110 Castlegregory Junction to Castlegregory

TDR / 3ft gauge / mileposts measured from Castlegregory Junction

Castlegregory Junction to Castlegregory opened 01-04-1891 by the TDR.

Castlegregory Junction to Castlegregory closed completely 17-04-1939 by the GSR.

MPost Dist.	Miles & Chains	Place / Feature (notes)	Date Opened	Date Closed	Map Grid	Table Ref.
0		CASTLEGREGORY JUNCTION closed as junction; formerly CAMP JUNCTION, re-named 1895	1891	1939	24 D2	109
2½		DEELIS	1891 ?	1939	24 D2	
4		AUGHACASLA	by 1895	1939	24 C2	
6		CASTLEGREGORY	1891	1939	24 C2	

111 Ennis to Kilkee

WCR – Ennis to Miltown Malbay
SCR – Miltown Malbay to Kilkee
3ft gauge / mileposts measured from Ennis

Ennis to Miltown Malbay opened 02-07-1887 by the WCR.
Miltown Malbay to Moyasta Junction opened for goods 07-11-1892 by the SCR.
Miltown Malbay to Moyasta Junction opened for passengers 23-12-1892 by the SCR.
Kilkee to Kilrush opened to goods 11-05-1892 by the SCR.
Kilkee to Kilrush opened to passengers 13-08-1892 by the SCR.
Kilkee to Moyasta Junction opened 13-08-1892 by the SCR.

Passenger services suspended 24-02-1947 due to fuel shortage.
Passenger services resumed 24-05-1947.

Ennis to Kilkee and Kilrush closed completely 01-02-1961 by CIE.

A short length of track has been relaid at Moyasta Junction by a preservation group called the West Clare Railway. The track runs from immediately north of Moyasta No.4 Crossing through the Kilkee side platform to a point a little to the north of the station. This length of track was opened to traffic 01-08-1997.

MPost Dist.	Miles & Chains	Place / Feature (notes)	Date Opened	Date Closed	Map Grid	Table Ref.
0	0:00	ENNIS bay platform at WLR Station	1887	1961	19 C4	17
1¼	1:20	Curravorrin Crossing	1887	1961	19 C4	
1¾	1:60	Lifford Halt Crossing also called Asylum Gates	1887	1961	19 C4	
1¾		LIFFORD railcar stop, opened 05-05-1952	1952	1961	19 C4	
3½	3:44	Erinagh Crossing	1887	1961	19 C4	
4¾	4:60	Ballygriffey Crossing	1887	1961	19 C3	
4¾		Ballygriffey Ballast Siding	1904	?	19 C3	

6¾		RUANE	1888	1961	19 C3	
		originally RUAN, closed 1898, re-opened 1904,				
		closed 31-03-1921, re-opened as RUANE on				
		05-05-1952 as a railcar stop				
6¼	6:27	Ruan Crossing	1887	1961	19 C3	
7	7:05	Laurel Vale Crossing	1887	1961	19 C3	
7¼	7:30	Dromcavan Crossing	1887	1961	19 C3	
		also called Murphy's Crossing				
7½	7:44	Ballycullinan No.1 Crossing	1887	1961	19 C3	
		also called Cragmoher No.1 Crossing				
8¼	8:28	Ballycullinan No.2 Crossing	1887	1961	19 C3	
		also called Cragmoher No.2 Crossing				
8¾	8:54	COROFIN	1887	1961	19 C3	
8¾	8:61	Corofin Station Gates	1887	1961	19 C3	
9¾		ROXTON	?	?	19 C3	
		platform here during early years				
9¾	9:69	Roxton Crossing	1887	1961	19 C3	
10¾	10:53	Newtown Crossing	1887	1961	19 C3	
11¾		WILLBROOK	1888	1961	10 C3	
		opened 1888, closed 1898, re-opened 1904,				
		closed 1921, re-opened 1929				
11¾	11:61	Willbrook Crossing	1887	1961	19 C3	
14		CLOUNA	1954	1961	19 B3	
		also called CLOONEY, opened 04-05-1954				
		as a railcar stop				
14		Clooney Crossing	1887	1961	19 B3	
		also called Clouna				
15¾		MONREAL	1952	1961	19 B3	
		opened 14-09-1952 as a railcar stop				
15¾	15:63	Monreal Crossing	1887	1961	19 B3	
17½	17:31	Knockdromagh No.1 Crossing	1887	1961	19 B3	
17½	17:36	Knockdromagh No.2 Crossing	1887	1961	19 B3	
18½		ENNISTYMON	1887	1961	19 B3	
19½		WORKHOUSE	?	1961	19 B3	
		opened in early years for Workhouse staff,				
		closed 1925, re-opened for public use 29-06-1953				
19½	19:44	Workhouse Crossing	1887	1961	19 B3	
20	20:07	Lahinsey No.1 Crossing	1887	1961	19 B3	
20¼	20:25	Lahinsey No.2 Crossing	1887	1961	19 B3	
21		LAHINCH	1887	1961	19 B3	
		LEHINCH up to c.1900				
21	20:73	Lahinch Station Gates	1887	1961	19 B3	
21¼	21:13	Cregg Crossing	1887	1961	19 B3	
22¼		HANRAHAN'S BRIDGE	1958	1961	19 B3	
		also called MOY BRIDGE,				
		opened 01-10-1958as a railcar stop				
22¾	22:60	Moymore No.1 Crossing	1887	1961	19 A3	
23¾	23:51	Moymore No.2 Crossing	1887	1961	19 A3	
24½		RINEEN	1952	1961	19 A3	
		trains did call here in early days,				
		re-opened 05-05-1952 as a railcar stop				
24½		Rineen Crossing	1887	1961	19 A3	
24½		Rineen Ballast Siding	1887	c.1926	19 A3	
27		MILTOWN MALBAY	1887	1961	19 A4	
27	27:01	Miltown Malbay Stn Gates	1892	1961	19 A4	
27¼	27:27	Flag Road No.1 Crossing	1892	1961	19 A4	
27½	27:37	Flag Road No.2 Crossing	1892	1961	19 A4	
28½	28:41	Braffa Crossing	1892	1961	19 A4	
28¾	28:66	Annagh No.1 Crossing	1892	1961	19 A4	
29½	29:45	Annagh No.2 Crossing	1892	1961	19 A4	
29½		ANNAGH NO.2	1952	1961	19 A4	
		opened 05-05-1952 as a railcar stop				
30	29:70	Emalough Crossing	1892	1961	19 A4	
31	30:72	Quilty East Crossing	1892	1961	19 A4	
31	31:06	Quilty Station Gates	1892	1961	19 A4	
31½		QUILTY	1892	1961	19 A4	
32¼	32:25	Kilmurry Station Gates No.1	1892	1961	19 A4	
32½		KILMURRY	1892	1961	19 A4	
		'KILMURRY & MULLAGH' on 1" OS map c.1905				
32½	32:40	Kilmurry Stn Gates No.2	1892	1961	19 A4	
33½	33:36	Clonadrum Crossing	1892	1961	19 A4	
33¾	33:66	Lisseynealon Crossing	1892	1961	19 A4	
34½	34:37	Craggaknock Station Gates	1892	1961	19 A4	
34½		CRAGGAKNOCK	1892	1961	19 A4	
35		Ballast Siding and Quarry	1913	c.1926	19 A4	
35¼	35:29	Clohans No.1 Crossing	1892	1961	19 A4	
35½	35:34	Clohans No.2 Crossing	1892	1961	19 A4	
36¼	36:18	Caherfeenich No.1 Crossing	1892	1961	19 A5	
36¼	36:25	Caherfeenich No.2 Crossing	1892	1961	19 A5	
36½	36:36	Caherfeenich No.3 Crossing	1892	1961	19 A5	
37¼	37:29	Caherfeenich No.4 Crossing	1892	1961	19 A5	
37½	37:42	Doonbeg Station Gates	1892	1961	19 A5	
37¾		DOONBEG	1892	1961	19 A5	
39¾	39:51	Shragh Siding Crossing	1892	1961	19 A5	
39½		SHRAGH	1952	1961	19 A5	
		opened 05-05-1952 as a railcar stop				
39¾		Shragh Siding	?	1961	19 A5	
		open in SCR/GSR days				
41¾	41:50	Monmore Crossing	1892	1961	19 A5	
43		MOYASTA JUNCTION	1892	Open	19 A5	112
		closed 01-02-1961 by CIE,				
		re-opened 01-08-1997 by the West Clare Railway				
43	43:01	Moyasta No.4 Crossing	1892	1961	19 A5	
43¼		Moyasta (West Junction)	1892	1961	19 A5	112
43¾	43:65	Moyasta West No.5 Crossing	1892	1961	19 A5	
44	44:11	Bawnmore Crossing	1892	1961	18 D5	
44¾	44:59	Gurrane Crossing	1892	1961	18 D5	
45¼		BLACKWEIR	1892	1961	18 D5	
45¼	45:18	Blackweir Station Gates	1892	1961	18 D5	
46¾	46:52	Lisdeen Crossing	1892	1961	18 D5	
47	47:08	Dough Crossing	1892	1961	18 D5	
48		KILKEE	1892	1961	18 D5	

112 Moyasta Junction to Kilrush & Cappagh Pier

SCR / 3ft gauge / mileposts measured from Ennis

Kilrush to Kilkee opened 13-08-1892 by the SCR.
Moyasta Junction to Kilrush and Cappagh Pier opened to goods 11-05-1892 by the SCR.
Moyasta Junction to Kilrush and Cappagh Pier opened to passengers 13-08-1892 by SCR.

Passenger services suspended 24-02-1947 due to fuel shortage.
Passenger services resumed 24-05-1947.

Moyasta Junction to Kilrush and Cappagh Pier closed 01-02-1961 by CIE.

A short length of track has been relaid at Moyasta Junction by a preservation group called the West Clare Railway. The track runs from immediately north of Moyasta No.4 Crossing through the Kilkee side platform to a point a little to the north of the station. This length of track was opened to traffic 01-08-1997.

MPost Dist.	Miles & Chains	Place / Feature (notes)	Date Opened	Date Closed	Map Grid	Table Ref.
43		MOYASTA JUNCTION	1892	Open	19 A5	111
		closed 01-02-1961 by CIE,				
		re-opened 01-08-1997 by the West Clare Railway				
43	42:73	Moyasta No.1 Crossing	1892	1961	19 A5	
43	43:02	Moyasta No.2 Crossing	1892	1961	19 A5	
0		Moyasta (West) Junction	1892	1961	19 A5	111
		MOYASTA LOOP PLATFORM	1892	by 1954	19 A5	
		platform out of use by 1954				
	43:49	Moyasta No.3 Crossing	1892	1961	19 A5	
0½		Moyasta (East) Junction	1892	1961	19 A5	
43¼		Moyasta (East) Junction	1892	1961	19 A5	
43¾	43:69	Carnacalla No.1 Crossing	1892	1961	19 A5	
44¾	44:62	Carnacalla No.2 Crossing	1892	1961	19 A5	
46	46:01	Leadmore No.1 Crossing	1892	1961	19 A5	
		also called Shanakyle Crossing				
46¼		Skagh Point Ballast Siding	1892	1904	19 A5	
46¾	46:65	Leadmore No.2 Crossing	1892	1961	19 A5	
46¾		Merchants Quay Siding	?	1961	19 A5	
47	46:79	Dock Crossing	1892	1961	19 A5	
47		KILRUSH	1892	1961	19 A5	
47	47:00	Kilrush Station Gates	1892	1961	19 A5	
47¾	47:55	Cappagh Crossing	1892	1961	19 A5	
		also called Supples Crossing				
47½		CAPPAGH PIER	1892	1916	19 A5	
		closed 1916 after cessation of regular passenger trains				
		and steamer services to and from Limerick; excursion Train				
		for Cappagh Regatta ran once a year after 1916 to ?				

?		Pier accessed by Wagon Turntable	1892	?	19 A5	

113 Portrush to Giant's Causeway

GCPBVT / 3ft gauge / Distances measured from Portrush

Portrush to Bushmills opened 29-01-1883 by the GCPBVT.
Portrush to Portrush Harbour opened 1883 by the GCPBVT.
Bushmills to Giant's Causeway opened 01-07-1887 by the GCPBVT.

Portrush Harbour to Portrush Station closed 01-06-1887 by the GCPBVT.
Portrush to Giant's Causeway closed 01-10-1949 by the GCPBVT.

Portrush Harbour to Portrush tramcar depot and Portballintrae Road, Bushmills to Giant's Causeway – steam hauled from opening until 26-07-1899.
Portrush Tramcar depot to Portballintrae Road, Bushmills raised outside third rail at 250V DC from opening until 26-07-1899. Regular electric services commenced 05-11-1883.
Portush Station to Giant's Causeway converted to overhead trolley system at 250V DC on 26-07-1899. Voltage increased to 550V DC in 1900.
World's first Hydro-electric railway.

MPost Dist.	Miles & Chains	Place / Feature (notes)	Date Opened	Date Closed	Map Grid	Table Ref.
0		PORTRUSH line was extended 75yds in 1888	1883	1949	4 D3	
0¼		Portrush Harbour mixed gauge with NCC from harbour.	1883	1888	4 D3	73
		PORTRUSH POST OFFICE	1883	1949	4 D3	
0¾		Depot passing loop	1883	1949	4 D3	
		ROYAL PORTRUSH GOLF CLUB	1883	1949	4 D3	
1¾		Passing Loop near Craigahulliar Quarry	1883	1949	4 D3	234
2½		BALLYMONEY ROAD passing loop	1883	1949	4 D3	
3¼		WHITE ROCKS	1883	1949	4 D3	
3¼		Long Gilbert Quarry Siding laid 02-1883	1883	?	4 D3	235
3¼		Punchbowl Passing Loop	1888	1949	4 D3	
3¾		Giant's Head Passing Loop	1883	1949	4 D3	
4¼		Dunluce Crossing	1883	1949	4 D3	
4¼		DUNLUCE CASTLE passing loop	1883	1949	4 D3	
5		PORTBALLINTRAE passing loop	1883	1949	4 D3	
5		Portballintrae Crossing	1883	1949	4 D3	
5½		GORTNEE passing loop	1888	·1949	4 D3	
6¼		STANALANE passing loop	1883	1949	4 D3	
?		Level Crossing	1883	1949	4 D3	
6¾		BUSHMILLS passing loop	1883	1949	4 D3	
0		BUSHMILLS	1883	1949	4 D3	
0¼		BUSHMILLS MARKET YARD also siding for market use	1883	1890	4 D3	
6¾		Level Crossing	1887	1949	4 D3	
7¼		BUSHFOOT GOLF LINKS passing loop	1887	1949	4 D3	
7¾		Sandhills Siding passing loop	1887	1949	4 D3	
8		Victoria Jubilee Bridge	1887	1949	4 D3	
8¼		BUSHFOOT STRAND passing loop	1887	1949	4 D3	
8½		RUNKERRY passing loop	1887	1949	4 D3	
9		Level Crossing	1887	1949	4 D3	
9¼		GIANT'S CAUSEWAY	1887	1949	4 D3	

114 Islandbridge Junction, Glasnevin Junction & Drumcondra Junction to the North Wall

GSWR / 5ft3in gauge / mileposts measured from Islandbridge Junction

Islandbridge Junction to Glasnevin Junction opened 02-09-1877 by the GSWR.
West Road Junction to Church Road Junction opened 02-09-1877 by the GSWR.
East Wall Junction to Church Road Junction opened 01-12-1877 by the GNR(I).
Drumcondra Junction to Church Road Junction opened 01-04-1901 by the GSWR.
Church Road Junction to North Wall (LNWR) opened 02-09-1877 by the LNWR.
North Strand Road Junction to Amiens Street Junction Station opened 01-12-1906 by the GSWR.
Ossory Road Junction opened 02-04-1973 by CIE (see note below).
Ossory Road Junction to Suburban Junction opened 09-08-1981 by CIE (see note below).
Church Road Junction to North Wall (Point) opened 06-09-1886 by the GSWR.
North Wall Extension opened ?
Granaries to Alexandra Quay opened 1971 by the DPDB.

Drumcondra Junction to Glasnevin Junction Closed 30-11-1906 by GSWR and MGWR, lifted 1921.
West Road Junction to North Wall closed to passengers 11-1922 by the GSWR.
East Wall Junction to North Wall closed to passengers 17-01-1921 by the GNR(I).
North Strand Road Junction to Church Road Junction closed to passengers 11-1922 by GSWR.
Ossory Road Junction closed 1981 by CIE (see note below).

Glasnevin Junction opened 22-11-1936 by GSR.

New Glasnevin Junction was a reversal of the original Drumcondra-Glasnevin Junctions link to allow trains diverted from Dublin Broadstone to use the easier graded GSWR route via North Strand Road Junction to Amiens Street Station.

Ossory Road Junction installed 1973 to allow Sligo/Galway trains access from former GNR(I) platforms to Link Line. Removed 1981 and replaced with another crossover near station. New Ossory Road Junction/Suburban Junction opened 09-08-1981 as part of electrification remodelling to allow double track access from GNR(I) lines to suburban platforms and Loop Line.

MPost Dist.	Miles & Chains	Place / Feature (notes)	Date Opened	Date Closed	Map Grid	Table Ref.
Islandbridge Junction to Glasnevin Junction						
0	0:00	Islandbridge Junction	1877	Open	32 B2	8
0½	0:30	Liffey Bridge Junction freight lines from Islandbrige Junction trail in	1877	Open	32 B2	
0½	0:32	River Liffey Bridge	1877	Open	32 B2	
0½	0:34	Phoenix Park Tunnel 757 yards long	1877	Open	32 B2	
2	1:68	Cabra Siding former cattle sidings, now a cement terminal	1877	Open	32 B2	
2½	2:38	Drumcondra Junction former Facing Junction to MGWR lines	1901	1906	32 C2	115
2¾	2:53	Glasnevin Junction former junction before reversal in 1933	1877	1906	32 C2	115
Drumcondra Junction to North Wall						
2½	2:38	Drumcondra Junction former Facing Junction to MGWR lines	1901	1906	32 C2	115
0	0:00	Drumcondra Junction	1901	1906	32 C2	115
0¼	0:15	GLASNEVIN JUNCTION	1877	1906	32 C2	115
2¾	2:53	Glasnevin Junction trailing Junction from ex-MGWR lines	1936	Open	32 C2	115
3	2:75	GLASNEVIN Closed 01-12-1910. Island platform	1901	1910	32 C2	
3¼	3:28	DRUMCONDRA closed 01-12-1910; IRRS premises in station buildings 1969 to 1983; station re-opening in 1998	1901	1910	32 C2	
4¼	4:18	North Strand Road Junction	1901	Open	32 D2	
4¼	4:18	North Strand Road Junction	1906	Open	32 D2	
0	0:00	Suburban Junction double track junction opened 09-08-1981 from GNR(I) Lines to Link Line	1981	Open	32 D2	50
?	?	Ossory Road Junction	1981	Open	32 D2	50

4½	4:37	Ossory Road Junction double track junction opened 09-08-1981 from GNR(I) Lines	1981	Open	32 D2	50
?	?	Ossory Road Junction former link installed 1973 to allow access from GNR(I) platforms to link line; removed 1981 and replaced with new junction nearer station	1973	1981	32 D2	50
4¾	4:50	Junction from GNR(I) joins GNR(I) Lines	1906	Open	32 D2	50
4¾	4:54	Amiens Street Junction junction with North Strand Road Junction lines	1906	Open	32 D2	50
4¾	4:54	Amiens Street Junction junction from GNR(I) Lines	1906	Open	32 D2	50
4¾	4:56	Amiens Street Junction junction with Newcomen Bridge Junction lines	1906	Open	32 D2	115
4¾	4:61	Amiens Street Junction Station	1906	Open	32 D2	31
		MILEAGE CHANGE (mileposts measured from Liffey Junction)				
2¼	2:35	West Road Junction	1877	Open	32 D2	114
2½	2:45	Church Road Junction	1877	Open	32 D2	114
4¾	4:50	MILEAGE CHANGE (mileposts now measured from Islandbridge Junc)				
		MILEAGE CHANGE (mileposts measured from Church Road Junction)				
0½	0:32	East Wall Junction	1877	Open	32 D2	50
0	0:00	Church Road Junctions	1877	Open	32 D2	114
4¾	4:52	MILEAGE CHANGE (mileposts now measured from Islandbridge Junc)				
4¾	4:50	Church Road Junction trailing Junction from Newcomen Junction Line	1892	Open	32 D2	50, 115
4¾	4:52	Church Road Junction trailing Junction from East Wall Junction Line	1877	Open	32 D2	50, 115
4¾	4:53	Church Road Junction facing Junction to Alexandra Road Line	1886	Open	32 D2	50, 115
4¾	4:53	Church Road Junction	1886	Open	32 D2	
4¾	4:79	North Wall (LNWR Cattle)	1877	?	32 D2	
5	5:01	NORTH WALL (LNWR) by 11-1922, regular timetabled passenger trains – GSWR / MGWR and GNR(I) – had stopped	1877	1922	32 D2	
5	5:03	North Wall Goods (LNWR) now called North Wall Container Depot	1877	Open	32 D2	
	5:11	End of Quay	1877	?	32 D2	
4¾	4:53	Church Road Junction	1886	Open	32 D2	
5	4:73	Granaries	1886	Open	32 D2	
5	4:73	Granaries	1886	Open	32 D2	
5	5:11	Sherriff Street Crossing	1886	Open	32 D2	
5¼	5:28	North Wall Point Depot	1886	Open	32 D2	
5¼	5:29	North Wall Crossing	?	Open	32 D2	
5½	5:35	North Quay Extension	?	Open	32 D2	
?		East Wall Yard	1886	Open	32 D2	
5¼	5:17	East Wall Crossing	1886	Open	32 D2	
5¼	5:17	Alexandra Road Tramway line owned by Dublin Port, road tramway	1971	Open	32 D2	
5¼	5:28	Alexandra Terminal Siding Lead & Zinc Concentrates discharge bunkers	?	Open	32 D2	
5¾	5:74	IE Fuel Terminal Siding	?	Open	32 D2	
5¾	5:76	Irish Tar Siding	?	Closed	32 D2	
5¾	5:78	Texaco Siding	?	Closed	32 D2	
6	6:08	Esso Ireland & Texaco Siding	?	Open	32 D2	
6¼	6:12	Irish Shell Siding	?	Open	32 D2	
?		Ferryport Teminal	?	Open	32 D2	
6½	6:30	Asahi Sidings on spur from tramway	?	Open	32 D2	
6½	6:41	End of Tramway	?	Open	32 D2	

115 Liffey Junction to North Wall

MGWR – Liffey Junction to North Wall
CDJR – Newcomen Bridge Junction to Amiens Street
5ft3in gauge / mileposts measured from Dublin Broadstone

Liffey Junction to North Wall Midland opened for goods 01-03-1864 by the MGWR.
Glasnevin Junction to North Wall LNWR opened to GSWR Passenger trains 02-09-1877.
Liffey Junction to Glasnevin Junction opened to passengers 11-1887 by the MGWR.
West Road Junction to Church Road Junction opened 02-09-1877 by the GSWR.
Newcomen Bridge Junction to Amiens Street Junction Station opened 02-06-1892 by the CDJR .
North Wall CDSPC Station opened 15-09-1873 by the CDSPC .

Drumcondra Junction to Glasnevin Junction Closed 1906 by GSWR / MGWR, lifted 1921.

Glasnevin Junction opened 22-11-1936 by GSR.

New Glasnevin Junction was a reversal of the original Drumcondra-Glasnevin Junctions link to allow trains diverted from Dublin Broadstone to use the easier graded GSWR route via North Strand Road Junction to Amiens Street Station.

MPost Dist.	Miles & Chains	Place / Feature (notes)	Date Opened	Date Closed	Map Grid	Table Ref.
1½	1:33	LIFFEY JUNCTION opened as a junction; platforms provided in 1881; closed as a junction in 1961.	1864	1937	32 B1	34
0	0:00	MILEAGE CHANGE (mileposts now measured from Liffey Junction)				
0	0:00	Liffey Junction	1864	1961	32 C2	
0½	0:34	North City Mills Siding Junction lifted 1977	1866	1977	32 C2	
1½	1:30	North City Mills lifted 1977	1866	1977	32 C2	
0¾	0:57	Glasnevin Junction (new) facing Junction to ex-GSWR lines	1936	Open	32 C2	
0¼	0:57	Drumcondra Junction	1901	1906	32 C2	114
0	0:65	Glasnevin Junction (old)	1877	1906	32 C2	114
0¾	0:65	Glasnevin Junction (old) trailing Junction from GSWR lines	1877	1906	32 C2	114
1	0:73	Cross Guns Tunnel 292 yards long	1864	Open	32 C2	
1¾	1:51	Clonliffe Mills Junction	?	?	32 C2	
0	0:00	Clonliffe Mills Junction	?	?	32 C2	
?	?	Clonliffe Mills	?	?	32 C2	
2¼	2:21	Newcomen Bridge Junction	1892	Open	32 C2	
2¼	2:21	Newcomen Bridge Junction	1892	Open	32 C2	
2½	2:41	Amiens Street Junction junction from North Strand Road Junction and GNR(I)	1906	Open	32 2	114
2½	2:46	AMIENS STREET JUNCTION Station	1892	Open	32 C2	31
2¼	2:24	Newcomen Bridge Junction	1873	?	32 C2	
2¾	2:62	Sherrif Street Junction end-on junction with CDSPC property	1873	?	32 C2	
3	2:79	NORTH WALL (CDSPC)	1873	?	32 D2	
2½	2:39	West Road Junction	1864	Open	32 D2	
3	2:78	North Wall (MGWR Yard) now the North Wall Freight Depot	1864	Open	32 D2	
2½	2:39	West Road Junction	1877	Open	32 D2	
2½	2:49	Church Road Junctions	1877	Open	32 D2	114

116 Central Junction to Ballymacarrett Junction, Queen's Bridge and Donegall Quay Junction

BCR / 5ft3in gauge

Central Junction to Ballymacarrett Junction opened for goods 09-08-1874 by the BCR.
Central Junction to Ballymacarrett Junction opened to passengers 05-08-1878 by the BCR.
East Bridge Street Junction to Queen's Bridge opened for goods 12-06-1876 by the BCR.
East Bridge Street Junction to Queen's Bridge opened to passengers 05-08-1878 by the BCR.
Queen's Bridge to Donegall Quay Junction opened to goods 12-06-1876 by the BCR.
Westlink Junction to City Junction opened 30-09-1995 by NIR.

Belfast Central Railway closed to passengers 30-11-1885 by the GNR(I), except for excursions etc. to and from BCDR.

East Bridge Street Junction to Donegall Quay Junction closed 03-06-1963 by the UTA. BCR closed 31-07-1965 by UTA when the Middlepath Street bridge was removed.

Ballymacarrett Junction to Belfast Central re-opened to passengers 12-04-1976 by NIR. Belfast Central to Central Junction re-opened to passengers 26-04-1976 by NIR.

New mileposts when reopened in 1976, continuing the GNR(I) series from Dublin Connolly (shown in brackets).

MPost Dist.	Miles & Chains	Place / Feature (notes)	Date Opened	Date Closed	Map Grid	Table Ref.
0	0:00	Central Junction	1874	Open	34 C3	50
(112)	(112:00)	formerly Ulster Junction				
0	0:00	ULSTER JUNCTION	1878	1885	34 C3	50
(112)	(112:00)	exchange platforms opened 05-08-1878, closed 30-11-1885				
0	0:00	Westlink Junction	1995	Open	34 C3	50
		section known as 'Blythefield Curve'				
0¼	0:17	City Junction	1995	Open	34 C3	
0¼	0:15	City Junction	1995	Open	34 C3	
(112¼)	(112:15)					
0¼	0:22	CITY HOSPITAL	1986	Open	34 C3	
(112¼)	(112:22)	opened 06-10-1986				
0½	0:29	WINDSOR	1878	1885	34 C3	
(112¼)	(112:29)	closed 30-11-1885				
0½	0:38	Lisburn Road Tunnel	1874	Open	34 C3	
(112½)	(112:38)	107 yards long				
0½	0:49	BOTANIC	1976	Open	34 C3	
(112½)	(112:49)	opened 26-04-1976				
1	1:01	ORMEAU	1878	1885	34 C3	
(113)	(113:01)	closed 30-11-1885				
?	?	Gasworks Siding	?	?	34 C3	
1¼	1:23	Maysfields Goods Depot	1914	1965	34 C3	
(113¼)	(113:24)	closed 31-05-1963 to all traffic except coal, sand and livestock				
1½	1:39	BELFAST CENTRAL	1976	Open	34 C3	
(113½)	(113:39)	opened 12-04-1976				
1½	1:50	East Bridge Street Junction	1876	1963	34 C3	
(113½)	(113:50)					
0	0:00	East Bridge Street Junction	1876	1963	34 C3	
0½	0:18	QUEEN'S BRIDGE	1878	1885	34 C3	
		closed 30-11-1895, station demolished 1960				
0¼	0:24	Queen's Bridge Subway	1881	1963	34 C3	
		originally a surface tramway, replaced by 131 yard long tunnel in 1881				
0¼	0:38	Donegall Quay Junction	1876	1963	34 C3	129
		end-on junction with Belfast Harbour Commissioners Line				
1¾	1:53	Lagan Viaduct	1874	Open	34 C3	
(113¾)	(113:53)	also called 'the Shaky Bridge'. replaced with a new bridge built by NIR c.1976				
1¾	1:60	Lagan Junction	1994	Open	34 C3	117
(113¾)	(113:60)					
2¼	2:20	BRIDGE END	1977	Open	34 C3	
(114¼)	(114:20)	opened 09-05-1977 replacing BALLYMACARRETT which closed the same day				
2¼	2:31	Ballymacarrett Junction	1874	1994	34 D3	78,79
(114¼)	(114:31)	junction with BCR, BHC and Downpatrick line, opened 24-04-1950; closed as a junction with the BHC and BCH 31-07-1965; re-opened as a junction with the BCR 12-04-1976; finally closed as a junction to the Central Services Depot 28-11-1994				

117 Belfast Central to Lagan Junction and York Road North Junction

NIR / 5ft 3in gauge / mileposts measured from Dublin (Connolly)

York Road North Junction to Yorkgate opened 17-10-1992 by NIR.
Lagan Junction to Yorkgate opened 28-11-1994 by NIR.
Opened officially 09-03-1995.

NCC main line mileposts changeover point is in line with the buffer stops of the old York Road Station.

MPost Dist.	Miles & Chains	Place / Feature (notes)	Date Opened	Date Closed	Map Grid	Table Ref.
113½	113:39	BELFAST CENTRAL	1976	Open	34 C3	116
113¾	113:53	Lagan Viaduct	1994	Open	34 C3	116
113¾	113:60	Lagan Junction	1994	Open	34 C3	116
113¾	113:75	Queens Quay Junction	1994	Open	34 C3	
		double track becomes single at this point				
113¾	113:75	Dargan Bridge	1994	Open	34 C3	
		626ft long bridge across River Lagan, although the bridge is part of a 4,675ft viaduct				
114¼	?	DONEGALL QUAY	–	–	34 C3	
		proposed station				
114¼	114:20	Donegall Quay Loop	1994	Open	34 C3	
		passing loop				
114¾	114:60	YORKGATE	1992	Open	34 C2	67
		opened 17-10-1992, replacing York Road				
115	115:00	Adjacent to York Road Depot	–	–	–	–
		mileposts now read 0 from a point adjacent to the rear wall of Maintenance Shed				
0	0:00	MILEAGE CHANGE				
		(mileposts measured from rear wall of Maintenance Shed)				
0	0:03 ?	York Road South Junction	1994	Open	34 C2	67
		junction to York Road Depot				
0		York Road Depot	1992	Open	34 C2	67
		on site of former York Road Station				
0¾	0:56	York Road North Junction	1994	Open	34 C2	67
		junction from York Road Depot, temporary connection to Depot in yard area 1992-1994				

118 Parsonstown to Portumna Bridge

PPBR – worked by the GSWR
5ft 3in gauge / mileposts measured from Birr

Opened 05-11-1868 by the PPBR.

Parsonstown to Portumna Bridge closed 29-11-1878 by the PPBR.
The line closed as the GSWR refused to continue to work the line after the initial ten year working agreement had expired.

MPost Dist.	Miles & Chains	Place / Feature (notes)	Date Opened	Date Closed	Map Grid	Table Ref.
0		PARSONSTOWN	1868	1878	21 A2	24
0¼ ?		Parsonstown Junction	1868	1878	21 A2	24
0¼ ?		Riverstown No.1 Crossing	1868	1878	21 A2	
		crossed minor road south of Riverstown Village				
0½ ?		Riverstown No.2 Crossing	1868	1878	21 A2	
		crossed minor road south of Riverstown Mill				
0¾ ?		Riverstown Viaduct	1868	1878	21 A2	
		crossed Little Brosna River on 6 span girder bridge				
4 ?		Derrylahon Cossing	1868	1878	20 D2	
		crossed minor road in Derrylahon Wood				
7¼ ?		Curraghglass East Crossing	1868	1878	20 D2	
		crossed minor road 1 mile east of Curraghglass				
7¾		Curraghglass Crossing	1868	1878	20 D2	
		crossed road near Curraghglass House				
9 ?		Lorrha Road Crossing	1868	1878	20 D2	
		crossed road to Lorrha ½ mile north of village				
12		PORTUMNA BRIDGE	1868	1878	20 D2	
12¼ ?		Portumna Bridge Quay	1868	1878	20 D2	
		spur ran from station to River Shannon				

Level crossing and bridge distances measured from Ordnance Survey maps

119 Dublin to Blessington and Poulaphouca

DBT / BPT (worked by DBT but nominally independent)
5ft 3in gauge / distances measured from Terenure

Dublin to Blessington opened 01-08-1888 by DBT.
Blessington to Poulaphouca opened 01-05-1895 by BPT.

Blessington to Poulaphouca closed completely 30-09-1927 by the BPT.
Dublin to Blessington closed completely 01-01-1933 by the DBT.

MPost Dist.	Miles & Chains	Place / Feature (notes)	Date Opened	Date Closed	Map Grid	Table Ref.
0		TERENURE	1888	1933	32 C4	220
		connection to Dublin United Tramways				
?		KIMMAGE ROAD	1888	1933	32 B4	
		roadside stopping place				
1¼		TEMPLEOGUE DEPOT	1888	1933	32 B4	
		TEMPLEOGUE BRIDGE	1888	1933	32 B4	
		roadside stopping place				
?		TEMPLEOGUE MILL	1888	1933	32 B4	
		roadside stopping place				
		BALROTHERY	1888	1933	32 B4	
		roadside stopping place				
?		STUBBS' LANE	1888	1933	32 B4	
		roadside stopping place				
3¼		TALLAGHT	1888	1933	23 A1	
?		CLONDALKIN ROAD	1888	1933	23 A1	
		roadside stopping place				
?		Aerodrome Siding	c.1918	c.1923	23 A1	230
		used for delivering materials for Aerodrome construction, siding about 1 mile long.				
?		THE COMMON	1888	1933	23 A1	
		roadside stopping place				
?		FOX'S LANE	1888	1933	23 A1	
		roadside stopping place				
?		FORTUNESTOWN LANE	1888	1933	23 A1	
		roadside stopping place				
5½		JOBSTOWN	1888	1933	23 A1	
?		MOUNT SESKIN ROAD	1888	1933	23 A1	
		roadside stopping place				
6¾		EMBANKMENT	1888	1933	23 A1	
?		MAHON'S LANE	1888	1933	23 A1	
		roadside stopping place				
?		OLD SAGGART ROAD	1888	1933	23 A1	
		roadside stopping place				
?		KENNY'S	1888	1933	22 D1	
		roadside stopping place				
?		GLENARANEEN	1888	1933	22 D1	
		roadside stopping place				
8½		CROOKSLING	1888	1933	22 D1	
		roadside stopping place				
10		BRITTAS	1888	1933	22 D2	
?		THE LAMB	1888	1933	22 D2	
?		TINODE POST OFFICE	1888	1933	22 D2	
		roadside stopping place				
?		HEMPSTOWN	1888	1933	22 D2	
		roadside stopping place				
?		SLATE QUARRIES ROAD	1888	1933	22 D2	
		roadside stopping place				
14½		CROSS CHAPEL	1888	1933	22 D2	
		roadside stopping place				
?		REDLANE	1888	1933	22 D2	
		Roadside stopping place				
15½		BLESSINGTON	1888	1933	22 D2	
?		CORNER OF NAAS ROAD	1895	1927	22 D2	
		roadside stopping place				
?		BALTIBOYS ROAD	1895	1927	22 D2	
		roadside stopping place				
?		BURGAGE ROAD	1895	1927	22 D2	
		roadside stopping place				
?		FEATHERBED LANE	1895	1927	22 D2	
		roadside stopping place				
?		BALLYMORE ROAD	1895	1927	22 D2	
		roadside stopping place				
20¼		POULAPHOUCA	1895	1927	22 D2	

120 Athy to Wolfhill (Gracefield and Modubeagh Collieries)

BoW – worked by GSWR / 5ft 3in gauge / mileposts measured from Athy

Opened 24-09-1918 by the British Government.

Vested in GSR on 01-01-1929.

Ballylinan to Wolfhill closed 1929 by the GSR.
Athy Asbestos Cement Factory to Ballylinan closed 01-04-1963 by CIE.

MPost Dist.	Miles & Chains	Place / Feature (notes)	Date Opened	Date Closed	Map Grid	Table Ref.
0	0:00	ATHY	1846	Open	22 B3	2
0¼	0:26	Carlow Road Crossing	1918	Open	22 B3	
0½	0:37	Asbestos Cement Factory	?	Open	22 A3	
		Tegral Company siding				
0¾	0:68	Fortbarrington Crossing	1918	1963	22 A3	
2	2:07	Lanigan Lane Crossing	1918	1963	22 A4	
3½	3:31	Drimroe Crossing	1918	1963	22 A4	
4¼	4:25	Ballylinan Crossing	1918	1963	22 A4	
4½		Ballylinan Beet Siding	1918	1963	22 A4	
		used for seasonal Beet traffic until 01-04-1963				
5½ ?		Crossing	1918	1929	22 A4	
6¼ ?		Crossing	1918	1929	22 A4	
7¼ ?		Crossing	1918	1929	22 A4	
7¼ ?		Junction	1918	1929	22 A4	
7¼ ?		Junction	1918	1929	22 A4	
7¾ ?		Gracefield Colliery	1918	1929	22 A4	
8¼		Crossing	1918	1929	22 A4	
9½ ?		Modubeagh Colliery	1918	1929	22 A4	

Mileages from Ballylinan are estimated

121 Dublin to Leixlip

DLT (Dublin to Lucan) / LLCT (Lucan to Leixlip)
Gauge – see notes

Dublin to Chapelizod opened 01-06-1881 by the DLT.
Chapelizod to Palmerstown opened 11-1881 by the DLT.
Palmerstown to Lucan opened 20-02-1883 by the DLT.
Lucan to Leixlip opened 1890 by the LLCT.

Dublin to Lucan
Dublin to Lucan was opened in stages to Lucan as a 3ft gauge steam tramway. This was converted to a 3ft 6in gauge electric tramway using the overhead trolley system at 500v DC. The line commenced electric operation 08-03-1900 as the Dublin & Lucan Electric Tramway; the line closed 29-01-1925. The line was subsequently purchased by the Dublin United Tramway Company who commenced regauging in 1927 to 5ft 3in, but only as far as Lucan (for Lucan to Dodsborough see below). The line re-opened as an O'Connell Bridge to Chapelizod service 14-05-1928, extending to Lucan on 27-05-1928. This section finally closed 14-04-1940 (see Table 220).

Lucan to Leixlip
Lucan to Leixlip was opened 1889 by the Lucan, Leixlip and Celbridge Steam Tramway as a 3ft gauge steam tramway worked by DLT. This section closed 31-10-1897. The ½ mile section from Lucan to Dodsborough (a short walk from the Spa Hotel) was re-gauged to 3ft 6in, electrified and re-opened in 1911 by a new called the Lucan & Leixlip Electric Railway using the defunct LLCT trackbed. This company used the overhead trolley system at 500v DC. This section of the line also closed 29-01-1925. When the system was purchased by the DUTC they abandoned this section.

Closed – see above notes

MPost Dist.	Miles & Chains	Place / Feature (notes)	Date Opened	Date Closed	Map Grid	Table Ref.

0	DUBLIN CONYNGHAM ROAD	1881	1940	32 B2	
?	ISLANDBRIDGE	1881	1940	32 B2	
1¾	CHAPELIZOD	1881	1940	32 A2	
?	ST LAURENCE	1881	1940	32 A2	
4½	PALMERSTOWN	1881	1940	32 A2	
?	QUARRYVALE	1883	1940	23 A1	
?	CURSIS STREAM	1883	1940	23 A1	
?	HERMITAGE	1883	1940	23 A1	
?	BALLYDOWD	1883	1940	23 A1	
7	LUCAN	1883	1940	23 A1	
7½	DODSBOROUGH called DODSBOROUGH (SPA HOTEL) from 1911	1890	1940	22 D1	
?	SPA HOTEL	1890	1897	22 D1	
9	Leixlip	1890	1897	22 D1	

122 Warrenpoint and Rostrevor Tramway, Co Down

Warrenpoint & Rostrevor Tramways Co / 2ft 10in gauge

Warrenpoint to Mourne Hotel opened 01-08-1877.
Rostrevor Quay extension opened 10-1877.

Closed February 1915.

MPost Dist.	Miles & Chains	Place / Feature (notes)	Date Opened	Date Closed	Map Grid	Table Ref.
0	0:00	WARRENPOINT RAILWAY STATION	1877	1915	10 D6	60
2½	2:48	ROSTREVOR	1877	1915	10 D6	
?		MOURNE HOTEL later called the GREAT NORTHERN HOTEL	1877	1915	10 D6	
3¼	3:24	Rostrevor Quay section used for goods	1877	1915	10 D6	

123 Bray to Enniskerry

Bray and Enniskerry Street Tramway Company / 3ft 6in gauge Electric Tramway

Company incorporated 16-07-1874 to construct a 3'6" gauge roadside tramway. Work started with some rails laid but project was abandoned and never opened.

Map reference 23 B2.

124 Bessbrook to Newry

BNT / 3ft gauge / mileposts measured from Bessbrook

Bessbrook to Newry opened 01-10-1885 by the BNT.

Bessbrook to Newry closed 12-01-1948 by the BNT.

Electrified tramway. Unusual track with additional rails on the outside of the running rails which allowed use of flangeless rail wagons which could be used on roads. Electrified centre third rail at 245V DC, overhead trolley for 50yds through Millvale Crossing.

MPost Dist.	Miles & Chains	Place / Feature (notes)	Date Opened	Date Closed	Map Grid	Table Ref.
0	0:00	BESSBROOK	1885	1948	10 C5	
0½		MAYTOWN also called MAYTOWN & MULLAGHGLASS and MULLAGHGLASS & DERRAMORE, re-named 1901	1885	1948	10 C5	
1		MILLVALE	1885	1948	10 C5	
1		Millvale Crossing overhead trolley through crossing	1885	1948	10 C5	
1½		CRAIGMORE	1885	1948	10 C5	
3	3:02	NEWRY adjacent to Edward Street Station	1885	1948	10 D6	60

125 Keane's Points to Limerick Junction

GSWR / 5ft 3in gauge / mileposts measured from Limerick

Opened 03-07-1848 by the WLR.

Passenger services suspended 24-02-1947 due to fuel shortage.
Passenger services resumed 24-05-1947.

MPost Dist.	Miles & Chains	Place / Feature (notes)	Date Opened	Date Closed	Map Grid	Table Ref.
0	21:56	Keane's Points	1848	Open	26 D1	13
?		TEMPORARY PLATFORM opened 20-07-1880 in 'V' of junction; closed very soon after opening	1880	1880	26 D1	13
0¼	21:78	LIMERICK JUNCTION	1848	Open	26 D1	8

126 Kyle Crossing to Milltown Crossing

IE / 5ft 3in gauge / mileposts measured from Dublin Kingsbridge

Opened 16-10-1967 by CIE.

MPost Dist.	Miles & Chains	Place / Feature (notes)	Date Opened	Date Closed	Map Grid	Table Ref.
106¼	106:23	Kyle Crossing	1967	Open	26 D1	8
106¾	106:70	Milltown Crossing	1967	Open	26 D1	13

127 Limerick Check to Castlemungret

IE / 5ft 3in gauge / mileposts measured from Limerick

Opened 01-10-1957 by CIE.

In 1957 a junction was made with Foynes Branch to serve Castlemungret Cement Works. Due to the level of traffic, a second parallel line was laid from a new Junction at Limerick Check which diverges at 'Rossbrien Curve'. This new line opened 11-08-1968 whereupon Cement Factory Junction closed.

MPost Dist.	Miles & Chains	Place / Feature (notes)	Date Opened	Date Closed	Map Grid	Table Ref.
0½	0:45	Limerick Check	1859	Open	20 A6	13
1	1:00	Foynes Junction	1856	1975	20 A6	18
1¼	1:26	Rathbane Crossing	1957	Open	20 A6	18
1¾	1:62	Rossbrien Crossing line diverges at this point	1957	Open	20 A6	18
2	1:78	Cement Factory Junction closed 11-08-1968	1957	1968	20 A6	18
2¾	2:58	Ballincurra Crossing	1957	Open	20 A6	
3½	3:38	Ballykeefe Crossing	?	Open	20 A6	
4	3:72	Sheheacreggaun Crossing opened 11-09-1990	1990	Open	20 A6	
4	4:02	Dock Road Crossing	1957	Open	20 A6	
4½	4:45	Castlemungret Cement Works Irish Cement Limited	1957	Open	20 A6	

128 Silvermines Junction to Silvermines

IE / 5ft 3in gauge / mileposts measured from Silvermines Junction

Opened December 30-12-1966 by CIE.

Closed ? Last train ran 29-10-1993 when mine closed.

MPost Dist.	Miles & Chains	Place / Feature (notes)	Date Opened	Date Closed	Map Grid	Table Ref.
0	0:00	Silvermines Junction	1966	1993	20 C5	23
0¼	0:14	Shallee Road Crossing	1966	1993	20 C5	
1¼	1:14	Silvermines	1966	1993	20 C5	289

129   Belfast Harbour

BHC / 3ft gauge and 5ft 3in gauge

Opened, first section (5ft 3in) 1867; reached a length of about 16 miles.

Closed in stages from 1967 to 1970.

A Passenger Boat Train from the NCC, at Dufferin Dock Junction, ran along the BHC to the Heysham Boat c.1930.
BHC also owned a 4ft 8½in gauge urban street tramway operated by BCT (see Table 221). This was about one mile long and was in Queen's Road. It closed in 1954.
BHC also owned a 3ft gauge line for use in slobland reclamation for the construction of the Harbour c.1860 to 1900.

MPost Dist.	Miles & Chains	Place / Feature (notes)	Date Opened	Date Closed	Map Grid	Table Ref.
West Bank of River Lagan						
0	0:00	Dufferin Dock Junction	1867	1960s	34 C2	67
?		Duncrue Street Crossing	?	1960s	34 C2	
?		Dufferin Dock	?	1960s	34 C2	
?		Dufferin Dock	?	1960s	34 C2	
?		Spencer Basin	?	1960s	34 C2	
?		Princes Dock	?	1960s	34 C2	
?		Clarendon Dock	?	1960s	34 C2	
0¾	0:75	Donegall Quay Junction	?	1960s	34 C3	116
East Bank of River Lagan						
0	0:00	Ballymacarrett Junction	1874	1969	34 D3	78
		some sections laid from 1855 and extended				
?		Abercorn Basin	1874	1969	34 D2	

Queen's Bridge to Dufferin Dock Junction ceased to be through route in 1962.

130   Ballyaghagan Quarry to Belfast

Cavehill Tramway / 4ft 9in gauge

Opened 05-09-1840; closed 02-1896.

The tramway ran from the Ballyaghagan Quarry on the south side of Cave Hill to the Victoria Channel in Belfast. The tramway was cable operated on the steep section near the quarry and gravity operated to the Quay, horse worked on the return journey. The line was double track for most of its length. The tramway ran on the west side of the present Cavehill Road, passed under the Antrim Road and continued on the east side of Limestone Road to a terminus near York Road.

Distance (Miles)	Place / Feature (notes)	Date Opened	Date Closed	Map Grid	Table Ref.
0	Ballyaghagan Quarry	1840	1896	34 C2	
?	Tunnel	c.1843	1896	34 C2	
	at the juction of the Cavehill and Antrim Roads				
?	Alexandra Road Tunnel	?	1896	34 C2	
?	York Road Tunnel	?	1896	34 C2	
4	BELFAST	1840	1896	34 C2	

131   Guinness Brewery Railway, Dublin

St James's Gate Brewery, Dublin / 1ft 10in and 5ft 3in gauges

Opened 1875

Closed broad gauge 15-05-1965; closed narrow gauge 05-08-1975.

Internal 1ft 10in gauge railway begun in 1874, closed 05-08-1975.
Narrow gauge system was on two levels, originally connected by a hydraulic lift, replaced by a spiral tunnel of 2.65 turns and 865ft long.

5ft 3in gauge street tramway from brewery to Kingsbridge Station, 31 chains long, opened 1875, closed 15-05-1965.

Map reference 32 C2, also see Table 8.

132   Portstewart Station to Portstewart Town

NCC / 3ft gauge / Distances measured from Portstewart Station

Opened 28-06-1882 by the Portstewart Tramway.
Closed 31-01-1926 by the NCC.

Halts and features marked * do not appear on the map in the atlas section, owing to the shortness of the line.

MPost Dist.	Miles & Chains	Place / Feature (notes)	Date Opened	Date Closed	Map Grid	Table Ref.
0	0:00	PORTSTEWART STATION	1882	1926	4 C3	73
?		MILLBANK *	1882	1926	4 C3	
		request stop				
?		GOLF LINKS HALT *	1882	1926	4 C3	
		request stop				
?		VICTORIA TERRACE *	1882	1926	4 C3	
?		PARADE *	1882	1926	4 C3	
		later called PROMENADE				
1¾	1:62	Portstewart Town	1882	1926	4 C3	
		Montagu Arms Hotel				
		Depot *	1882	1926	4 C3	

133   Cork Coal Gantry Railway

GSWR / 5ft 3in gauge

Opened 09-01-1885 by the GSWR.

Closed 1964 by CIE. Dismantled about 1970.

Built to transport coal from the wharves at Penrose Quay to the Coal Bank at Glanmire Road Locomotive Shed.

Distance (Mls & Chns)	Place / Feature (notes)	Date Opened	Date Closed	Map Grid	Table Ref.
0	Penrose Quay	1885	1964	33 D2	
0:17	Glanmire Road Depot	1885	1964	33 D2	

This system ran on an elevated gantry 15ft 2½in from rail to ground level. It was totally unconnected to any other railway. Possibly Ireland's shortest standard gauge railway!

134   Magilligan to Magilligan Point

LCR / 4ft 8½in gauge

Opened 06-1855 by LCR.
Closed 10-1855 by LCR.

MPost Dist.	Miles & Chains	Place / Feature (notes)	Date Opened	Date Closed	Map Grid	Table Ref.
0		MAGILLIGAN	1855	1855	4 C3	67
?		DRUMMOND	1855	1855	4 B3	
4½		MAGILLIGAN POINT	1855	1855	4 B3	

135   Londonderry Port & Harbour Commissioners

5ft 3in and 3ft mixed gauge (mixed gauge from 1885)

Opened 01-1868.

Closed 31-08-1962.

Total length of about 6 miles, mixed gauge.

LLSR trains ran through to Middle Quay from 1869 until 1888 (weekdays only).

Line across Carlisle Bridge was at right angles to the lines on either bank, wagons crossed bridge by means of wagon turntables and capstans. Locomotives only worked on the West bank.

MPost Dist.	Miles & Chains	Place / Feature (notes)	Date Opened	Date Closed	Map Grid	Table Ref.
East Bank Lines						
?		LONDONDERRY WATERSIDE	1868	1962	3 D4	67
?		Carlisle Bridge (East end) replaced by Craigavon Bridge in 1933	1868	1962	3 D4	
?		VICTORIA ROAD	1900	1955	3 D5	
West Bank Lines						
?		GRAVING DOCK	1868	1962	3 D4	101
?		MIDDLE QUAY used by LLSR trains 1869 to 1888	1868	1962	3 D4	101
?		City Goods Station opened 1877 by BNCR	1877	1962	3 D4	
?		Carlisle Bridge (West end) replaced by Craigavon Bridge in 1933	1868	1962	3 D4	
?		FOYLE ROAD	1868	1962	3 D4	49
?		Cow Market	1868	1962	3 D5	49

136   Bangor Erris Group of Bogs, Co Mayo

Bord na Móna / 3ft gauge

Opened 1964.

An unconnected part of the Owenniny Group (Table 137). This bog system lies to the west of Bellacorick Power Station. Milled peat is transported to a tip head where lorries complete the journey to Bellacorick. The line has two gated level crossings.

Map reference 6 C4.

137   Owenniny Group of Bogs, Co Mayo Tionnasca Abhainn Einne (T.A.E.) including the Bellacorick Bog Railway

Bord na Móna / 3ft gauge

Opened 1953.

This system is part of the Peat Energy Division of Bord na Móna and produces milled peat for use in ESB's Bellacorick Power Sation. Peat is also delivered by road from the associated Bangor Erris system (Table 136).

Bord na Móna did run a tourist train – the Bellacorick Bog Railway – around part of the system; this commenced 11-07-1994. The train ran out to the Windfarm Control Centre, a distance of 1 mile 47 chains, and back again, giving a round trip of 3 miles 14 chains. The service ceased at the end of 1996.

Map reference 6 D5.

138   Keel Harbour to Quarry, Achill Island

Irish Industrial Minerals Company / 2ft gauge

Opened 1910.

Closed 1916.

Built to transport whitestone from the quarry to the harbour for use in pottery making.

Approximate length, three miles. Line ran from a whitestone quarry southwards to Keel Harbour. It crossed the main Achill-Doagh road near the Achill Head Hotel before descending steeply to the harbour.

Irish Industrial Minerals also operated a second line from Darby's Point Pier to Kildownet (see Table 225).

Map reference 6 A6

139   Creevelea Ironworks Tramway, Co Leitrim

2ft or 2ft 6in gauge

Operated circa 1852-4.

Horse operated tramway.

Distance (Miles)	Place / Feature (notes)	Date Opened	Date Closed	Map Grid	Table Ref.
0	Creevelea Iron Works	c.1852	c.1854	8 C5	
1½	Tullynamoyle	c.1852	c.1854	8 C5	

140   Glenfarne Forestry Railway, Co Leitrim

Lees and Nixon / 2ft gauge

Opened 1919; closed 1920.

Approximately 4½ miles long excluding sidings. Used for transporting timber from the forest for onward transhipment on the SLNCR (see Table 108) from Glenfarne Station.

Line ran from a loading bank on the north side of Glenfarne (SLNCR) Station. The line then ran north for a while through the estate of Lord Massey, crossed the Kiltyclogher road on the level then crossed a river on a concrete bridge. The line then continued past Glenfarne Hall and on for about three miles through woods down to the lake. Six sawmills were established and branch lines ran to all of these. In addition there were many temporary sidings serving places where trees were being felled.

Map reference 8 D4.

141   Admiralty Rly, Haulbowline Island, Co Cork

British Admiralty / 3ft 6in gauge

Opened 1875 by the British Admiralty.

Closed late 1920s, track still in situ in 1957.

First railway was a temporary system to enable the island to be enlarged for the Navy's purposes. These temporary lines were laid in 1875 and continued in use until the completion of the project in 1887.

The second railway was of a more permanant nature and was started in the 1890s. This system totalled about 3 miles of track. Until 1914 it consisted of two circuits connected to each other. One circled the dock basin and the other the stores and buildings. A third circuit was added in 1914 to include the Army Barracks at the western end of the island. Near this western end was the pier used by the Cork, Blackrock and Passage Railway steamboats. There was also a short tramway from the Pier to a goods shed c.1850s. Haulbowline Island was handed over to the Irish Government on 01-04-1923. The Irish Board of Trade worked the railway spasmodically until the late 1920s.

Map reference 33 F4.

142   Arigna Ironworks Tramway, Co Roscommon

4ft 2in gauge

Opened 1836 by the Arigna Ironworks Co.

Closed 1838.

Distance (miles)	Place / Feature (notes)	Date Opened	Date Closed	Map Grid	Table Ref.
0	Arigna Iron Works	1832	1838	8 C6	
3⅛	Aughabehy Coke Yard	1832	1838	8 C6	

Completed February 1832 but not used until 1836. Horse worked. Lifted c.1857-8. Most of the trackbed was later used by the Arigna Valley Railway (see Table 98).

An earlier tramway existed here from c.1805 to c.1808, about 300yds long. It ran from the lower (rolling) part of the works to the upper (smelting) part of the works.

Also see Table 143.

143   Arigna Mining Company, Co Roscommon

4ft 2in gauge and 2ft gauge

Operating dates, see below.

Cable operated, inclined plane tramway, operating c.1832-1838, running from
Aughabehy Coke Yard to Aughabehy Mine Adit. 4ft 2in gauge, the line was cable
operated, about 200yds long and had a gradient of 1:3. Used in conjunction with the
line detailed in Table 142. Lifted c.1857.

A second incline plane tramway, was built in 1919. This was 650yds long, and ran for
part of the way on the formation of the earlier tramway. This was built to 2'0" gauge,
was cable operated and had an average gradient of 1:3. Unusually it had three rails,
ascending wagons using the centre and left rails while descending wagons used the
centre and right rails. At the halfway point, the track opened up to four rails forming a
passing loop. This tramway closed in 1927 and was lifted 1930/1.

Map reference 8 C6.

144   Eglinton Lime Company, Glenarm, Co Antrim

2ft 6in gauge

Opened ?   Closed c.1952.

The line ran from 'Town' and 'Mill' quarries down to the harbour. The line also served a
basalt quarry at the top of the hill. It is thought that the line may have been worked by a
steam locomotive around the 1916 to 1925 period.

Map reference 5 C5.

145   Ballintoy Inclined Plane, Co Antrim

? gauge

Opened ?   Closed ?

Situated on the hillside south of the main coast road. Stone was carted from the foot of
the inclined plane to Ballintoy Harbour, presumably by horse and cart.

Map reference 5 A3

146   Irish Hill Bauxite Mines, Straid, Co Antrim

? gauge

Operating c.1906.

Two inclined planes, side by side, of about ½ mile in length.

Map reference 11 B1.

147   Admiralty Railway, Lisahally, Co Derry

British Admiralty / 2ft gauge

British Admiralty diesel locomotive worked line during the 1939-1945 war period. Line
ran along pier. (Also see Table 67)

Map reference 4 A4.

148   Upperlands Horse Railway, Co Derry

William Clark and Sons Ltd / 2ft gauge

Opened 1900;   closed 1959 ?

Built to transport consignments of linen from Main Works to the 'Examining Room'.

Approximate length ¼ mile, horse worked. This narrow gauge railway ran from the Main
Works, crossing the siding from Upperlands NCC station (See table 74), up a steep slope
to the Examining Room. In later years, a Ferguson tractor was used to shunt standard
gauge wagons in the yard and to assist the horse (Fanny) on the 2ft gauge.

Map reference 4 D6.

149   United Kingdom Peat Moss Litter Co Ltd, Co Derry

2ft 7½in gauge / 2ft gauge / 1ft 8in gauge

New Ferry, near Bellaghy, 2ft 7½in gauge, opened ? , closed c.1972.
Ballylease, near Portglenone, 2ft gauge, opened ? , lifted by 1966.
Creagh, near Toome, 1ft 8in gauge, opened ? , closed by 1972.

Private peat producer with sites at Ballylease, New Ferry and Creagh. The Ballylease and
New Ferry systems were locomotive worked and it is thought that the Creagh system
may have been locomotive worked at some stage. The New Ferry site was later acquired
by the Bulrush Peat Co (see Table 356).

Map references 4 D6 (Ballylease and New Ferry), 10 C1 (Creagh).

150   Glenties Turf Co-op Society Ltd, Co Donegal

2ft gauge

Opened 1939 by the Turf Development Board. Still currently operating.

Site is situated on the N56 Glenties-Adara Road just beyond the junction with the R262.

Formerly the Turf Development Board Limited, taken over in 1946 by Bord na Móna.
Later became an independent privatised turf producer in 1989 called Glenties Turf
Co-op Society Ltd. The line is about 3 to 4 miles long. Produces sod peat.

Map reference 2 C6.

151   City of Derry Tramways

4ft 8½in gauge

Graving Dock to Shipquay Place opened 01-04-1897.
Shipquay Place to Carlisle Bridge opened December 1897.

Closed 1920.

Approximate length 1½ miles, horse worked. Ran from the LLSR station at Graving Dock
south along Strand Road into Shipquay Place, along Foyle Street ending at John Street at
the north western end of the Carlisle Bridge.

Map reference 3 D4.

152   Courtaulds Works Railway, Co Antrim

5ft 3in gauge

Opened 1950;   closed 1968.

Courtaulds had sidings off the main Belfast-Larne railway at Mount (see Table 76). These
sidings ran into the works and were operated by the company's two steam locomotives.

Map reference 11 B1.

153   Baldonnel Aerodrome Railway, Co Dublin

British War Department / 2ft gauge

Opened 1917;   closed 1919 ?

Built by the British War Department to transport people and materials for the
construction of Baldonnel Aerodrome.

Approximate length of 2½ miles. Ran from exchange sidings (Baldonnel Siding, GSWR
Table 8) near Lucan South southwards. It crossed the Grand Canal near the Twelfth
Lock Bridge. The railway then ran alongside the Milltown-Newcastle road for a short
distance and continued across some fields after which it crossed the Clondalkin-
Newcastle road at right angles and ran along a byroad skirting the grounds of Castle
Bagot before passing the ruins of Kilbride Castle and entering Baldonnel Airfield. There
were extensive sidings at the airfield.

Map reference 22 D1.

154   Trostan Mineral Railway, Co Antrim

Antrim Iron Ore Co / 2ft gauge ?

Opened c.1872; Abandoned c.1874.

Length about 2 miles. The tramway linked various iron ore mines around the scarp of the east and north slopes of Trostan Mountain to the roadway. The ore was then transported to Red Bay. The sites were worked by the Antrim Iron Ore Co.

Map reference 5 B4.

155   Glenariff Iron Ore & Harbour Company, Co Antrim

3ft gauge

Opened 1873;   closed 1885.

Irelands first 3ft gauge railway, constructed to carry Iron Ore from Cloughcor Mines to Milltown Pier.

Distance (Miles)	Place / Feature (notes)	Date Opened	Date Closed	Map Grid	Table Ref.
0	Cloughcor	1873	1885	5 B5	
2½	Greenahan Viaduct	1873	1885	5 B4	
4½	Milltown Pier	1873	1885	5 C4	

Map reference 5 B4.

156   Antrim Wire Tramway Company, Co Antrim

Ran from Cargan Mines to near Red Bay Pier.

Opened end of 1872; bankrupt at end of 1873, bought by BCRBR 09-1875.
Cargan to Retreat dismantled Autumn 1876.
Retreat to Red Bay disposed of Spring 1881.

Owned by parent company The Wire Tramway Company. Completed early 1873. About 8 miles in length and reached a height of 800-900ft. Powered by four 12hp steam stationary engines. Buckets suspended from an endless wire rope which reached a speed of about 4mph.

Map reference 5 B4.

157   Carnlough Lime Company Tramways, Co Antrim

Carnlough Limestone Quarries Ltd / 3ft 6in and 4ft 8½in gauges

Opened 08-1854 by Carnlough Lime Company Limited; closed late 1970s ?

The 4ft 8½in gauge cable operated line was opened in August 1854 by CLCL and ran from the quarry at Gortin to the harbour at Carnlough. At a point 150 yards from the Gortin terminus another line at right angles ½ mile in length went up to the Creggan Quarries. A short tunnel separated the Upper and Lower Quarries. The 3ft 6in gauge, opened 1890 and steam locomotive worked from 1898 to c.1920, ran from a quarry at Tullyaughter to Carnlough Harbour. Both gauges met near Carnlough and formed a section of dual gauge track for a short distance. The Tullyaughter line closed in 1922 but the harbour section remained for some time. Around 1948 the line came under the control of the CLQL. There were also some other works lines of 1ft 8in, 2ft 4in and 4ft 8½in gauge at Carnlough.

Map reference 5 C5.

158   Donegal Peat Development Company, Fintown, Co Donegal

2ft gauge

Opened ?   Closed c.1969.

Diesel locomotive worked railway used for transporting peat around bogs.

Map reference 3 A5.

159   Lough Meela Quarry Tramway, Co Donegal

? gauge

Opened ?   Closed ?

Stone Quarry Line from Quarry at Lough Meela to loading pier.

Map reference 2 C4.

160   Ballycastle Harbour Tramway, Co Antrim

3ft gauge

Opened 1740;   closed c.1743.

The tramway, built by Hugh Boyd, opened about 1740 for conveying stone for harbour construction. This 3ft gauge wooden tramway started at the base of the cliffs to the west of the town. The tramway, laid with oak and fir scantling rails, ran 310 yards to the Harbour construction site. Four waggons were used but it is unknown if these were hand or animal operated.

Map reference 5 B3.

161   Ballyheady Ballast Pit Tramway, Co Cavan

? gauge

Operating c.1929.

Internal system to allow ballast to be transported from the point of quarrying to the CLR's siding at Ballyheady. Manually operated. Also see Table 97.

Map reference 9 A6.

162   Cork City Tramways

Cork Tramways Company opened Alfred Street to Victoria Road in 12-09-1872 as a 2 mile 5ft 3in gauge horse tramway, closed 12-1875. Line was extended to Navigation Walk (later site of Ford Factory), the extension is believed to have been worked only on Sundays. The horse tram depot was near the CBPR Victoria Road Station.

Cork Electric Tramways and Lighting Company tramways opened 22-12-1898 (except Ballintemple to Blackrock which opened 1900 and Gaol Cross to Sunday's Well which opened 1901) as a 2ft 11½in gauge electric tramway. Maximum route mileage, 9¾ miles. Closed 30-09-1931.

Map reference 33 C2.

163   Northern Brick and Sand Company, Toome Bridge, Co Antrim

2ft gauge

Opened ?   Closed 1948 ?

Diesel locomotive worked sand quarry railway.

Map reference 10 C1.

164   Shane's Castle Railway, Co Antrim

2ft gauge and 3ft gauge

The 2ft gauge line was in existence here from 1940 to 1956, to and from a bomb dump, operated by the British Army (War Department).

The leisure railway 3ft gauge track was laid by NIR staff in their spare time using 75lb/yd rail with curves to CDRJC specification and worked by a variety of locomotives. Opened 30-04-1971. Closed 31-10-1995.

Distance (Miles)		Place / Feature (notes)	Date Opened	Date Closed	Map Grid	Table Ref.
0	0:00	Loco Depot	1971	1995	10 D1	
0	0:04	ANTRIM	1971	1995	10 D1	
0¼	0:10	Level Crossing	1971	1995	10 D1	
0¼	0:17	Level Crossing	1971	1995	10 D1	
1	0:78	MILLBURN	1971	1995	10 D1	
1½	1:36	SHANE'S CASTLE	1971	1995	10 D1	
1½	1:40	Headshunt	1971	1995	10 D1	

165   Annaghmore Turf Railway, Co Armagh

Irish Peat Development Company Ltd / 3ft gauge
Peatlands Railway

Opened 1901;   closed 1962.

Originally worked by horses. Later worked by electric locomotives working from a 500v DC overhead system with trolley wires to one side of the track. Diesel locomotives started to replace the electrics in 1954, with the electrics being out of use by 1957.

Approximately eight miles in length. Earliest railway ran from the company's factory at Maghery to the River Blackwater, where the finished product was transported to Belfast by boat. This was horse worked. The 1907 system went from reception sidings at the Maghery factory out to the bogs where various sidings served areas being worked. There were four level crossings.

Since closure, two railways have been opened and are operating on parts of the original system: they are the Peatlands Park Railway (see Table 441) and the Sunshine Peat Company (see Table 442).

Map reference 10 C3.

166   Drumglass Colliery Railway, near Coalisland, Co Tyrone

Gauge – not known

In 1754 a wooden tramway opened at the Coalisland Colliery. Some four years later it was reported to be in bad repair and it is believed to have closed down around that time. Later, in 1777, Davis Ducart built a canal including three inclined planes (known as 'dry hurry's') to allow small boats to be transported from the Coalisland Canal, then under construction, to the pits. The inclined planes were not a success and it was planned to replace them by conventional tramways, although it seems that this was never carried out. The colliery was offered for sale in 1793 and amongst the list of equipment advertised was 'a wagon road which leads to the navigation'.

Map reference 10 B2

167   Dungannon Brick Company, Co Tyrone

2ft gauge

Opened 1945 ?   Closed 1962 ?

A diesel locomotive was used on this works railway. The works are sometimes referred to as the Tyrone Brickworks. Served by a GNR(I) siding on the Dungannon to Cookstown line, see Table 56.

Map Reference 10 B3.

168   Glen Anne and Loughgilly Tramway, Co Armagh

George Gray and Sons. / 1ft 10in gauge

Opened 1897;   closed 1917.

Built to transport coal and linen between factory and station, horse worked.

Distance (Miles)	Place / Feature (notes)	Date Opened	Date Closed	Map Grid	Table Ref.
0	GLEN ANNE passenger terminus outside factories main gates, but line continued into company's premises to a tramcar shelter	1897	1917	10 C5	
?	BARBOUR'S CROSS ROADS level crossing	1897	1917	10 C5	
?	TULLYALLEN CROSS ROADS level crossing	1897	1917	10 C5	
?	Sandpits Siding branch to Sandpits	1897	1917	10 C5	
2½	LOUGHGILLY Line continued beyond station yard for a further 20yds to a point between the running line and a siding	1897	1917	10 C5	60

There was also an earlier manually operated tramway connecting the three parts of the Glen Anne Works known as 'main factory', 'wee mill' and 'upper mill'. Between the 'main mill' and the 'wee mill' there was a steep section on a public road. This section was manually cable operated. When the Loughgilly Railway was constructed in 1897 a new inter-works connecting railway was provided avoiding this steep incline.

169   Belfast Zoo Railway, Bellevue Park, Belfast

15in gauge

Opened 1933;   closed ?

A 15" gauge pleasure railway in the grounds of Belfast Zoo. The line ran from one station at Bellevue to another at Bell Hazel, sometimes called Hazelwood. There were run-round loops at each end.

Map reference 34 C1.

170   Silent Valley Railway, Co Down

S. Pearson and Company Ltd / 2ft gauge / 4ft 8½in gauge

Opened May 1923; closed 1930.

Locomotive worked contractors' line used in construction of a dam. The 4ft 8½in gauge line, about 5 miles long, ran from Annalong to the dam wall at the southern end of the valley. There was also an extensive network of 2ft gauge tracks around the dam itself.

Map reference 11 A6.

171   Wicklow Harbour Tramway, Co Wicklow

5ft 3in gauge

Wicklow Town Goods Yard to Harbour opened 23-11-1869.
Harbour to Quay opened 11-07-1906.

Harbour to Quay closed 1922. Goods Yard to Quay closed c.1930.

The original tramway, opened 23-11-1869, ran from Wicklow Town Goods Yard to the Harbour. In 11-07-1906 the Quay Extension to the tramway was made at request of the Earl of Fitzwilliam. The tramway was then worked by the DSER. The tramway finally closed in 1922 and was lifted by the early 1930s.

MPost Dist.	Miles & Chains	Place / Feature (notes)	Date Opened	Date Closed	Map Grid	Table Ref.
?		Wicklow	1869	c.1930	23 B4	31
?		Wicklow Harbour	1869	c.1930	23 B4	
?		Wicklow Harbour North Quay	1906	1922	23 B4	

172   Cavehill & Whitewell Tramway, Co Antrim

4ft 8½in gauge

Opened 01-07-1882; closed 23-01-1949.

Opened as a four mile steam and horse operated passenger tramway. Electrified 1906 and worked by Belfast Corporation Tramways from 1911 (see table 221) as their Chichester Park to Glengormley route.

Map reference 34 C1.

173 Marconi Railway, Co Galway

2ft gauge

Opened 1906; closed 1922.

Built to transport construction materials, coal, turf and people to and from the Radio Station.

The line ran from the Ballyconneely road to Clifden Radio Station.
The various buildings on the site were connected by the railway and temporary tracks were laid in the surrounding bog to transport peat for burning in the stations boilers. Length approximately 1½ miles.

Map reference 12 C4.

174 Leckavrea Mine Tramway, Co Galway

? gauge

Opened c.1870; closed c.1878.

Distance (Miles)	Place / Feature (notes)	Date Opened	Date Closed	Map Grid	Table Ref.
0	Leckavrea Mine	c.1870	c.1878	13 A4	
1	Maam Bridge Quay	c.1870	c.1878	13 A4	

175 Anglinham Lime Quarry Tramway, Co Galway

Marble and Stone Company of Ireland / ? gauge

Operating c.1865.

Distance (Miles)	Place / Feature (notes)	Date Opened	Date Closed	Map Grid	Table Ref.
0	Anglinham Lime Quarry	?	?	13 D6	
4	Quay	?	?	13 C6	

176 Galway and Salthill Tramway, Co Galway

3ft gauge

Opened 01-10-1879; closed 01-1918.

Approximate length 2¼ miles, horse worked. Ran from Eyre Square near the MGWR station through Williamsgate Street, Shop Street, Mainguard Street, Dominic Street, Swivel Bridge, Salthill Road, King's Hill, Salthill.

Map reference 13 C6 to D6.

177 Attymon Group of Bogs, Co Galway

3ft gauge

Opened 1947 (Attymon) and 1951 (Clonkeen).

Two unconnected systems either side of the Athlone-Galway main line. Originally opened and worked by Bord na Móna, the system was privatised as the Attymon Peat Co-op Ltd c.1992. Works at Attymon and Clonkeen. The southern bog is Attymon, with the works situated 6 miles east of Athenry on the L99 road 1½ miles south of Attymon Junction Station. The northern bog is Clonkeen, situated 1½ miles west of Attymon

Junction Station on the minor road to Athenry. Consists of Derrydoo and Woodlough bogs. Locomotives from Clonkeen are moved by road to Attymon for maintainence. The Attymon Group produces sod peat.

Map reference 14 B6.

178 Mountdillon Group of Bogs, Counties Longford and Roscommon

Bord na Móna / 3ft gauge

Opened 1948.

An extensive system north of Lough Rea, supplying peat to ESB Power Stations at Lanesborough. The system used to take sod peat to Lanesborough 'A' Power Station, wagons were then hauled by ESB locomotives to the point of unloading (see Table 283), but upon the closure of this power station, the system now supplys Lanesborough 'B' and 'C' Power Stations with milled peat. System includes Edera, Derrymacar, Derrycolumb, Derraghan, Corlea, Derryad, Killashee, Clooneeny, Clonard, Cloonbony and Derryaroge Bogs on the Longford side of the Shannon. On the Roscommon side are Cloonaddra, Moher, Cloontusker, Mountdillon, Erenagh, Curraghroe, Granaghan, Derrycashel, Cloonshanagh and Derrymoylin bogs.

The main works are at Mountdillon (Derryarogue) situated on the N63 Lanesborough to Longford Road. The original works were at the southern end of the Mountdillon bog, now called Mountdillon Yard.

Map reference 15 A3.

179 Blackwater Group of Bogs, Counties Offaly, Roscommon and Westmeath

Bord na Móna, including the Clonmacnoise & West Offaly Railway / 3ft gauge

Opened 1959.

The Blackwater system originally produced peat for horticultural use, latterly it has produced milled peat for the ESB Shannonbridge Power Station (125MW).

The workshops are at Blackwater. The Blackwater group consists of Blackwater, Kilcummin, Belmount, Derryharney, Clonlyon, Ballynashawn, Ballyderg, Ballyduff, Bloomhill, Clonascra, Curraghboy, Cloncraff Killgarvan, Bunnahinly, Ballaghuff 1 and Ballaghuff 2 Bogs.

The Garryduff system is to the south of the River Shannon, part of the system runs along the dried up bed of the Ballinasloe Arm of the Grand Canal from Fannings Lock to Lismanny Bog. The main feature is Kylemore Lock, still with lock gates and 3ft gauge railway running through it. The works are at Clonfert Bridge. The system includes Kilmacshane, Garryduff, and Lismanny bogs. Crossing over the River Suck are Creggan, Culliaghmore, Clooniff 1, Clooniff 2, Coolumber, Cloonbeggaun, Drumlosh and Cornafulla Bogs.

The two systems were connected with the construction of the 595ft long Shannon Viaduct just south of Shannonbridge Power Station c.1965.

The Blackwater Group was connected to the Boora Group in 1995 with a link from Ballaghuff 2 bog to Lemanaghan Bog, see Table 194

The Clonmacnoise and West Offaly Railway is a tourist railway which opened in March 1991 and takes a circular tour of western part of Blackwater Bog and traverses a 4 mile 26 chain circuit in about 45 minutes.

Map reference 15 A6.

180 Carnagh Tramway, Co Cavan

Ritchie / narrow gauge

Opened 1867; closed 1876

The narrow gauge line ran for a distance of about a mile, from the quay to exchange sidings with the MGWR at Carnagh. Iron ore was extracted from the Cleenragh Iron Mines and transported across Lough Gowna to the quayside for transhipment on the tramway. Also see Table 38.

Map reference 15 D2.

181　Coolnagun Group of Bogs, Co Westmeath

Bord na Móna / 3ft gauge

Opened 1952.

Opened by Bord na Móna in 1952, the system is now leased to the Coolnagun Peat Company and produces sod peat. The system includes Coolnagun, Kiltareher and Milternagh Bogs. The works are at the southern end of the system at Coolnagun.

Map reference 15 D4.

182　Ballivor Group of Bogs, Counties Meath and Westmeath

Bord na Móna / 3ft gauge

Opened 1952.

Opened by Bord na Móna in 1952 and produces sod peat. The system includes Ballivor, Bracklin and Lisclogher Bogs. The works are to the north of Ballivor Bog.

Map reference 16 B5.

183　Derrygreenagh Group of Bogs, Counties Offaly and Westmeath

Bord na Móna / 3ft gauge

Opened 1958.

Produces milled peat for the ESB Rhode Power Station (80MW) and Croghan Briquette Factory. Group includes Derryarkin, Derryhinch, Drumman, Ballybeg, Esker, Cavemount, Derrycricket, Clongreen, Monagh, Toar, Clonad, Ballykean and Mountlucas Bogs.

Connected to the Clonsast Group in April 1977, from a link at Derrycricket Bog (see Table 192). Connected to the Ballydermot-Timahoe System with a link from Clongreen Bog c.1992 (see Table 199).

Map reference 16 A6.

184　River Fergus Reclamation Schemes, Co Clare

2ft 6in gauge / 600mm gauge

First system operated 1870s to 1883; second system operated 1893 to c.1940

First railway was a 2'6" gauge steam worked line some four to five miles long, operated by the River Fergus Reclamation Company from 1870s to 1883 and run by H. C. Drinkwater. It connected Drumquin, Islandavanna, Islandmagrath and Teermaclane. The line started at Islandmagath were large stone boulders arrived by boat and were transported by train along the sea wall to various points. The railway also moved amounts of mud and clay to various dumping grounds.

Second Railway was a 600mm gauge steam worked line from Islandavanna to Islandmagrath. Operated by the Fergus Reclamation Syndicate Ltd from 1893. It is suggested that steam working ceased around 1900, though up until around 1940 some part of the system near Islandavanna is reputed to have been horse worked in connection with a farm.

Map reference 19 C5

185　Bianconi Farm Railway, Co Clare

2ft gauge

Opened 1910;　closed 1929.

Line approximately one mile long. Ran from the Bianconi Farm, connecting the Mills, Barns, Foundry and Brickworks at Lacknashannagh to Kildysart Quay with a branch known as the 'Corcass Line' about 700yds in length. There was one level crossing just before the 'Corcass Line' branch. The line was horse and oil burning lorry worked.

Bianconi also had a wooden, horse or donkey worked, waggonway within the confines of the farmyard used between 1908 and 1910.

Map reference 19 C5.

186　Watson's Quarry Tramway, Co Clare

G. O. Watson and Co / 4ft 8½in gauge

Opened 1903 ?　Closed 1915 ?　Operating circa 1905.

Steam locomotive worked quarry railway approximately 3 miles in length, near Doonagore.

Map reference 19 B2.

187　Castleconnell Tramway, Co Limerick

? gauge

Opened ?　Closed ?

Probably used for moss peat extraction.

Map reference 20 B5.

188　Shannon Hydro-electric Scheme, Counties Clare and Limerick

Siemens Bauunion AG. /
900mm gauge 'main line' – Steam and Electric worked
600mm gauge subsidiary lines – Steam worked

Opened 1925;　closed 1930.

Built to transport materials and for earthworks in connection with the building of the Shannon Hydro-electric Power Station.

Approximately eight miles of 900mm gauge line. Ran from Thomondgate near Limerick, across the Limerick to Ennis line (See Table 17) on the level and carried on to to O'Briensbridge. A short length of electric railway was also in use powered by 500V DC.

When project was nearing completion, a GSR branch was built to Ardnacrusha Power House resulting with some mixed gauge 900mm and 5ft 3in railway (See Table 17).

Map reference 20 A5.

Also related lines at Banagher and Meelick (See tables 236 and 237).

189　Coolnamona Group of Bogs, Co Laois

Bord na Móna / 3ft gauge

Opened 1964.

Serves Coolnamona horticultural factory. Produces peat for horticultural use. The bogs are either side of the Dublin-Cork main line and include Cashel, Coolnacarten and Coolnamona Bogs. The main feature of this system is the bridge under the IE line just north of Clonkeen Crossing. The system was served by a CIE spur from Portlaoise on the former Kilkenny line (see Table 6).

Map reference 21 D3.

190　Pope Brothers Limited, Co Tipperary

2ft gauge

Opened August 1959; closed 1976.

The line was opened in August 1959 when Pope Brothers Limited, of Co Tipperary moved their peat operation from a site in Co Kerry to Longfordpass near Urlingford, Co Tipperary . The main works were just by the side of the T36 road with the railway running in a north westerly direction. The permanent way was laid by the contractor's on steel sleepers. A new road was built (N8, c.1971) which crossed the line from the works to the bogs, as a result, new works were constructed (March 1971) ½ mile away on the northern side of the new road to avoid trains crossing the busy Dublin-Cork road. In the interim, there was a level crossing. Rail haulage ceased in 1976. Bord na Móna acquired most of the bog as part of their expansion of the Littleton Group (see Table 191). Pope Brothers subsequently worked a small area but using tractors and trailers. The maximum length of the railway was about 2½ miles.

Map reference 21 B6.

191   Littleton Group of Bogs, Co Tipperary

Bord na Móna / 3ft gauge

Opened – see notes.

Started off as two separate systems, the Littleton System opening in 1950 and the Templetouhy System (sod peat) opening in 1955. Littleton and Templetouhy were connected in 1982 as part of an expansion of this bog area. All other bog areas were opened in 1982.

Part of this area was previously worked by Pope Brothers (see Table 190).

Group includes Templetouhy, Carrickhill, Derryville, Baunmore, Inchirourke, Longfordpass, Littleton, Ballybeg, Derryvella, Lanespark and Killeen Bogs. Serves Lanespark Briquette Factory. Workshops at Templetouhy and Littleton. Littleton Works closed 09-1983. New works opened adjacent to Lanespark Briquette Factory.

Map reference 21 B5.

192   Clonsast Group of Bogs, Co Offaly

Bord na Móna / 3ft gauge

Opened 1939 by the Turf Development Board.

Served ESB Portarlington Power Station (see Table 262) with sod peat. Formerly owned by the Turf Development Board Limited, taken over in 1946 with the establishment of Bord na Móna.

Bogs in this system are Garryhinch, Derryounce, Clonsast, Clonsast North, Bulge and Derrylea. Works at Clonsast and Garryhinch (1954).

Connected to the Derrygreenagh Group in April 1977 via a link from Derrycricket Bog, see Table 183. Since the closure of Portarlington Power Station in 1986, milled peat is taken to Rhode and Allenwood via the Derrygreenagh Group. Sod peat is still produced from the Garryhinch Bog and taken to a tip head at Clonygowan.

Map reference 21 D2.

193   Rahan Peat Works Railway, Co Offaly

? gauge

Opened 1890s; closed 1914.

This railway, approximately 1 mile long, ran from the peat workings to a loading point on the Grand Canal. Owned by David Sherlock.

Map reference 21 C1.

194   Boora Group of Bogs, Co Offaly

Bord na Móna / 3ft gauge

Opened 1957.

Serves the ESB Ferbane Power Station (90MW) and Derrinlough Briquette Factory.

Group includes Clongawny More, Galros, Drinagh West, Drinagh East, Boora West, Boora East, Noggulsboy, Derries, Tumduff, Turraun, Oughter, Pollagh and Killaranny Bogs. Produces milled peat for Ferbane Power Station.

The isolated Lemanaghan Bog (Table 362) was connected to this system c.1988/9 with a swing bridge over the Grand Canal and a fixed bridge over the River Brosna. In turn, a link to the Blackwater group was completed in 1995 by a line from Lemanaghan to Ballaghuff 2 Bog.

Map reference 21 B1.

195   Turraun Peat Works Railway, Co Offaly

Possibly 2ft gauge

Operating c.1934.

Early peat works railway operated by Leinster Carbonising Co Ltd, with line running from bog workings via the works to the Grand Canal. Understood to have had one internal combustion locomotive. Bord na Móna now work this area as part of the Boora Group (see Table 194).

Map reference 21 B1.

196   Irish Steam Preservation Society, Stradbally Hall, Stradbally, Co Laois

3ft gauge

Opened 1969.

A 48-chain purpose-built circuit in a balloon type loop in the hall grounds.

Map reference 22 A3.

197   Kilberry Group of Bogs, Co Kildare

Bord na Móna / 2ft gauge – 1947 to c.1988
3ft gauge – c.1988 to present

Opened 1947.

This bog system was one of the two 2'0" gauge systems operated by Bord na Móna. The system was converted to 3'0" circa 1988. The system was served by a CIE siding on the Cherryville Junction to Waterford line (see Table 2).

Produced peat moss for fertiliser factory, now also served by road deliveries from the Ummeras Bog (see Table 334). There was a previous company who were working this bog called the Electro-Peat Syndicate (see Table 247).

Map reference 22 B3.

198   Edenderry Peat Works, Co Offaly

? gauge

Opened ?   Closed ?

Operating at the turn of the century, this early peat works line ran from the bog workings to the Grand Canal.

Map reference 22 A1.

199   Ballydermot-Timahoe Group of Bogs, Counties Kildare and Offaly

Bord na Móna / 3ft gauge

Opened 1948.

This group produced sod peat for ESB's now closed Allenwood Power Station. The group includes Ballydermot South, Ballydermot North, Shean South, Shean North, Black River, Glashabaun South, Glashabaun North, Barnaran, Lullymore Lodge, Timahoe South and Timahoe North Bogs. The Lullymore system is situated in the middle of this system (See table 231) and was connected by a link from Lullymore Lodge Bog. The system was connected to the Derrygreenagh system (Table 183) from Clongreen Bog, c.1992. These bogs now produce sod peat for domestic consumption.

Bord na Móna acquired the Shamrock Machine Turf Company's Shane Valley site (see Table 303) in 1978 as part of an expansion of this system.

Allenwood Power Station had its own ESB railway which connected to this system (see Table 254). There was also connection to the Irish C.E.C.A. Ltd factory, see Table 282.

Map reference 22 B1.

200   Grand Canal Tramway, Co Kildare

2ft gauge ?

Quarry line dating from about 1900. Possibly used for transporting special soil for sealing leaks in the canal banks.

Map reference 22 C1.

201   Ummaras Peat Moss Works Railway, Co Kildare

? gauge

Opened 1910;   closed 1917.

Possibly electrified in early days.

Bord na Móna started development in part of this bog c.1978, see Table 334.

Map reference 22 A2.

202   Derrylea Peat Company Railway, Co Kildare

5ft 3in gauge

Opened c.1860;   closed c.1867.

Peat Briquette Factory opened by Charles Hodgson, later appears to be owned by the Patent Peat Company. Went bankrupt c.1867 due to coal competition. The first section of line, completed c.1860, ran from the works to the bog workings on Derrylea Bog.

The second line ran from the works to a loading point on the Athy Branch of the Grand Canal by Macartney's Bridge near the 24th Lock. Completed in 1865 the line was some three miles long and replaced a canal which had previously ran from the works to the Grand Canal.

Map reference 22 A2.

203   Gleniff to Mullaghmore, Co Sligo

Barium Consolidated / 2ft gauge /
Distances measured from Gleniff Quarry

Opened October 1928; closed 1931.

Approximately seven miles long. Built to transport barytes from Gleniff Quarry to the harbour at Mullaghmore. Part of the northern end of the line was possibly on the trackbed of the former Mullaghmore Harbour Tramway (see Table 224).

Distance (Miles)	Place / Feature (notes)	Date Opened	Date Closed	Map Grid	Table Ref.
0	Gleniff Quarry	1928	1931	8 B3	
0¾	Timber Trestle Bridge	1928	1931	8 B3	
1¾	Ballintrillick 'Pilot Factory' served by spur from 'main line', trains could avoid factory, which was used to purify and crush barytes.	1928	1931	8 B3	
4½	Creevykeel Crossing also called Hannon's Cross	1928	1931	8 B3	
7	Mullaghmore	1928	1931	8 B2	

At the Gleniff Quarry end there were two more railways. The first was an 18" gauge manual or gravity worked track on top of the mountain about one mile in length from the borings to a point overlooking the head of Gleniff Valley.

The second was also of 18" gauge and ran from the end of the first line to the foot of the mountain adjacent to the 2'0" gauge line to Mullaghmore. This line was cable worked. The track consisted of three rails, that is to say the two lines shared a common centre rail. At the middle of the incline was a passing loop, so the three rails became four. Full wagons at the top were lowered down pulling empty wagons back up, crossing at the passing loop.

204   Bonmahon Copper Mine Railway, Co Waterford

Mining Company of Ireland Ltd / Bonmahon Copper Mines Syndicate
? gauge – horse worked

Opened late 1860s ? Closed 1907

The Mining Company of Ireland Ltd was using this line from the late 1860s to the late

1880s. It ran from a large mine shaft at Tankardstown along the cliff edge and then steeply descended to a place called the 'Copper Yard'. From here another line ran in the opposite direction by the side of a public road to Knockmahon cross-roads, crossed a stream and then headed north to a series of shafts. For a short time an 'Aerial Ropeway' was in use from the 'Copper Yard' to the seashore to transport washed copper ore to waiting boats.

In 1906 and 1907 the Bonmahon Copper Mines Syndicate started renewed borings. No railway was in use except for short sections of underground track.

Map reference 27 D4.

205   Hodgson's Tramway, Co Wicklow

Wicklow Copper Mine Co / 3ft 6in gauge

Opened 1847

Avoca to Arklow closed 1870.
Ballymurtagh to Avoca still operating in 1878, closed ?

Ran from the Ballymurtagh and Ballygahan Mines to Arklow North and South Quays. There was a tunnel under a road near Avoca. The line was absorbed by the Dublin, Wicklow and Wexford Railway on 01-05-1861. Line worked by Wicklow Copper Mine Co until 05-05-1863. The line was horse worked from the mines to Avoca station. Locomotive worked from Avoca Station to Ballyraine and horse worked from Ballyraine to Arklow Quays. Length about 8 miles.

A double line of inclined plane was relaid c.1940 from Ballymurtagh to a loading point.

Map reference 23 A5.

206   Fenit Pier and Harbour Commissioners, Co Kerry

5ft 3in gauge

Opened 1887;   closed 05-06-1978 by CIE

Line was approximately ½ mile long and ran from an end on junction with the Tralee and Fenit Railway (see Table 20) at Fenit to the Pier. The line was worked by the WL&WR until a dispute broke out. The line was then worked by Fenit Pier and Harbour Commisioners from 1899 to 1900. Thereafter it was worked by the GSWR and successors until closure.

Closed in 1941 as Pier was declared unsafe. Pier was rebuilt and and the line reopened in October 1955 by CIE.

Map reference 24 D2.

207   Lyracrumpane Group of Bogs, Co Kerry

Bord na Móna / 3ft gauge

Opened 1939 by the Turf Development Board Ltd; closed c.1980.

Works at Lyrecrumpane. Produced sod peat.

Formerly owned by the Turf Development Board Limited. Taken over by Bord na Móna in 1946.

Map reference 25 B2.

208   Carrigcannon Group of Bogs, Co Kerry

Bord na Móna / 3ft gauge

Opened 1958;   closed c.1985 ?

Works at Carrigcannon.

Map reference 25 B2.

209   Barna Group of Bogs, Co Kerry

Bord na Móna / 3ft gauge

Opened 1960;   closed c.1985.

This bog was sold to private owners c.1985. The railway was being lifted for re-use elsewhere as the new owners were going to use road transport.

Map reference 25 C3.

210   Derryfadda Group of Bogs, Co Galway

Bord na Móna / 3ft gauge

Opened 1979.

Bogs at Killeglan, Castlegar, Newtown, Cloonboley, Clara Island, Cloonbeggaun, Clooniff and Cornaveagh. Milled peat factory at Ballyforan.

This system is partly built on the old CSET Gowla Farm Railway, see Table 285.

Map reference 14 C5.

211   British Aluminium Works, Larne, Co Antrim

3ft gauge

Opened 1900;   closed 1960.

The line ran from the quay at Larne Harbour to the factory and was used to carry ore. There was a connection with the NCC narrow gauge line. The works had mainly closed by 1953.

Map reference 5 D6.

212   Killeady Quarry Line, Co Cork

Probably 3ft gauge

Opened about 1900; closed about 1924.

Ran from quarry north of Kinsale Junction to the north end of Kinsale Junction where it crossed over the Bandon lines on an overbridge and terminated at sidings, where loads could be tipped into standard gauge wagons below. Also see Table 85.

Map reference 31 C1.

213   Duncrue Salt Mine Tramway, Co Antrim

Belfast Mining Co / 5ft 3in gauge and narrow gauge plateway

Opened 1860s;   closed ?

Standard gauge siding off Belfast-Larne line at Trooperslane (see Table 76). Narrow gauge tramway from broad gauge siding to mine. Certainly working in 1865, as Belfast Mining Co private wagons were taking rock salt on the BNCR to a Salt Works near York Road.

Map reference 11 B1.

214   Drinagh Limeworks Railway, Co Wexford

H J Cooper Ltd / 3ft 7in gauge

Opened c.1885; closed 1918.

Three lines radiated from the works. Two were animal worked apart from the quarry line which was a cable operated 1:2 incline.

Was served by a DSER siding (see Table 31)

Map reference 29 A3.

215   Ballinhassig Aerial Ropeway, Co Cork

Opened 09-09-1901 by CBSCR; closed early 1913.

A 3½ mile long aerial ropeway from Ballinhassig station (see Table 85) to Ballinphelic Brickworks. Used to transport bricks. Iron trestles 140 yds apart supported an endless rope on which were attached 126 buckets. The rope was powered by a 30hp engine at Ballinhassig.

Map reference 31 C1.

216   Cork Exhibition Railway (1889)

2ft or 2ft 2in gauge

Opened 22-10-1889; closed c.1890.

Electrically worked by the overhead trolley system at 110V DC.

Built by George Percival for the 1889 Cork Exhibition on the Corn Exchange site behind the Municipal Buildings off Albert Quay and Anglesea Street. The line was of a circular nature (length not known) running around the exhibition. Line closed at the end of the exhibition.

Map reference 33 D2 (Inset).

217   Cork Exhibition Railway (1932)

1ft 1in gauge

Opened May 1932; closed October 1932.

Built for the Cork Industrial Fair and Exhibition of 1932 on a site on the Carrigohane Straight to the west of Cork City. A special platform was built on the Cork and Muskerry section of the GSR (see table 83) for the duration of the exhibition. The line encircled half of the showground, length unknown.

Map reference 33 B2.

218   Ford Motor Company Rooftop Railway, Cork City

2ft gauge

Opened 1930;   closed 1948.

Built to transport coal from the riverside wharf to the factory bunkers across the top of the roof of the factory. Length was about 200yds.

In 1941, during the Second World War, the railway was dismantled and moved to Caheraveelane Bog (see Table 219). After the war the line was reinstated on top of the factory roof were it worked until about 1948. It was finally dismantled in 1950.

Map reference 33 D2 (Inset).

219   Caheraveelane Turf Railway, Co Cork

Ford Motor Company / 2ft gauge

Opened Spring 1941; closed Autumn 1941.

Built to transport turf from the bog to a public road for onward transhipment to the Ford Factory at Cork.

This line was originally on the rooftop of the Ford Motor Company's factory at Cork. It was removed and taken to Caheraveelane and re-erected to extract peat for use as fuel at the company's factory. See also table 218.

The line ran from a public road to the bogs. Total mileage about ½ mile. The bog was only worked during the summer of 1941.

Map reference 26 A4.

220   Dublin Tramways
5ft 3in gauge, 550v DC overhead trolley system

Opened 1872-1906; closed 1929-1949.

Dublin Tramway Company, Dublin Central Tramways and the North Dublin Street Tramways (all 5'3" gauge horse drawn) amalgamated in 1881 to form the Dublin United Tramway Company. Electrified between 1897 and 1907.

In 1896 the DUTC absorbed the Dublin Southern Tramways, a 5'3" gauge horse and steam worked system, electrified in 1896. Part of the DST system was 4'0" gauge, but this was regauged to 5'3" and electrified in 1896.

The DUTC absorbed the Blackrock and Kingstown (opened 1883) in 1893. This was electrified in 1896.

From 1907, the DUTC worked the Clontarf and Hill of Howth Tramway (opened 1900 as a 5'3" gauge electric tramway) which closed in 1941.

Maximum route mileage, 54¼ miles, 92½ track miles. Closed 1949.

Map reference, page 32.

221   Belfast Corporation Tramways
4ft 8½in gauge, 550V DC overhead trolley system

Opened 28-08-1872; closed 10-02-1954.

Opened 1872, originally as a 5'3" gauge horse drawn line. Converted to 4'8½" gauge in 1878 and absorbed by Belfast Corporation in 1904. Electrified in 1905. Worked the Ligionel and Sydenham systems. After 1911 the Corporation also worked the Cavehill and Whitewell system (see Table 172)

Maximum route mileage, 51 miles.

Map reference page 34.

222   Aghada Harbour Tramway, Co Cork
? gauge

Opened c.1892; closed c.1900 ?

Short tramway from the pier to a goods shed, used in conjunction with the CBPR steamer services from Cork.

Map reference 31 D1.

223   Ballycraigy Brickworks Tramway, Co Antrim
? gauge

Opened 1880s at Ballycraigy, near Carncastle, Co Antrim; closed 1900s.

¼ mile long tramway from the clay pits to the brickworks.

Map reference 5 C6.

224   Mullaghmore Harbour Tramroad, Co Sligo
? gauge

Opened 1822;   closed 1842.

Line was a horse or donkey worked tramway built to transport stone from the hills near Mullaghmore for use in construction of Mullaghmore Harbour, causeway and pier. The project was financed by Lord Palmerston and took about twenty years to complete.

When Barium Consolidated built their line to Mullaghmore Harbour it is possible that they used some of the original trackbed (see Table 203).

Map reference 8 B2.

225   Kildownet to Darby's Point Pier, Achill Island
Irish Industrial Mineral Company / 2ft gauge ?

Opened 1910 ?   Closed 1916 ?

Built to transport whitestone from quarry to harbour for use in pottery making.

Line ran from quarry near Kildownet to pier at Darby's Point. For part of the way the line ran by the side of a public road. Full wagons were worked by gravity from the quarry to the harbour and hauled back by horses.

Irish Industrial Minerals also operated a line on Achill Island (see table 138).

Map reference 6 A6.

226   Ballyshannon Hydro-Electric Scheme, Co Donegal
Bord Solathair an Leictreachais (Electricity Supply Board, ESB) / 2ft 6in gauge

Opened 1946 ?   Closed 1947 ?

Locomotive worked railway used in the construction of the hydro-electric scheme.

Map reference 8 C2.

227   Roundwood Reservoir Scheme, Co Wicklow
3ft gauge

Opened circa 1908; closed circa 1925

Railway used in construction of Roundwood Resevoir, Co Wicklow. Project started 1908 with P. J. Kinlen as contractor, then McKee and McNally, then to J. Mackay in 1914, to H. and J. Martin from 1915 until completion

Map reference 23 A3

228   Poulaphouca Reservoir Scheme, Co Wicklow
Cementation Co / 2ft gauge and 1ft 10in gauge

Opened 1937;   closed 1942.

Used in construction of dam at the Poulaphouca Resevoir.

Map reference 22 D2.

229   River Bann Improvements
3ft gauge

Opened 1930;   closed 1939.

Railway used in River Bann improvement scheme. Site not located at present.

230   Tallaght Aerodrome Railway, Co Dublin
British War Department / 2ft gauge

Opened 1918;   closed 1919.

Originally called Cookstown, but renamed 08-08-1918 to avoid confusion with Cookstown, Co Tyrone. Used for transporting materials for the construction of Tallaght Aerodrome. A 5'3" gauge siding also ran to the site from the Dublin and Blessington Tramway (see table 119).

Map reference 23 A1.

231 Lullymore Bog and Briquette Factory, Co Kildare

Bord na Móna / 3ft gauge

Opened ? by the Peat Fuel Company.

Formerly the Peat Fuel Company, it was taken over in 1940 by the Turf Development Board Limited which was subsequently taken over in 1946 by the newly formed Bord na Móna.

A self-contained system in the midst of the larger Ballydermot-Timahoe Group (see Table 199) taking peat to Lullymore Briquette Factory. The system was later linked to the Ballydermot-Timahoe group with a link from Lullymore Lodge Bog.

Map reference 22 B1.

232 Courtown Brick & Tile Works Railway, Co Wexford

Wallace Brothers Ltd / 1ft 8in gauge

Opened ? Closed 1971.

Factory situated about a mile from Courtown Harbour, on the Gorey Road. The narrow gauge line ran from the Clay mill, past the locomotive shed (served by a trailing spur), down a steep hill to the quarry. Here there was another trailing point to a switchback along the quarry face. Worked by horses until 1948 when a diesel locomotive was acquired.

Inside the works there was an extensive 2ft gauge tramway used to transport the clay pipes etc through the various stages of production on shelved trolleys.

Map reference 29 B1.

233 Dalkey Quarry Railway, Co Dublin

Kingstown Harbour Commissioners / ? gauge

Opened 1816; closed 1836.

Built to transport stone from Dalkey Quarry to Kingstown (Dun Laoghaire) for the construction of the new harbour. Part of this trackbed was later used by the Dublin and Kingstown Railway (see table 31). Length about 2 miles.

Dalkey Quarry had an extensive system which was apparently used until the late 19th century.

Map reference 23 B1.

234 Craigahulliar Quarry Railway, Co Antrim

Giant's Causeway Columnar Basalt Company, Portrush Columnar Basalt Co / 2ft 6in gauge

Opened c.1914; closed c.1943.

Line ran from Craigahulliar Quarry to Ballycraig.

Map reference 4 D3.

235 Long Gilbert Quarry Railway, Co Antrim

A. Gray / 3ft gauge – Rope worked incline

Opened ? Closed ? – in use in 1939.

Long Gilbert Limestone Quarry was just to the east of White Rocks in Co Antrim. Quarry was served by a siding from the Giant's Causeway, Portrush and Bush Valley Railway (see table 113).

A 3'0" gauge rope worked incline went from the quarry floor to the siding. The winding gear was powered by a petrol engine.

Map reference 4 D3.

236 Shannon Hydro-Electric Scheme – Banagher Works, Co Offaly

Siemens Bauunion AG / 600mm gauge

Opened 1925? Closed 1930?

Works in relation to the Shannon Hyro-Electric scheme at Ardnacrusha, see Table 188.

Map reference 21 A1.

237 Shannon Hydro-Electric Scheme – Meelick Works, Co Galway

Siemens Bauunion AG / 600mm gauge

Opened 1925? Closed 1930?

Works in relation to the Shannon Hydro-Electric scheme at Ardnacrusha, see Table 188.

Map reference 20 D2.

238 Porthall Lime Kiln Railway, Co Donegal

? gauge

Opened ? Closed ?

Lime kilns owned by Mr. McGuinness, later reference as Hoffman's Lime Kilns. Ran from the south side of Porthall Station (Table 49) to Lime Kilns.

Map reference 3 D5.

239 Belfast Corporation

2ft gauge

Opened 1924; closed ?

No details of this line at present other than two locomotives were supplied new to the Corporation.

Map Reference 34.

240 Roughfort Quarry Railway, Co Antrim

James Boyd and Sons (Carnmoney) Ltd / 2ft gauge

Opened mid 1940s; closed early 1970s.

Map reference 11 B1.

241 Magheramorne Cement Factory Railway, Co Antrim

British Portland Cement Manufacturers Ltd / 5ft 3in gauge / 2ft gauge

Broad gauge private sidings at Magheramorne Station. Narrow gauge quarry lines lifted c.1947. The narrow gauge line went under the NCC line just past the northern end of the platforms of Magheramorne Station.

Map reference 5 D6

242 Harland and Wolff Ltd, Belfast

5ft 3in gauge

Opened ? Closed ?

Works railway at Queen's Island, Belfast.

Map reference 34 D2.

243   Carnduff Quarry Rly, Larne, Co Antrim

Hugh Foster (until 1908), Howden Brothers Ltd / 2ft gauge

Opened 1905;   closed 1950 and lifted.

Line ran from Quarry to exchange sidings on the Belfast-Larne railway (see table 76). Horse operated until 1921 when replaced by a locomotive.

Map reference 5 C6.

244   Sulphate of Ammonia Co Ltd, Larne, Co Antrim

2ft gauge

Opened 1910;   closed 1912.

Works railway.

Map reference 5 D6.

245   Carlow Sugar Factory, Co Carlow

Comhlucht Suicre Éireann Teoranta / 5ft 3in and narrow gauge

Opened 1926;   closed ?

The narrow gauge railway was used in the construction of the sugar factory. It transported material carried by barge from the nearby River Barrow Navigation to the building site. The narrow gauge remained in use for a number of years after opening. The broad gauge works sidings were connected to GSR (see Table 2). Originally a private sugar factory opened in 1926, the industry was nationalised in 1934 to form CSET.

Map reference 22 B5.

246   Mallow Sugar Factory, Co Cork

Comhlucht Suicre Eireann Teoranta / 5ft 3in gauge

Opened 1934;   closed c.1965.

Re-opened about 1990.

Works sidings connected to GSR (see Table 8).

Map reference 26 B4.

247   Electro-Peat Syndicate, Co Kildare

? gauge

Opened 1906;   closed 1914.

Rope hauled tramway used for transporting peat **at** Kilberry Bog, Co Kildare.

This was the first peat railway at this site. In 1947 Bord na Móna opened their system on the same site (see Table 197).

Map reference 22 B3.

248   Dublin Port and Dock Board

3ft gauge

Opened ?   Closed ?

Railway used in construction of the Alexandra Basin Extension.

Map reference 32 D2.

249   Irish Engineering & Harbour Construction Co Ltd, Leixlip, Co Kildare

2ft gauge

Opened Summer 1970; closed Autumn 1970.

Contractors railway employed by the ESB when it was erecting a high tension pylon route. Marshy ground near the River Liffey off the Celbridge to Kill road near Celbridge, Co Kildare, caused a problem. Deep foundations were necessary and as lorries were unable to traverse the marshy ground, a temporary railway almost ¼ mile long was built. The railway carried concrete from the main road to the site.

Map reference 22 D1.

250   Irish Shell Ltd, Dublin

5ft 3in gauge

Opened 1951 ? Closed ?

Private sidings at No. 2 Site, North Wall Docks, Dublin, worked by a locomotive.

Map reference 32 D2

251   Manor Whinstone Quarry Rly, Co Dublin

2ft gauge

Opened c.1929; closed ?

Locomotive worked quarry railway Woodtown, Co Dublin.

Map reference 23 A1.

252   Balbriggan Waterworks Railway, Co Dublin

Daniel Thompson and Sons Ltd / 2ft gauge

Opened 1929 ? Closed 1930 ?

Contractors railway used in construction of Balbriggan Waterworks.

Map reference 17 B5.

253   Tuam Sugar Factory, Co Galway

Comhlucht Suicre Eireann Teoranta / 5ft 3in gauge

Opened 1934;   closed June 1985.

Works sidings connected to the GSR Athenry-Claremorris railway (see Table 17).

Map reference 14 A4.

254   Allenwood Power Station Rly, Co Kildare

Bord Solathair an Leictreachais (Electricity Supply Board, ESB) / 3ft gauge

Opened 1952;   closed 1991

ESB railway at Allenwood Power Station (40MW) connected to the Ballydermot-Timahoe Bord na Móna System (Table 199). Also connected to the Irish C.E.C.A. Ltd Allenwood Carbon Factory system (Table 282). Allenwood was a sod peat fired power station. Bord na Móna wagons were left in reception sidings from where ESB locomotives brought them forward to the unloading point.

Map reference 22 B1.

255   **Sutton Sand Co Ltd, Newbridge, Co Kildare**

2ft gauge

Opened 1933 ?   Closed ?

Locomotive worked quarry railway.

Map reference 22 C2.

256   **Carnanee Quarry Railway, Co Derry**

Unknown owner c.1909; R.Faris 1930 to 1939 / 3ft gauge

R. Faris used quarry to supply materials for the River Bann improvement works of Coleraine Harbour Commissioners. Approximately two miles long. Stone was delivered to the breakwater construction site where the Government of Northern Ireland lines (see Table 257) took over.

Map reference 4 C3.

257   **Bann Navigation Railway, Co Derry**

Government of Northern Ireland / 2ft gauge

Opened 1937;   closed 1937.

Used in connection with River Bann Improvements. Stone was delivered from Carnanee Quarry (see Table 256). Two diesel locomotives were in use.

Map reference 4 C3.

258   **Harbour and General Works Ltd, Coleraine, Co Derry**

2ft gauge

Opened c.1940; closed ?

Locomotive worked construction railway for Coleraine Harbour Contract.

Map reference 4 D4.

259   **Black Braes Embankment Rly, Co Derry**

Ministry of Agriculture, Lough Foyle / 2ft gauge

Opened 1955;   closed 1955 ?

Lifted by 1966.

Locomotive worked railway used in embankment maintainence.

Map reference 4 A4.

260   **Unidentified Quarry, near Dunkitt, Co Kilkenny**

? gauge

Operating ? Shown on 1908 OS Map.

A quarry tramway running from area called Smartcastle to a site near Mullinabro House. Although it was only ¼ mile from Dunkitt (se Table 6), it did not connect with either of the broad gauge railways which met there.

Map reference 28 B3.

261   **David Patton Ltd, Monaghan, Co Monaghan**

2ft gauge

No details known other than that it had one locomotive.

Map reference 9 D5.

262   **Portarlington Power Station Rly, Co Laois**

Bord Solathair an Leictreachais (Electricity Supply Board, ESB) / 3ft gauge

Opened 1941 ?   Closed c.1986.

37.5MW Sod peat fired power station served by the Bord na Móna Clonsast System. Bord na Móna wagons were left in reception sidings and taken to the unloading point by ESB locomotives.

Also see Bord na Móna Clonsast Group of Bogs, Table 192 and Clonsast Siding, Table 4

Map reference 21 D2.

263   **Thurles Sugar Factory, Co Tipperary**

Comhlucht Suicre Eireann Teoranta / 2ft gauge and 5ft 3in gauge

Opened 1934;   closed ?

Various standard gauge works sidings connected to Dublin-Cork Main Line (see table 8). Also 2'0" gauge line running from the boiler house, the locomotive(s) and wagons are used to remove ash.

Map reference 21 A6.

264   **J. Howard & Company, Cluntoe, Co Tyrone**

2ft gauge

Opened 1926;   closed 1930.

Locomotive worked railway used for an Air Ministry contract.

Map reference 10 B1.

265   **Parnell Whinstone Tramway, Co Wicklow**

? gauge

Opened ?   Closed ?

Tramway running north from quarries near Arklow, Co Wicklow, to Arklow South Quay.

Map reference 23 B6.

266   **Kynoch Ltd, Arklow, Co Wicklow**

2ft gauge

Opened ?   Closed ?

Extensive works railway at Kynoch Ltd Cordite Factory. Lines were extended southwards from the factory to Arklow North Quay and northwards for a distance.
Locomotive worked.

Map reference 23 B5.

267   Black Hill Railway, Belfast

Inclined plane, No details known other than it was in use in 1956.

Map reference 11 A2.

268   Clowney Brickworks, Belfast

Narrow gauge

Opened ?   Closed ?

Shown on 1901 and 1932 OS Maps. A 1932 OS map shows two parallel lines leaving two separate buildings and running in a north westerly direction to the clay pits.

Map reference 34 B3.

269   Colinward Limestone Quarry, near Whitewell, Belfast

4ft 9in gauge

Opened 1840.

Closed 1896.

Quarry tramway. No locomotives worked this system.

Map reference 34 C1.

270   Kellswater, Co Antrim

Possible site of an industrial railway or tramway, no details known about location, operating dates or purpose.

Map reference 5 A6.

271   Kilcoan Quarry Railway, Islandmagee, Co Antrim

? gauge

Opened c.1920.

Closed c.1930.

An inclined plane of about ½ mile in length running from Kilcoan Quarry to the Pier.

Map reference 11 C1.

272   Knocknadona Quarry Railway, Lisburn, Co Antrim

Narrow gauge

Opened ?

Closed ?

Narrow gauge lines on quarry floor.

Map reference 11 A3.

273   Haypark Brickworks, Ava Avenue, Belfast

H. & J. Martin Ltd / narrow gauge

Opened ?

Closed ?

Map reference 34 C4.

274   Ballymurphy Brickworks, Belfast

Thomas Murphy and Son Ltd / narrow gauge

Opened ?

Closed ?

A 1932 OS map shows two lines. One at the northern end of the works runs a short distance in a south easterly direction, the other is at the southern end of the works and also runs in a south easterly direction but is about twice as long. Both lines go to the clay pits.

Map reference 34 B3.

275   Forth River Brickworks, Springfield Road, Belfast

Thomas Murphy and Son Ltd / narrow gauge

Opened ?   Closed ?

Map reference 34 B3.

276   Craig Park Quarry, Bushmills, Co Antrim

W. Peden / narrow gauge

Opened ?   Closed ?

Map reference 4 D3.

277   Skegoneil Brickworks, Skegoneil Avenue, Belfast

Skegoneil Brick Co Ltd / narrow gauge

Opened ?   Closed ?

A 1938 OS map shows a line leaving the works on the east side, the line then turns sharply south and appears to cross Skegoneil Avenue.

Map reference 34 C2.

278   Roosky Harbour Railway, Main Street, Roosky, Co Roscommon

2ft gauge

A 2'0" gauge railway built in the garden of a private house. Two locomotives operate on the 200yd straight line, both were supplied by FMB Engineering Ltd, Oakhanger, Hampshire. Three toast rack carriages are used, one carriage being converted to an enclosed carriage. The carriages were built in 1928 for the Lilleshall Park and Woodland Railway, Shropshire and were put into store upon closure in 1939. They re-emerged in 1952 at Alton Towers, Staffordshire and came to Roosky in September 1993. In addition a number of wooden and steel bodied coal hutches of various gauges from collieries in the Arigna mines area are present.

Map reference 15 B2.

279   Scrabo Quarry, Newtownards, Co Down

? gauge

Opened c.1858; closed ?

Tramway from workings to dressing station.

Map reference 11 C2.

280 Newcastle, Co Down

? gauge

Opened ?   Closed ?

Inclined plane, working in 1956.

Map reference 11 C2.

281 Howth Harbour, Co Dublin

? gauge

Opened ?   Closed ?

Tramway used in construction of harbour.

Map reference 17 C6 (Inset).

282 Allenwood Carbon Factory, Co Kildare

Irish C.E.C.A. Ltd / 3ft gauge

Opened 1965;   closed May 1983.

Irish C.E.C.A operated a factory making carbon from peat on a site adjacent to the ESB's Allenwood Power Station. Peat was supplied by Bord na Móna and left in reception sidings. Irish C.E.C.A. Ltd locomotives would collect these wagons and forward them to the processing plant.

Also see Tables 199 and 254.

Map reference 22 B1.

283 Lanesborough 'A' Power Station Railway, Co Longford

Bord Solathair an Leictreachais (Electricity Supply Board, ESB) / 3ft gauge

Opened ?   Closed 1983

Peat was supplied by Bord na Móna and left in reception sidings. ESB's own locomotives would then collect these wagons and take them to the unloading point. Lanesborough 'A' Power Station (sod peat fired) closed in early 1983 and the 3ft gauge railway lifted.

Lanesborough 'B' and 'C' Power Stations (80MW, milled peat fired) are supplied directly by Bord na Móna.

Also see Table 178.

Map reference 15 A3.

284 Carrownanalt Coal Mine, Co Roscommon

2ft gauge

Opened 1940s;   closed 1961.

A series of short tramways served this coal mine near Dereenavoggy, Co Roscommon. The mine had originally been worked by both Arigna Iron Works Co and Arigna Mining Co. Between here and the Rover Mine (Table 372) were various smaller lines. At Wynn's there were at least two adits with single track tramways. Further west was 'Grogan's', two adits served by tramways. The main adit tramway was a single track, 2ft gauge, locomotive operated tramway. The next west was 'McDermott's', an adit with a tramway, probably a single line.

All the above were working in the 1940s, closing c.1947-1950.

Later the site appears to have been worked by Broderick & Ryan also using a locomotive operated, 2'0" gauge tramway. This seems to have been worked until about 1961.

Map reference 8 C6.

285 Gowla Farm Railway, near Ballinasloe, Co Galway.

Comhlucht Suicre Éireann Teoranta / 2ft gauge

Opened c.1950; closed 1978.

This was a grass farm for manufacturing feed stuffs, extensive 2'0" gauge locomotive worked lines were used for transporting the grass to the factory and distribution of fertilizers. Some of the 'main line' track is laid with very heavy rail from the Cavan & Leitrim Railway. After closure the site was acquired by Bord na Móna for their Derryfadda Group development (see Table 210).

Map reference 14 C5.

286 Keelogues Limestone Quarry, Co Roscommon

Western Industries (Boyle) Ltd / 2ft gauge

Opened ?   Closed 1961

Locomotive worked quarry railway. Few details known.

Map reference 14 D1.

287 Glen Ballynashee Colliery Railway, Co Sligo

McTiernan Brothers, Glen Ballynashee Colliery, Geevagh, Co Sligo/ 2ft gauge

Opened ?   Closed 1983 ?

Working in 1966.

A small location high up in the Bralieve Mountains where coal was being extracted from a small adit. Wagons were drawn out of the adit by the locomotive which retired to the loco shed spur, the wagons were then hand pushed to the tipplers.

Map reference 8 B6.

288 Ballinagarry Colliery Railway, Co Tipperary

Ballinagarry Collieries (Production) Ltd, Gurteen, near Coalbrook, Co Tipperary / 2ft gauge

Opened 1946 ?   Closed ?

Part of the colliery railway was underground and worked by battery electric locomotives. Traffic was rope hauled up a steep incline from underground. Diesel locomotives worked the surface trains but all were out of use by 1966, being replaced by haulage by rope or hand.
The company also operated another mine at Clashduff, see Table 316.

Map reference 21 B6.

289 Shalee Silver Mines Railway, Co Tipperary

Mogul of Ireland Ltd / 2ft 6in gauge

Opened 1968;   closed July 1982.

The underground 2ft 6in gauge lines in this mine near Nenagh, Co Tipperary, were up to a mile in length with a total of some 4,000ft of track in use. The locomotives hauled 140cu.ft. capacity wagons which were loaded and unloaded whilst in motion. There were two 12 seat man-riders to transport staff underground. Later the mine was working on six different levels with rail working on the first four levels.

Also see Silvermines Siding, Table 128.

Map reference 20 C5.

290   Derryard Ballast Pit Tramway

? gauge

Opened 1878;   closed ?

Leased in 1878, a tramway costing £600 was built by J. Edwards to connect the Quarry to the MGWR siding.

Map reference ?

291   Silvermines Railway, Co Tipperary

Silvermines Lead and Zinc Company Ltd / 2ft gauge

Opened ?   Closed ?   The mines were worked by one diesel locomotive.

Map reference 20 C4.

292   St Patrick's Copper Mine Rly, Co Wicklow

St Patrick's Copper Mines Ltd, Avoca / 3ft gauge and 1ft 11½in gauge

Opened ?   Closed ?

Two sites were worked, that on the eastern side had ceased by 1966 and was served by the 3ft gauge line. The mine on the western side were still being worked in 1966 and were served by the 1ft 11½in gauge track which went underground. Worked by one battery electric locomotive. The mines were later taken over by the American backed Avoca Mines Ltd , who used one unidentifed Wingrove & Rogers battery-electric locomotive underground on a short length of line.

Map reference 23 A5.

293   Portrush Miniture Railways, Co Antrim

7¼in & 9½in mixed gauge / 9½in gauge

West Strand site – 7¼in / 9½in mixed gauge. Opened c.1961; closed 1972.

Caravan Park site – 9½in gauge. Opened and Closed 1992 – ran for one year only.

Map reference 4 D3.

294   Container Refurbishing Co Ltd, Newry, Co Down

3ft gauge

Opened 1975 ?   Closed ?

Locomotive worked railway used for hauling containers through the works whilst the containers undergo repair and cleaning. The company were not traceable by 1980 but may have changed its name to Ulcon Ltd of Tandragee Road, Newry.

Map reference 10 D5.

295   Erin Peat Products Ltd, Birr, Co Offaly

2ft gauge

Opened 1971;   closed 1980.

Erin Peat Products Ltd had two sites. One works was about 3 miles from Birr on the T41 road to Tullamore (N090066), the other works was about 1½ miles down the L113 road off the L115 Birr to Banagher Road (N020108).

The railway was bought as a complete 'railway outfit' from M.E. Engineering Ltd, London, and included track, wagons and a locomotive. Three other locomotives were bought from Pope Brothers in 1977 who had ceased rail operations in 1976 (see Table 190). Rail operations ceased here in 1980, with some of the track, wagons and locomotives going to Midland Irish Peat Moss Ltd, Rathowen (see Table 300).

Map reference 21 A2.

296   Mr Holwell, Bangor, Co Down

Nothing known other than Mr Holwell had one Motor Rail locomotive acquired from Ballylumford Power Station and which subsequently went to the Ulster Folk & Transport Museum, Cultra.

Map reference 11 C2.

297   Irish Mining, Athlone, Co Westmeath

No details known other than the company sold two locomotives to Priority Drilling Co. They are possibly heavy plant dealers.

Map reference 15 A5.

298   McGill, Eglinton, Co Derry

1ft 10in gauge

Opened ?   Closed ?

No details other than on Hibberd locomotive was owned by McGill.

Map reference 4 A4.

299   W. P. McCormick, Knock, Belfast

3ft gauge

Opened 08-63   Closed 11-67

Mr McCormick had about 80yds of heavy 3ft gauge track in his back garden. He had also acquired an ex-British Aluminium 0-4-0T in 1960 along with a former BNCR 4-wheel open wagon and a 4-wheel flat from the aluminium works and a CDRJC signal. The locomotive had been restored by 1964 and was in occasional use until 1967. The locomotive later went to the Shane's Castle Railway in 1969.

Map reference 34 E3.

300   Midland Irish Peat Moss Limited, Rathowen, Co Westmeath

2ft gauge

Opened 1983.

The operation currently occupies three sites, called Mill (the main works), Landsale Yard and Smith's Bog. Operations started in 1983 when the company bought redundant trackwork and locomotives from the Erin Peat Products system near Birr (see Table 295). There is thought to be some 4km of permanent line and some 2km of temporary line in use among the three sites.

Map reference 15 C4.

301   O'Connell Peat Ltd, near Ballyshannon, Co Donegal

2ft gauge

Opened 1983;   closed ?

Private peat extraction operation. The complete railway, supplied by Alan Keef Ltd, included ½ mile of new 20lb rail, fifteen ex-RAF Fauld four wheel wagons converted into turf wagons and one Keef diesel locomotive. Upon closure the locomotive went to Midland Irish Peat Moss Ltd (see Table 300).

Map reference 8 2C.

302   Rio Tinto Finance and Exploration, Co Longford

No details known.

303 Shamrock Machine Turf, Shane Valley, Co Offaly

2ft gauge

Opened ?   Closed 1978.

Locomotive worked railway used for transporting peat from the bog workings to the loading point. Rolling stock consisted of five wooden slatted tipper wagons (08/1972). In 1978 the bog was sold to Bord na Móna to allow the Bord to extend its operation at Ballydermot (see Table 199). Upon closure one of the two locomotives went to Midland Irish Peat Moss Ltd.

Map reference 22 A1.

304 Tramore Leisure Railway, Tramore, Co Waterford

15in gauge

Opened 1973.

Miniature railway using a steam outline locomotive. Uses a circular circuit giving a running length of 18 chains. Still currently operating.

Map reference 28 B4.

305 Butlin's Railway, Mosney, Co Meath

Site at Butlin's Holiday Camp, Mosney, Co Meath.

Map reference 17 B4.

306 Lagan Vale Estate Brick and Terracotta, Stranmillis, Belfast

2ft gauge

Opened ?   Closed ?

No details known but a 1937 OS map shows several lines leaving the works on all sides. There was one locomotive working on the site.

Map reference 34 C4.

307 Foyle Reclamation Schemes, Co Derry

4ft 8½in gauge and 5ft 3in gauge

Opened 1843;   closed 1848.

Various lines and contractors used for reclaiming the sloblands on the south bank of Lough Foyle in connection with the construction of the Londonderry & Coleraine Railway.

Two lines ran from the mouth of the Faughan River; one to what was later a tile works at Campsie, the other to gravel pits. At Longfield a line ran out to the main embankment from a large depot with sidings and engine shed. William Dargan had a line in 1843 running to Ballykelly and Ballymacran banks, whose course is now untraceable. A line from Binevenagh Quarry ran to the mouth of the River Roe.

Map reference 4 A4 & B4.

308 Gormanston Aerodrome Railway, Co Meath

British War Department / 2ft gauge

Opened 1918;   closed 1920.

Locomotive worked railway used in the construction of the aerodrome.

Map reference 17 B4.

309 Camden Fort, Ram's Head, Crosshaven, Cork Harbour

British Admiralty / 1ft 6in gauge / 12in gauge

Opened c.1870-1871; closed c.1920.

The 1ft 6in gauge system consisted of about ¼ mile of track on two unconnected levels. Double tracks ran from two piers with many wagon turntables giving access to adjoining lines. One of these lower level lines ran to what was called the 'Torpedo Pier'. The higher level line was some 30ft above the latter system, transfer being by crane, this line ran into storehouses excavated into the hillside. The system was used for transporting ammunition and general supplies. It is believed that a locomotive worked here, this too could be 'craned' from one level to another.

The other, railway of 12in gauge and approximately 50ft long, ran to the 'Torpedo Pier' and was used for transporting torpedos to a location where they could be fired at possible approaching enemy vessels.

Map reference 31 D1.

310 Ravenhill Patent Brick and Tile Company, Belfast

Thos. H. Rea / 2ft gauge

Works railway system. It is thought that a locomotive might have worked here, although no proof of this exists.

Map reference 34 D3.

311 Marley Park Leisure Railway, Co Dublin

3½in / 5in / 7¼in gauges

Opened ?

Still currently operating.

Elevated level mixed gauge railway running in the grounds of the Marley Park Estate, Grange Road, Rathfarnham, Co Dublin. Owned and operated by the Dublin Society of Mechanical Engineers who run public services on summer Saturdays in the afternoon. Track length of the circular circuit is 15 chains.

Map reference 23 A1.

312 Arranmore Whaling Station Tramway, Co Mayo

Opened 1908;   closed 1913.

Norwegian owned tramway which ran from the pier at Rusheen Island, Co Mayo to the whaling station buildings. Wagons were hand pushed.

Map reference 6 A4.

313 Blacksod Whaling Station Tramway, Co Mayo

Opened 1910.

Closed 1923 (Closed during war).

Norwegian owned tramway which ran from the pier at Blacksod Point, Co Mayo to the whaling station works, a distance of some 175yds. Wagons were hand pushed.

Map reference 6 A5.

314   Malcomsons Compressed Peat Factory, Birdhill, Co Tipperary

2ft 6in gauge

Operating c.1870.

In about 1869, William Malcomson started a compressed peat factory on a bog about one mile south-west of Birdhill Station. It used a 16hp steam engine on 20ft of track, working two pug mills which processed the peat prior to drying. The peat was collected by portable 2ft 6in gauge railways.

Map reference 20 B5.

315   Dinsmore Factory Tramway, Co Antrim

2ft 6in gauge

Opened ?   Closed ?

Used for coal transfer from the NCC station at Kells to the linen factory, hand pushed.

Map reference 5 B6.

316   Clashduff Colliery Railway, Co Kilkenny

Ballinagarry Collieries (Production) Ltd / 2ft gauge

Opened ?   Closed ?

Locomotive worked railway used in coal extraction. The locomotives were later moved to the nearby Gurteen site worked by the same company (see Table 288).

Map reference 21 C6.

317   Altnahinch Dam Railway, Lough Fiel, Ballymena, Co Antrim

Reed & Mallick Ltd / probably 2ft gauge

Opened 1963;   closed 1965.

Locomotive worked railway used in construction of the Altnahinch Dam, Lough Fiela.

Map reference 5 A4.

318   Balbriggan Coke Oven Tramway, Co Dublin

Dublin and Drogheda Railway / ? gauge

Opened 1844;   closed ?

Used to transport coal from the quay to the coke ovens for use in DDR locomotives.

Map reference 17 B4.

319   Hannahstown Quarries Ltd, Co Antrim

2ft gauge

Opened ?   closed ?

Locomotive worked quarry railway at Hannahstown, Co Antrim. Formerly Black Mountain Quarries Ltd.

Map reference 11 A2.

320   Irish Steel Limited, Haulbowline Island, Cork

4ft 8½in gauge

Opened 1982;   still currently operating.

Used to carry steel and materials from the dockside to the steelworks. This railway is unusual on two counts, one is that it is built to the British Standard gauge of 4ft 8½in, which, of course, makes it a narrow gauge railway in Irish terms. The second unusual feature is that it uses three of the Unilok road/rail locomotives.

Map reference 33 F4.

321   Admiralty Tramway, Rocky Island, Cork Harbour

British Admiralty / ? gauge

Opened ?   Closed ?

Hand operated tramway used for moving stocks of Gunpowder. Rails were made of brass in an effort to minimise the danger of sparks. It is likely that the gunpowder came from the Ballincollig Royal Gunpowder Mills (see Table 322).

Map reference 33 F4.

322   Royal Gunpowder Mills Tramway, Ballincollig, Co Cork

? gauge

Opened by 1898; closed c.1903.

Two tracks connected at right angles to the west of the main works, total length of about 400 yards, gauge unknown. The tramways connected Magazine No.1, Magazine No.2, the Cannister Store and the Dusting House.

It is thought that the barrels of gunpowder left the works by boat and went to the Admiralty storage facility on Rocky Island, Cork Harbour (see Table 321).

Map reference 33 A2.

323   Tipperary Anthracite, Lickfinn, Ballinunty, Thurles, Co Tipperary

2ft gauge

Opened ?   Closed by 1991.

No details known other than one Clayton Equipment battery-electric locomotive was reported to have worked here.

Map reference 27 C1.

324   Board of Works, near Inch, Co Donegal

2ft gauge

Opened late 1950s ? Closed c.1978 ?

The line was used by Office of Public Works to maintain the causeway which carried the Londonderry and Lough Swilly Railway between OS Map reference C359234 and C353225. One diesel locomotive worked the line and had been removed by mid-1983.

Map reference 3 D4.

325   River Lee Hydro-Electric Scheme Railway, Co Cork

? gauge

Opened c.1955. Closed c.1959.

Railway equipment was shipped from Germany to the site by the contractors. However, it is understood that the locomotives, wagons and tracked were never used and were shipped back to Germany upon completion of the contract.

Map reference 26 B6.

326 River Erne Hydro-Electric Scheme, Co Donegal

2ft gauge

Opened ?   Closed c.1955 ?

Railway used to transport materials used in connection with the construction of the River Erne Hydro-Electric Scheme, near Cliff, Belleek, Co Donegal.

Map reference 8 C2.

327 Tynagh Mines, Co Galway

3ft gauge

Opened ?   Closed ?

Mineral railway serving Tynagh Lead and Zinc mines.

Map reference 20 B1.

328 St John of God Brothers, Drumcar, Co Louth

2ft gauge

Opened c.1967; closed c.1974.

This railway ran in the grounds of a large school for mentally handicapped children. The equipment was aquired c.1967. The locomotive reputedly coming from Layden's Coal Mine, Arigna (see Table 330). The track was very light Jubilee track of about 10lbs/yard spiked to wooden sleepers and was well laid on broken stone ballast. The line was about 600 yards in length twisting through trees and climbing dangerously steep gradients. The line had fallen into disuse a number of years before disposal.

Upon closure the whole railway was aquired by the Rosminian Fathers, Upton (see Table 329).

Map reference 17 A2.

329 Rosminian Fathers, Upton, Co Cork

2ft gauge

Opened 1974;   closed 1997.

The entire railway was aquired in 1974 from the St John of God Brothers, Drumcar (see Table 328). The line operated during the annual steam rally. The locomotive had a steam outline casing fitted and was painted in a black livery. The line was straight and was 9 chains long.

Map reference 31 B1.

330 Derreenavoggy Coal Mine, Co Roscommon

2ft gauge

Opened c.1927; closed ?   In use in 1964.

This mine was beside Arigna village and was worked by various parties including both the Arigna Iron Works Co and the Arigna Mining Co. In 1927, Laydens took over the working. The ropeways from Rock Hill Mine (Table 371) and Rover Mine (Table 372) came here. There was another ropeway, 600yds long, which went from here to the village loading stage of the Arigna Valley Railway (Table 98). This ropeway was built by the British Ropeway Engineering Company. The mine was worked by a 2ft gauge, double track, cable operated tramway.

Map reference 8 C6.

331 Spelga Dam Railway, Co Down

John Laing & Son Ltd / probably 2ft gauge

Opened 1954 ?   Closed 1957 ?

Railway used in conjuction with the construction of the Spelga Dam. The dam is situated in the Mourne Mountains close to the source of the River Bann about three miles north-west of the Silent Valley. The dam was constructed for the Portadown & Banbridge Regional Waterworks Joint Board with the contract awarded to John Laing & Sons Ltd. The line ran from the Batching Plant to the Dam. It started underneath the loading hoppers at the Batching Plant, situated upstream of the dam. It then ran along a temporary embankment on the west bank of the River Bann and crossed the river by a Bailey bridge to reach the dam. A number of derrick tracks were laid out beside the line on each wing of the dam.

Map reference 11 A6.

332 Banagher Water Scheme, Co Derry

2ft gauge

Opened 1930;   closed c.1932 ?

Railway used in construction of the Banagher Water Scheme. It is believed that the railway may have been locomotive worked.

Map reference 4 B4.

333 Limerick Dock Extension Railway, Co Limerick

T. J. Moran & Co Ltd / 2ft gauge

Operating 1934.

Railway used for transporting materials used in the construction of the dock extension. Possibly locomotive worked.

Map reference 20 A5.

334 Ummeras Bog, Co Kildare

Bord na Móna / 3ft gauge

Opened 1978 ?   Still currently operating.

Opened c.1978 (OS N623146) to provide a secondary source of moss peat for the Kilberry factory. Peat is hauled from the bog to a lorry loading point for onward transhipment by road to Kilberry.

Part of this bog had been worked previously by different companies, notably Ummeras Peat Co Ltd (see Table 201).

Map reference 22 B2.

335 Bellair Bog, Co Offaly

Bord na Móna / 3ft gauge

Opened 1980;   still currently operating.

Line runs from the tip head through Bellair North Bog and passes under the Iarnród Éireann Portarlington-Athlone line (Table 4). The line then continues to Bellair South Bog.

Map reference 15 B6.

336 Parkmore Siding, Parkmore, Co Antrim

2ft 6in gauge

Operating 1860s; line ran from Parkmore Station for a distance of some 2 miles to Glenravel and Ballynatralva Mines. Also see Table 72.

Map reference 5 B5.

**337   Glenconway Bog Railway,
        Dungiven, Co Derry**

Charles Tennant & Co (N.I.) Ltd / 3ft gauge

Opened ?   Closed ?

This locomotive worked railway was in use in 1973 by a consortium of local farmers who were working the bog. OS Grid reference C62 14.

Map reference 4 B5.

**338   Tramore Drainage Scheme Railway,
        Co Waterford**

Department of Defence, Construction Corps / 2ft gauge

Opened 1944;   closed 1946.

Used in connection with a drainage scheme at Tramore. Believed to have been diesel locomotive worked.

Map reference 28 B4.

**339   Meelick Flood Defence Contract,
        Co Galway**

2ft gauge

Opened late 1971; closed February 1972.

Locomotive worked railway used in connection with flood defence work on the west bank of the River Shannon just south of Meelick Lock, Co Galway.

Map reference 20 D1.

340   Portumna, Unknown Contract, Co Galway

2ft gauge

Opened 1972;   closed ?

Nothing known about this contract other than that there were supposed to be two locomotives from the Meelick Flood Defence Contract delivered here.

Map reference 20 D2.

**341   Shannon Stakes Ltd, Mountshannon,
        Co Clare**

probably 2ft gauge

Opened 1979;   still currently operating ?

This company manufactures fencing stakes. The railway is used to transport untreated stakes to a chemical treatment tank. The wagons appear to hauled by chain with the length of line somewhere in the region of 75yds length.

Map reference 20 B3.

**342   CIE Sleeper Treatment Works, LMS Yard,
        North Wall, Dublin**

probably 3ft gauge

Opened ?   Closed 1974 ?

A narrow gauge line running parallel to the standard gauge line in the LMS Yard at the North Wall. The line was used to transport wooden sleepers from the storage area to a treatment plant. The line was about 250yds long. Some 10 4-wheeled wagons were moved by a road tractor. With concrete sleepers now being used this site fell into disuse, although the track was still visible in 1984.

Map reference 32 D2.

343   Irish Army, Curragh Camp, Co Kildare

No.1 Maintainance Company, Irish Army, Curragh / 2ft gauge

Opened by 1909; still operating

The line had appeared on a 1909 OS map but the actual opening date has not yet been found out. By 1946, only a short length of line was in use due to disrepair. It appears that the line was worked by either animals or man. In 1950, one locomotive, rolling stock and track were transferred from the nearby Baldonnel Camp (Table 361). By 1952 the railway had been relaid and was back in use. The line is used to transport targets from the camp to the ranges.

Map reference 22 B2.

**344   Albert Brickworks, Carrickfergus,
        Co Antrim**

? gauge

Opened ?   Closed ?

The Albert Brickworks was served by John Kelly's siding, off the headshunt of Carrickfergus Station (NCC) goods yard. This siding had been removed by 09-1953. The brickworks also had a narrow gauge tramway which ran north, under the Belfast-Larne line, to the quarry.

Map reference 11 C1.

**345   Belfast & County Down Miniature Railway
        Society, Co Down**

7¼in gauge

Opened April 1995; still currently operating.

This miniature railway at Four Road Ends, between Newtownards and Donaghadee, Co Down, consists of 80 chains of 7¼in gauge track in a 'dog bone' shape. It has a 1-chain double track tunnel and a 30ft long bridge.

Map reference 11 C2.

**346   Pickie Family Fun Park Railway,
        Bangor, Co Down**

7¼in gauge

Opened June 1993; still currently operating.

The line gives a 28 chain long run and serves the Pickie Family Fun Park at the western end of the Bangor Marina complex. The line runs from the end of Kinnegar Terrace under a short tunnel then forms a loop travelling by Swan Lake and back. At the Kinnegar end there is a passing loop and a turntable for turning the locomotive. The locomotive is a steam outline 2 stroke diesel and is named 'Pickie Puffer'.

Map reference 11 C2.

**347   Antrim Road Waterworks Miniature Railway,
        Belfast**

7¼in gauge

Opened c.1954; closed c.1971.

This was a small oval in a paddock near the lakeside path close to the landing stage. The line was closed due to vandalism and transferred to Cultra (See table 348).

Map reference 34 C2.

**348   Ulster Folk & Transport Museum,
        Cultra Manor, Holywood, Belfast**

5ft 3in, 3ft, 2ft, 1ft 10in, 7¼in, 5in and 3½in gauges

Opened 1980.

The Ulster Folk and Transport Museum has a number of railway features. Apart from the static exhibits in the main building there are two other railway systems. A 2ft gauge system and 7¼in, 5in and 3½in gauge systems are run in the grounds. The miniature lines are operated by the local Model Engineers Society.

2ft gauge system: This was a demonstration line which was never actually used. Coaches were to be built on the frames of four Cravens wagons from the MoD line at Lisahally (see Table 67). A number of locomotives were to have run services. The line was straight and 7 chains long, with a station at one end.

7¼in gauge system: An oval shape layout giving a 17 chain circuit. Passing loop by station and two spurs to MPD's. It is the former Antrim Road Waterworks system and is used at ground level.

5in and 3½in gauge system: This elevated loop is situated within the 7¼in gauge loop and has a length of 20 chains.

Map reference 11 B2.

349 Dublin Gas Company Tramway

? gauge

Opened ?   Closed ?

A double track horse-drawn railway running from the quayside along Forbes Street to the big Retort House.

Map reference 32 D2.

350 Hussey, Pickmere & Egan, Co Kildare

2ft gauge

Opened c.1946; closed ?   Contractors for the ESB using a locomotive worked railway.

Map reference 22 D1.

351 Nicholl's Sawmill Tramway, Ballycastle, Co Antrim

2ft gauge

Opened ? certainly in use by 1924; closed ?

Tramway ran from Nicholl's Sawmill under the Tow Viaduct to ?

Map reference 5 B3.

352 Ulster Minerals Ltd, Curraghinalt, near Gortin, Co Tyrone

2ft gauge

Opened ?   Closed ?

Locomotive worked railway. Nothing known other than site was reportedly under a care and maintainance basis from 03-1989.

Map reference 9 C1.

353 Leisureland Express, Salthill, Co Galway

15in gauge

Opened 1975;   still currently operating.

Line ran in the grounds of the former Leisureland Amusement Park and included a tunnel. The Park was reported to have been cleared and bulldozed in 1993 but the track has been relaid. The current circuit forms a circular loop 16 chains long with a short tunnel . The railway uses a steam outline diesel locomotive.

Map reference 13 C6.

354 Westport House Country Estate Railway, Co Mayo

15in gauge

Opened 1990;   still currently operataing.

Miniature leisure railway in the grounds of Westport House using a steam outline diesel locomotive. The track layout is of the 'dumbell' type giving an out and back run of 37 chains.

Map reference 13 A1.

355 Turlough Hill Railway, Co Wicklow

Priority Drilling Co / 2ft gauge

Opened ?   Closed ?

The Priority Drilling Company of Killimor, Co Galway, is a Canadian firm that has interests in Ireland. It had a tunnelling contract to construct an outlet tunnel from Lough Nahanagan for the Turlough Hill pump storage power station in Co Wicklow. Although the contract was in Co Wicklow the company's base was on the Loughrea Road, Killimor Co Galway. Two locomotives were used for the contract.

Map reference 23 A3.

356 Bulrush Peat Company

New Ferry Road, Bellaghy & Tyanee (Co Derry); Randlestown (Co Antrim); Carrickmore (Co Tyrone) and Baronstown East (Co Kildare) / 750mm gauge

Opened 1979 ?

This is a subsidiary of a Danish company who operate a number of sites. The one on the New Ferry Road, near Bellaghy, is the former UK Peat Moss Litter Company site (see Table 149) and is the main processing plant. A smaller site to the north at Tyanee and a larger site at Randalstown both use railways to transport peat from the bog to a tiphead for onward transhipment by road to New Ferry. Another site at Carrickmore was undergoing clearance for extraction in 1997; this site is believed to be the old Irish Peat Development Co site (see Table 430). The site at Baronstown East, Co Kildare, also uses a railway from bog to tiphead and road transport to New Ferry.

Map references: 4 D6 (New Ferry); 10 D1 (Randalstown); 4 D6 (Tyanee); 9 D2 (Carrickmore); 22 B2 (Baronstown East).

357 Ballylumford Power Station, Co Antrim

2ft gauge

It is believed that a 2'0" gauge locomotive worked railway was used during construction.

Map reference 5 D6.

358 Howth Sewage Works Railway, Co Dublin

? gauge

Opened ?   Closed ?

Tramway ran from the works to nearby waste banks. Hand pushed tubs.

Map reference 17 B6 (inset).

359 Falls Brickworks, Belfast

? gauge

Opened ?   Closed ?

Tramway running from brickworks out to the claypits. A 1932 OS map shows a line commencing in a clay pit running north east, the line turns south east and runs into the works. It exits on the southern side of the building following the original line before turning again to a westerly direction terminating in another clay pit.

Map reference 34 B4.

360   Belfast Pottery, Brick and Tile Works, Limestone Road, Belfast

J. Thompson / ? gauge

Opened ?   Closed ?

Works tramway system.

Map reference 34 C2.

361   Irish Army, Baldonnel Camp, Co Kildare

2ft gauge

Opened ?   Closed 1950 ?

Nothing much known about this system which apparently had a system using a diesel locomotive. This locomotive and stock was later transferred from here to the nearby Curragh Camp in 1950. (see Table 343)

Map reference 22 D1.

362   Lemanaghan Bog, Co Offaly

Bord na Móna / 3ft gauge

Opened ?

Formerly a privately worked bog for sod peat using an isolated railway to a tip head reached by a flat crossing over the former CIE Banagher Branch (Table 5). The system was linked to the BnM Boora System c.1988/89 from the north end of Derries Bog (Table 194) with a line running over a swing bridge across the Grand Canal and a fixed bridge across the River Brosna. The system now produces milled peat. The line was continued in 1995 to connect with the Blackwater System (see Table 179) at Ballaghuff No.2 Bog.

Map reference 21 B1

363   Altagowlan Coal Mine Tramway, Co Roscommon

1ft 10in gauge

Opened 1950s;   closed ?

A few workings date from early days but serious working commenced in the 1950s when Laydens acquired the site. Laydens installed a 1'10" gauge double track, cable operated tramway of some 1000yds in length. 600 yds of this tramway were underground in the adit.

Map reference 8 C6.

364   Aughabehy Coal Mine Tramways, Co Roscommon

2ft gauge

Opened 1832;   closed 1931.

Early wokings existed from 1780s. From 1832 until the late 1830s, the adit begun by the O'Reilly's, was served by the Arigna Iron Works Tramway (see Table 142). The mine was then unused for about 50 years until the Arigna Mining Co started mining again from 1883 to 1929, and then for a year by Laydens. The mine closed in 1931 by which time it was worked out. During the 40 year woking period, mining was carried out at two sites. No.1 Site was originally worked by shafts from 1888 to c.1892. About 1912 it was re-opened with a new adit served by a 2ft gauge tramway, which later connected to with the Incline Railway (Table 160) leading to the terminus of the Arigna Valley Extension Railway (Table 98). This 2ft gauge tramway was opened in 1912 and closed in 1931, it was cable operated.

The second site, No.2 Site, was opened in 1893, on the closure of site No.1. The tramway here was double track, cable operated and probably 2ft gauge. It was in use from the 1890s to 1919.

Map reference 8 C6.

365   Geevagh Coal Mines, Ballynashee, Co Sligo

? gauge

Opened c.1900; closed ?

Worked in the mid-1800s and then later in the early 1900s. Two short tramways were in use for a brief period during the latter period of working. The Glen Ballynashee Colliery started working this area later (see Table 287).

Map reference 8 B6.

366   Greaghnageeragh Coal Mine, Co Roscommon

2ft gauge

Opened ?   Closed ? In use in 1964.

Worked from about 1800 to the early 1900s. Latterly there was at least one tramway in use. Working recommenced in the mid-1950s. A steeply inclined adit was served by double track, 2'0" gauge, cable operated tramway extending some 20yds outside the adit. This was later abandoned due to legal difficulties. A second tramway was the constructed also of 2'0" gauge but single track. Winch operated for part of the way, the hutches were then manually brought to a small screen. There were also a couple of sidings.

Map reference 8 C6.

367   Tullynahaw Coal Mine, Co Roscommon

? gauge

Opened ?   Closed ?

Originally worked by Hibernian Mining Co for a short time in 1825. Irish Mining Co also were working the area in the same period but continued a lot longer. Laydens finally worked out the site using tramways.

Map reference 8 C6.

368   Gubbarudda Coal Mine, Co Roscommon

2ft gauge

Opened c.1955. Closed ?

Worked from an early period but by Noone from about 1955. Noone used a 2'0" gauge, double track, steeply graded cable operated tramway from the adit. Part of the tramway apparently crossed a public road.

Map reference 8 C6.

369   Lugmore Coal Mine, Co Leitrim

? gauge

Operating c.1910; closed ?

Worked by various parties from 1830. From the 1870s Lugmore was worked by Laydens. In 1910 there was a tramway in use connecting the two adits.

Map reference 8 C5.

370   Greaghnaglough Coal Mine, Co Roscommon

2ft gauge

Opened ?   Closed 1957.

Some very early workings are known. Some time up until 1940s, Lynch was working the mine using a 2'0" gauge mine tramway. A further 2'0" gauge line went from the mine to the nearest road, a distance of some 1½ miles. This second tramway was diesel locomotive worked.

From the mid-1940s, Laydens started working this mine using the adit tramway, but dismantled the rest of Lynch's line. At one stage there was a third line in use. Working ceased about 1957.

Map Reference 8 C6.

371   Rock Hill Coal Mine Tramway, Co Roscommon

1ft 10in gauge

Opened 1917.   Closed ?

This mine South West of Arigna was opened in 1917 and worked for a number of years by Irish Exploration & Development Co. It is thought that it was later worked by the Arigna Mining Co. Laydens worked it from 1930 until recently (still in use in 1964). The small adit was served by a double track, steeply graded, cable operated tramway built to 1'10" gauge. In the 1920s there was a tramway from the adit mouth to the nearby Keadue road, a distance of some 500yds on an average gradient of 1:6. It is suspected that this tramway was a single line. There was a ropeway from here to Dereenavoggy (Table 330), some 2 miles in length and built by the British Ropeway Engineering Company.

Also see Table 330.

Map reference 8 C6.

372   Rover Mines, Co Roscommon

? gauge

Opened ?   Closed by 1938.

Rover Mine was originally owned by the Archbishop of Tuam in the 18th century. The mine was intermittantly worked in the 1800s. From 1885 until closure in 1938, the mine was worked by Laydens. There was a ropeway from here to Dereenavoggy in later years. This ropeway was about ¼ mile long and built by the British Ropeway Engineering Company. The Ropeway was not used after about 1938. There were two tramways here at various times. The adit was served by a single line in 1910. There are remains of a second adit near the main site; this is presumed to have also had a tramway.

Also see Table 330.

Map reference 8 C6.

373   Seltannaveeny Coal Mine, Co Roscommon

? gauge

Opened ?   Closed ?

Two systems.

In 1896 the Arigna Mining Co opened three shafts and an adit. In 1903 a tramway was in operation connecting the mine with the roadside, a distance of about ½ mile. The tramway was removed in 1931 and is said to have been hand operated.

In 1950 the mine was reopened by Laydens, who worked the mine for a few years using a small tramway.

Map reference 8 C6.

374   Seltenaskeagh Coal Mine, Co Roscommon

? gauge

Opened 1960s; closed ? Still extant in 1969.

Originally worked in from 1860 to 1880. A 'wire tramway' was installed in 1875, erected by Fawcett Brothers, from the adit mouth to the roadside. Later, Laydens were working the site using a steeply inclined, winch operated, single line tramway.

Map reference 8 C6.

375   Spion Kop Coal Mine, Tullymurray, Co Roscommon

? gauge

Opened ?   Closed 1957.

Worked by Laydens at various sites until about 1957 using tramways. The Creevelea Co (see Table 139) are thought to have worked some levels and to have had brick ovens. It is also thought that there was a ropeway from here to a brickworks at Spencer Harbour on Lough Allen.

Map reference 8 C6.

376   Ardclinis Inclined Plane, Co Antrim

? gauge

Opened c.1870s; closed 1901 ?

A ¼ mile long gravity powered inclined plane from Ardclinis Mine to the pier at Fallowvee. Climbed 500ft and was known locally as 'The Drum'. Served bauxite/iron ore mines.

Map reference 5 C4.

377   Murlough Bay Collieries Tramways, Co Antrim

? gauge

Operating ?

Various tramways serving the collieries.

Map reference 5 B3.

378   Ballycastle Collieries Tramway, Co Antrim

? gauge

Opened c.1752; closed c.1780.

A double track tramway running from the collieries along the coast to the harbour at Ballycastle.

Map reference 5 B3.

379   West Lighthouse Inclined Plane, Rathlin Island

? gauge

Opened c.1912; Closed c.1917.

200 yard long, four horse winch operated inclined plane used in the construction of lighthouse.

Map reference 5 B2.

380   Glencar Barytes Mine, Co Leitrim

? gauge

Operated ?

No details known.

Map reference 8 B3.

381   Courtown Harbour Tramway, Co Wexford

? gauge

Operating c.1846.

Horse operated tramway.

Map reference 29 B1.

382   Rathnew Brickworks Tramway, Co Wicklow

? gauge

Operating c.1900.

No details known.

Map reference 23 B4.

383   Luganure Lead Mine Tramway, Co Wicklow

? gauge

Operating c.1866.

Mule worked line from the lead mines to the lead works, length about ¾ mile.

Map reference 23 A4.

384   Carrickfergus Waterworks Railway, Co Antrim

McCrea & McFarland / ? gauge

Operating c.1885.

Railway used in construction of waterworks; possibly one or two locomotives.

Map reference 11 C1.

385   Alexandra Dock Construction Railway, Belfast

McCrea & McFarland / ? gauge

Operating c.1885 ?

Locomotive worked railway used in the construction of the Alexandra Dock.

Map reference 34 D2.

386   Graving Dock, North Wall, Dublin

William Dargan / ? gauge

Operating c.1859-1860.

Locomotive worked railway used in the construction of the Graving Dock.

Map reference 32 D2.

387   Vartry Waterworks Railway, Co Wicklow

? gauge

Operating c.1858.

Locomotive worked railway used in the construction of Vartry Waterworks.

Map reference 23 A3.

388   Rosslare Pier Extension Railway, Co Wexford

C. Brand & Co / ? gauge

Operating 1902.

Contractors locomotive worked railway used for building pier extension.

Map reference 29 B4.

389   Diatomite Co Ltd, New Ferry, Co Derry

Narrow gauge

Operating ?   Peat Railway, no other details known.

Map reference 4 D6.

390   Lyles Hill Bauxite Mine, Templepatrick, Co Antrim

? gauge

Opened c.1890s; Closed 31-12-1945.

Line originally opened c.1890s serving six adits around the circumference of Lyle's Hill, closed c.1902.

During the Second World War, Britain's normal supply of aluminium from France was cut off. In 1941 it was decided to re-open the bauxite mines at Lyles Hill, near Templepatrick. Mining was done by digging six horizontal shafts at intervals around the hill. The bauxite ore was transported in 'bogies' from the mining shafts to the loading bay, from where it was taken by lorry to Templepatrick Station. Most of the bauxite went by rail to Belfast, but about 1000 tons a week went along the narrow gauge line to Larne to shipped to processing plants in England.

Map reference 11 A1.

391   Colin Glen Brickworks, Springfield Road, Belfast

S. McGladdery & Sons / 2ft gauge

Opened ?   Closed ?

Locomotive worked railway. Possibly used for transporting clay from the clay pits to the brickworks.

Map reference 34 A4.

392   Cranmore Brickworks, Charleville Avenue, Belfast

Henry Laverty & Sons / ? gauge

Opened ?   Closed ?

Works tramway system.

Map reference 34 B4.

393   Clonard Brickworks, Springfield Road, Belfast

Clonard Brick & Estate Co Ltd / ? gauge

Opened ?   Closed ?

Works tramway system.

Map reference 34 B3.

394   Marquis's Brickworks, Ava Avenue, Belfast

J. Kennedy / ? gauge

Opened ?   Closed ?

Works tramway system.

Map reference 34 C4.

395   Prospect Brickworks, Belfast

? gauge

Opened ?   Closed ?

Works tramway system.

Map reference 34 C4.

396   Blackstaff Flax Spinning & Weaving Mill, off Springfield Road, Belfast

? gauge

Opened ?   Closed ?

Works tramway system. Shown on a 1901 map, but had disappeared by 1930.

Map reference 34 B3.

397   Bottle Works, Stranmillis Road, Belfast

? gauge

Opened ?   Closed ?

Works tramway system.

Map reference 34 C4.

398   Oldpark Brickworks, Ardilea Avenue, Belfast

James Wallace & Sons / ? gauge

Opened ?   Closed ?

Works tramway system.

Map reference 34 B2.

399   Falls Foundry Tramway, Belfast

? gauge

Opened ?   Closed ?

Ran along North Howard Street between the Falls and Shankhill Roads. Branches off into various workshops along the route. Shown on 1901 & 1932 OS Maps.

Map reference 34 C3.

400   Lagan Foundry Tramway, Ravenhill Road, Belfast

? gauge

Opened ?   Closed ?

Works tramway system.

Map reference 34 D3.

401   Londonderry Brickworks, off Bligh's Lane, Londonderry

? gauge

Opened ?   Closed ? by 1905.

Two lines running from works to clay pits.

Map reference 3 D4 (See inset page 2).

402   Belfast City Council

2ft gauge

Opened ?   Closed ?

Locomotive worked railway used in connection with River Lagan Improvement Scheme. Site unknown.

Map reference 34.

403   C. V. Buchan, Belfast

2ft gauge

Opened ?   Closed ?

Locomotive worked railway used in connection with the Belfast Sewer Contract.

Map reference 34.

404   Fetherstone's Bog Railway

? gauge

Operating c.1830s. Nothing known.

Map Reference ?

405   King Williamstown Wagonway

? gauge

Operating c.1834. Nothing known.

Map reference ?

406   Edgeworthstown Bog Railways, near Edgeworthstown, Co Longford

? gauge

Operating c.1786/7.

Worked in boglands of Co Longford and Co Westmeath. Used man-handled side tipping wagons.

Map reference 15 C4.

407   Mountrath Peat Works

? gauge

Opened ?   Closed ?

Nothing known.

Map reference 21 C3.

408   Inchicore Works Tramway, Inchicore, Dublin

GSWR / ? gauge

Opened 1864;   closed 1877.

Narrow gauge tramway from the 3rd lock of the Grand Canal to Inchicore Works for the conveyance of coal and iron brought up from Dublin by barge. Horse and gravity worked.

Map reference 32 B3.

409   Killeany Limestone Quarries Tramway, Rathlin Island

3ft gauge ?

Operating c.1922.

The limestone quarries were situated to the west of Church Bay. A ¾ mile long tramway went from the quarries to the pier. The stone was shipped from here to Glasgow. Owned by a Mr Johnson.

Map reference 5 B2.

410   Kirkcubbin Brickworks Tramway, Castle Espie Estate, Co Down

? gauge

Operating c.1866/7.

Map reference 11 C3.

411   Ballygowan Quarries, Ballygowan, Co Down

? gauge

Opened ?   Closed ?

Served by various sidings on the BCDR Comber-Downpatrick line (see Table 79).

Map reference 11 B3.

412   Athlumney Mill Tramway, near Navan, Co Meath

? gauge

Opened c.1906; closed 03-1933.

Tramway ran from the Timber Yard to the Sawmills and Furniture Factory, which was a converted Flax Mill. Continued to work until March 1933 when the mill was destroyed by fire.

Map reference 16 D4.

413   Clay Lake Railway, Clay Lake, near Keady, Co Armagh

2ft gauge

Operating c.1910.

Railway used in reclaiming bog land near Clay Lake. One locomotive was used.

Map reference 10 B5.

414   Rathkenny Mines Tramway, Rathkenny, Co Antrim

2ft gauge ?

Operating.

Tramway system at mines. Loads were transfered to the 3ft gauge NCC branch to Parkmore (see Table 72).

Map reference 5 B5.

415   Leinster Coalfields Railways

? gauge

Operating c.1829. Nothing known.

Map reference ?

416   Lisamoney Medical Depot Railway, near Cookstown, Co Derry

5ft 3in gauge

Operating c.1940s.

USAAF Medical Depot. Extensive internal rail network connected to NCC Magherafelt-Cookstown line (see Table 66).

Map reference 10 B1.

417   Bangor Brickworks Tramway, Donaghadee Road, Bangor, Co Down

? gauge

Opened ?   Closed ?   Operating in 1903.

Short tramway from the brickworks going south to clay pits.

Map reference 11 C2.

418   Cambricville Brewery Tramway, Dundalk, Co Louth

? gauge

Opened ?   Closed ?

Short tramway from GNR(I) siding (Table 50) to brewery complex.

Map reference 17 A1.

419   Dundalk Sawmills Tramways, Co Louth

? gauge

Opened ?   Closed ?

Complex of tramway lines in Sawmill just west of Barrack Street, Dundalk.

Map reference 17 A1.

420   Gilltown Bog, Co Kildare

Bord na Móna / 3ft gauge

Opened late 1980s; still currently operating.

Short railway from bog to tiphead just to the east of Timahoe North Bog.

Map Reference 22 C1.

421 Monettia Bog, Co Offaly

Bord na Móna / 3ft gauge

Opened late 1980s.

Still currently operating.

Associated with but unconnected to the Boora Group (Table 194). Short line from bog to loading area.

Map reference 21 C1.

422 Allen Bog, Co Kildare

Bord na Móna / 3ft gauge

Opened ?

Map reference 22 B2.

423 Kinnegad Bog, Co Meath

Bord na Móna / 3ft gauge

Opened ?

Short line situated at the northern end of bog area.

Map reference 16 B6.

424 Van Diemen's Land Mine, Co Wicklow

Mining Company of Ireland / ? gauge

Operating c.1868-70.

Short inclined tramway from mine to road. Served adit above Glenealo River and a shaft. Mined lead and copper pyrites.

Map reference 23 A4.

425 New Ross Minature Railway, New Ross, Co Wexford

7¼in gauge

Opened ?

A circular 7¼in gauge minuature railway operating in Kennedy Park, New Ross. Track length is 20 chains with one platform and an engine shed on a spur.

Map reference 28 C3.

426 Causeway Safari Park Railway, Co Antrim

9½in gauge

Opened ?

Park closed in 1996.

Circular pleasure line in the grounds of the Safari Park giving a length of 7 chains.

Map reference 4 D4.

427 Coleraine Model Engineers Railway, Turnakibbuck, Coleraine, Co Londonderry

3½in / 5in / 7¼in gauges

Opened ?

Still currently operating.

A circle of mixed gauge track 8 chains in length. Has one station and a locomotive depot inside the loop served by a turntable.

Map reference 4 D4.

428 W. Scott, Belfast Graving Dock construction

4ft 8½in gauge

Opened ?   Closed ?

Steam locomotive worked railway used in the construction of dock.

Map reference 34 D2.

429 Graceys Concrete Products Ltd, Tanderagee, Co Armagh

2ft gauge

Opened ?   Closed ?

Nothing much known apart from that a Lister petrol locomotive was delivered new in 1950.

Map reference 10 C4.

430 Irish Peat Development Company, Carrickmore

? gauge

Opened ?   Closed ?

It is believed that the company had a line operating here served by a siding on the GNR(I) Portadown to Omagh line (see Table 53). The company also had another site near Annaghmore (see Table 165). The Carrickmore site is now being developed by the Bulrush Peat Co (see Table 356)

Map reference 9 D2.

431 Carnance Quarry, Portstewart, Co Londonderry

3ft gauge ?

Opened ?   Closed ?

This quarry was alleged to have had a Kerr, Stuart locomotive from the nearby Carnanee Quarry (Table 256) sometime in the 1930s.

Map reference 4 D3.

432 Cahir Railway Centre, Cahir Station, Co Tipperary

2ft gauge / 3ft gauge

Opened 1990;   closed 1992.

This railway centre/museum adjacent to Cahir railway station had a short a length of 3ft gauge straight track 4 chains long and a very small length of 2ft gauge track.

Map reference 27 B2.

433   Parkview Brickworks, Ballygomartin Road, Belfast

? gauge

Opened ?   Closed ?   Tramway ran from Brickworks to clay pits.

Map reference 34 B2.

---

434   Ailwee Show Cave Railway, Ballyvaughan, Co Clare

2ft gauge

Opened ?   In use c.1991; closed ?

Tramway for removing spoil during the opening up of the cave. Used one skip wagon.

Map reference 19 C2.

---

435   Kilworth Camp Military Tramway, Kilworth, Co Cork

British Army / probably 2ft gauge

Opened ?   Closed ?

Tramway at the firing ranges of Kilworth Camp, possibly used for moving targets as at Curragh Camp. Nearly 1¼ mile long the tramway ran on a north-south axis. The line was extant in 1905.

Map reference 26 D3.

---

436   Beilbeag Mine Tramway, Co Leitrim

2ft gauge

Opened 1948;   closed 1963. Mine tramway from adit, operated by P.J. Wynne.

Map reference 8 D6.

---

437   Red Hill Mine Tramway, Co Leitrim

2ft gauge

Opened 1963;   closed 1990. Mine tramway from adit, operated by P. J. Wynne.

Map reference 8 D6.

---

438   ESB Pole Yard, near Limerick Junction, Co Tipperary

Bord Solathair an Leictreachais (Electricity Supply Board) / ? gauge

Opened ?   Still currently operating.

Short length of tramway used to transport electricity poles around the site.

Map reference 26 D1.

---

439   Cookstown Lime Company, Co Tyrone

Narrow gauge ?

Opened ?   Closed ?

The Cookstown Lime Company had a private siding off and to the north of Cookstown (NCC) Goods Yard. From here a narrow gauge tramway ran under a public road to a quarry. The tramway was in ruins by 1950.

Map reference 10 B2.

---

440   O'Beirne's Bog Reclamation Railway, Co Leitrim

Narrow gauge ?

Operating c.1869.

M. O'Beirne used a portable railway, with wagons, for transporting clay as part of a bog reclamation scheme on his property. It is unknown exactly where this railway operated.

Map reference unknown.

---

441   Peatlands Park Railway, Derryhubbert Rd, The Birches, Co Armagh

3ft gauge ?

Opened 1988.

Built on part of the Irish Peat Development Company site at Annaghmore, an entirely new railway has been built, called the Peatlands Railway. It has been built by the Department of the Environment (N.I.) as a leisure railway. The line is more or less circular in form with three platforms called Deerpark Halt, Turf Halt and Joe's Halt, and a locomotive shed on a long spur; running distance is 1 mile 29 chains.
It uses some of the original trackbeds and is worked by the diesel locomotives from the original system plus a new Alan Keef locomotive. Also see Tables 165 and 442.

Map reference 10 C3.

---

442   Sunshine Peat Company, Derryhubbert Rd, The Birches, Co Armagh

3ft and 2ft 6in gauges

Opened 1984 (3ft) and 1997 (2ft 6in).   Closed 1988 (3ft).   2ft 6in gauge still operating.

The Sunshine Peat Company acquired some of the southern part of the former Irish Peat Development Company at Annaghmore in 1984. Using part of the abandoned lines still in situ, a homebuilt 4w petrol mechanical locomotive was used to haul the peat from the bog to a loading site. The locomotive and railway went out of use in 1988 and the track was lifted c.1996/7 to allow enough clearance under a motorway bridge for lorries to haul peat out of the bog. Upon closure of the MoD Broughton Moor site in Cumbria the locos and stock were moved into storage at Thelkeld Quarry, Cumbria, by dealers W.Hocking of Cardiff. In May 1997 the Peat company acquired two Hunslet locomotives and some 24 flat wagons and some rail from Thelkeld Quarry, plus Hunslet 2264, which had gone to Cardiff and was transported from there. Although only some 300yds of track has since been laid, the intention is to reinstate the railway from various parts of the bog out to a roadside loading site. Also see Tables 165 and 441.

Map reference 10 C3.

---

443   Dun Laoghaire Sewer Contract, Dun Laoghaire, Co Dublin

? gauge

Opened ?   Closed ?

Construction railway used in the building of a new sewer scheme in Dun Laoghaire. The pumping station is in the old harbour area and from here the sewage is pumped to Ringsend via the new sewer, where it is loaded on a boat and disposed of. The course of the sewer is believed to run under the sea but close to the shore. The railway is understood to have run inside the large diameter pipes and been used for the transportation of materials and removal of spoil.

Map reference 32 F4.

---

444   Lispople Miniature Railway, Swords, Co Dublin

7¼in gauge ?

Opened ?

A miniature railway running in the private grounds of a house in north Dublin.

Map reference 17 B6.

445 Listowel & Ballybunion Railway Museum, Ballygowan, Lisselton, Co Kerry

Lartigue Monorail gauge

About 100ft of the former Listowel & Ballybunion Monorail (Table 92) have been single-handedly salvaged and restored by local farmer Michael Barry over the past 40 years and re-erected in the private grounds of his farmhouse. There is also a carriage and some of the pulleys from the drawbridge-type level crossings, plus numerous other L&B artifacts and drawings.

Map reference 25 B1.

446 Riverstown Mill Railway, Riverstown, Dundalk, Co Louth

4ft 8½in gauge

Opened 1997.

A British standard gauge railway built to connect a car park to the Riverstown Mill Restaurant, some 550yds away. Also present is a Hunslet 0-6-0ST locomotive, No.4 named *Robert Nelson* (works number 1800 of 1936) that was formerly with the Gloucestershire and Warwickshire Railway.

Map reference 17 A1.

MIDLAND BOOKS ON IRISH RAILWAYS

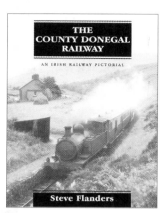

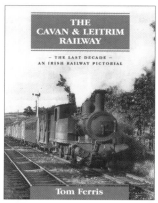

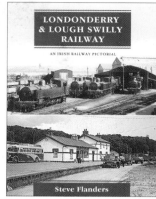

We hope you enjoyed this book . . .

Midland Publishing titles are edited and designed by an experienced and enthusiastic team of specialists.

Further titles are in preparation but we always welcome ideas for future publications.

In addition, our associate company, Midland Counties Publications, offers an exceptionally wide choice of books and videos in the following interest areas, for sale by mail-order around the world: aviation, spaceflight, astronomy, military, naval, merchant shipping, modelling, urban transport, railways, buses and trams, inland waterways and commercial vehicles.

For a copy of the appropriate catalogue, or to order further copies of this book, and any of the titles mentioned elsewhere on this page, please either write, telephone, fax or e-mail to:

Midland Counties Publications
Unit 3 Maizefield,
Hinckley, Leics, LE10 1YF,
Great Britain

Tel: (+44) 01455 233 747
Fax: (+44) 01455 233 737
E-mail: midlandbooks@compuserve.com

THE COUNTY DONEGAL RAILWAY
Softback, 282 x 213 mm, 64 pages
158 black/white photographs
Post free UK / Ireland
£7.99 Stg

THE CAVAN & LEITRIM RAILWAY
Softback, 282 x 213 mm, 64 pages
c160 b/w photographs
Post free UK / Ireland
£8.99 Stg

THE LONDONDERRY & LOUGH SWILLY RAILWAY
Softback, 282 x 213 mm, 64 pages
c170 b/w photographs
Post free UK / Ireland
£8.99 Stg

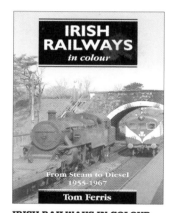

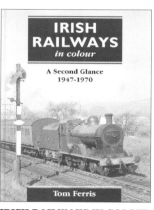

IRISH RAILWAYS IN COLOUR
From Steam to Diesel 1955-1967
Laminated hardback, 282 x 213 mm,
120 pages, 225 colour photographs
Post free UK / Ireland
£16.99 Stg

IRISH RAILWAYS IN COLOUR
A Second Glance 1947-1970
Laminated hardback, 282 x 213 mm,
144 pages, 350 colour photographs
Post free UK / Ireland
£19.99 Stg

Earlier titles that are still available:

THE IRISH NARROW GAUGE
A Pictorial History by Tom Ferris
Vol.1: From Cork to Cavan
Hardback, 112 pages, 250 b/w photos
15.99 Stg
Vol.2: The Ulster Lines
Hardback, 128 pages, 287 b/w photos
15.99 Stg

LOCOMOTIVES & RAILCARS OF BORD NA MÓNA
Stephen Johnson
A detailed survey of the motive power fleet that operates in the peat bogs of Ireland.
£4.99 Stg

MIDLAND GREAT WESTERN RAILWAY OF IRELAND
An illustrated history by Ernie Shepherd
Hardback, 144 pages, 130 b/w photos, locos, buildings and rolling stock drawings.
£18.99 Stg

All of the above Midland titles are mailed post free to UK and Ireland addresses.

MIDLAND VIDEOS ON IRISH RAILWAYS etc

Midland Publishing offer an expanding range of VHS/PAL videos on railways and allied subjects. Most of these programmes feature archive material carefully transferred to video and are accompanied by detailed commentaries to form rounded and enjoyable programmes, which are of interest not only to railway enthusiasts, but to those absorbed in the history and heritage of the areas covered in the various programmes.

Two major series are underway, featuring British and Irish Railways. Details of the most relevant and recent releases are shown here:

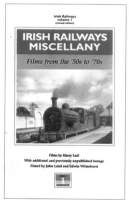

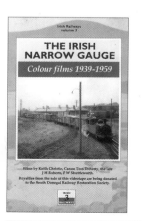

IRISH RAILWAYS MISCELLANY
Irish Railways vol 1 – revised edition
VHS, running time 55 min. New material by John Laird and Edwin Wilmshurst added to original films by Harry Luff and Wilf Watters **£14.99** Stg

THE IRISH NARROW GAUGE
Colour films, 1939-1959
VHS, running time approx 50 min
Films featuring five systems: L&LSR, CDR, C&L, T&D and the West Clare.
£16.99 Stg

The complete series of Irish Railway videos:

1: Irish Railways Miscellany
Films from the '50s to the '70s
55 min, colour & b/w, £14.99 Stg
2: Steam Swansong in Ulster
55 min, all colour, £14.99 Stg
3: Irish Narrow Gauge 1939-59
50 min, all colour, £16.99 Stg
4: Twilight of Steam in Ulster
55 min, colour & b/w, £15.99 Stg
5: Irish Railways in '40s & '50s
45 min, colour & b/w, £14.99 Stg
6: The Peat Railways of Ireland
Narrow Gauge Rlwys of Bord na Móna
55 min, colour, £16.99 Stg
7: Irish Railways in the 1960s
From Steam to Diesel
55 min, colour & b/w, £16.99 Stg

Other titles:

Trolleybus Days in Belfast
38 min, colour & b/w, £10.99 Stg
The Irish Narrow Gauge Today
20 locations and 5 different gauges
55 min, colour, £14.99 Stg